A Literary Atlas
& Gazetteer
of the British Isles

A Literary Atlas
& Gazetteer
of the British Isles

Michael Hardwick

Cartography by
Alan G Hodgkiss

David & Charles: Newton Abbot

0 7153 5923 1

Filmset in Photon Times 9 on 8 pt, by
Richard Clay (The Chaucer Press) Ltd Bungay Suffolk
Printed in Great Britain by
Fletcher & Son Ltd Norwich
for David & Charles (Holdings) Limited
South Devon House Newton Abbot Devon

Contents

Map numbers appear in brackets after each entry

5

Introduction

This book contains nearly 4,500 entries ranging in period from the beginnings of English literature to the present day. Every entry is keyed to a number on the relevant map and supported by an entry in the indices to enable anyone seeking an immediate reference to find it by starting in any of the three sections—text, indices or maps. Just as there are several ways of using this book to find information, there are several purposes for which it is intended. It is meant to serve the busy reference librarian faced with an urgent enquiry; the biographer contemplating the scope of a potential subject; the local journalist seeking a signpost to a writer worthy of attention; the literary-minded browser; and, far from least, the tourist who wishes to see the places connected with an author or explore the literary associations of an area. Publications are cited under birth entries.

The problems of creating a work of this nature are vast, and one of the chief of them is deciding who is included in it, and who is left out. Inevitably, anyone who scrutinises this volume for omissions, rather than for information or pleasure, will find them, and may feel duly gleeful. Others, whose use of it will be more purposeful and may not find what they seek, may be caused some inconvenience, regret and perhaps irritation, and it is to them that I apologise in advance. I hope they will draw my attention to omissions of people or significant place-associations, in the interest of a revised edition. There is one stipulation: admission is by death. Particulars of living literary figures are available in a number of publications; my concern is confined to those whose record is complete.

The idea for this work came from its publishers, who originally envisaged something much more modest in scope. I duly consulted the various encyclopedias of literary biography and dealt with the élite who figure in them all: though, I may add, such works by no means always agree with one another in the matter of dates and particulars, so that part of my task was not so simple as it might sound. While performing it, again and again I encountered side-references to other people who, while not of 'classic' stature, had produced poetry, or books, or journalism, or works of scholarship which might justifiably be classed as literature, and which are, or were once, popular or useful or respected. I extended my researches to include many hundreds of such people. It is not easy to define 'literature' to precise limits, and I expect to be told that, by comparison with some of the more obscure people I have included, I have left out deserving candidates. Again, I shall be grateful for details.

This additional contingent enlarged the book considerably; and yet I was also conscious of an anxious host of the shades of still others who are renowned or remembered regionally rather than nationally. Clearly, they had to be sought after, and I wrote to dozens of county and city librarians for assistance. A few could not spare the time or staff to find such information; but the majority of librarians gave me what help they could; and when they could not, it was because they had no such information available, which, I feel, goes towards justifying this publication. At any rate, I am much indebted to many librarians, and most especially to Miss Jean Mauldon, reference librarian at Royal Tunbridge Wells, who epitomises her profession at its best.

My other individual acknowledgement is to Judith Glover, who has worked on the book since its inception. But for her relentless pursuit of information it would have been immensely longer in the making and deficient in much detail. She also shared the writing of the entries and undertook the major task of compiling the indices.

Of the many printed sources to which I have had recourse, and in which greater detail of the people's lives and works may be found, I will list just the principals: *The Concise Dictionary of National Biography*, *Chambers's Biographical Dictionary*, *The Oxford Companion to English Literature*, *Everyman's Dictionary of Literary Biography* (J. M. Dent), *Who Was Who*, *The Author's and Writer's Who's Who* and *A General Analytical Bibliography of the Regional Novelists of the British Isles 1800–1950* by Lucien Leclaire. Brian Doyle's *Who's Who of Children's Literature* (Hugh Evelyn, 1968) proved useful, as did *Twentieth Century Writing* edited by Kenneth Richardson (Newnes, 1969), *The Penguin Companion to Literature* edited by David Daiches (1971) and *Brief Lives*: a biographical guide to the Arts edited by Louis Kronenberger (first English publication 1972), both the latter published by Allen Lane The Penguin Press.

MICHAEL HARDWICK
Royal Tunbridge Wells

The Maps

The National Grid Reference System

The county maps in this book are based on the Ordnance Survey 10-mile series (1/25,000) on which the National Grid Reference System is superimposed.

The National Grid is a kilometric system which breaks the country down into a series of 100-kilometre squares each of which is identified by a two-letter reference. The 10-mile maps are also gridded at 10-kilometre intervals. A diagram illustrating the 100-kilometre squares and their reference letters is provided opposite and the letters are repeated on the county maps. The numbers of the 10-kilometre squares are indicated on two sides of each map.

Readers who wish to use the National Grid system—perhaps to locate entries on larger-scale maps—can determine four-figure references by the following method. The double-letter reference is given first—if as an example entry 37 for Devonshire is being dealt with on Map 2, it will be seen that it lies in the 100-kilometre square labelled SX. An easting is then taken from the 0 point of square SX and entry 37 will be found to lie slightly east of 70 kilometres as indicated by the figure 7 in the southern margin. The number of kilometres east of 7 has to be estimated and will be seen to be 2. This gives an easting of 72. A northing has now to be taken and reference to the figure in the westerly margin will indicate that entry 37 has a northing of exactly 40 kilometres. The complete four-figure reference will be SX 7240.

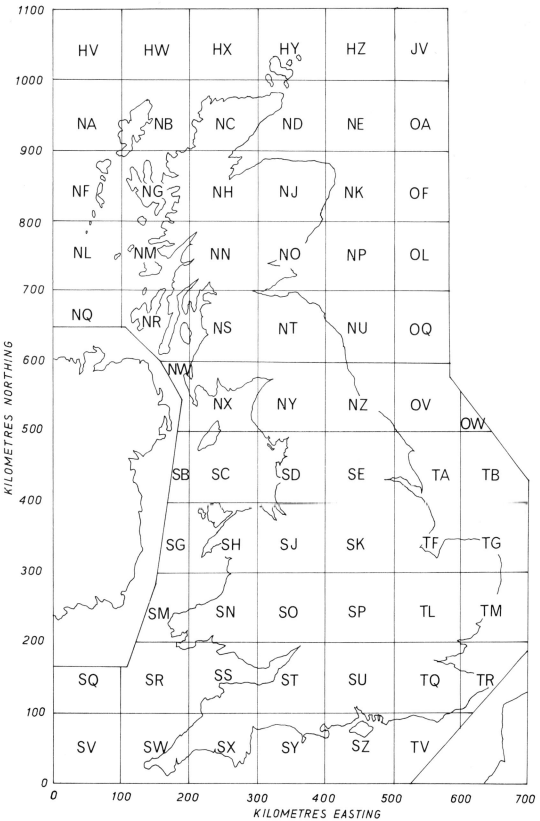

England
&
Wales

Cornwall (*Map 1*)

1 Bodmin HAMLEY, GENERAL SIR EDWARD (1824–93), author, born here. He edited the first series of *Tales from Blackwood*, 1858, and wrote a variety of works, including *Lady Lee's Widowhood*, 1854, *The War in the Crimea*, 1855, and *Voltaire*, 1877.

MCNEILE, HERMAN CYRIL (1888–1937), novelist, born here. He was author of the *Bulldog Drummond* series under the pseudonym 'Sapper'.

QUILLER-COUCH, SIR ARTHUR (1863–1944), literary scholar and novelist, born here. Author of many works on literature and compiler of *The Oxford Book of English Verse*, 1900, and other notable anthologies. His novels were written under the pseudonym 'Q'.

2 Camborne HARRIS, JOHN (1820–84), miner and poet, born here. He published *Lays of the Mine, the Moor and the Mountain*, 1853.

3 Carbis Bay ELLIS, HAVELOCK (1859–1939), psychologist and author, wrote several of his books while living here.

4 Coombe HAWKER, ROBERT STEPHEN (1803–75), poet, owned a cottage near the water mill and here wrote *Song of the Western Men* ('And shall Trelawney die?'), 1832.

5 Duloe SCOTT, ROBERT (1811–87) rector here c1840. He collaborated with H. G. Liddell in compiling the Greek–English lexicon, 1843.

6 Falmouth FOX, CAROLINE (1819–71), diarist and translator, born and lived at Penjerrick. Extracts from her journal recording her friendships with John Stuart Mill, John Sterling and Thomas Carlyle were edited in 1882.

HARRIS, JOHN (1820–84), miner and poet, died here (see **Camborne**).

SPRING, HOWARD (1889–1965), novelist, lived at The White Cottage and used Falmouth and its neighbourhood as a setting for several novels, eg *All the Day Long* is set in Mylor.

7 Flushing BUCKINGHAM, JAMES SILK (1786–1855), author and traveller, born here. He wrote about his travels and also in the Temperance cause.

8 Fowey ATTWELL, MABEL LUCIE (1879–1964), book illustrator, lived at Fowey for many years and died here.

GRAHAME, KENNETH (1859–1932), essayist and children's author, was married here in 'the little grey sea town that clings along one side of the harbour': described by the Sea Rat in *Wind in the Willows*.

QUILLER-COUCH, SIR ARTHUR (1863–1944), literary scholar and novelist lived at The Haven during his last years, and died here. He was elected mayor of Fowey in 1937 (see **Bodmin**).

9 Godolphin GODOLPHIN, SIDNEY (1610–43), poet and 'little Sid' of Sir John Suckling's works, born here. His *Passion of Dido* was contained in Dryden's *Miscellany*.

10 Helston COLERIDGE, DERWENT (1800–83), son of Samuel Taylor Coleridge, headmaster of the grammar school 1825–41. He published various works, including a biography of his brother, Hartley.

JOHNS, CHARLES ALEXANDER (1811–74), author of popular works on natural history, was second master at the grammar school under Derwent Coleridge, and then headmaster 1843–47.

11 Kilkhampton Old Stowe House is described in CHARLES KINGSLEY's *Westward Ho!*

12 Launceston FOX, GEORGE (1624–91), founder of the Society of Friends, imprisoned here for six months in 1656 for distributing his religious tracts.

13 Looe BOND, THOMAS (1765–1837), topographer, was town clerk. He published a topography of the town in 1823.

14 Ludgvan BORLASE, WILLIAM (1695–1772), Cornish antiquary, rector from 1722 until his death and buried here (see **Pendeen**).

15 Morwenstow HAWKER, ROBERT STEPHEN (1803–75), poet, rector 1834–74 (see **Coombe**).

16 Mylor MANSFIELD, KATHERINE (1888–1923), short story writer, and her husband, J. Middleton Murry (1889–1957), critic, lived here.

17 Pendeen BORLASE, WILLIAM (1695–1722), Cornish antiquary, born at Pendeen House. Correspondent of Pope, he supplied him with geological samples for the grotto at Twickenham.

18 Penryn DELANY, MRS MARY (1700–88), lived at the manor house of Roscrow 1718–48. Correspondent of Swift and Fanny Burney, her London salon was a meeting place for artists and men of letters.

REDDING, CYRUS (1785–1870), journalist and author, born here. He published numerous works, including a *History and Description of Modern Wines*, 1833.

TEMPLE, WILLIAM JOHNSTONE (1739–96), essayist, vicar of Gluvias from 1776. He was a lifelong friend of Boswell and of Gray, of whom he wrote an appreciation that was included by Dr Johnson in his *Lives of the Poets*.

19 Penzance DAVIDSON, JOHN (1857–1909), poet, committed suicide here.

HUDSON, WILLIAM HENRY (1841–1922), naturalist and author, travelled widely in the Land's End area and wrote about it in his book *The Land's End*.

TREGARTHEN, JOHN COULSON (1854–1933), novelist, born here. His novels of Cornish life are *John Penrose*, 1923, and *The Smuggler's Daughter*, 1932.

20 Polperro CROUCH, JONATHAN (1789–1870), naturalist and historian, born at Polperro, practised medicine here from 1809 until his death, and is buried here. He was the author of a history of Polperro.

21 Polruan WALMSLEY, LEO (1892–1966), novelist, lived at Pont Creek. Most of his stories have Cornish settings.

22 St Germans CAREW, RICHARD (1555–1620), antiquary, lived and died at Antony House. He translated the first five cantos of Tasso's *Godfrey of Bulloigne*, 1594, and wrote a *Survey of Cornwall*, 1602.

23 St Ives ELLIS, MRS HAVELOCK (*née* Edith Mary Lees, 1861–1916), novelist, born here. She married Havelock Ellis in 1891. Her novels include *Seaweed: A Cornish Idyll*, 1898.

HOCKING, JOSEPH (1860–1937), novelist, died here (see **St Stephen**).

WOOLF, VIRGINIA (1882–1941), novelist, lived here during 1926 and wrote *To the Lighthouse* (generally thought to be Godrevy lighthouse). As a child she spent every summer at Talland House.

24 St Juliot HARDY, THOMAS (1840–1928), novelist and poet, restored the church here. His first wife, Emma Lavinia Gifford, whom he married in 1874, was sister-in-law of the rector.

25 St Stephen-in-Brannel HOCKING, SILAS (1850–1935), and his brother JOSEPH (1860–1937) born here. Each wrote some fifty novels with considerable success.

26 Truro FOOTE, SAMUEL (1720–77), actor and dramatist, born in Boscawen Street and lived as a child at the Red

Lion Inn opposite. He was nicknamed 'the English Aristophanes' in his day, but his plays have not endured.

LOWRY, HENRY DAWSON (1869–1906), novelist, born here. His publications include *Women's Tragedies*, 1895, and *A Man of Moods*, 1896.

POLWHELE, RICHARD (1760–1838), topographical and miscellaneous writer, born here. He published histories of Devon and Cornwall.

WALPOLE, SIR HUGH SEYMOUR (1884–1941), novelist, lived here in childhood and set many of his novels in the county. *The Cathedral*, 1922, was the first of a series set in the town of 'Polchester', based largely on Truro. He was born in New Zealand.

WOLCOT, JOHN ('Peter Pindar', 1738–1819), satirist and poet, practised medicine here 1773–80.

27 Tresillian HALS, WILLIAM (1656–c1737), Cornish historian, born at Merther. He contributed to the *History of Cornwall* published c1750.

28 Treslothian HARRIS, JOHN (1820–84), miner and poet, buried here (see **Camborne**).

29 Zennor LAWRENCE, DAVID HERBERT (1885–1930), novelist and poet, lived at Higher Tregarthen from 1916 to 1917 when he was working on *Women in Love*. KATHERINE MANSFIELD and J. MIDDLETON MURRY stayed with him and took a house called The Eagle's Nest before moving to Mylor (qv). Lawrence also lived briefly at Porthcothan, Dec 1915–Feb 1916.

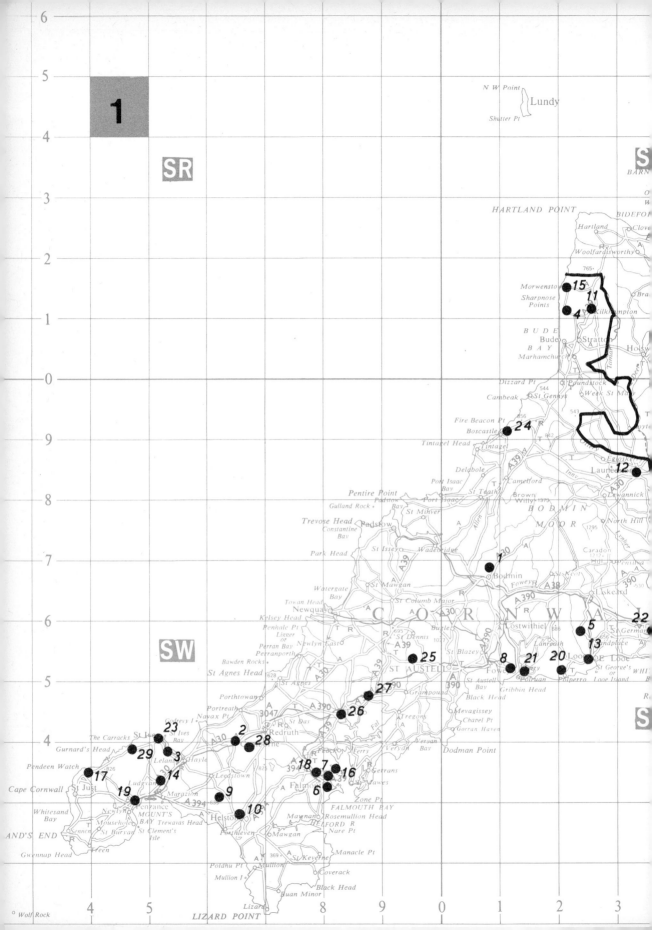

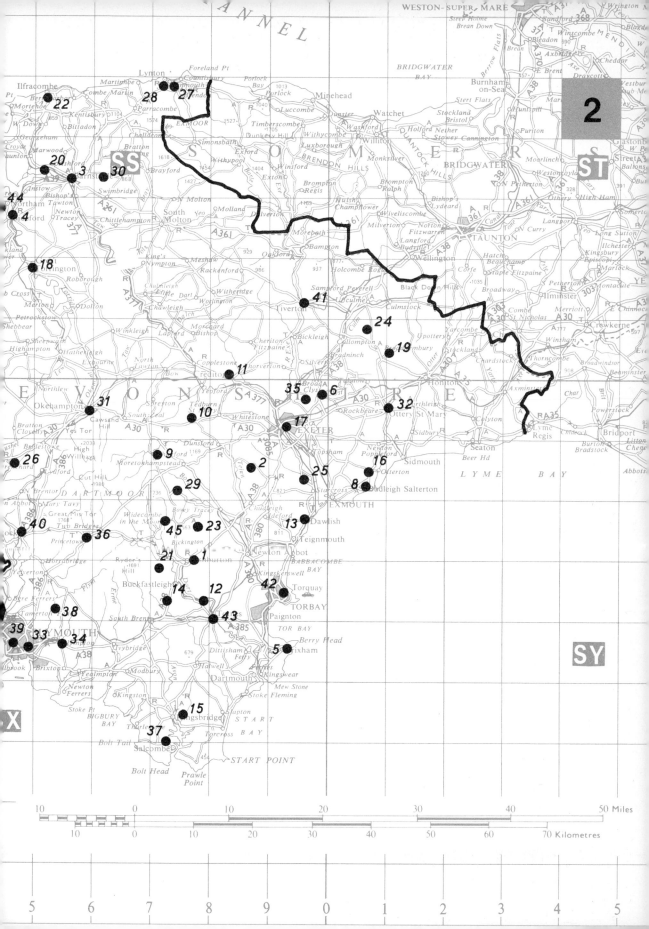

Devonshire (*Maps 1 & 2*)

1 Ashburton GIFFORD, WILLIAM (1756–1826), poet, translator and critic, born here. His *Baviad*, 1794, and *Maeviad*, 1796, satirised the affectations of a contemporary group of poets. *Epistle to Peter Pinder*, 1800, was an attack on Dr John Wolcot (see **Dodbrooke**). Gifford edited the plays of Ben Jonson, Ford and Massinger.

MOORMAN, FREDERICK (1872–1919), author, born here. His publications are mostly associated with Yorkshire where he spent the greater part of his life; they include *Tales of the Ridings*, 1920.

2 Ashton CHUDLEIGH, LADY MARY (1656–1710), poet and essayist, is buried here.

3 Barnstaple BARBELLION, W. N. P. (pseudonym of Bruce Frederick Cummings, 1889–1919), author, born here. His *Journal of a Disappointed Man* was published in 1919.

CHICHESTER, SIR FRANCIS (1901–72), solo circumnavigator of the world, born here. He is buried at nearby Shirwell, where his father had been rector 1894–1936. Also a notable aviator, he reflected his experiences in a number of books, including *Alone Across the Atlantic*, 1962, *Gipsy Moth Circles the World*, 1967, and his autobiography *The Lonely Sea and the Sky*, 1964.

GAY, JOHN (1685–1732), poet and dramatist, born at 35 High Street. His *Beggar's Opera* was produced in 1728.

SAUNDERS, JOHN (1810–95), author, born here. His works include *Abel Drake's Wife*, 1862, and *Hirell*, 1869.

4 Bideford KINGSLEY, CHARLES (1819–75), author, lived here from 1854. It is the chief setting for his *Westward Ho!* 1855 (see also **Holne**).

5 Brixham LYTE, HENRY (1793–1847), poet and hymn writer, vicar here for twenty-five years.

6 Broad Clyst PHILLPOTTS, EDEN (1862–1960), novelist, spent his last years here. He was born in India. His best-known works are about Dartmoor and include *Secret Woman*, 1905, *Widecombe Fair*, 1913, and the play *The Farmer's Wife*, 1916. He is said to have done for Devon what Thomas Hardy did for Dorset.

7 Buckland Brewer CAPERN, EDWARD (1819–94), poet, born here. Known as 'the rural postman of Bideford', he published his verses by subscription in 1856, with much success.

8 Budleigh Salterton TROLLOPE, THOMAS ADOLPHUS (1810–92), novelist and brother of Anthony Trollope, lived in Cliff Terrace.

9 Chagford GODOLPHIN, SIDNEY (1610–43), poet, lived here and was killed at the inn during the Civil War: he was the 'little Sid' of Sir John Suckling's works.

10 Cheriton Bishop MALLOCK, WILLIAM HURRELL (1849–1923), novelist, born at Cockington Court. His publications include *The New Republic*, 1877, and *The New Paul and Virginia*, 1878.

11 Crediton ROWE, SAMUEL (1793–1853), Devonshire topographer, vicar of Crediton 1835 and buried here.

12 Dartington FROUDE, JAMES ANTHONY (1818–94), historian, born here. His great twelve-volume *History of England* appeared 1856–70.

13 Dawlish BARHAM, RICHARD (1815–86), poet, son and biographer of RICHARD HARRIS BARHAM, the author of *The Ingoldsby Legends*, lived at Broxmore from 1863 and is buried here.

14 Dean Prior HERRICK, ROBERT (1591–1674), lyrical poet, vicar 1629–47 and again in 1662, and is buried here.

15 Dodbrooke WOLCOT, JOHN (1738–1819), poet who wrote under the name Peter Pindar, born here. His many poetical pamphlets included *The Apple-dumplings and a King*, *Bozzy and Piozzi*, *Lyrical Odes* and a number of ballads.

16 East Budleigh RALEIGH, SIR WALTER (1552–1618), explorer, poet, and author of *History of the World*, 1614, born at Hayes Barton.

17 Exeter AINSWORTH, WILLIAM FRANCIS (1807–96), travel writer, born here. He published numerous works on the Near East, including *Travels and Researches in Asia Minor, Mesopotamia, etc*, 1842.

BARING-GOULD, SABINE (1834–1924), novelist, folklorist and hymn writer, born here. He wrote voluminously about religion, myths, superstitions and the West Country. His best-known hymn is 'Onward, Christian Soldiers'.

BRICE, ANDREW (1690–1773), printer and topographer, born and buried here. He issued a local newspaper c1715–73, and published his *Grand Gazetteer, or Topographic Dictionary* in 1759.

D'URFEY, THOMAS (1653–1723), dramatist and song writer, born here. *Pills to Purge Melancholy*, 1719–20, is a collection of songs; his plays include *Madame Fickle*, 1677, and *The Virtuous Wife*, 1680.

HOOKER, RICHARD (1554–1600), theologian and author of *The Laws of Ecclesiastical Polity*, 1594–97, born here.

LEOFRIC (d1072), first bishop of Exeter, was a notable collector of books, and bestowed the poetry collection known as the *Liber Exoniensis* on the church. It is kept in the cathedral library.

The Turks Head Inn was the scene of Pickwick's encounter with Joe, the Fat Boy, in *Pickwick Papers*. CHARLES DICKENS settled his parents into Mile End Cottage, Alphington, in 1839.

18 Great Torrington JOHNSON, WILLIAM, poet, born here in 1823.

19 Broad Hembury TOPLADY, AUGUSTUS MONTAGUE (1740–78), hymn writer, vicar here 1768–75.

20 Heanton Punchardon CAPERN, EDWARD (1819–94), poet, buried here (see **Buckland Brewer**).

21 Holne KINGSLEY, CHARLES (1819–75), author, born at the vicarage. His *Westward Ho!* was published in 1855, and *The Water Babies* in 1863.

22 Ilfracombe JEWEL, JOHN (1522–71), theological writer and bishop of Salisbury, born at Berrynarbor nearby. He was a leading opponent of Rome with such works as *Apologia Ecclesiae Anglicanae*, 1562.

KERNAHAN, COULSON (1858–1943), author, born here. His publications include *Captain Shannon*, 1897, and *Swinburne as I knew him*, 1919.

23 Ilsington FORD, JOHN (1586–c1640), dramatist, born here; called by Charles Lamb 'the last of the Elizabethans'. His chief works include *Lover's Melancholy*, 1629, and *'Tis Pity She's a Whore*, 1633.

24 Kentisbeare SCOTT, SIR WALTER (1771–1832) wrote the epitaph on the memorial to George Scott, a relative buried here.

25 Kenton POLWHELE, RICHARD (1760–1838), author and poet, curate 1782–93.

26 Lew Trenchard BARING-GOULD, SABINE (1834–1924), novelist, folklorist and hymn writer, succeeded to the family estate here in 1872, became rector in 1881, and is buried here (see **Exeter**).

27 **Lynmouth** SHELLEY, PERCY BYSSHE (1792–1822) wrote *Queen Mab* while living here 1812–13.

28 **Lynton** NEWNES, SIR GEORGE (1851–1910), editor and founder of *Tit-Bits*, 1881, *The Strand Magazine*, 1891, etc, is buried here.

29 **Manaton** GALSWORTHY, JOHN (1867–1933), novelist, lived at Wingstone Farm 1906–23.

30 **Northleigh** CARPENTER, NATHANIEL (1589–1628), author and philosopher, born here. His treatises on philosophy were largely directed against Aristotelianism.

31 **Okehampton** GODOLPHIN, SIDNEY (1610–43), poet, is buried here (see **Chagford**).

32 **Ottery St Mary** BARCLAY, ALEXANDER (1475–1552), poet, was a priest at the college here when his *Ship of Fools* appeared in 1508.

BROWNE, WILLIAM (1591–c1643), poet, lived here (see **Tavistock**).

COLERIDGE, SAMUEL TAYLOR (1772–1834) born at the vicarage. His first publication was *Poems on Various Subjects*, 1796, but his great step to fame was through *Lyrical Ballads*, 1798, written with Wordsworth and including Coleridge's *Rime of the Ancient Mariner*.

THACKERAY, WILLIAM MAKEPEACE (1811–63) lived from 1825 to 1828 with the Smyths at nearby Larkbeare. In his largely autobiographical novel *Pendennis*, 1848, Ottery St Mary becomes Clavering St Mary, Exeter is Chatteris and Sidmouth is Baymouth.

33 **Plymouth** CARRINGTON, NOEL (1777–1830), poet, born here. His verse is largely descriptive of Devonshire.

CHICHESTER, SIR FRANCIS (1901–72), solo circumnavigator of the world, and author, died at the Royal Naval Hospital.

COLLINS, MORTIMER (1827–76), poet, novelist and bohemian, born here. Among his works are *The Inn of Strange Meetings, and other Poems*, *The Vivian Romance*, *Transmigration* and *From Midnight to Midnight*.

DOBSON, HENRY AUSTIN (1840–1921), poet and critic, born here. His series of essays *Eighteenth Century Vignettes* appeared in 1892, 1894 and 1896; he also published popular biographies and light verse.

HAWKER, ROBERT STEPHEN (1803–75), poet and antiquary, buried here (see **Stoke Damerel**).

MACCARTHY, SIR DESMOND (1877–1952), critic, born here. Much of his work was written for the *New Statesman* and *The Sunday Times* and collected later, eg *Drama*, 1940, and *Humanities*, 1953.

MCCULLOCH, DEREK (1897–1967), children's author, born here. His widest fame was as 'Uncle Mac' of Children's Hour on the radio.

SQUIRE, SIR JOHN (1884–1958), poet and critic, born here. As literary editor of the *New Statesman*, 1919–34, and editor of the *London Mercury*, he helped many writers and poets to their first successes.

STRONG, LEONARD ALFRED GEORGE (1896–1958), poet

and novelist, born here. His best known novel is *Dewar Rides*, 1929, set on Dartmoor.

34 **Plympton** STRODE, WILLIAM (1602–45), lyrical poet, born here. His play *The Floating Island* was produced in 1633.

35 **Poltimore** BAMPFYLDE, JOHN (1754–96), poet, born here. His *Sixteen Sonnets* appeared in 1778.

36 **Princetown** The Dartmoor area is the setting for SIR ARTHUR CONAN DOYLE's most celebrated Sherlock Holmes story, *The Hound of the Baskervilles*, 1902.

37 **Salcombe** FROUDE, JAMES ANTHONY (1818–94), historian, lived at Woodcot and buried here (see **Dartington**).

38 **Shaugh Prior** CARRINGTON, NOEL (1777–1830), poet, lived here (see **Plymouth**).

39 **Stoke Damerel** HAWKER, ROBERT STEPHEN (1803–75), poet and antiquary, born here. Many of his poems concern the West Country; the best known is 'And shall Trelawney die?'

40 **Tavistock** BRAY, ANNA (1790–1883), novelist, lived here.

BROWNE, WILLIAM (1591–c1643), poet, born here. His works include *Britannia's Pastorals*, 1613–16 and 1852 (Percy Society), and *The Shepheard's Pipe*, 1614.

41 **Tiverton** COWLEY, MRS HANNAH, *née* Parkhouse (1743–1809), dramatist, born, died and buried here. Her works include *The Belle's Stratagem*, 1782.

42 **Torquay** BROWNING, ELIZABETH BARRETT (1806–61), poet, lived here 1832–34 and worked on her translation of the *Prometheus Bound* of Aeschylus, 1833.

BUDGES, THOMAS CHARLES (1868–1944), prolific author of boys' stories, spent his last years at Torquay and died here. He also wrote under the pseudonyms Christopher Beck, Martin Shaw and John Stanton.

HOPE, ANNE (1809–87), author, died at St Marychurch.

KIPLING, RUDYARD (1865–1936), poet and novelist, lived at Maidencombe 1896–97 and here wrote some of his best stories, included in *The Day's Work*, 1898.

KNOWLES, JAMES SHERIDAN (1784–1862), Irish-born dramatist, died here. His works include *Virginius*, 1820, and *The Love Chase*, 1837.

O'CASEY, SEAN (1884–1964), Irish-born playwright, lived at Torquay from 1926 and died here. Plays of this period include *Red Roses for Me*, 1942, and *Cock-a-doodle Dandy*, 1949; the six volumes of his autobiography appeared between 1939 and 1945.

PHILLPOTTS, EDEN (1862–1960), novelist, lived here before moving to Broad Clyst (qv).

PROWSE, WILLIAM (1836–70), poet, born and buried here. His chief success was with humorous contributions to periodicals.

SAVAGE, MARMION (1803–72), novelist, died here.

43 **Totnes** CROSS, JOHN KEIR (1914–67), children's author and writer of many radio plays, farmed at Diptford nearby for several years up to his death.

44 **Westward Ho!** KIPLING, RUDYARD (1865–1936), poet and novelist, was educated at the United Services College. He based *Stalky and Co*, 1899, on his experiences there, with himself in the character of Beetle.

45 **Widecombe** CHASE, BEATRICE (1874–1955), novelist, lived at Venton House.

Somerset (*Map 3*)

1 **Aisholt** NEWBOLT, SIR HENRY (1862–1938), poet, lived here towards the end of his life.

2 **Ansford** WOODFORDE, JAMES (1740–1803), diarist, born at the parsonage and was curate to his father here until 1771. His diary, covering the years 1758–1802, was published 1924–31 as *Diary of a Country Parson*.

3 **Bath** ANSTEY, CHRISTOPHER (1724–1805), poet, lived and is buried here.

ATHERSTONE, EDWIN (1788–1872), poet, died here.

BAYLY, THOMAS HAYNES (1797–1839), author and song writer, born here. He produced novels and plays, but is best known for such songs as 'She Wore a Wreath of Roses' and 'We Met—'twas in a Crowd'.

BECKFORD, WILLIAM (1759–1844), author of *Vathek*, 1787, moved to Bath from Fonthill in 1822 and built Lansdown Tower.

BOWDLER, THOMAS (1754–1825) born at Ashley. His expurgating of Shakespeare and other authors introduced the term 'bowdlerise' into the language.

BROOME, WILLIAM (1689–1745), translator of Homer and poet, is buried in Bath Abbey.

BURNEY, FANNY (Madame Francis d'Arblay, 1752–1840), diarist and author, died in Bath and is buried in Walcot churchyard.

BUTLER, JOSEPH (1692–1752), theological writer, died here.

EWING, MRS JULIANA HORATIA (1841–85), children's author, died here.

HONE, WILLIAM (1780–1842), author and compiler, born here. He published political satires and collections of curious information.

KILVERT, FRANCIS (1793–1863), antiquary, born in Westgate Street. In 1837 he moved to Claverton Lodge, where he lived until his death, and is buried in Old Widcombe churchyard. His publications include papers on Bath's literary associations.

MONTGOMERY, ROBERT (1807–55), poet, born here. He was successful with his work *Satan, or Intellect without God*, 1830, until Macaulay determinedly destroyed his reputation.

MORE, HANNAH (1745–1833), dramatist and religious writer, moved to a house in Great Pulteney Street in 1789.

RUSSELL, WILLIAM CLARK (1844–1911), American-born author of sea stories, spent his last years at 9 Sydney Place.

SHERIDAN, RICHARD BRINSLEY (1751–1816), dramatist, lived at Terrace Walk 1770–73, and began *The Rivals* here. In 1772 he eloped with Elizabeth Linley, of the Royal Crescent, marrying her in the following year.

SPENDER, LILY (1838–95), novelist, lived here from 1858, died, and is buried here.

VACHELL, HORACE ANNESLEY (1861–1955), novelist and playwright, lived at Widcombe Manor.

WORDSWORTH, WILLIAM (1770–1850), poet laureate, lived at 9 North Parade in 1841.

4 **Beckington** DANIEL, SAMUEL (1562–1619), poet and dramatist, spent the last months of his life at Ridge Farm, and is buried here (see **Taunton**).

5 **Blagdon** LANGHORNE, JOHN (1735–79), poet and translator of Plutarch's *Lives*, 1770, rector from 1766 and buried here.

6 **Bruton** BATMAN, STEPHEN (d1584), translator and author, born here. Shakespeare is said to have derived material from his works of history and religion.

7 **Charlcombe** FIELDING, SARAH (1710–68), novelist, sister of Henry Fielding, buried here.

8 **Charlton Mackrell** LYTE, HENRY (c1529–1607), antiquary, lived at Lyte's Cary and is buried here.

9 **Clevedon** COLERIDGE, SAMUEL TAYLOR (1772–1834), poet, lived here in 1795 after marrying Sara Fricker.

HALLAM, ARTHUR HENRY (1811–33), poet, buried here. His early death inspired Tennyson's poem *In Memoriam*, 1850.

THACKERAY, WILLIAM MAKEPEACE (1811–63), novelist, wrote part of *Henry Esmond* and much of *Vanity Fair* while staying at Clevedon Court.

10 **Combe Florey** SMITH, SYDNEY (1771–1845), clergyman, author and wit, was rector 1829–45.

11 **Combe Hay** CARRINGTON, NOEL (1777–1830), poet, is buried here.

12 **Doulting** ALDHELM, ST (c640–709), Saxon poet, died at the original wooden church there.

13 **Frome** KEN or KENN, THOMAS (1637–1711), devotional writer, poet and bishop of Bath and Wells, buried here.

14 **Holford** WORDSWORTH, WILLIAM (1770–1850), poet laureate, and his sister DOROTHY, rented Alfoxden Manor 1797–98 to be near Coleridge at Nether Stowey (qv). It was during this period that *Lyrical Ballads*, 1798, was planned.

15 **Ilchester** BACON, ROGER (c1214–94), philosopher and writer, born here. His extensive knowledge won him the title 'Doctor Mirabilis'.

ROWE, ELIZABETH (1674–1737), poet, born here. Her *Poems on Several Occasions by Philomela* were published in 1696.

16 **Langport** BAGEHOT, WALTER (1826–77), author and editor, was born, died and is buried here. He was a banker, and edited *The Economist* from 1860, but was better noted for his literary criticism, principally collected in five volumes, 1879 and 1895.

17 **Misterton** MATHERS, HELEN (1853–1920), novelist, born and lived here. *Coming through the Rye*, her most noted work, was published 1875.

18 **Nether Stowey** COLERIDGE, SAMUEL TAYLOR (1772–1834), poet, lived at what is now Coleridge Cottage from 1797 to 1799—the time of the *Lyrical Ballads* and *Kubla Khan*. The house is open to the public.

19 **Odcombe** CORYATE, THOMAS (c1577–1617), traveller, born here. In 1608 he walked some 2,000 miles on the Continent and described his experiences in *Coryate's Crudities*, 1611.

20 **Orchardleigh** NEWBOLT, SIR HENRY (1862–1938), poet, buried here.

21 **Sharpham Park, nr Glastonbury** DYER, SIR EDWARD (c1545–1607), poet, born here. His poems include 'My mind to me a kingdom is'.

FIELDING, HENRY (1707–54), novelist and playwright, born at the manor house, now a farmhouse. His celebrated work, *The History of Tom Jones, a Foundling*, appeared in 1749.

22 **Swainswick** PRYNNE, WILLIAM (1600–69), Puritan pamphleteer, born here. His *Histriomastix*, 1632, offended Queen Henrietta Maria and brought Prynne much punishment; his most notable work is *Brevia Parliamentaria Rediviva*, 1662.

23 **Taunton** DANIEL, SAMUEL (1562–1619), poet and dramatist, born here or nearby. His sonnet series *Delia* appeared in 1592, and his masques *Tethys Festival* and *Hymen's Triumph* in 1610 and 1615 respectively.

KINGLAKE, ALEXANDER (1809–91), historian, born at Wilton House. His big history of the Crimean War appeared 1863–87.

NORRIS, EDWIN (1795–1872), orientalist and Cornish scholar, born here. He published *The Ancient Cornish Drama*, with a Cornish grammar, 1859.

24 Timberscombe MARTIN, JOHN PERCIVAL (c1880–1966), children's author, was Methodist minister here from 1932 until his death.

25 Trull EWING, MRS JULIANA HORATIA (1841–85), children's author, buried here. A window in the parish church commemorates her.

26 Wellington BENSON, ARTHUR CHRISTOPHER (1862–1925), essayist, born at Wellington College, son of the headmaster, E. W. Benson (later archbishop of Canterbury). He wrote biographies of Tennyson, 1904, Walter Pater, 1906, and others, beside several volumes of essays, novels and verse, including 'Land of Hope and Glory'.

BENSON, EDWARD FREDERICK (1867–1940), biographer and novelist, brother of A. C. Benson, born at Wellington College. He was the biographer of several royal figures, but is best remembered for his humorous Miss Mapp novels.

27 Wells STILL, JOHN (c1543–1608), dramatist, bishop of Bath and Wells from 1593 until his death, and is buried in the cathedral.

28 Weston-super-Mare EDWARDS, AMELIA ANN BLANFORD (1831–92), novelist and Egyptologist, died here.

WEBB, MARY GLADYS (1881–1927), novelist, lived here from 1912–14 after her marriage.

29 Widcombe Prior Park was the home of Ralph Allen, a patron of HENRY FIELDING. Fielding completed *Tom Jones*, 1749, while staying at Widcombe Lodge; and ALEXANDER POPE completed his *Dunciad* while a guest of Ralph Allen.

BRAMAH, ERNEST (pseudonym of Ernest Bramah Smith, 1868–1942), novelist, lived at the manor house.

30 Wrington LOCKE, JOHN (1632–1704), philosopher, born here. His *Essay on the Human Understanding* appeared in 1690.

MORE, HANNAH (1745–1833), dramatist and religious writer, lived at Cowslip Green from 1802 and is buried here.

31 Yeovil EDWARDS, RICHARD (c1523–66), poet and playwright, probably born hereabouts. His only extant play is *Damon and Pithias*, 1571.

ELIOT, THOMAS STEARNS (1888–1965). American-born poet and playwright, is buried at East Coker nearby, the village from which his ancestors had gone to America. His best-known works include *The Waste Land*, 1922, *Murder in the Cathedral*, 1935, and *Four Quartets*, 1943, one of which is entitled 'East Coker'.

RAYMOND, WALTER (1852–1931), author, born here. His publications include *Misterton's Mistake*, 1890, *Book of Simple Delights*, 1906, *English Country Life*, 1910, and *Under the Spreading Chestnut Tree*, 1928.

Dorsetshire (*Maps 3 & 4*)

1 **Affpuddle** Egdon Heath is the setting of THOMAS HARDY's *The Return of the Native*.

2 **Batcombe** The home of Conjuror Minterne, the quack in HARDY's *Tess of the d'Urbervilles*.

3 **Beaminster** Emminster in HARDY's *Tess of the d'Urbervilles*.

SPRAT, THOMAS (1635–1713), bishop, born here. His best known work is *History of the Royal Society*, 1667.

4 **Bere Regis** Kingsbere, home of the d'Urberville family in HARDY's *Tess*.

5 **Bincombe** The setting of scenes in HARDY's *The Trumpet Major* and *The Melancholy Hussar*.

6 **Blandford** Shottsford Forum in HARDY's Wessex.

BASTARD, THOMAS (1566–1618), satirist and versifier, born here. He published *Chrestoleros: Seuen Books of Epigrames*, 1598.

CREECH, THOMAS (1659–1700), translator of Latin classics, buried here.

JAMES, JOHN ANGELL (1785–1859), minister and author, born here. His works include *The Anxious Inquirer after Salvation*, 1834.

PITT, CHRISTOPHER (1699–1748), poet and translator, buried here.

7 **Blandford St Mary** WILLIS, BROWNE (1682–1760), antiquary, born here. Among his works is *Notitia Parliamentaria; or, A History of the Counties, Cities and Boroughs in England and Wales*, 1715–50.

8 **Bradford Peverel** HUTCHINS, JOHN (1698–1773), Dorset historian, born here. His *History of Dorset* first appeared in 1774.

9 **Bridport** Port Bredy in HARDY's *Fellow Townsmen*.

10 **Broad Windsor** FULLER, THOMAS (1608–61), historian, rector here 1634–c1641. During his incumbency he wrote his *History of the Holy War*, 1643, and *The Holy State and the Profane State*, 1642.

11 **Cerne Abbas** AELFRIC 'the Grammarian' (fl1006), first abbot, was probably at Cerne 987–1005. Many of his sermons, biographies and translations from the scriptures are still extant.

12 **Chaldon Herring** POWYS, LLEWELLYN (1884–1939), novelist and essayist, lived at 'Chydyok' 1931–36 (see **Dorchester**).

13 **Charminster** In *A Group of Noble Dames* THOMAS HARDY places Lady Penelope at 'Wolfeton'.

14 **Corscombe** HOLLIS, THOMAS (1720–74), benefactor of foreign universities, editor of Toland's *Milton* and the works of Algernon Sidney, buried here.

15 **Dorchester** BARNES, WILLIAM (1801–86), Dorset dialect poet, kept a school here 1835–62, and composed his *Hwomely Rhymes*, 1859, and other poems.

HARDY, THOMAS (1840–1928), novelist and poet, lived in Shire Hall Lane 1883–85, while writing *The Mayor of Casterbridge*. In 1885 he moved into Max Gate, the house he had built for himself, and remained here until his death. Major works written here were *The Woodlanders*, 1887, *Tess of the d'Urbervilles*, 1891, and *Jude the Obscure*, 1895. Dorchester is the Casterbridge of Hardy's novels.

POWYS, LLEWELLYN (1884–1939), novelist and essay-ist, born at Rothesay House. He wrote of his native county and of places visited during his wide travels, and collaborated with John Cowper Powys in the auto-biography *Confessions of Two Brothers*, 1916.

16 **East Chaldon** POWYS, THEODORE FRANCIS (1875–1953), novelist brother of Llewellyn and John Cowper Powys, lived here 1904–40.

17 **East Stour** FIELDING, HENRY (1707–54), author of *Tom Jones*, lived at the manor house throughout his childhood, and for a time after his marriage in 1734. His sister, SARAH FIELDING (1710–68), novelist, was born here. Her works include *The Adventures of David Simple in Search of a Faithful Friend*, 1744.

18 **Ferndown** TREVENA, JOHN (pseudonym of Ernest George Henham, 1870–1946), novelist, buried here.

19 **Forde Abbey** BENTHAM, JEREMY (1748–1832), philo-sopher and political economist, lived here 1815–18.

20 **Higher Bockhampton** HARDY, THOMAS (1840–1928), novelist and poet, born here. The cottage where he was born and spent his childhood is described in *Under the Greenwood Tree*. Dorset is the heart of the Wessex of Hardy's novels, the most popular of which is *Tess of the d'Urbervilles*, 1891. The longest of his many poems is *The Dynasts*, an epic drama, 1904–8.

21 **Hinton St Mary** FREKE, WILLIAM (1662–1744), mystical writer, lived here for most of his life and is buried here.

22 **Iwerne Minster** WILLIS, JOHN (died c1628), whose *Art of Stenographie*, 1602, foreshadowed modern short-hand, buried here.

23 **Long Bredy** MOTLEY, JOHN LOTHROP (1814–77), American-born historian and diplomat, died at Kingston Russell House. His best known work is *The Rise of the Dutch Republic*, 1856.

24 **Lyme Regis** Setting for part of JANE AUSTEN's *Persuasion*, 1815. She was here in 1804 and possibly in the previous year.

DAY LEWIS, CECIL (1904–72), poet laureate and novelist, lived near here from 1938–50.

25 **Mappowder** POWYS, THEODORE FRANCIS (1875–1953), novelist, lived at Mappowder from 1940 and is buried here.

26 **Marnhull** Marlott, the home of HARDY's *Tess of the d'Urbervilles*.

27 **Milborne St Andrew** MORTON, JOHN (c1420–1500), archbishop of Canterbury, born here. It is probable that he was the author of the Latin version of the *History of Richard III*, generally ascribed to Sir Thomas More.

28 **Minterne Magna** Great Hintock in HARDY's *Woodlanders*; Minterne Parva is called Little Hintock in the same work.

29 **Morden** Welland House of HARDY's *Two on a Tower* is situated here.

30 **Moreton** LAWRENCE, THOMAS EDWARD (Lawrence of Arabia, 1888–1935), soldier and writer, buried here.

31 **Pentridge** Trantridge in HARDY's Wessex.

32 **Piddletrenthide** WIGHTMAN, RALPH (1901–71), writer and broadcaster on country subjects, born here. One of his best known radio series, *Rural Rides*, retraced William Cobbett's travels in modern terms and was also published in book form.

33 **Pilsdon** WORDSWORTH, WILLIAM (1770–1850), poet laureate, lived at Racedown Farm 1795–97, completed *The Borderers* and began *Margaret, or The Ruined Cottage*, which was later used in *The Excursion*, 1814.

34 **Pimperne** PITT, CHRISTOPHER (1699–1748), poet and translator, rector from 1722 until his death.

35 Poole Poolhaven in HARDY's Wessex.
WEBSTER, JULIA (1837–94), poet, born here. She wrote under the name of Cecil Home, and also published plays, translations and a novel.

36 Poxwell Oxwell in HARDY's *Trumpet Major*.

37 Puddletown Weatherbury, in HARDY's Wessex and the main setting for *Far from the Madding Crowd*. Waterston House here was the original of Bathsheba Everdene's home.
WIGHTMAN, RALPH (1901–71), writer and broadcaster on country subjects, lived at the Tudor House (see **Piddletrenthide**).

38 Rushay BARNES, WILLIAM (1801–86), Dorset dialect poet, born here. He published series of *Poems of Rural Life in the Dorset Dialect*, 1844, 1859 and 1863.

39 Shaftesbury Shaston in HARDY's writings.
GRANGER, JAMES (1723–76), biographer, born here. He published *A Biographical Dictionary of England*, 1769, with blank pages where the reader could insert enlarged portraits. The practice of interleaving books with one's own collection of engravings became popular and was known as 'grangerising'.

40 Sherborne Sherton Abbas in HARDY's Wessex.
RALEIGH, SIR WALTER (c1552–1618), adventurer and author, lived here 1592–95.
The Sherborne Missal was written between 1396 and 1407 by JOHN WHAS, a monk at the abbey.

41 Stinsford The Mellstock of *Under the Greenwood Tree*; THOMAS HARDY's heart is buried here; his ashes lie in Westminster Abbey.
DAY LEWIS, CECIL (1904–72), poet laureate and novelist, is buried in the parish churchyard.

42 Stoke Abbott CROWE, WILLIAM (1745–1829), poet, rector 1782–87.

43 Sturminster Newton Stour Castle of HARDY's Wessex stands here. The author was frequently in Sturminster while writing his early books, and lived at Riverside Villa 1876–78. It was here that he wrote *The Return of the Native*, 1878.
YOUNG, ROBERT (1811–1908), poet, born and buried here. He published dialect verse under the pseudonym Robin Hill.

44 Sutton Poyntz Overcombe in HARDY's Wessex; the Trumpet Major's father was miller here.

45 Tarrant Crawford POORE, RICHARD (d1237) born and buried here. He may possibly have been the author of the *Ancren Riwle*, one of the first books in English (c1200), a work of guidance for nuns.

46 Tincleton Stickleford in HARDY's Wessex.
WALKER, CLEMENT (1651), presbyterian writer, born at Clyffe House. He was imprisoned in the Tower of London from 1649 for his *History of Independency* and died there.

47 Tolpuddle The Tolpuddle Martyrs have been the subject of many books, plays and poems.

48 Upwey The mill here is the original portrayed by HARDY in *The Trumpet Major*. He wrote the opening scene of his epic drama *The Dynasts*, 1904–8, in Upwey.

49 Wareham Anglebury in HARDY's Wessex.
AGNUS, ORME (pseudonym of John C. Higginbotham, d1919), novelist, was a teacher here from the age of eighteen until his death. His novels are almost all set in Dorset.
HUTCHINS, JOHN (1698–1773), Dorset historian, buried here (see **Bradford Peverel**).
WESTERMAN, PERCY FRANCIS (1876–1960), boys' novelist, lived and died here.

50 Weymouth Budmouth in HARDY's Wessex; the novelist lodged at 3 Wooperton Street in 1869.
COLLINGWOOD, HARRY (pseudonym of W. J. C. Lancaster, 1851–c1924), boys' author, born here. *The Secret of the Sands*, 1879, was followed by many more novels about the sea and flying.
HENTY, GEORGE ALFRED (1832–1902), boys' novelist, died on his yacht in the habour.
PEACOCK, THOMAS LOVE (1785–1866), novelist, born here. An intimate friend of Shelley, his best works include *Headlong Hall*, 1816, *Nightmare Abbey*, 1818, and *Crotchet Castle*, 1831.

51 Whatcombe HOLLOWAY, WILLIAM (1761–1854), poet, born here.

52 Whitcombe BARNES, WILLIAM (1801–86), Dorset dialect poet, curate here 1847–52 (see **Rushay**).

53 Wimborne Warborne in HARDY's Wessex; the novelist lived at Llanherne, The Avenue, 1881–83, and wrote *Two on a Tower*, 1882.
PRIOR, MATTHEW (1664–1721), poet and diplomat, born here. With Charles Montagu he parodied Dryden's *Hind and the Panther* as *The Town and Country Mouse*, 1687. He is best remembered for his lyrics and epigrams, including *To a Child of Quality*.

54 Winterborne Came BARNES, WILLIAM (1801–86), Dorset dialect poet, rector from 1862 until his death and buried here (see **Rushay**).

55 Winterborne Whitchurch TURBERVILLE, GEORGE (c1540–c1610), poet and translator, born here. A pioneer of blank verse, his publications include *Epitaphs, Epigrams, Songs and Sonets*, 1567, and *The Booke of Faulconrie*, 1575.

56 Woodbury Hill Scene of Greenhill Fair in HARDY's *Far from the Madding Crowd*.

57 Wool LAWRENCE, THOMAS EDWARD (Lawrence of Arabia, 1888–1935), soldier and writer, owned Clouds Hill cottage from 1923 and worked here on *The Seven Pillars of Wisdom*, 1926. He was killed when he crashed his motor-cycle on the road outside. The cottage is preserved for public viewing (see **Moreton**).

58 Wraxall LAWRENCE, HENRY (1600–64), puritan statesman and pamphleteer, lived here. His son is mentioned in one of Milton's sonnets.

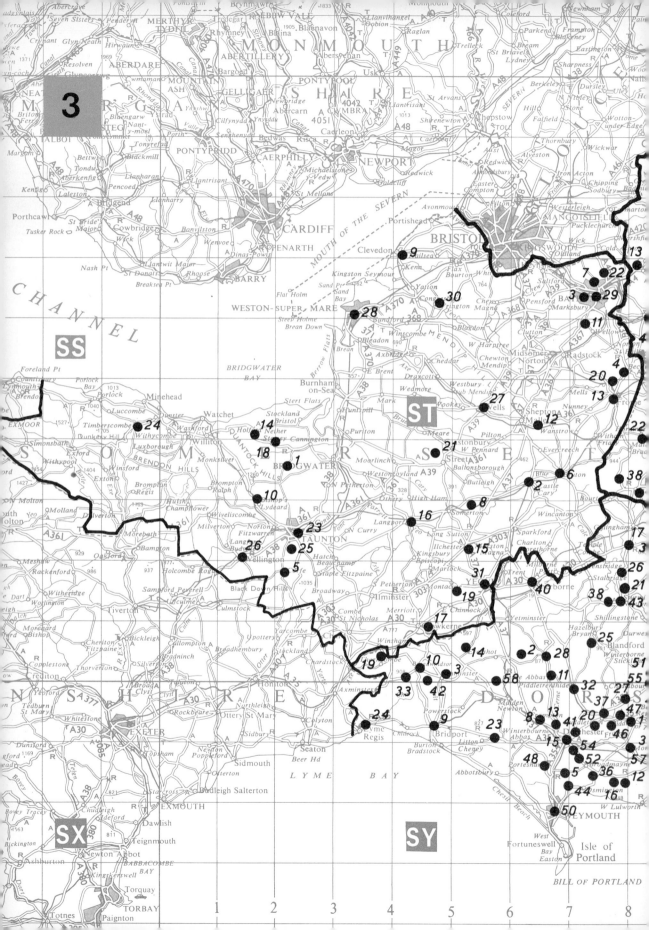

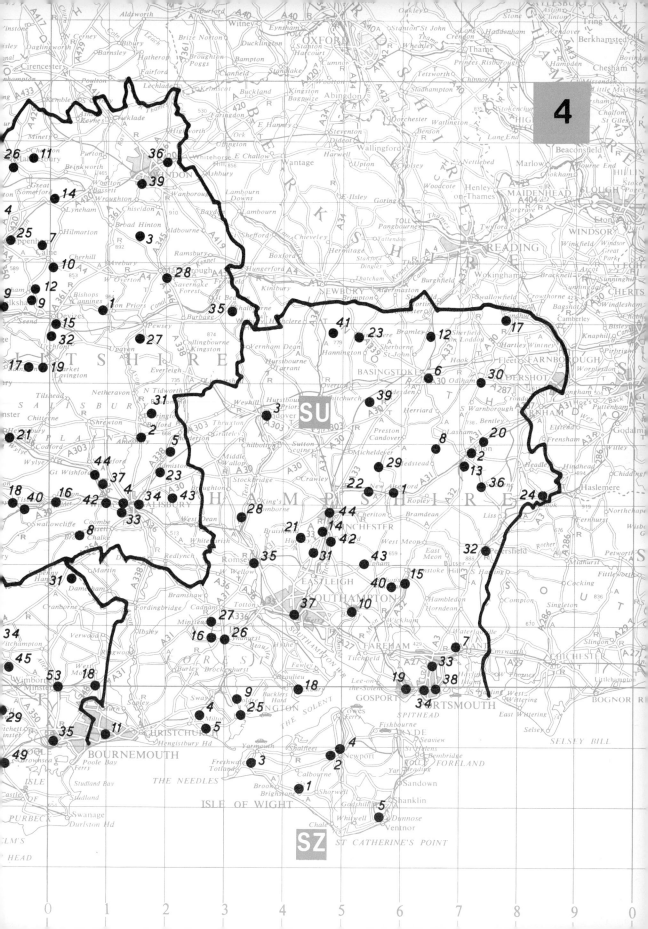

Hampshire and Isle of Wight
(*Map 4*)

HAMPSHIRE

1 **Alresford** MITFORD, MARY RUSSELL (1787–1855), novelist, born in Broad Street. *Our Village*, her most notable work, appeared in parts in the *Lady's Magazine*, 1819–32.

2 **Alton** CURTIS, WILLIAM (1746–99), writer on botany and entomology, born here. He translated Linnaeus's *Fundamenta Entomologiae*, 1772.

PINNOCK, WILLIAM (1782–1843), educational publisher and writer, born here. He made highly successful abridgments of Goldsmith's histories and collected his own instructional works into a *Juvenile Cyclopaedia*.

SPENSER, EDMUND (c1552–99), poet, lived in Amery Street.

3 **Andover** AÏDÉ, HAMILTON (1830–1906), French-born writer and musician, settled in the neighbourhood after leaving the British Army in 1852.

HATTON, JOSEPH (1841–1907), novelist and journalist, born here. He wrote volumes of theatrical reminiscences for the actors Henry Irving and J. L. Toole.

4 **Ashley, New Milton** HOUSMAN, LAURENCE (1865–1959), novelist and dramatist, lived here.

5 **Barton-on-Sea** HARRADEN, BEATRICE (1864–1936), novelist, lived and died here.

6 **Basingstoke** WARTON, THOMAS (1728–90), poet laureate 1785, born here. He edited classical texts and wrote a notable *History of English Poetry*, 1774–81.

7 **Bedhampton** KEATS, JOHN (1795–1821), poet, completed 'The Eve of St Agnes' while staying at the Old Mill House with Mr and Mrs John Snook in 1819.

8 **Bentworth** WITHER, GEORGE (1588–1667), poet, born here. His *Juvenilia*, a collection containing most of his best work, was published in 1622.

9 **Boldre** GILPIN, WILLIAM (1724–1804), author, vicar from 1777 and buried here.

SOUTHEY, ROBERT (1774–1843), poet laureate and biographer, married Caroline Anne Bowles (1786–1854), poet, here in 1839 (see **Lymington**).

10 **Botley** COBBETT, WILLIAM (1763–1835), author and agriculturalist, farmed here from 1805 until his imprisonment in Newgate in 1809.

11 **Bournemouth** BOYD, ANDREW KENNEDY HUTCHINSON (1825–99), essayist, died here.

HALL, MARGUERITE RADCLYFFE (1886–1943), novelist, born here. Her novel *The Well of Loneliness*, 1928, a sympathetic treatment of a lesbian theme, caused a sensation and was banned in Britain.

HUDSON, WILLIAM HENRY (1841–1922), naturalist and author, lived here.

KEBLE, JOHN (1792–1866), Tractarian leader and poet, died here.

MACDONALD, GEORGE (1824–1905), poet and novelist, lived here.

MACGREGOR, ROB ROY (d1892), travel writer, buried here.

PAYN, JAMES (1830–98), novelist, lived here.

RUSSELL, GEORGE WILLIAM ('Æ', 1867–1935), poet, critic and painter, buried here.

SHELLEY, PERCY BYSSHE (1792–1822) poet and dramatist: his heart was buried at St Peter's Church in 1851, in the coffin of his son, Sir Percy Shelley. Shelley's second wife Mary lived at Boscombe Manor with her parents and is buried at St Peter's, as are her father, WILLIAM GODWIN (1756–1836), author, and her mother, MARY WOLLSTONECRAFT GODWIN (1759–97), poet.

STEVENSON, ROBERT LOUIS (1850–94), novelist and poet, lived at Skerryvore in Alum Chine 1884–87 and here wrote *Kidnapped*, 1886, *Dr Jekyll and Mr Hyde*, 1886, and some of *A Child's Garden of Verses*, 1885.

TAYLOR, SIR HENRY (1800–86), colonial officer and dramatist, died here.

12 **Bramley** SHAW, THOMAS (1694–1751), travel writer, vicar from 1742 until his death and is buried here.

13 **Chawton** AUSTEN, JANE (1775–1817), novelist, lived here 1810–17 and completed *Emma*, 1816, and *Persuasion*, 1815. Her house is preserved for the public to visit (see **Steventon**).

14 **Compton** PHILPOTT, JOHN (1516–55), poet and martyr, born here.

15 **Droxford** WALTON, IZAAK (1593–1683), author of *The Compleat Angler*, 1653, married Anne Hawkins, the rector's daughter, in 1626.

16 **Emery Down** BRADDON, MRS MARY ELIZABETH (1837–1915), novelist, lived at Amresley Bank.

17 **Eversley** KINGSLEY, CHARLES (1819–75), novelist, curate and then rector 1842–59. He died and is buried here.

18 **Exbury** MITFORD, WILLIAM (1744–1827), Greek historian and friend of Edward Gibbon the historian, lived and is buried here.

19 **Gosport** UPFIELD, ARTHUR (1888–1964), novelist, born here. He made his home in Australia and produced a long series of popular detective novels featuring the half-aborigine Inspector Napoleon Bonaparte.

20 **Holybourne, nr Alton** GASKELL, MRS ELIZABETH CLEGHORN (1810–65), novelist and biographer, died here.

21 **Hursley** KEBLE, JOHN (1792–1866), Tractarian leader and poet, vicar from 1836 until his death and is buried here.

STERNHOLD, THOMAS (d1549), co-author of the metrical version of the Psalms, lived and is buried here.

22 **Itchen Abbas** KINGSLEY, CHARLES (1819–75), novelist, wrote *The Water Babies*, 1863, here.

23 **Kingsclere** SPENCE, JOSEPH (1699–1768), anecdotist, born here. He recorded the talk of Pope and his circle, published as *Anecdotes*, 1820.

24 **Liphook** WEBB, SIDNEY (1859–1947) and his wife BEATRICE (1858–1943), authors and economists, lived here.

25 **Lymington** BOWLES, CAROLINE ANNE (1786–1854), poet and second wife of Robert Southey (1774–1843), poet and biographer, born here. Her narrative poem *Ellen Fitzarthur*, sent anonymously to Southey in 1820, effected their introduction. She died here at Buckland Cottage.

26 **Lyndhurst** LIDDELL, ALICE, later Mrs Reginald Hargreaves (1852–1934), the original of LEWIS CARROLL's Alice in *Alice's Adventures in Wonderland*, 1865, lived much of her life at Lyndhurst and is buried here.

VACHELL, HORACE ANNESLEY (1861–1955), novelist, came here to live in 1899.

27 **Minstead** DOYLE, SIR ARTHUR CONAN (1859–1930), creator of Sherlock Holmes, buried in the churchyard.

28 **Mottisfont Abbey** MEINERTZHAGEN, RICHARD (1878–1967), writer and diarist, lived here.

29 **Northington** WHITE, GILBERT (1720–93), naturalist, curate c1757.

30 Odiham LILY, WILLIAM (1468–1522), grammarian, born here.

LYLY, JOHN (c1554–1606), dramatist, born here. His literary style in the play *Euphues*, 1579, gave the word euphuism to the English language.

31 Otterbourne KEBLE, JOHN (1792–1866), Tractarian leader and poet, was vicar before 1836.

YONGE, CHARLOTTE MARY (1823–1901), novelist, born, lived all her life, and is buried here. She made her name with *The Heir of Redclyffe*, 1853. Most of her many books were popular with both adult and young readers.

32 Petersfield THOMAS, EDWARD (1878–1917), poet and critic, lived at Steep nearby.

33 Portsea BESANT, SIR WALTER (1836–1901), novelist, born here. He founded the Society of Authors, 1884, and the Authors' Club, 1892. Much of his writing was in collaboration with James Rice (1843–82).

34 Portsmouth ALDINGTON, RICHARD (1892–1962), poet, novelist and biographer, born here. He was one of the 'Imagist' poets of the years before and during World War I, and wrote a notable war novel *Death of a Hero*, 1929.

DICKENS, CHARLES JOHN HUFFHAM (1812–70), novelist, was born at 1 Mile End Terrace, Landport (now 393 Commercial Road, and open to the public as a Dickens museum). The family moved shortly to 16 Hawke Street, now vanished. The font in which he was baptised in the parish church of St Mary, Kingston, is now in St Stephen's Church, Portsea, and there is a tablet to his memory in the church which has replaced St Mary's.

MADDEN, SIR FREDERIC (1801–73), antiquary, born here. He edited *Wyclif's Bible*, 1850, and collected the Caedmon MSS for Oxford University.

MEREDITH, GEORGE (1828–1909), poet and novelist, born here. *The Ordeal of Richard Feverel*, for which he is best known, appeared in 1859. The best of his poetry is in *Modern Love* and *Poems of the English Roadside*, 1862.

WESTERMAN, PERCY FRANCIS (1876–1960), boys' author, born here. He published over 150 adventure novels from 1908, many of them flying stories featuring 'Standish of the Air Police'.

35 Romsey LATHAM, JOHN (1740–1837), author of *A General History of Birds*, 1821–28, buried here.

36 Selborne WHITE, GILBERT (1720–93), naturalist, born here, lived at The Wakes, and is buried here. His *Natural History and Antiquities of Selborne* was published in 1789.

37 Southampton DIBDIN, CHARLES (1745–1814), dramatist and song writer, born here. He is best remembered for his sea songs, epitomising the life and sentiments of the British tar of the Nelson age.

SAINTSBURY, GEORGE EDWARD BATEMAN (1845–1933), historian and critic, born here. He wrote widely on English and French literature, and also on his other interest, wine.

WATTS, ISAAC (1674–1748), hymn writer, born here. 'O God our help in ages past' and 'As I survey the wondrous Cross' are two of his best-known hymns.

38 Southsea DOYLE, SIR ARTHUR CONAN (1859–1930), novelist, practised as a doctor at 1 Bush Villas (now vanished) 1882–91, during which time he created Sherlock Holmes in *A Study in Scarlet*, 1887.

KIPLING, RUDYARD (1865–1936), poet and novelist, from 1871 suffered five unhappy years as a foster-child here which had a lasting effect on his character and writing.

39 Steventon AUSTEN, JANE (1775–1817), novelist, born at the parsonage and lived here until 1801. The first version of *Pride and Prejudice*, 1813, was written here under the title *First Impressions*, but it failed to achieve publication in this form.

40 Swanmore, nr Bishops Waltham LEACOCK, STEPHEN BUTLER (1869–1944), humorist, born here. His long series of humorous books began with *Literary Lapses*, 1910. He spent most of his life in Canada.

41 Sydmonton FINCH, ANNE, COUNTESS OF WINCHILSEA (c1661–1720), poet, born here. Her *Miscellany Poems* appeared in 1713.

KINGSMILL, ANDREW (1538–69), devotional writer, born here.

42 Twyford FRANKLIN, BENJAMIN (1706–90), American statesman, philosopher and writer, wrote most of his autobiography while staying at Twyford House in 1771.

43 Upham YOUNG, EDWARD (1683–1765), poet, born here, where his father was rector. His chief work, *The Complaint, or Night Thoughts on Life, Death and Immortality*, 1742–44, in blank verse, was occasioned by his sorrow at losing his wife and stepdaughter.

44 Winchester AUSTEN, JANE (1775–1817), novelist, died in College Street and is buried in the cathedral (see **Steventon**).

BOORDE, ANDREW (c1490–1549), physician, traveller and writer, lived here from c1540 until his death in London.

MILNER, JOHN (1752–1826), Winchester historian, lived here c1798–1801.

WALTON, IZAAK (1593–1683), author of *The Compleat Angler*, 1653, lived here from 1678 until his death at 7 The Close, and is buried in the cathedral.

ISLE OF WIGHT

1 Brightstone KEN, or KENN, THOMAS (1637–1711), devotional writer and poet, rector 1669–72 and here composed his celebrated hymns 'Awake, my soul' and 'Glory to Thee, my God, this night'.

2 Carisbrooke MORLEY, HENRY (1822–94), English literary scholar and editor, died here.

3 Freshwater TENNYSON, ALFRED, LORD (1809–92), poet laureate, lived at Farringford 1853–69 and composed *Idylls of the King*, 1859 (with further parts later) and *Maud: a Monodrama*, 1855.

4 Newport REYNOLDS, JOHN HAMILTON (1796–1852), poet and friend of Keats and his circle, clerk to the county court and died here.

RICHMOND, LEGH (1772–1827), author, curate of Brading and Yaverland 1798–1805.

SEWELL, ELIZABETH (1815–1906), novelist, born here. She taught privately at Bonchurch 1852–91 and founded St Boniface School for middle-class girls at Ventnor in 1866.

5 Ventnor STERLING, JOHN (1806–44), critic and poet, died here.

Wiltshire (*Maps 3 & 4*)

1 **Alton Barnes** CROWE, WILLIAM (1745–1829), poet, rector from 1787 until his death.

2 **Amesbury** DOUGLAS, CATHERINE, DUCHESS OF QUEENSBERRY (d1777), friend and correspondent of many eminent literary men, lived at the Abbey House. She was Matthew Prior's 'Kitty'.
GAY, JOHN (1685–1732), poet, lived with the Queensberrys from 1729 until his death.
The George Inn claims to be the Blue Dragon of CHARLES DICKENS's *Martin Chuzzlewit*, 1843–44.

3 **Barbury Camp** Memorials here commemorate RICHARD JEFFERIES (see **Swindon**) and ALFRED WILLIAMS (see **South Marston**).

4 **Bemerton** HERBERT, GEORGE (1593–1633), poet, rector from 1630 until his death and buried here.

5 **Boscombe** HOOKER, RICHARD (c1554–1600), theological writer, rector 1591–95. Here he completed four of the proposed eight books of *Laws of Ecclesiastical Polity*, 1594.

6 **Bradford on Avon** WILLMOTT, ROBERT (1809–63), poet, writer and anthologist, born here. He was a prolific contributor to journals and wrote on literature, travel and the poets. His own *Poems* appeared in 1841.

7 **Bremhill** BOWLES, WILLIAM LISLE (1762–1850), poet and antiquary, vicar from 1804 until his death.

8 **Broadchalke** HEWLETT, MAURICE (1861–1923), novelist and poet, lived and died here.

9 **Bromham** MOORE, THOMAS (1779–1852), Irish poet and author, buried here.

10 **Calne** GROSSETESTE, ROBERT (d1253), theological author and bishop of Lincoln, rector 1225.
PRIESTLEY, JOSEPH (1733–1804), scientist and theologian, was literary companion to the Earl of Shelburne at Bowood House 1772–80.

11 **Charlton** DRYDEN, JOHN (1631–1700), poet and dramatist, lived here from 1665–66, having married Lady Elizabeth Howard here in 1663.
DUCK, STEPHEN (1705–56), poet, born here. Once a farm labourer, he became librarian to Queen Caroline.

12 **Chittoe** MOORE, THOMAS (1779–1852), Irish poet and author, lived and died at Sloperton Cottage.

13 **Colerne** GROCYN, WILLIAM (c1446–1519), Greek scholar, born here. He tutored Sir Thomas More at Oxford, where he introduced the study of Greek, and shared his home with Erasmus, to whom he was 'patronus et praeceptor'.

14 **Corsham** BLACKMORE, SIR RICHARD (d1729), physician and poet, born here. His epics *Prince Arthur* and *King Arthur*, 1695 and 1697, were widely scorned, but Dr Johnson and others thought highly of the later *Creation*.

15 **Devizes** REYNOLDS, STEPHEN (1881–1919), Wiltshire topographer, born here. His works include *Devizes and Roundabout*, 1906.

16 **Dinton** HYDE, EDWARD, 1ST EARL OF CLARENDON (1609–74), statesman and historian, born here. His *History of the Rebellion and Civil Wars in England* appeared in 1704–7.

17 **East Coulston** DELANY, MRS MARY (1700–88), friend of eminent literary people, born here. She corresponded with Swift and her salon became a meeting place for foremost writers and artists.

18 **Fonthill** BECKFORD, WILLIAM (1759–1844), author of *Vathek*, 1786, lived here until 1822.

19 **Great Cheverell** STONHOUSE, SIR JAMES (1716–95), doctor of medicine and devotional writer, Hannah More's 'Shepherd of Salisbury Plain', rector from 1779 and is buried here.

20 **Hardenhuish** KILVERT, ROBERT FRANCIS (1840–79), clergyman and diarist, born here. His diary, covering the years 1870–79, was first published in three volumes in 1938–40. It relates largely to his observations on nature and social life during his years in Radnorshire and Herefordshire.

21 **Heytesbury** CUNNINGTON, WILLIAM (1754–1810), antiquary, buried here.

22 **Horningham** KEN, or KENN, THOMAS (1637–1711), devotional writer and bishop of Bath and Wells, stayed at Longleat as the guest of Lord Weymouth from 1691, and died here.

23 **Idmiston** BOWLE, JOHN (1725–88), writer on Spanish literature, vicar from c1778 until his death and is buried here.

24 **Kington St Michael** AUBREY, JOHN (1626–97), antiquary, born at Easton Piercy. His *Topographical Collections* were edited in 1862 and his *Brief Lives of Contemporaries* in 1898.
BRITTON, JOHN (1771–1857), antiquary and topographer, born here. He published *Architectural Beauties of Great Britain*, 1805–14, and *Beauties of Wiltshire*, 1801.

25 **Langley Burrell** KILVERT, ROBERT FRANCIS (1840–79), diarist, curate to his father here before moving to a Welsh parish in 1865.

26 **Malmesbury** ST ALDHELM (c640–709), writer of devotional treatises and verse, was abbot of Malmesbury c673–705, and is buried here.
HOBBES, THOMAS (1588–1679), philosopher, born here. Known as 'the Sage of Malmesbury', he published *Leviathan* in 1651.
WILLIAM OF MALMESBURY (c1090–1143), historian, was a monk at the monastery.

27 **Manningford Bruce** FALKNER, JOHN MEADE (1858–1932), novelist, born here. His celebrated adventure novel, *Moonfleet*, appeared in 1898.

28 **Marlborough** FARRAR, FREDERICK WILLIAM (1831–1903), author of the school story *Eric, or Little by Little*, 1858, was a master at Marlborough College 1854–55 and headmaster from 1871.

29 **Melksham** RUTTY, JOHN (1689–1775), physician and diarist, born here. He wrote on medical subjects and published a *History of the Quakers in Ireland*, 1751.

30 **Mere** BARNES, WILLIAM (1801–86), the Dorsetshire poet, began his literary career while running a school here at The Chantry, 1823–35.

31 **Milston** ADDISON, JOSEPH (1672–1719), poet, essayist and statesman, born at the rectory. With Sir Richard Steele (1672–1729) he started the *Spectator* in 1711, contributing his Sir Roger de Coverley essays to it.

32 **Potterne** BALCHIN, NIGEL MARLIN (1908–71), novelist, born here. His best-selling works include *The Small Back Room*, 1943, *Mine Own Executioner*, 1945, and *A Sort of Traitors*, 1949.

33 **Quidhampton** OLIVIER, EDITH (1879–1948), writer on country life, lived at Daye House.

34 **Salisbury** BENNET, THOMAS (1673–1728), religious polemicist, born here. His many publications included

treatises against dissenters and a paraphrase of the *Book of Common Prayer, with Annotations*, 1708.

COXE, WILLIAM (1747–1828), historian and archdeacon of Wiltshire, died here.

FIELDING, HENRY (1707–54), novelist, wrote part of *Tom Jones*, 1749, at a house near St Anne's Gate.

HARRIS, JAMES (1709–80), grammarian, born in The Close. Wrote *Hermes, or a Philosophical Inquiry concerning Universal Grammar*, 1751.

HAYTER, RICHARD (1611–84), theological writer, born here. His *The Meaning of Revelation*, was published in 1675.

HERBERT, MARY, COUNTESS OF PEMBROKE (1561–1621), sister of Sir Philip Sidney, is buried in the cathedral choir. She revised and added to his *Arcadia*, 1580–81.

JEWEL, JOHN (1522–71), theological writer, appointed bishop of Salisbury 1559.

JOHN OF SALISBURY (c1118–80), theological writer, born at Old Sarum nearby. Bishop Stubbs declared him to have been 'for thirty years the central figure of English learning'.

MASCHIART, MICHAEL (d1598), Latin poet, born here.

MASSINGER, PHILIP (1583–1640), dramatist, probably born here: he was christened at St Thomas's Church. Author of fifteen plays, including *A New Way to Pay Old Debts*, 1633, he also collaborated with Dekker, Fletcher and others.

MATTHEW, SIR TOBIE (1577–1655), Catholic churchman and polemicist, born here. His works include *A Rich Cabinet of Precious Jewels*, 1623.

THORNBOROUGH, JOHN (1551–1641), churchman and radical writer, born here. He advocated union of England and Scotland in several of his works.

TOBIN, JOHN (1770–1804), dramatist, born here. His works include *The Curfew*, 1807, and *The School for Authors*, 1808.

TROLLOPE, ANTHONY (1815–82), novelist, had the idea for *The Warden*, 1855, the first book in his Barsetshire saga featuring many of the same characters, while strolling beside the stream adjoining the Close one summer's evening in 1851, during his two-year assignment to examine Post Office services in the West Country. Attempts have been made to identify Salisbury (and also Winchester) with Barchester, but the author refused to accept these and Barchester and Barsetshire would seem to be simply the epitome of cathedral towns and their surroundings.

35 Shalbourne TULL, JETHRO (1674–1741), author of works on husbandry, lived at Prosperous Farm from 1709 until his death.

36 South Marston WILLIAMS, ALFRED (1877–1930), poet, born and lived here until c1889. He returned at the end of World War I and lived at Ranikhet until his death. He is buried at South Marston.

37 South Newton STREET, ARTHUR GEORGE (1892–1966), novelist and agricultural writer, lived and died at Mill Farm (see **Wilton**).

38 Stourton HOARE, SIR RICHARD COLT (1758–1838), historian of Wiltshire, buried here. His home was at Stourhead nearby.

39 Swindon JEFFERIES, JOHN RICHARD (1848–87), naturalist and novelist, born at Coate Farm and lived in Victoria Road, Swindon, while writing for the *North Wilts Herald*, c1866. He lived in a house on Victoria Hill for three years after his marriage in 1874. His *Gamekeeper at Home* appeared in 1877 and *The Story of My Heart*, 1883.

40 Tisbury DAVIES, SIR JOHN (1569–1626), poet and attorney-general for Ireland, born here. His poem on the immortality of the soul, *Nosce Teipsum*, appeared in 1599, and his drama *Contention between a Wife, a Widdow, and a Maide* was performed before the queen in 1602.

KIPLING, LOCKWOOD (1837–1911) and his wife, **Rudyard Kipling**'s parents, buried here. Lockwood Kipling illustrated some of his son's works.

41 Trowbridge CRABBE, GEORGE (1754–1832), poet, rector from 1814 until his death.

42 Wilton Wilton House was the home of Mary Herbert, Countess of Pembroke (1561–1621). SIR PHILIP SIDNEY (1554–86), her brother, wrote *Arcadia* while staying here in 1580. WILLIAM HERBERT, 3RD EARL OF PEMBROKE (1580–1630), born here, was a poet and patron of the arts, to whom, with his brother Philip, William Shakespeare dedicated the first folio of his works in 1623, and he has been identified with Shakespeare's 'Mr W.H.'. The first performance of *As You Like It* was given in the great hall before James I by Shakespeare's players in 1595.

OLIVIER, EDITH (1879–1948), author of country works, was the daughter of the rector and was mayor of Wilton 1938–41.

STREET, ARTHUR GEORGE (1892–1966), novelist and agricultural writer, born at Ditchampton Farm. A practical farmer, editor of *Country Life*, and well-known broadcaster, his publications include *Farmer's Glory*, 1932, *Strawberry Roan*, 1932, *Country Calendar*, 1935, and *The Endless Furrow*, 1934.

43 Winterslow HAZLITT, WILLIAM (1778–1830), essayist and critic, lived here 1808–12. Returning frequently in later years, he wrote his *Winterslow Essays* while staying at the Pheasant Inn, also known as the Winterslow Hut.

44 Wishford HAYWARD, ABRAHAM (1802–84), essayist, born here. He wrote three series of *Essays*, 1858, 1873 and 1874, and other works including *The Art of Dining*, 1852.

Berkshire (*Map 5*)

1 Abingdon CARTE, THOMAS (1686–1754), historian, died at Caldecott House.

ORWELL, GEORGE (Eric Blair, 1903–50), novelist, buried at All Saints church, Sutton Courtenay, nearby.

RICHARDSON, DOROTHY MILLER (1873–1957), novelist, born here. Her 'stream-of-consciousness' novels bear the collective title *Pilgrimage*.

RUSKIN, JOHN (1819–1900), author and artist, lived at the Crown and Thistle Inn in 1871 while first Slade Professor of Art at Oxford.

2 Basildon TULL, JETHRO (1674–1741), agricultural writer, born and buried here. Author of *The Horse-hoing Husbandry*, 1733, and many other treatises.

3 Bear Wood WALTER, JOHN, II (1776–1847), proprietor of *The Times*, bought the estate in 1816 and built the house. He is buried here. He also built the church of St Catherine and appointed ROBERT WILLMOTT, poet and writer, as first incumbent, 1846–62.

4 Binfield MACAULAY, CATHERINE (1731–91), radical and historian, buried here.

POPE, ALEXANDER (1688–1744), poet and satirist, divided his time between London and his father's home, Whitehill House, Binfield, until 1716 when his father moved.

5 Blewbury GRAHAME, KENNETH (1859–1932), author, lived at Boham's Farm 1910–20.

6 Boar's Hill BRIDGES, ROBERT (1844–1930), poet laureate, built and lived at Chilswell House 1907–30, where he composed his *Testament of Beauty*, 1929.

7 Bracknell SHELLEY, PERCY BYSSHE (1792–1822), poet, lived for a time with his wife at High Elms House in 1813, and later stayed alone with the de Boinville family here, 1814.

8 Bradfield PORDAGE, SAMUEL (1633–c91), poet, lived here with his father John Pordage, the rector and mystic, who may have collaborated in some of his works.

9 Brightwell GODWIN, THOMAS (d1642), scholar, vicar from 1626. He died and is buried here.

10 Bucklebury ST JOHN, HENRY, LORD BOLINGBROKE (1678–1751). Patron of authors and associate of Pope and Swift, lived here 1700–15.

11 Childrey POCOCK, EDWARD (1604–91), orientalist writer, rector 1642–60.

12 Compton Beauchamp SENIOR, NASSAU (1790–1864), biographer, born here. His biographies largely took the form of interviews with his subjects.

13 Cookham GRAHAME, KENNETH (1859–1932), author, lived here 1906–10 and wrote *The Wind in the Willows*, 1908, here; as a child, 1864–66, he lived at The Mount.

WALKER, FREDERICK (1840–75), prolific book-illustrator, buried here.

14 Easthampstead FENTON, ELIJAH (1683–1730), poet, spent his last years in Easthampstead and is buried here.

15 Faringdon PYE, HENRY JAMES (1745–1813), poet laureate 1790, born here. His official odes were much abused and parodied.

16 Hungerford TULL, JETHRO (1674–1741), agricultural writer, practised his revolutionary farming methods at Prosperous Farm, where he lived from 1709 until his death (see **Basildon**).

WHITELOCKE, BULSTRODE (1605–75), lawyer, writer and Keeper of the Great Seal, lived at Chilton Park nearby.

17 Hurley MAVOR, WILLIAM FORDYCE (1758–1837), compiler of educational works, vicar from 1789 until his death.

18 Knowl Hill COLLINS, MORTIMER (1827–76), poet, novelist and bohemian, lived here from 1862 until his death.

19 Lambourn SYLVESTER, JOSHUA (1563–1618), poet and translator, attached to the household of the Earl of Essex at Lambourn Place.

20 Long Wittenham GIBBINGS, ROBERT (1889–1958), author, engraver and book designer, spent his last years here at Footbridge Cottage.

21 Longworth BLACKMORE, RICHARD DODDRIDGE (1825–1900), novelist, born at the vicarage where his father was curate-in-charge. The family moved to the West Country when he was a few months old. His best-known novel, *Lorna Doone*, was published in 1869.

22 Maidenhead COLLIER, JOHN PAYNE (1789–1883), Shakespearean critic and literary forger, lived here from 1850 and died at Riverside.

LOFTING, HUGH (1886–1947), children's author, born here. His *Dr Doolittle* series emerged from letters to his children from the Western Front in World War I. He died in California.

NOEL, THOMAS (1799–1861), poet, lived at Boyne Hill.

23 Midgham CROWE, WILLIAM (1745–1829), poet and clergyman, born here. His best-known poem is 'Lewesdon Hill', 1788.

24 Newbury HUGHES, JOHN (1790–1857), author, moved to Donnington Priory here in 1833 from Uffington (qv).

LAWRENCE, DAVID HERBERT (1835–1940), novelist and poet, lived in a cottage at Hermitage nearby, Dec 1917–April 1918 and again in 1919.

MONTAGU, ELIZABETH (1720–1800), author and leader of society, inherited the Sandleford estate at the death of her husband, Edward Montagu, 1775.

PENROSE, THOMAS (1742–79), poet, born here. He became his father's curate at Newbury after serving at sea with privateers. Published several collections of verse.

RUDYERD, SIR BENJAMIN (1572–1658), poet and politician, lived at West Woodhay 1634–58 and died here. His son, WILLIAM (d1661), who inherited the house, also published verse.

25 Pangbourne GRAHAME, KENNETH (1859–1932), author, lived at Church Cottage from 1920 until his death. He is buried at Oxford.

MORTON, THOMAS (c1764–1838), dramatist, lived here 1793–1828.

MORTON, JOHN MADDISON (1811–91), a highly successful writer of farces and son of the author Thomas Morton, born here. His *Box and Cox*, 1847, was re-written by F. C. Burnand for Arthur Sullivan's music as *Cox and Box*, 1867.

26 Pusey PUSEY, EDWARD BOUVERIE (1800–82), scholar and author, born here. Leader of the Oxford Movement, he began *Tracts for the Times* in 1833 with Newman and Keble. His father was Philip Bouverie, his name being changed to Pusey upon inheriting the family estates here.

27 Reading BACON, PHANUEL (1700–83), dramatist, born here. He wrote five plays and some verse; his best-known poems are 'The Kite' and 'The Snipe'.

BAKER, WILLIAM (1742–85), printer and essayist, born here. His *Theses Graecae et Latinae Selectae*, 1783, was an anthology of classical authors.

DUCK, STEPHEN (1705–56), poet, committed suicide by drowning, behind the Black Lion Inn.

LATTER, MARY (1725–77), poet and dramatist, lived and is buried here.

MERRICK, JAMES (1720–69), poet and classical scholar, born here. His poem 'The Chameleon' was once a stock item for reciters.

MILMAN, HENRY HART (1791–1868), poet and historian, became vicar of St Mary's in 1816.

SMITH, GOLDWIN (1823–1910), historian, born here. His works include *Lectures on the Study of History*, 1883.

TALFOURD, SIR THOMAS NOON (1795–1854), dramatist and judge, born here. His best-known work was the tragedy *Ion*, 1835.

WHITE, WALTER (1811–93), travel writer, born here. He wrote widely about his travels around Britain and elsewhere. He was librarian to the Royal Society 1861–84.

WILDE, OSCAR FINGAL O'FLAHERTIE WILLS (1854–1900), dramatist and poet, underwent his imprisonment 1896–98 in the gaol which still stands and wrote the confessional *De Profundis* here. His *Ballad of Reading Gaol* was published in 1898.

28 Shinfield MITFORD, MARY RUSSELL (1787–1855), novelist, lived in Shinfield 1802–20. Her father, George Mitford, is buried here.

29 Swallowfield MITFORD, MARY RUSSELL (1787–1855), novelist, lived here from 1851 until her death and is buried here.

30 Three Mile Cross The Mitford family occupied a 'labourer's cottage' here from 1820–51, after George Mitford had dissipated MARY RUSSELL MITFORD'S fortune. Most of her works were written here, and her classic *Our Village, Sketches of Rural Character and Scenery*, 1823–32, is about this neighbourhood.

31 Twyford PENN, WILLIAM (1644–1718), founder of Pennsylvania and Quaker campaigner, died at his home at Field Ruscombe nearby.

32 Uffington HUGHES, JOHN (1790–1857), author, lived here before 1833.

HUGHES, THOMAS (1822–96), author, born here. His classic, *Tom Brown's Schooldays*, was published in 1857 under the pseudonym 'An Old Boy'.

33 Wallingford BLACKSTONE, SIR WILLIAM (1723–80), legal writer and poet, buried here.

34 Waltham St Lawrence GIBBINGS, ROBERT (1889–1958), author, engraver and book designer, bought the Golden Cockerel Press at Waltham St Lawrence from its founder Harold Taylor in 1923 and produced some notable work there.

NEWBERY, JOHN (1713–67), publisher and author, born here. He published the first books for children, including *The History of Little Goody Two-Shoes*, 1765, which he may have written with Oliver Goldsmith (1728–74). He also published the first children's periodical *The Lilliputian Magazine*, 1751.

35 Wantage BUTLER, JOSEPH (1692–1752), bishop and theological writer, born here. His *Analogy of Religion, Natural and Revealed* gained him the appellation 'the Bacon of theology'.

KIMBER, ISAAC (1692–1755), biographer, journalist and Baptist minister, born here. He founded the *Morning Chronicle*, edited it 1728–32, and wrote several biographical works.

36 Wargrave DAY, THOMAS (1748–89), author, lived at Bear Place and is buried here.

EDGEWORTH, RICHARD LOVELL (1744–1817), author and educational theorist, lived at Hare Hatch 1765–71. He later collaborated with his daughter Maria (1767–1849) in a number of his own works and some of those better known ones which bear her name alone.

37 White Waltham HEARNE, THOMAS (1678–1735), antiquary, born at Littlefield Green and buried here. His *Curious Discourses upon English Antiquities* appeared in 1720.

38 Windsor HALLAM, HENRY (1777–1859), historian, born here. His three major works are his *View of the State of Europe during the Middle Ages*, 1818, a *Constitutional History of England from Henry VII's Accession to the Death of George II*, 1827, and *Introduction to the Literature of Europe*, 1837–39.

KNIGHT, CHARLES (1791–1873), author and publisher, born here. He helped his father found the *Windsor and Eton Express* in 1812; later supervised the periodicals of the Society for Diffusion of Useful Knowledge, and wrote serial publications on various subjects.

ROBINSON, MARY (1758–1800), actress ('Perdita'), author and poet, buried in Old Windsor churchyard.

SHELLEY, PERCY BYSSHE (1792–1822), poet, lived in a furnished house here for a time in 1813 and again in 1814.

39 Yattendon BRIDGES, ROBERT (1844–1930), poet laureate, buried here.

CARTE, THOMAS (1686–1754), historian, buried here.

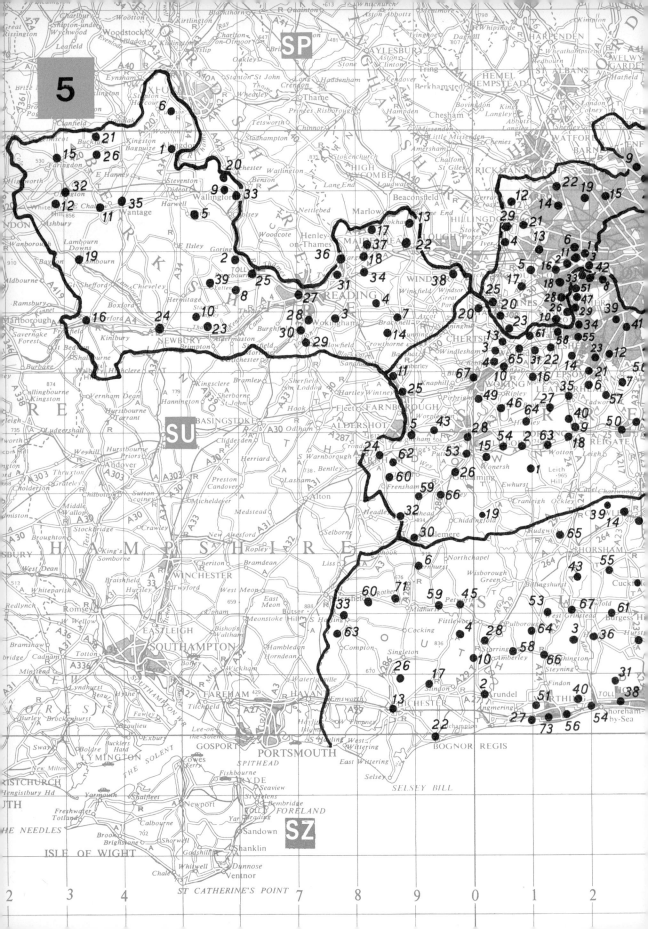

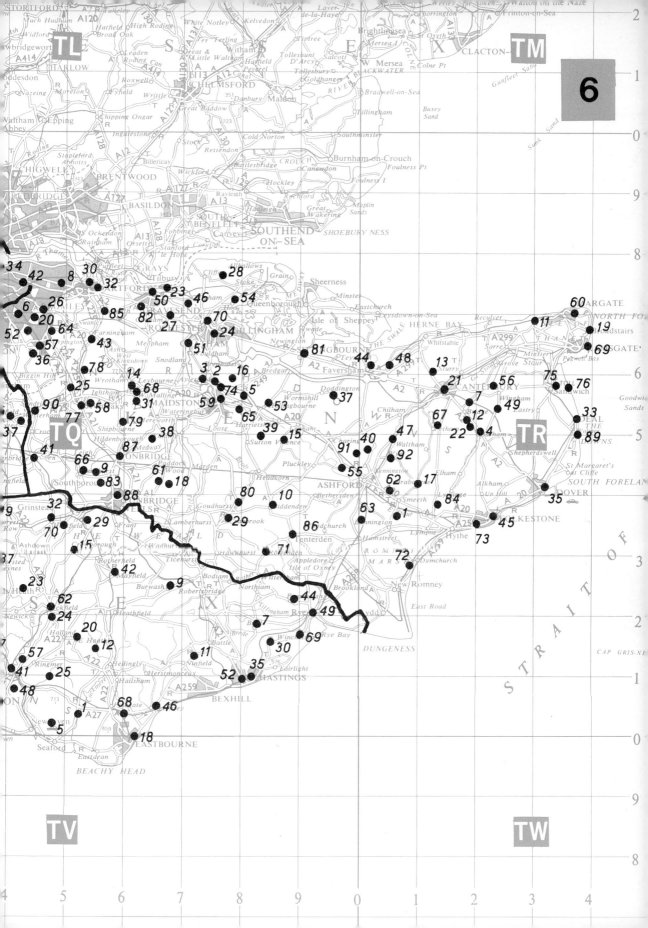

Middlesex (*Maps 5 & 6*)

1 Acton BAXTER, RICHARD (1615–91), author and clergyman, lived here from 1662–c1685.

LYTTON, EDWARD GEORGE EARLE LYTTON BULWER-, 1ST BARON LYTTON (1803–73), novelist, dramatist and statesman, lived at Berrymead Priory, Salisbury Street, for a time.

2 Brentford TOOKE, JOHN HORNE (1736–1812), philologist, curate of St Lawrence's church, 1760.

TRIMMER, SARAH (1741–1810), children's author, lived here after her marriage in 1762 and founded a school for girls.

3 Chiswick CARY, HENRY FRANCIS (1772–1844), translator, lived in Hogarth Lane.

FOSCOLO, UGO (1778–1827), Italian author, lived at Turnham Green from 1817 and died here.

POPE, ALEXANDER (1688–1744), poet and satirist, lived in Mawson Terrace, Chiswick Lane, 1716–18. While here, he issued a collected edition of his works, 1717, and translated much of the *Iliad*.

WAINEWRIGHT, THOMAS GRIFFITHS (1794–1852), writer and poisoner, born here. His writings were journalistic, including art criticism. He was transported to Tasmania in 1837 and died there still a convict.

4 Cowley DODD, WILLIAM (1729–77), editor and compiler, buried here after being hanged for forgery.

LIGHTFOOT, JOHN (1735–88), naturalist, buried here.

5 Cranford FULLER, THOMAS (1608–61), antiquary, was vicar from 1658 until his death and is buried here.

WILKINS, JOHN (1614–72), bishop of Chester, author of *The Discovery of a World in the Moone*, 1638, rector here from 1660–2.

6 Ealing FIELDING, HENRY (1705–54), novelist, lived at 'Fordhook' from March to June 1754, before his departure to Lisbon, where he died and is buried.

HUXLEY, THOMAS HENRY (1825–95), scientist and author, born at the Old Rectory, formerly the Great Ealing School. His works include *Man's Place in Nature*, 1863, *Science and Morals*, 1886, and *Ethics and Evolution*, 1893.

RICHARDS, FRANK (pseudonym of Charles Harold St John Hamilton, 1876–1961), boys' author, born here. He wrote an immense number of stories and books and created some fifty fictional schools, but none more celebrated than Greyfriars, with its Billy Bunter, Harry Warton & Co, whose first appearance was in 1908.

SHUTE, NEVIL (pseudonym of Nevil Shute Norway, 1899–1960), novelist, born here. His best-selling novels include *A Town Like Alice*, 1950, and *On the Beach*, 1957.

TOOKE, JOHN HORNE (1736–1812), philologist, buried here.

TRIMMER, SARAH (1741–1810), children's author, buried here.

7 Edmonton LAMB, CHARLES (1775–1834) and his sister MARY (1764–1847), poets and essayists, lived at Bay Cottage (now Lamb's Cottage) from 1833. Both died and are buried here.

8 Enfield CLARKE, CHARLES COWDEN (1787–1877), author, born here. He published several literary guides to other authors' works, and with his wife, Mary Victoria Cowden Clarke (1809–98), edited *Cassell's Illustrated Shakespeare*, 1865–69, and produced *Recollections of Writers*, 1878. He died in Genoa.

D'ISRAELI, ISAAC (1766–1848), author and father of Benjamin Disraeli, Lord Beaconsfield, born here. He wrote novels and popular works on literature.

GOUGH, RICHARD (1735–1809), antiquary, lived here.

LAMB, CHARLES (1775–1834) and his sister MARY (1764–1847), poets and essayists, lived here 1829–33, first in Gentleman's Row, then in Chase Side, at the Poplars, and later in Westwood Cottage next door.

9 Friern Barnet WALKER, JOHN (1732–1807), lexicographer, born at Colney Hatch. His *Rhyming Dictionary* appeared in 1775 and his *Critical Pronouncing Dictionary* in 1791.

10 Hampton GARRICK, DAVID (1717–79), actor and dramatist, lived at Hampton House from 1745 until his death.

JOHNS, CAPTAIN WILLIAM EARL (1893–1968), boys' novelist, lived here.

STEELE, SIR RICHARD (1672–1729), essayist and dramatist, lived for a time in a house (which he termed 'the hovel') by the Green.

11 Hanwell DOBSON, HENRY AUSTIN (1840–1921), poet and critic, is buried in the Westminster cemetery.

KILLIGREW, THOMAS (1612–83), WILLIAM (1606–95) and HENRY (1613–1700), dramatist brothers, born here. Thomas was responsible for the building of the first Drury Lane theatre.

12 Harefield STANLEY, FERDINANDO, 5TH EARL OF DERBY (c1559–94), lived here. He was the patron of EDMUND SPENSER, who panegyrised him as 'Amyntas' and his wife Alice as 'Amaryllis'. Spenser dedicated his *Tears of the Muses* to her, and she was the subject of poems by George Chapman and Thomas Nash. On the earl's death she married, and resided here with, SIR THOMAS EGERTON (c1540–1617), patron of Bacon, Jonson and others. In 1635, JOHN MILTON, living nearby at Horton, wrote the masque *Arcades* for the Dowager Countess, and it was first performed here in that year.

13 Harlington TRAPP, JOSEPH (1679–1747), poet and pamphleteer, was rector from 1732 until his death and is buried here.

14 Harrow ARNOLD, MATTHEW (1822–88), poet and critic, lived for many years at Byron House, Byron Hill.

CHASE, BEATRICE (Olive Katharine Parr, 1874–1955), novelist, born here. Her books include several about Dartmoor, where she lived much of her life.

GILBERT, SIR WILLIAM SCHWENCK (1836–1911), dramatist, lived at Grim's Dyke and died here.

SIEVEKING, LANCE (Lancelot de Giberne Sieveking, 1896–1972), author and radio playwright, born here. He wrote books on various subjects, among them the novel *Stampede*, 1924, illustrated by G. K. Chesterton. He produced what may have been the world's first television play in 1927.

STEEL, FLORA ANNIE (1847–1929), novelist, born at Sudbury Priory. Her novels are set in Scotland, where she lived in her youth.

Many important literary figures have taught, or been students, at Harrow School. EDWARD BOWEN (1836–1901) became a master in 1859 and remained here for the rest of his life. He wrote the Harrow School Song, 1872, and published *Harrow Songs and other Verses*, 1886. Students have included: LORD BYRON (1788–1824), poet; SIR WINSTON CHURCHILL (1874–1965), statesman and author; JOHN GALSWORTHY (1867–1933), novelist and dramatist; RICHARD BRINSLEY SHERIDAN (1751–1816), dramatist; ANTHONY TROLLOPE (1815–82), novelist; and HORACE ANNESLEY VACHELL (1861–1955), novelist, whose celebrated school story *The Hill*, 1905, has Harrow as its setting.

15 Hendon AYLOFFE, JOSEPH (1709–81), antiquary, buried here.

PARSONS, JAMES (1705–70), antiquary and physician, buried here.

16 Heston BANKS, SIR JOSEPH (1744–1820), naturalist and writer, buried here.

17 Hounslow ANDREW, STEPHEN (pseudonym of Frank G. Layton, 1872–1941), novelist, born here. His publications include *Doctor Grey*, 1911, and *Sable and Motley*, 1912.

18 Isleworth BANKS, SIR JOSEPH (1744–1820), naturalist and writer, lived and died at Spring Grove.

HALIBURTON, THOMAS CHANDLER (1796–1865), humorist, said to have founded the American school of humour, died and is buried here.

KEATE, GEORGE (1729–97), poet and essayist, buried here.

SIDNEY, LADY DOROTHY (1617–84) born at Syon House. She was courted by the poet EDMUND WALLER, who termed her his 'Sacharrisa' and wrote to her 'Go, lovely rose'.

19 Kingsbury GOLDSMITH, OLIVER (1728–74), dramatist and novelist, lodged at Hyde Farm and here wrote *She Stoops to Conquer*, 1773, and part of *The Vicar of Wakefield*, 1766.

20 Laleham ARNOLD, MATTHEW (1822–88), poet and critic, born and lived here until 1831, returning soon after to spend a further two years in Ashford Road as a pupil of his uncle. He is buried in Laleham churchyard.

21 Northolt MAPLET, JOHN (d1592), author, was vicar from 1576 until his death and is buried here.

OWEN, GORONWY (1723–69), Welsh poet termed 'the Burns of Wales', was curate from 1755–58.

22 Pinner COMPTON-BURNETT, DAME IVY (1884–1969), novelist, born here. Her books include *Brothers and Sisters*, 1929, *Men and Wives*, 1931, *Daughters and Sons*, 1937, and *A Heritage and its History*, 1959, all written in a highly formalised style.

PYE, HENRY JAMES (1745–1813), poet laureate, lived and is buried here.

23 Shepperton ELIOT, GEORGE (1819–80), novelist, wrote *Scenes from Clerical Life*, 1857, at the old manor house.

MEREDITH, GEORGE (1828–1909), novelist, lived at Vine Cottage with his first wife, who died in 1860. She was the daughter of THOMAS LOVE PEACOCK (1785–1866), novelist, who lived at Elmbank, Lower Halliford, and is buried at Shepperton.

24 Southgate HOOD, THOMAS (1799–1845), poet lived at Rose Cottage, Winchmore Hill.

HUNT, JAMES HENRY LEIGH (1784–1859), essayist and poet, born at Eagle House. He started several periodicals and through these and his contributions to others, did much to spread interest in literature.

MASSEY, GERALD (1828–1907), poet, buried here.

25 Staines MIDDLETON, RICHARD BARHAM (1882–1911), poet, born here. He was a straw-plaiter and errand boy before having his first volume of poems published at the age of twenty. *Babe Christabel*, 1854, brought him to public notice.

26 Teddington BLACKMORE, RICHARD DODDRIDGE (1825–1900), novelist, lived at Gomer House from 1860 and is buried here.

TRAHERNE, THOMAS (c1638–74), mystical writer and poet, was minister at Teddington and is buried here.

WALTER, JOHN (1739–1812), founder of *The Times*, buried here.

WHITEHEAD, PAUL (1710–74), poet, buried here.

27 Tottenham BAXTER, WILLIAM (1650–1723), antiquarian, taught at the old grammar school here.

BEDWELL, WILLIAM (1562–1632), a translator of the Authorised Version of the Bible, was vicar from 1607 until his death and is buried in High Cross church.

28 Twickenham BERRY, MARY (1763–1852), author and literary executor of Horace Walpole, lived at Little Strawberry Hill.

CAMBRIDGE, RICHARD OWEN (1717–1802), poet, lived at Cambridge House and is buried in St Mary's church.

CROKER, JOHN WILSON (1780–1857), Irish-born author and critic, died at nearby Moulsey.

DE LA MARE, WALTER JOHN (1890–1956), poet and novelist, died here. His ashes are buried in the crypt of St Paul's cathedral.

DICKENS, CHARLES (1812–70) wrote *Oliver Twist* at Ailsa Park Villas, St Margaret's Road, 1837–39.

FIELDING, HENRY (1707–54) wrote *Tom Jones*, 1749, where Fielding Cottages now stand in Holly Road, formerly Back Lane.

FRANCIS, FRANCIS (1822–86), novelist and writer on angling, lived for many years until his death at The Firs, and is buried in Twickenham. Born at Seaton, Devonshire, he was angling editor of *The Field* for more than 25 years. His novels include *The Real Salt*, 1854, *Newton Dogvane*, 1859, and *Sidney Bellew*, 1870, but he is best remembered for his definitive work *A Book on Angling*, first published 1867.

MAYHEW, AUGUSTUS (1826–75), novelist, lived at 7 Montpelier Row.

MONTAGUE, CHARLES EDWARD (1867–1928), novelist and journalist, born here. He was C. P. Scott's assistant editor of the *Manchester Guardian*.

OLIPHANT, LAURENCE (1829–88), journalist and travel writer, died here.

POPE, ALEXANDER (1688–1744), poet and satirist, lived here from 1718 until his death, and is buried in Twickenham church.

SUCKLING, SIR JOHN (1609–42), poet and dramatist, born here. His ballads and songs have proved more enduring than his plays.

WALPOLE, HORACE, 4TH EARL OF ORFORD (1717–97), author and wit, lived at Strawberry Hill from 1747.

29 Uxbridge ST JOHN, HENRY, LORD BOLINGBROKE (1678–1751), writer on history and politics, lived c1725–39 at Dawley Court.

Surrey (*Maps 5 & 6*)

1 Abinger HOOLE, JOHN (1727–1803), translator and dramatist, lived here.

2 Abinger Hammer FORSTER, EDWARD MORGAN (1879–1970), novelist, lived at Piney Copse. Crossways farm is featured in a novel by GEORGE MEREDITH (1828–1909), *Diana of the Crossways*, 1885, the book which brought him first public acclaim.

3 Addlestone HALL, SAMUEL CARTER (1800–89), author and editor, and his wife ANNA MARIA (1800–81), author, lived, died and are buried here.

4 Anningsley DAY, THOMAS (1748–89), author of the *History of Sandford and Merton*, 1783, 1787, 1789, lived here.

5 Ash YOUNG, EDWARD (1683–1765) is believed to have written *Night Thoughts*, 1742–45, while staying at his brother-in-law's rectory here.

6 Ashtead MACDONALD, GEORGE (1824–1905), poet and novelist, died here.

7 Banstead BROWNE, GORDON (1858–1932), book illustrator, born here. The son of Hablôt K. Browne (Phiz), he illustrated countless classics and contemporary works and wrote several of his own, including *Nonsense for Somebody, Anybody and Everybody, Particularly the Baby-Body*, 1895.

8 Barnes JERROLD, DOUGLAS WILLIAM (1803–57), playwright and journalist, lived in Barnes for nine years and wrote *Mrs Caudle's Curtain Lectures*, 1846, here.
MAYHEW, AUGUSTUS (1826–75), novelist, buried here.

9 Box Hill BURNEY, FANNY (Frances, 1752–1840), novelist and diarist, lived for a time at Camilla Cottage, bought with the proceeds from her *Camilla*, 1796.
The last 500 lines of JOHN KEATS'S *Endymion*, 1818, were probably inspired during a visit here in 1817. He completed the poem at the Burford Bridge Hotel here.
MEREDITH, GEORGE (1828–1909), novelist, lived at Flint Cottage from 1867 until his death here.
SHERIDAN, RICHARD BRINSLEY (1751–1816), dramatist, owned Polesden Lacey and lived there with his second wife after 1795.

10 Byfleet DUCK, STEPHEN (1705–56), poet, was rector here until his death by suicide.
SMITH, GEORGE (1824–1901), publisher, died at St George's Hill and is buried here.
SPENCE, JOSEPH (1699–1768), anecdotist, lived here from 1749, died by drowning, and is buried in Byfleet church.

11 Camberley HARTE, FRANCIS BRETT (Bret Harte, 1839–1902), American author, died here.

12 Cheam COWLEY, ABRAHAM (1618–67), poet, died at the Porch House.
TOMSON, LAURENCE (1539–1608), theological author and transcriber, buried here.

13 Chertsey COWLEY, ABRAHAM (1618–67), poet lived at Cowley House, Guildford Street, 1665–7.
SMITH, ALBERT (1816–60), humorous novelist, born here. He wrote *The Adventures of Mr Ledbury*, 1844; *The Scattergood Family*, 1845, etc.

14 Chessington BURNEY, FANNY (Frances, 1752–1840), novelist and diarist, often stayed at Chessington Hall, home of Samuel Crisp (d1783), dramatist, her 'Daddy

Crisp'. It was here that she learned of the success of *Evelina*, 1778.

15 Chilworth STRACHEY, JOHN ST LOE (1860–1927), editor and proprietor of the *Spectator*, 1898–1925, lived and died at Newlands Corner.

16 Cobham ARNOLD, MATTHEW (1822–88), poet and critic, lived at Pains Hill Cottage, 1873–88.

17 Coulsdon LYALL, SIR ALFRED COMYN (1835–1911), Indian administrator and author, born here. His publications include *Warren Hastings*, 1889; *Tennyson*, 1902; and *Studies in Literature and History*, 1915.

18 Dorking AUBREY, JOHN (1626–97), antiquary, lived here briefly.
DISRAELI, BENJAMIN, 1ST EARL OF BEACONSFIELD (1804–81), statesman and novelist, wrote most of *Coningsby*, 1844, while staying at Deepdene.
EVELYN, JOHN (1620–1706), diarist and versatile writer, born at Wotton House and is buried at Wotton church. His *Diary*, first published 1818, covers the period 1641–1706.
HOOLE, JOHN (1727–1803), poet and dramatist, buried here.
MARKLAND, JEREMIAH (1693–1776), classical scholar, lived at Milton Court and is buried here.

19 Dunsfold WARTON, JOSEPH (1722–1800), poet and critic, born here. He published *Odes*, 1744 and 1746, a translation of Virgil, 1753, and an *Essay on the Writings and Genius of Pope*, 1756 and 1782.

20 Egham DENHAM, SIR JOHN (1615–69), poet, lived here. His poem 'Cooper's Hill', describing the scenery about Egham, is the earliest example of descriptive poetry in English.
ROBINSON, MARY (1758–1800), actress and author known as Perdita, lived here.

21 Epsom PARKHURST, JOHN (1728–97), biblical lexicographer, buried here.

22 Esher HOWITT, WILLIAM (1792–1879) and his wife MARY (1800–88), miscellaneous authors, lived here 1837–39 and wrote some of their most successful books.
PORTER, ANNA MARIA (1780–1832) and JANE (1776–1850), novelist sisters, buried here.
WHITELAW, DAVID (1875–1971), novelist and inventor of the card game 'Lexicon', died here.

23 Ewell CORBET, RICHARD (1582–1635), bishop and poet, born here. His collected poems were published 1647. He was bishop of Oxford and of Norwich.

24 Farnham BOURNE, GEORGE (pseudonym of George Sturt, 1863–1927), novelist and poet, born here. His reflections of Surrey life include *A Farmer's Life*, 1922, and *The Wheelwright's Workshop*, 1923. He lived in the nearby village of Lower Bourne from 1891 until his death.
COBBETT, WILLIAM (1763–1835), essayist, radical journalist and agriculturalist, born at the Jolly Farmer Inn and buried at Farnham church. His *Rural Rides* appeared 1830.
TOPLADY, AUGUSTUS MONTAGUE (1740–78), author of 'Rock of Ages' and other hymns, born here.
WALTON, IZAAK (1593–1683), author, lived at Farnham Castle from 1662 with GEORGE MORLEY (1597–1684), bishop of Winchester and author of theological works, to whom he dedicated his life of Richard Hooker, 1665, and life of George Herbert, 1670, both probably written here.

25 Frimley HARTE, FRANCIS BRETT (Bret Harte, 1839–1902), American author, buried here.

26 Godalming CLUTTON-BROCK, ARTHUR (1868–1924), author and essayist, buried nearby.

34

HUXLEY, ALDOUS LEONARD (1894–1963), novelist and essayist, born here. His novels include the conversation-pieces *Crome Yellow*, 1921, and *Antic Hay* 1923, and the more seriously intentioned *Point Counter Point*, 1928, and *Brave New World*, 1932.

MANNING, OWEN (1721–1801), Surrey historian, rector 1763–1801 and buried here.

STRONG, LEONARD ALFRED GEORGE (1896–1958), novelist and poet, lived here.

27 Great Bookham BURNEY, FANNY (Frances, 1752–1840), novelist and diarist, lived here after her marriage to Alexandre d'Arblay in 1793, and wrote *Camilla*, 1796.

28 Guildford CARROLL, LEWIS (pseudonym of Charles Lutwidge Dodgson, 1832–98), author of *Alice in Wonderland*, died while visiting his sisters at The Chestnuts. He is buried in the Mount cemetery. The museum exhibits items associated with him.

SMITH, CHARLOTTE (1749–1806), poet and novelist, buried here.

TUPPER, MARTIN FARQUHAR (1810–89), poet, lived and died at nearby Albury and is buried in the churchyard there.

29 Ham DOUGLAS, CATHERINE (d1777), Duchess of Queensberry, correspondent of Swift and other eminent literary figures, lived here.

30 Haslemere ELIOT, GEORGE (pseudonym of Mary Anne Evans, 1819–80), novelist, stayed at Shottermill for three months in 1871 where she wrote most of *Middlemarch*, 1871–72.

MACDONALD, GEORGE (1824–1905), poet and novelist, lived here for a time.

31 Hersham LILLY, WILLIAM (1602–81), astrologer and historian, Samuel Butler's 'Sidrophal', lived here after 1660 and died here.

32 Hindhead DOYLE, SIR ARTHUR CONAN (1859–1930), creator of Sherlock Holmes, lived at 'Undershaw', 1897–1907.

33 Kew COBBETT, WILLIAM (1763–1835), political writer, worked here as a gardener, 1777–8.

34 Kingston Hill GALSWORTHY, JOHN (1867–1933), novelist and dramatist, born here. His many successful works include the *Forsyte Saga* sequence of novels, first published collectively in 1922, and such plays as *Justice*, 1910, and *Loyalties*, 1922.

35 Leatherhead BETHUNE, COLONEL DRINKWATER (1762–1844), historian of the siege of Gibraltar 1779–83, lived at Thorncroft, Gimcrack Hill.

HOPE, ANTHONY (pseudonym of Sir Anthony Hope Hawkins, 1863–1933), novelist, buried here.

36 Limpsfield BARCLAY, FLORENCE (1862–1921), novelist, born and buried here. Her highly popular book *The Rosary* was published in 1909.

RACKHAM, ARTHUR (1867–1939), book illustrator, died here.

THOMSON, SIR JOHN ARTHUR (1861–1933), author of popular scientific works, buried here.

37 Limpsfield Chart GARNETT, EDWARD (1868–1937), critic, and his wife CONSTANCE (1861–1946), translator, lived at the Cearn.

38 Merstham MILLES, JEREMIAH (1714–84), antiquary, rector from 1745 until his death.

RAVIS, THOMAS (c1560–1609), rector from 1591 until his death, assisted in translating the New Testament from 1604.

39 Merton FORD, FORD MADOX (born Ford Madox Hueffer, 1873–1939), novelist, born here. His memorable work is the tetralogy subsequently published as *Parade's End*, 1950, depicting social attitudes engendered by World War I.

MORRIS, WILLIAM (1834–96), poet, artist and socialist visionary, bought a print factory here in 1881 and produced wallpapers and household decorations in it with William de Morgan (1839–1917), novelist and potter.

SHERIDAN, RICHARD BRINSLEY (1751–1816), dramatist and politician, rented Church House for a time in the late 18th century.

40 Mickleham MILL, JOHN STUART (1806–73), philosopher, lived here before 1857.

SHARP, RICHARD (1759–1835), poet and politician, lived here.

STAËL, ANNA LOUISE GERMAINE, MADAME DE (1766–1817), French novelist and political writer, established herself at Juniper House in 1793 with other refugees, among them General Alexandre d'Arblay, to whom FANNY BURNEY, the novelist, was married at Mickleham church in 1793.

41 Mitcham DONNE, JOHN (1573–1631), poet and churchman, lived in a house here, bought for him by the wife of Sir Walter Raleigh, from 1605 until 1608 or thereabouts.

42 Mortlake BURTON, SIR RICHARD FRANCIS (1821–90), travel writer and translator, buried here.

FRANCIS, SIR PHILIP (1740–1818), reputed author of *Letters of Junius*, 1769–72 and 1812, buried here.

PARTRIDGE, JOHN (1644–1715), astrologer and almanac maker, born here. Swift wrote a pamphlet in 1708 under the name Isaac Bickerstaff satirising Partridge's predictions.

43 Normandy, nr Guildford COBBETT, WILLIAM (1763–1835), political writer, farmed at Normandy after 1821 and died here.

44 Norwood COLVIN, SIR SIDNEY (1845–1927), critic, born here. His publications include lives of Landor, 1881, and Keats, 1887, and he edited the letters of his friend Robert Louis Stevenson.

DOYLE, SIR ARTHUR CONAN (1859–1930), creator of Sherlock Holmes, lived at 12 Tennison Road, South Norwood 1891–93.

RUSKIN, JOHN (1819–1900), writer on art and sociology, lived at 26 Herne Hill.

45 Nutfield CHARLESWORTH, MARIE LOUISA (1819–80), author of *Ministering Children*, 1854, and other inspirational tales, spent her last years at Nutfield and is buried here.

46 Ockham MILLBANKE, RALPH, 2ND EARL OF LOVELACE (1839–1906), lived at Ockham Park. Grandson of Byron, he wrote *Astarte*, 1905, defending Lady Byron against Harriet Beecher Stowe's aspersions.

47 Petersham ASHFORD, DAISY (1881–1972), author of *The Young Visiters*, born here. This best-selling story was written when she was nine and published in 1919 with a preface by Sir James Barrie, to whom its authorship was sometimes, but erroneously, ascribed.

48 Purley TOOKE, JOHN HORNE (1736–1812), politician and philologist, made his reputation in philology with his *Diversions of Purley*, 1782. Formerly named Horne, he adopted the name of Tooke from a Purley friend of his.

49 Pyrford DONNE, JOHN (1573–1631), poet and churchman, and his wife Anne lived at Pyrford Park, 1602–4, home of Anne's cousin, Francis Wolley.

MUNBY, ARTHUR JOSEPH (1828–1910), poet, barrister and diarist, lived at Wheeler's Farm from 1877 until his death there, and is buried in Pyrford churchyard.

50 Reigate AINSWORTH, WILLIAM HARRISON (1805–82), historical novelist, died here.

51 Richmond ADCOCK, ARTHUR ST JOHN (1864–1930), writer and poet, buried here.

BRADDON, MRS MARY ELIZABETH (1837–1915), novelist, lived and died here.

BRADY, NICHOLAS (1659–1726), poet, was rector 1696–1726 and is buried here.

ELIOT, GEORGE (pseudonym of Mary Anne Evans, 1819–80), novelist, lived here with GEORGE HENRY LEWES (1817–78), journalist and author.

MAYHEW, AUGUSTUS (1826–75), novelist, died at the infirmary.

SAUNDERS, JOHN (1810–95), novelist, died here.

TATE, NAHUM (1652–1715), poet laureate and dramatist, lived here.

THOMSON, JAMES (1700–48), poet, probably wrote 'Rule, Britannia' while living here, and is buried here.

52 **Sanderstead** HEAD, SIR FRANCIS BOND (1793–1875), travel writer and biographer, buried here.

53 **Shalford** BUNYAN, JOHN (1628–88), religious writer, is thought to have lived in hiding for a time at Horn Hatch Cottage, Shalford Common.

54 **Shere** BARRIE, SIR JAMES MATTHEW (1860–1937), playwright, lived at Anchor Cottage in 1892 and wrote *The Professor's Love Story*, 1894, here.

55 **Surbiton** JEFFERIES, RICHARD (1848–87), naturalist and novelist, lived here 1877–82 and wrote *The Story of My Heart*, 1883.

56 **Sutton** NORTHCLIFFE, LORD (Alfred Charles William Harmsworth, 1865–1922), journalist, owned Sutton Place from 1901.

57 **Tadworth** HOPE, ANTHONY (pseudonym of Sir Anthony Hope Hawkins, 1863–1933), novelist, lived and died at Heath Farm.

58 **Thames Ditton** HOOD, THOMAS (1799–1845), poet, frequently stayed at the Swan Inn and wrote 'The Song of the Shirt' here.

59 **Thursley** FREEMAN, JOHN (1880–1929), poet, buried here.

60 **Tilford, nr Farnham** SMITH, CHARLOTTE (1749–1806), poet and novelist, died here. She is buried in Stoke-Juxta-Guildford church.

61 **Walton-on-Thames** LILLY, WILLIAM (1602–81), astrologer and historian, buried here.

MAGINN, WILLIAM (1793–1842), Irish poet and journalist, buried here.

62 **Waverley** TEMPLE, SIR WILLIAM (1628–99), statesman and author, bought Moor Park in 1681 and spent most of his remaining years here. JONATHAN SWIFT (1667–1745), satirist, was his secretary here at intervals from 1689, and met ESTHER JOHNSON (1681–1728), the Stella of his *Journal to Stella*, as the 1948 collection of his letters to her was titled: she was daughter of the companion to Temple's widowed sister, perhaps by Temple himself.

63 **Westcott** MALTHUS, THOMAS ROBERT (1766–1834), economist, born at Rookery House. His *Essay on the Principle of Population*, advocating population control, appeared in 1798, and *The Nature and Progress of Rent* in 1815.

64 **West Horsley** West Horsley Place is thought to have been the home of SIR ANTHONY BROWNE (d 1548) and his wife, the Fair Geraldine of the Earl of Surrey's sonnets. SIR WALTER RALEIGH's head is believed to be buried in the Nicholas Chapel.

65 **Weybridge** HEWLETT, MAURICE (1861–1923), novelist and poet, born here. His novels include *Richard Yea-and-Nay*, 1900, and *The Queen's Quair*, 1904. His poetry is best represented in *The Song of the Plough*, 1916.

66 **Witley** LEWES, GEORGE HENRY (1817–78), journalist and philosophical writer, lived with GEORGE ELIOT (1819–80), novelist, here from the end of 1876 until his death.

67 **Woking** HENLEY, WILLIAM ERNEST (1849–1903), poet and critic, died here.

Sussex (*Maps 5 & 6*)

1 **Alfriston** DE BEER, SIR GAVIN (1899–1972), scientific writer and biographer, died here.

LOWER, RICHARD (1782–1865), dialect poet, born and lived most of his life in the neighbourhood. His best known work, *Tom Cladpole's Jurney to Lunnon*, appeared in 1830.

2 **Arundel** EDWARDES, TICKNER (1865–1944), clergyman and novelist, lived and ministered nearby and wrote his Sussex novels, including *The Honey Star*, 1913, and *Transy*, 1914.

HOWARD, HENRY, EARL OF SURREY (1517–47), poet, born here. With Wyatt, he introduced the sonnet form and blank verse into England.

SOUTHWELL, ROBERT (c1561–95), poet, was chaplain to the Countess of Arundel between 1589 and 1592, during which time he wrote much of his verse. He was brought up at, and closely associated throughout his life with, Roffey Place near Horsham.

3 **Ashurst** FAIRLESS, MICHAEL (pseudonym of Margaret Fairless Barber, 1869–1901), essayist, buried.

4 **Bignor Park, nr Arundel** SMITH, CHARLOTTE (1749–1806), poet and novelist, spent most of her life here.

5 **Bishopstone** HURDIS, JAMES (1763–1801), poet, buried here.

6 **Blackdown, nr Haslemere** TENNYSON, ALFRED, LORD (1809–92), poet laureate, built Aldworth on the Sussex slope of Blackdown and lived here from 1869 until his death.

7 **Brede** CRANE, STEPHEN (1871–1900), American journalist and novelist, lived here towards the end of his life. *The Red Badge of Courage* appeared in 1895.

KAYE-SMITH, SHEILA (1887–1956), novelist, spent most of her life here (see **St Leonards**).

8 **Brighton** BROWN, VINCENT (c1870–1933), novelist and journalist, lived his whole life here. His best known book is *The Glory and the Abyss*, 1910.

CARPENTER, EDWARD (1844–1929), socialist reformer, born here. His publications include *Towards Democracy*, 1883, and *Love's Coming of Age*, 1896.

DICKENS, CHARLES (1812–70), novelist, stayed here in 1837 and 1841 at the Old Ship Hotel, King's Road, and in 1847 wrote much of *Dombey and Son* at 148 King's Road, setting parts of the story in Brighton. He also used the Bedford Hotel for brief visits.

HALLIWELL-PHILLIPS, JAMES ORCHARD (1820–89), scholar, died at Hollingbury Copse.

HUGHES, THOMAS (1822–96), author of *Tom Brown's Schooldays*, 1857, died here.

LYALL, EDNA (pseudonym of Ada Ellen Bayly, 1857–1903), novelist and feminist, born here. Her most popular works were *We Two*, 1884, and *In the Golden Days*, 1885.

MACKINTOSH, EWART ALLEN (c1892–1917), soldier poet, born here. He published *A Highland Regiment*, 1917, and *War, The Liberator*, 1918.

MARRYATT, FLORENCE (1838–99), novelist, daughter of Captain Marryat, the novelist (1792–1848), born here. She published some eighty novels and *Life and Letters of Captain Marryat*, 1872, as well as works on spiritualism.

NOEL, THOMAS (1799–1861), poet, lived at Brighton from 1858 and died here.

PHILIPS, FRANCIS (1849–1921), novelist and playwright, born here.

SALA, GEORGE AUGUSTUS (1828–95), journalist and novelist, died at 59 Norton Road.

SMITH, WILLIAM (1808–72), novelist, died here.

SPENCER, HERBERT (1820–1903), philosopher and author, spent his last years at 5 Percival Terrace.

9 **Burwash** KIPLING, RUDYARD (1865–1936), poet and novelist, lived at Bateman's from 1902 until his death. It is the house of *Puck of Pook's Hill*, 1906, and *Rewards and Fairies*, 1910, and is preserved for the public to visit.

10 **Bury** GALSWORTHY, JOHN (1867–1933), novelist and dramatist, lived at Bury House from 1926 until his death. His ashes were scattered on the Downs in the neighbourhood.

11 **Catsfield** BROSTER, DOROTHY KATHLEEN (d1950), novelist, lived here.

12 **Chiddingly** LOWER, MARK ANTHONY (1813–76), antiquary, born. His *History of Sussex* appeared in 1870. His father, the schoolmaster, was the dialect poet RICHARD LOWER (see **Alfriston**).

13 **Chichester** COLLINS, WILLIAM (1721–59), poet, born at 21 East Street. His *Odes*, 1747, remain highly regarded, but his death in Chichester passed unnoticed by the press.

CROCKER, CHARLES (1797–1861), poet, was a verger of the cathedral.

FULLER, MAJOR-GENERAL JOHN FREDERICK CHARLES (1878–1966), military historian, born here. His *Decisive Battles of the Western World* was published 1954.

HAYLEY, WILLIAM (1745–1820), poet and biographer, born here. His *Triumphs of Temper* appeared in 1781. He was the friend of many well-known people, including William Blake, Robert Southey, George Romney and Emma, Lady Hamilton.

KEATS, JOHN (1795–1821), poet, began *The Eve of St Agnes* at 11 Eastgate Street (formerly Hornet Square) while visiting Chichester in 1819.

14 **Crawley** LEMON, MARK (1809–70), humorous writer and first editor of *Punch*, lived at Vine Cottage from 1858 and died here.

SIEVIER, ROBERT (d1939), sporting journalist, died and is buried here.

15 **Crowborough** DOYLE, SIR ARTHUR CONAN (1859–1930), author, lived at Windlesham from 1907 and died here. He wrote many of his Sherlock Holmes stories, and others, here. He was buried in the garden, but his remains were removed to Minstead, Hampshire, after World War II.

FULLER, MAJOR-GENERAL JOHN FREDERICK CHARLES (1878–1966), military historian, died at Forest Gate.

HUTCHINSON, ARTHUR STUART MENTETH (1879–1971), novelist, lived and died at New Forest Lodge, Beacon Road. His best-selling *If Winter Comes* appeared in 1920.

JEFFERIES, RICHARD (1848–87), naturalist and novelist, spent the winter of 1885–86 at The Downs, London Road, and here wrote his last essays, published posthumously as *Field and Hedgerow*, 1889.

16 **Cuckfield** BOORDE, ANDREW (c1490–1549), physician, traveller and writer, born here. He wrote about his travels and against the growing of beards.

KINGSLEY, HENRY (1830–76), novelist and brother of Charles Kingsley, buried here.

17 **Eartham** HAYLEY, WILLIAM (1745–1820), poet, lived as the self-styled 'Hermit of Eartham' 1774–1800 (see **Chichester**).

18 Eastbourne HUXLEY, THOMAS HENRY (1825–95), scientist and writer, spent his last years at Eastbourne and died here.

KEARY, ANNIE (1825–79), novelist, died here.

LYALL, EDNA (pseudonym of Ada Ellen Bayly, 1857–1903), novelist, lived here from 1883 until her death (see **Brighton**).

19 East Grinstead NEALE, JOHN MASON (1818–66), author of 'Jerusalem the Golden' and other hymns, was warden of Sackville College almshouses from 1846 until his death and is buried here.

PATMORE, COVENTRY KERSEY DIGHTON (1823–96), poet, bought an estate here in 1866 and described it in *How I managed my Estate*, 1886.

20 East Hoathly TURNER, THOMAS, diarist, buried here. His diary covers the period 1754–65.

21 Falmer WINN, GODFREY HERBERT (1908–71), journalist and author, lived at the Mill House until his death.

22 Felpham HAYLEY, WILLIAM (1745–1820), poet, lived at Turret House from 1800 until his death and is buried here. WILLIAM BLAKE (1757–1827) stayed here 1800–4 while illustrating Hayley's works. It was here in 1803 that he ejected a soldier, John Scholfield, from his garden, resulting in Blake's trial for assault and sedition at Chichester in January 1804. He was acquitted.

23 Fletching GIBBON, EDWARD (1737–94), historian, buried here.

24 Framfield ARNOLD, SIR ARTHUR (1833–1902), politician and writer, born here. He was editor of the evening paper *Echo* 1868–75, and published a *History of the Cotton Famine*, 1864, *Through Persia by Caravan*, 1877, and a collection of radical essays, *Social Politics*, 1878.

REALF, ROBERT (1834–78), journalist and a poet of the American Civil War, born here.

25 Glyndebourne HAY, WILLIAM (1695–1755), poet and philosopher, lived at Glynde Place and is buried here.

26 Goodwood Halnaker Mill is the subject of HILAIRE BELLOC's poem of that title.

27 Goring-on-Sea JEFFERIES, RICHARD (1848–87), naturalist and novelist, spent the last nine months of his life here and died at Sea View, now Jefferies House.

28 Greatham, nr Pulborough LAWRENCE, DAVID HERBERT (1885–1930), novelist, lived here from Jan–July 1915, while he was writing *The Rainbow*, 1915.

MEYNELL, WILFRED (1852–1948) and ALICE (1847–1922), poets and authors, lived here, at the home of their daughter VIOLA (1886–1956), poet and novelist.

29 Groombridge WALLER, EDMUND (1606–87), poet, was living here at the time of his unsuccessful courting of Lady Dorothea Sidney, to whom, as 'Sacharissa', he wrote 'Go, lovely rose', 1635, and other poems. Groombridge Manor is Birlstone Manor House in CONAN DOYLE's Sherlock Holmes novel *The Valley of Fear*, 1915.

30 Guestling MARTIN, GREGORY (d1582), translator, born at Maxfield. His translation of the Bible (1582 and 1610) is known as the Douay version.

31 Hangleton The manor house is believed to have been owned by SIR PHILIP SIDNEY (1554–86) at the time of his death, and he may have lived here for some time towards the end of his life.

32 Hartfield MILNE, ALAN ALEXANDER (1882–1956), children's author, lived at Gill's Lap. The house is the original of *The House at Pooh Corner*, 1928.

33 Harting TROLLOPE, ANTHONY (1815–82), novelist, lived at South Harting from 1880.

34 Hassocks HAMILTON, PATRICK ANTHONY WALTER (1904–62), novelist and dramatist, born here. His successful plays include *Rope*, 1929, and *Gaslight*, 1939, and his novels *Hangover Square*, 1941, and *The Slaves of Solitude*, 1947.

35 Hastings CROWLEY, ALEISTER (Edward Alexander, 1875–1947), magician, poet and autobiographer, spent his last years here and died in a boarding house, Netherwood, at The Ridge.

EDWARDS, MATILDA BARBARA BETHAM (1836–1919), novelist and writer on France, lived here.

'GREY OWL' (Archie Belaney, 1885–1938), author and lecturer, born here. He spent most of his life as a Canadian Indian and wrote and spoke widely on Indian ways. His book *Pilgrims of the Wild*, 1935, was an international bestseller.

MOGRIDGE, GEORGE (1787–1854), children's author, died here. He wrote as Old Humphrey and Peter Parley.

PATMORE, COVENTRY KERSEY DIGHTON (1823–96), poet, lived here 1875–91 and was instrumental in building the church of Our Lady of the Sea in the Old Town.

ROSSETTI, DANTE GABRIEL (1828–82), poet and painter, married the Pre-Raphaelite model Elizabeth Siddal at St Clement's church in 1860.

36 Henfield FAIRLESS, MICHAEL (pseudonym of Margaret Fairless Barber, 1869–1901), essayist, spent the last two years of her life at Mock Bridge House and composed *The Roadmender*, 1902, here.

HORNUNG, ERNEST WILLIAM (1866–1921), novelist, buried here.

37 Horsted Keynes MOORE, GILES (1617–79), diarist, rector 1656–79 and died here.

38 Hove ELLIOTT, CHARLOTTE (1789–1871), hymn writer, buried here.

SALA, GEORGE AUGUSTUS (1828–95), journalist and novelist, buried here.

39 Ifield LEMON, MARK (1809–70), humorous writer and first editor of *Punch*, buried in St Margaret's churchyard.

40 Lancing SEWELL, ANNA (1820–78), author, lived at Lancing for some time and here acquired the love of horses which led to her *Black Beauty*, 1877.

41 Lewes BELL, CLIVE (1881–1964), writer on art and literature and one of the original members of the Bloomsbury Group, lived at Charleston, Firle, near Lewes and died here.

BROWNE, SIR THOMAS (1605–82), author of *Religio Medici*, c1635, lived here for a time.

HUNTINGTON, WILLIAM (1745–1813), evangelist and author, buried here.

LUCAS, EDWARD VERRALL (1868–1938), essayist, lived at Kingston Manor nearby for several years before the World War I.

PAINE, THOMAS (1737–1809), political writer, lived at Bull House near the West Gate, 1768–74.

RICKMAN, THOMAS (1761–1834), bookseller and radical writer, known as 'Clio', born at The Cliffe. He returned to live in Lewes from 1778–83.

TWYNE, THOMAS (1543–1613), physician and translator, practised medicine and is buried here.

WOOLF, LEONARD (1880–1969), critic and historian and VIRGINIA (1882–1941), novelist and essayist, leased Asheham House nearby from 1912–19. It is the setting for Virginia Woolf's short story 'A Haunted House'.

42 Mayfield MAY, THOMAS (1595–1650), poet, author and dramatist, born here. His *History of the Long Parliament* appeared in 1647.

43 Nuthurst OLIVANT, ALFRED (1874–1927), novelist, born here. His books, set on the Sussex Downs, were widely popular, but he is best remembered for *Owd*

Bob, the Grey Dog of Kenmuir, 1898, set in Cumberland.

44 Peasmarsh PATTISON, WILLIAM (1706–27), poet, born here. Known as 'the Chatterton of Sussex', he died of smallpox and near-starvation.

45 Petworth BLUNT, WILFRED SCAWEN (1840–1922), poet, born here. He published several collections of poems, including *Sonnets and Songs of Proteus*, 1875, and also wrote against British imperialism in the East and in Ireland.

46 Pevensey BOORDE, ANDREW (c1490–1549), physician, traveller and writer, inherited property here from his brother, and was subsequently a frequent visitor after c1540 (see **Cuckfield**).

47 Plumpton DUDENEY, JOHN (1782–1852), shepherd and scholar, born here.

MASCALL, LEONARD (d1589), translator and writer on husbandry, lived at Plumpton Place.

48 Rodmell MARTIN, BASIL KINGSLEY (1897–1969), journalist, had a home here from 1954 until his death.

WOOLF, VIRGINIA (1882–1941), novelist and essayist, and LEONARD (1880–1969), critic and historian, lived and died at Monks House. They had been associated with neighbouring parts of Sussex, notably Firle, since 1910.

49 Rye The Mermaid Inn features prominently in RUSSELL THORNDIKE's *Dr Syn* stories.

FLETCHER, JOHN (1579–1625), dramatist, born here. His partnership with Francis Beaumont (1584–1616) lasted from 1606–16 and produced about a dozen plays, including *The Scornful Lady*, 1610, and *The Maid's Tragedy*, 1611.

HALL, MARGUERITE RADCLYFFE (c1886–1943), novelist, lived here.

JAMES, HENRY (1843–1916), novelist, lived at Lamb House from 1897 until his death, writing some of his most celebrated works here. The house, which is open to the public, belonged from 1916 to the novelist EDWARD FREDERICK BENSON (1867–1940), who used it as the setting for his Miss Mapp stories, and it was an occasional home of his brother, the scholar ARTHUR CHRISTOPHER BENSON (1862–1925).

50 Rottingdean KIPLING, RUDYARD (1865–1936), poet and novelist, lived at The Elms 1897–1903 and wrote *Kim*, 1901, and *The Just So Stories*, 1902. Other writers who have lived in Rottingdean for varying periods include SIR WILLIAM WATSON (1858–1935), poet; WILLIAM BLACK (1841–98), novelist, who is buried here; ALFRED NOYES (1880–1958), poet; and MAURICE BARING (1874–1945), poet and novelist.

51 Salvington, nr Worthing SELDEN, JOHN (1584–1654), historian, born here. He was known as the Father of Sussex literature and learning both for his many notable works and for his talk, which his secretary RICHARD MILWARD (1609–80) collected in *Selden's Table Talk*, 1689.

52 St Leonards KAYE-SMITH, SHEILA (1887–1956), novelist, born here. Her Sussex novels were highly popular, including *Sussex Gorse*, 1916, *Tamarisk Town*, 1919, *Joanna Godden*, 1921, and *End of the House of Alard*, 1923.

CHAMIER, FREDERICK (1796–1870), novelist, died at 29 Warrior Square.

WEBB, MARY GLADYS (1881–1927), novelist, died here.

53 Shipley BELLOC, JOSEPH HILAIRE PETER (1870–1953), poet, essayist and historian, lived at King's Land from 1906 until his death. The local windmill was restored as a memorial to him.

54 Shoreham DALMON, CHARLES (1862–1938), poet, lived here.

WESLEY, JOHN (1703–91), Methodist leader, was associated with Shoreham for forty years, frequently visiting his close friend VINCENT PERRONE (1693–1785), the 'archbishop of methodism' and father of EDWARD PERRONET (1721–92), an associate of the Wesleys and author of the hymn 'All hail the power of Jesu's name', 1780.

55 Slaugham TENNYSON, ALFRED, LORD (1809–92), poet laureate, and his wife lived at Warninglid shortly after their marriage in 1850.

56 Sompting TRELAWNY, EDWARD JOHN (1792–1881), author and biographer, spent his last days at Sompting and died here.

57 South Malling COURTHOPE, WILLIAM JOHN (1842–1917), poet and biographer, born here. His *History of English Poetry* appeared 1895–1910.

58 Storrington THOMPSON, FRANCIS (1859–1907), poet, wrote 'The Hound of Heaven', 1893, while visiting Storrington Priory.

59 Tillington LUCAS, EDWARD VERRALL (1868–1938), essayist, lived for some years at Tillington Cottage.

60 Trotton OTWAY, THOMAS (1652–85), dramatist, born at Milland rectory nearby. His *Venice Preserv'd* was first presented in 1682.

61 Twineham Hickstead Place was the home of the STAPLEY BROTHERS, 18th century diarists.

62 Uckfield PATMORE, COVENTRY KERSEY DIGHTON (1823–96), poet, lived at Heron's Ghyll in 1874.

63 Uppark, nr South Harting WELLS, HERBERT GEORGE (1866–1946), novelist and sociologist, began writing here as a child, when his mother was housekeeper to the family from 1880. It is the Bladesover of his novel *Tono Bungay*, 1909.

64 Warminghurst PENN, WILLIAM (1644–1718), founder of Pennsylvania and Quaker campaigner, lived here after his return from America in 1677.

65 Warnham, nr Horsham SHELLEY, PERCY BYSSHE (1792–1822), poet, born at Field Place.

66 Washington Washington and its neighbourhood, provide the setting for KIPLING's story 'They' in *Traffics and Discoveries*, 1904, though the original of Hawkin's Old Farm is his home at Burwash (qv), transferred to this district.

67 West Grinstead BELLOC, JOSEPH HILAIRE PETER (1870–1953), poet, essayist and historian, buried here.

BURRELL, SIR WILLIAM (1732–96), antiquary, lived at West Grinstead Park and is buried in the church.

HORNUNG, ERNEST WILLIAM (1866–1921), novelist, lived at Partridge Green nearby.

POPE, ALEXANDER (1688–1744), poet and satirist, wrote much of *The Rape of the Lock*, 1712, while staying at the house of John Caryll (c1666–1736), who is mentioned in the work.

68 Willingdon CLARKE, EDWARD (1769–1822), traveller and author, born at the vicarage. His *Travels* were published in six volumes 1810–23.

69 Winchelsea This town and the neighbouring Rye are the setting of WILLIAM MAKEPEACE THACKERAY's unfinished novel *Denis Duval*, 1864.

70 Withyham SACKVILLE, THOMAS, 1ST EARL OF DORSET (1536–1608), poet and dramatist, born here. With Thomas Norton he wrote *Gorboduc*, 1561, the first English tragedy in blank verse. CHARLES SACKVILLE, 6TH EARL (1638–1706), poet, is buried in the Sackville chapel here.

71 Woolbeding SMITH, CHARLOTTE (1749–1806), novelist, lived for a time at the manor house.

72 Worth BLUNT, WILFRED SCAWEN (1840–1922), poet, lived at Crabett Park from 1872 until his death. He died at Newbuildings Place, Southwater, and was buried in Newbuildings Wood without religious rites, as he wished (see **Petworth**).

73 Worthing HUDSON, WILLIAM HENRY (1841–1922), naturalist and author, buried in Broadwater cemetery.

JEFFERIES, RICHARD (1848–87), naturalist and author, buried in Broadwater cemetery.

Kent (*Map 6*)

1 **Aldington** FORD, FORD MADOX (1873–1939), novelist, lived at Pent Farm. JOSEPH CONRAD (1857–1924) worked with him there for some time from 1898 and rented the cottage until 1909.
GOWER, JOHN (1330–1408), poet and friend of Chaucer, lived at the manor.
LINACRE, THOMAS (c1460–1524), classical scholar, vicar 1509.

2 **Allington** WYATT, SIR THOMAS (1503–42), poet and diplomat, born and lived at Allington Castle. His verse style marked a change in English poetry and he introduced the sonnet into this country. The castle is the Castle Adamant of TENNYSON's *The Princess*, 1847, and hence of W. S. GILBERT's *Princess Ida*, 1884.

3 **Aylesford** SEDLEY, SIR CHARLES (c1639–1701), poet and courtier, born here. He wrote tragedies, comedies, poems and songs, but notably the plays *Bellamira*, 1687, and *The Mulberry Garden*, 1668.

4 **Barham** OXENDEN, HENRY (1609–70), poet, lived here.

5 **Bearsted** THOMAS, EDWARD (1878–1917), poet, lived here.

6 **Beckenham** Elizabeth, DR JOHNSON's wife ('Tetty') buried here 1752: her epitaph, in Latin, is by Johnson.
GROTE, GEORGE (1794–1871), banker and historian, born at Clay Hill. His *History of Greece* appeared 1846–56. He is buried in Westminster Abbey.

7 **Bekesbourne** COX, SIR GEORGE (1827–1902), mythologist, vicar here for a time.
FLEMING, IAN LANCASTER (1908–65), novelist, lived here for a period.

8 **Bexley Heath** MORRIS, WILLIAM (1834–96), poet, designer and socialist writer, built the Red House and lived there 1860–65.

9 **Bidborough** SIDNEY, DOROTHY (1617–84), EDMUND WALLER's 'Sacharissa', was living here when he sent her his poem 'Go, lovely rose', 1635.

10 **Biddenden** NARES, EDWARD (1762–1841), author, buried here.

11 **Birchington** ROSSETTI, DANTE GABRIEL (1828–82), poet, died at Westcliffe Bungalow and is buried here.

12 **Bishopsbourne** BROOKE, JOCELYN (1908–66), novelist and poet, lived here.
CONRAD, JOSEPH (1857–1924), novelist, spent his last years at Oswalds and died here.
HOOKER, RICHARD (1554–1600), theological writer, rector from 1595 and buried here.

13 **Blean** POSTGATE, RAYMOND WILLIAM (1896–1971), novelist and historian, lived here from 1967 until his death.

14 **Borough Green** CROWE, CATHERINE (1800–76), author, born here. She wrote tragedies, juvenile books, and *The Night Side of Nature*, 1848, a collection of stories of the supernatural.

15 **Boughton Melherbe** WOTTON, SIR HENRY (1568–1639), poet and diplomat, born at Boughton Hall. Several of his poems still find their way into anthologies, among them 'The Character of a Happy Life'.

16 **Boxley** SANDYS, GEORGE (1578–1643), travel writer and translator, lived and died at Boxley Abbey. He is buried in the church.

17 **Brabourne** GOWER, JOHN (1330–1408), poet and friend of Chaucer, possibly born here. His *Confessio amantis*, 1390, contrasts the claims of courtly love and the love of Christ.

18 **Brenchley** SASSOON, SIEGFRIED (1886–1967), poet and autobiographer, born here. As a writer he spoke for those who fought in World War I, especially in *Memoirs of a Fox-Hunting Man*, 1928 and *Memoirs of an Infantry Officer*, 1930.

19 **Broadstairs** Has associations with CHARLES DICKENS, who spent much time at this holiday resort. Bleak House (formerly Fort House) is preserved as a Dickens museum. Lawn House and the Albion Hotel were favourite lodgings of his, and considerable portions of several major works were written in the town, which holds an annual Dickens Festival.
ELIOT, GEORGE (pseudonym of Mary Ann Evans, 1819–80), novelist, lived here in 1852.
JOHNSON, LIONEL PIGOT (1867–1902), poet and critic, born here. His best criticism was collected posthumously in *Postliminium*, 1911, and his poetry, much derived from Celtic legend, is typified in *Ireland and Other Poems*, 1897.
NORTHCLIFFE, LORD (Alfred Charles William Harmsworth, 1865–1922), journalist, had his principal home, Elmwood, here from 1891 until his death.
RICHARDS, FRANK (pseudonym of Charles Harold St John Hamilton, 1875–1961), boys' author and creator of Billy Bunter, lived here for many years and died at Kingsgate nearby.

20 **Bromley** CRAIK, MRS DINAH MARIA (1826–87), novelist, lived at Shortlands from 1864 until her death.
WELLS, HERBERT GEORGE (1866–1946), novelist and sociologist, born over a shop in the High Street. His novels divide generally into comedies, eg *Kipps*, 1905, and *The History of Mr Polly*, 1910, and pseudo-scientific imaginings, eg *The Time Machine*, 1895, and *The Shape of Things to Come*, 1933. He also wrote works on history, science and economic questions.

21 **Canterbury** Has literary associations: eg CHAUCER's *Canterbury Tales*, first printed by Caxton 1475; KEATS's 'Eve of St Agnes', 1820, set in the cathedral close; and DICKENS's *David Copperfield*, 1849–50.
BARHAM, RICHARD HARRIS (1788–1845), poet and clergyman, born at 61 Burgate Street. He wrote the *Ingoldsby Legends*, set in Canterbury and other parts of Kent, for magazine publication. The stories were published in book form in 1840 and 1847.
CONRAD, JOSEPH (1857–1924), novelist, buried here.
GOSSON, STEPHEN (1554–1624), dramatist, born here. His works include *The Schoole of Abuse*, 1579, *The Ephemerides of Phialo*, 1579, and *Plays Confuted in Five Actions*, 1581.
LINACRE, THOMAS (c1460–1524), classical scholar, probably born here. He wrote works on grammar and medicine and made translations from the Greek.
MARLOWE, CHRISTOPHER (1564–93), dramatist and poet, born in St George's Street. Friend and contemporary of Shakespeare and second only to him in invention and quality. His best plays are *Tamburlaine*, 1587–8, *Dr Faustus*, 1588, *The Jew of Malta*, 1589, *Edward II*, 1593.

22 **Charlton** DE LA MARE, WALTER JOHN (1873–1956), poet and novelist, born here. He is chiefly renowned for his poems for children, some of them first published under the name Walter Ramel in *Songs of Childhood*, 1902.

23 **Chalk** DICKENS, CHARLES (1812–70), novelist, spent his honeymoon here in 1836 and found the original of

41

Joe Gargery's cottage and forge (*Great Expectations*, 1860–61), which is still to be seen. There are many Dickens associations with the neighbourhood.

24 Chatham Many associations with CHARLES DICKENS. His happiest childhood home was 2 (now 11) Ordnance Terrace, 1817–21. The town features in several of his works, notably *Pickwick Papers*, is Dullborough in *The Uncommercial Traveller* and Mudfog in *Mudfog Papers*.

25 Chevening PRATT, ANNE (1806–93), botanical writer, born here. Her popular works include *The Flowering Plants and Ferns of Great Britain*, 1855.

26 Chislehurst CAMDEN, WILLIAM (1551–1623), antiquary, spent his last years at Chislehurst and died here.

CROMPTON, RICHMAL (Richmal Crompton Lamburn, 1890–1969), children's author and creator of William, lived in Orpington Road and died here.

FIRBANK, RONALD (1886–1926), novelist, spent much of his life at his parents' house here.

27 Cobham The Leather Bottle Inn was CHARLES DICKENS's favourite hostelry during his last years, while he lived nearby at Gadshill. It now houses a Dickens collection. Cobham Hall, now a school, was the home of Dickens's friend Lord Darnley, and he often walked in the grounds there.

28 Cooling Cooling Castle was the home of Sir John Oldcastle (d1417), the original of Shakespeare's Falstaff. The castle was attacked once only and that was by SIR THOMAS WYATT (see **Allington**) during his rebellion against Mary I, 1554.

The line of small graves of eighteenth century Comport children in Cooling churchyard gave CHARLES DICKENS the notion for the tombstones of Pip's dead brothers and sister in *Great Expectations*, 1860–61.

29 Cranbrook DOBELL, SYDNEY THOMPSON (1824–74), poet, born here. The work which first brought him recognition, *The Roman*, 1850, was published under the name Sydney Yendys.

FLETCHER, PHINEAS (1582–1650), poet, born here. His most notable work is *The Purple Island or the Isle of Man*, 1633, an allegory on the human body.

30 Crayford BLACKWOOD, ALGERNON (1869–1951), author, born at the Manor House. He explored supernatural themes in many novels and short stories, beginning with *The Empty House*, 1906.

31 Crouch WELCH, DENTON (1915–48), novelist, lived and died here.

32 Dartford KEYES, SIDNEY (1922–43), poet, born here. The Hawthornden Prize was awarded posthumously for his second volume of verse, *The Cruel Solstice*, 1943.

33 Deal CARTER, ELIZABETH (1717–1806), author, poet and notable bluestocking, born and lived here. She was a close friend of Dr Johnson for many years and admired by him for her wide-ranging scholarship.

34 Deptford EVELYN, JOHN (1620–1706), diarist, lived at Sayes Court 1652–94.

MARLOWE, CHRISTOPHER (1564–93), dramatist and poet, is believed to have been killed in a tavern brawl at Deptford and buried here (see **Canterbury**).

35 Dover Shakespeare Cliff, dominating the eastern end of the sea front, is prominent in SHAKESPEARE's *King Lear*, c1605.

CHURCHILL, CHARLES (1731–64), satirist, buried here.

FOOTE, SAMUEL (1720–77), actor and dramatist, died here.

36 Downe DARWIN, CHARLES ROBERT (1809–82), naturalist, lived at Down House from 1842 until his death. Here he wrote his *Origin of Species*, 1859, and *Descent of Man*, 1871. The house is open to the public.

37 Eastling HASTED, EDWARD (1732–1812), historian,

born here. His notable *History and Topographical Survey of Kent* appeared in 1778–99.

38 East Peckham TWYSDEN, SIR ROGER (1597–1672), antiquary, born at Royden Hall. He wrote the important *Historiae Anglicanae Scriptores Decem*, 1652.

WELCH, DENTON (1915–48), novelist, lived here.

39 East Sutton FILMER, SIR ROBERT (c1590–c1653), political writer, born at East Sutton Place. His impressive advocacy of a divine right of kings was expressed in *Patriarcha*, 1679.

40 Eastwell FINCH, ANNE, COUNTESS OF WINCHILSEA (1661–1720), poet and friend of poets, died at Eastwell Park.

41 Edenbridge TIMBS, JOHN (1801–75), author and journalist, lived here and is buried here.

42 Eltham LILBURNE, JOHN (c1614–57), republican propagandist, died here.

LUCAS, EDWARD VERRALL (1868–1938), essayist, born here. His work is best represented in *Adventures and Misgivings*, 1938. He also wrote a notable *Life of Charles Lamb*, 1905.

NESBIT, EDITH (1858–1924), children's author, lived at Well Hall 1899–1921. It is the setting for her novel *The Red House*, and for some of her Bastable stories.

ROPER, WILLIAM (1496–1578), biographer of his father-in-law Sir Thomas More, lived at Well Hall.

43 Eynsford MEE, ARTHUR (1875–1943), journalist and editor, lived here.

44 Faversham Arden's House was the home of Thomas Arden, who was murdered here at his wife's instigation in 1550: this was the theme of a play *Arden of Faversham*, 1592, which has been attributed by some scholars to SHAKESPEARE.

FINLAY, GEORGE (1799–1875), historian, born here. His authoritative *History of Greece* from 146 BC to AD 1864 was published between 1843–61 (the additional years added in the corrective edition of 1877).

45 Folkestone CALVERLEY, CHARLES STUART (1831–84), parodist and poet, buried here.

COPPARD, ALFRED EDGAR (1878–1957), poet and short story writer, born here. His published collections of short stories include *Adam and Eve and Pinch Me*, 1921, and *The Field of Mustard*, 1926.

DICKENS, CHARLES (1812–70), novelist, rented 3 Albion Villas for the summer of 1855 and began *Little Dorrit* there.

GROSSMITH, GEORGE (1847–1912), actor and author, died here.

46 Gadshill The scene of Falstaff's attempt to rob the travellers in SHAKESPEARE's Henry IV part 1, c1597.

Gadshill Place, now a school, was CHARLES DICKENS's final home. He bought it in 1855 as a country residence, moved there permanently in 1860, and died in the house on 9 June, 1870. The Swiss garden chalet in which he worked at Gadshill is now at Rochester (*qv*).

47 Godmersham AUSTEN, JANE (1775–1817), novelist, spent much time at her brother's home, Godmersham Place, and worked on her novels there.

48 Goodnestone, nr Faversham JAMES, MONTAGUE RHODES (1862–1936), palaeographer and author, born here. His *Ghost Stories of an Antiquary* in two series, 1905 and 1911, are among the most notable examples of the genre.

49 Goodnestone, nr Wingham AUSTEN, JANE (1775–1817), novelist, was a frequent visitor to Goodnestone Park Manor, and worked there.

50 Gravesend ARNOLD, SIR EDWIN (1832–1904), poet, born here. He is notable for his attempt to express Eastern ways of thought in terms of English verse, eg in *The Light of Asia*, 1879.

JACOBS, WILLIAM WYMARK (1863–1943), short-story writer, lived here.

51 Halling LAMBARDE, WILLIAM (1536–1601), historian, lived here.

52 Hayes HALLAM, HENRY (1777–1859), historian, died here.

53 Hollingbourne GETHIN, LADY GRACE (1676–97), literary impostor, lived here and has an interesting memorial in the church.

54 Hoo GUNNING, PETER (1614–84), bishop of Ely and author, born here. He wrote *Paschal or Lent Fast*, 1662, and other theological works.

55 Hothfield AUSTIN, ALFRED (1835–1913), poet laureate, lived at Swinford Old Manor.

56 Ickham BRYDGES, SIR SAMUEL EGERTON (1762–1837), bibliographer, novelist and poet, lived here.

57 Keston CRAIK, MRS DINAH MARIA (1826–87), novelist, buried here.

58 Knole, nr Sevenoaks Family seat of the Sackvilles, several of whom have been notable literary figures: THOMAS SACKVILLE, 1ST EARL OF DORSET (1536–1608), collaborator with THOMAS NORTON on *Gorboduc*, 1561–62, the first English tragedy; CHARLES SACKVILLE, 6TH EARL OF DORSET (1638–1706), poet and benefactor of Dryden; VICTORIA SACKVILLE-WEST (1892–1962), poet and novelist (born here)—her works include *The Land*, 1927, *The Edwardians*, 1930, and *Knole and the Sackvilles*, 1923; EDWARD SACKVILLE-WEST (1901–65), novelist and music critic.

59 Maidstone HAZLITT, WILLIAM (1778–1830), critic and essayist, born in a house near the market buildings. His criticisms of his contemporaries appeared chiefly in *Table Talk*, 1821–22, and *The Spirit of the Age*, 1825.
TENNYSON, ALFRED, LORD (1809–92), poet laureate, had associations with the town and its neighbourhood. He lived at Park House for some time after the marriage of his sister Cecilia to the scholar Edmund Law Lushington (1811–93) and commemorated the marriage in the epilogue to *In Memoriam*, 1850. A fête held by Maidstone Mechanics Institute in 1842 inspired the prologue to *The Princess*, 1847.
WOODVILLE, ANTHONY, 2ND EARL RIVERS (c1442–83), lived at Mote Park. His translations from the French were printed by William Caxton.

60 Margate CLODD, EDWARD (1840–1930), banker and author, born here. He was a founder of the *Johnson Club*, 1884, and the *Omar Khayyam Club*, 1892.
HORNE, RICHARD HENGIST (1803–84), poet and author, died and was buried here.

61 Matfield SASSOON, SIEGFRIED (1886–1967), poet, lived here before the World War I. He describes this time in *The Weald of Youth*, 1942.

62 Mersham LINACRE, THOMAS (c1460–1524), classical scholar, rector 1509.

63 Orlestone CONRAD, JOSEPH (1857–1924), novelist, lived at Capel House for nine years from 1910.

64 Orpington FAWKES, FRANCIS (1720–77), poet and composer of the song 'The Brown Jug', rector here for 20 years.

65 Otham STEVENS, WILLIAM (1732–1807), biographer, whose pseudonym Nobody led to the founding of the Society of Nobody's Friends, c1800, is buried here.

66 Penshurst Penshurst Place, the family seat of the Sidneys, was the birth-place of SIR PHILIP SIDNEY (1554–86) and of his sister Mary (1561–1621), afterwards Countess of Pembroke, for whom he wrote his *Arcadia*, 1590. His grand-nephew ALGERNON SIDNEY (1622–83), political writer, was probably born here. He wrote *Discourses concerning Government*, published

posthumously in 1698, was executed on charges of treason and is buried at Penshurst.

67 Petham MARCHANT, BESSIE (1862–1941), girls' novelist, born here. Often referred to as 'the girls' Henty', she was immensely successful with adventure tales featuring girl heroines.

68 Platt WELCH, DENTON (1915–48), novelist, lived here.

69 Ramsgate BURNAND, SIR FRANCIS COWLEY (1836–1917), dramatist and editor of *Punch*, died here.

70 Rochester Many associations with CHARLES DICKENS. The Bull Inn, now the Royal Victoria and Bull, features in *Sketches by Boz* and *Pickwick Papers*; the cathedral, college gatehouse, Minor Canon Row, Eastgate House (now the museum, in whose grounds stands the Swiss chalet in which Dickens worked in his garden at Gadshill) all feature in *The Mystery of Edwin Drood*, the novel unfinished at his death in 1870. Cloisterham, the setting of *Edwin Drood*, is Rochester. Restoration House, Maidstone Road, is the original of Miss Havisham's Satis House, in *Great Expectations*.
BOTTOME, PHYLLIS (1884–1936), novelist, born here. Some of her best-regarded writing is in the autobiographical volumes *Search for a Soul*, 1947, *The Challenge*, 1953, and *The Goal*, 1961.
HEAD, SIR FRANCIS BOND (1793–1875), travel writer and biographer, born here. He published *The Emigrant*, 1846, *The Defenceless State of Britain*, 1850, *A Fortnight in Ireland*, 1852, and *The Royal Engineer*, 1860.

71 Rolvenden BURNETT, FRANCES ELIZA HODGSON (1849–1924), novelist, lived at Maytham Hall for twelve years from 1888.

72 St Mary's Bay NESBIT, EDITH (1858–1924), children's author, had her last home here from 1921 and died here. She is buried at St Mary-in-the-Marsh nearby.

73 Sandgate BROOKE, JOCELYN (1908–66), novelist and poet, born here. His most successful books are *The Military Orchid*, 1949, *A Mine of Serpents*, 1949, and *The Dog at Chamber-Crown*, 1955.
WELLS, HERBERT GEORGE (1866–1946), novelist and sociologist, built Spade House and lived here for eleven years from 1900. The house may be visited.

74 Sandling Cob Tree Hall is believed to have been the original of Wardle's Manor Farm, Dingley Dell, in CHARLES DICKENS's *Pickwick Papers*, 1837–39.

75 Sandwich PAINE, THOMAS (1737–1809), author of *The Rights of Man*, 1790–92, worked here for a time as a staymaker. His cottage still stands.
REYNOLDS, GEORGE (1814–79), author and politician, born here. He founded *Reynolds's Weekly Newspaper*, 1850.

76 Sandwich Bay FLEMING, IAN LANCASTER (1908–64), novelist, lived here.

77 Sevenoaks Weald NICOLSON, SIR HAROLD (1886–1968), author and diarist, and his wife VICTORIA SACKVILLE-WEST (1892–1962), author and poet, lived here until 1930.
THOMAS, EDWARD (1878–1917), poet, lived for five years at Else's Farm. W. H. DAVIES lived for a time there in a cottage lent him by Thomas and wrote *The Autobiography of a Super Tramp*, 1907.

78 Shoreham DUNSANY, LORD (Edward John Moreton Drax Plunkett, 18th Baron Dunsany, 1878–1957), poet and playwright, inherited Dunstall Priory at his mother's death in 1916. He died in Dublin, but is buried in Shoreham churchyard.
LANGDON-DAVIES, JOHN (1897–1971), South African-born author and journalist, died at Holly Place. A specialist in military-political affairs and science, he wrote the Home Guard training manuals in World War

II, and inaugurated in 1963 the *Jackdaws* series of educational publications.

79 Shipbourne SMART, CHRISTOPHER (1722–71), poet, born at Fairlawne. His most memorable work is *Song to David*, 1763.

80 Sissinghurst BAKER, SIR RICHARD (c1568–1644), religious and historical writer, born here. He translated Malvezzi's *Discourses on Tacitus*, 1642, wrote *Theatrum Redivivum*, and in 1643 published a chronicle of the kings of England from Roman times to 1625.

CHURCH, RICHARD THOMAS (1893–1972), poet, novelist, essayist and autobiographer, lived at nearby Curtisden Green for some twenty years until 1965. He spent his last years at the Priest's House, Sissinghurst Castle, and died here.

DOUGHTY, CHARLES MONTAGU (1843–1926), explorer, lived and died here.

NICOLSON, SIR HAROLD GEORGE (1886–1968), author and diarist, and his wife VICTORIA SACKVILLE-WEST (1892–1962), author and poet, lived at Sissinghurst Castle from 1930 until their deaths. The property is open to the public.

81 Sittingbourne THEOBALD, LEWIS (1688–1744), critic and translator, born here. He was assailed in Pope's *Dunciad* for his criticism of Pope's edition of Shakespeare.

82 Southfleet SEDLEY, SIR CHARLES (c1639–1701), courtier and poet, buried here (see **Aylesford**).

83 Speldhurst HICHENS, ROBERT (1864–1950), novelist, born here. His most successful books were *The Green Carnation*, 1894, and *The Garden of Allah*, 1904.

84 Stanford CONRAD, JOSEPH (1857–1924), novelist, lived at Pent Farm 1896–1907.

85 Sutton-at-Hone HASTED, EDWARD (1732–1812), historian, lived here.

86 Tenterden CAXTON, WILLIAM (c1422–91), translator and the first English printer, believed to have been born here, though Hadlow, near Tonbridge, has also been claimed for his birthplace.

87 Tonbridge LOWER, RICHARD (1782–1865), Sussex dialect poet, died here.

WELCH, DENTON (1915–48), novelist, lived here.

88 Tunbridge Wells CUMBERLAND, RICHARD (1732–1811), dramatist and novelist, lived and died here.

DOUGHTY, CHARLES MONTAGU (1843–1926), traveller and poet, lived here.

FOWLER, HENRY WATSON (1858–1933), lexicographer, born here. He and his brother, Francis George Fowler (1871–1918), produced *The King's English*, 1906, the *Concise Oxford Dictionary*, 1911, and *A Dictionary of Modern English Usage*, 1926, all of them enduring standard works.

GUTHRIE, SIR WILLIAM TYRONE (1900–71), playwright and theatrical producer, born here. He was one of the pioneers of broadcast drama with his play *The Squirrel's Cage*, 1931. His books include *Theatre Prospect*, 1932.

SMITH, HORACE (1779–1849), co-author of the *Rejected Addresses*, 1812, died here.

TENNYSON, ALFRED, LORD (1809–92), poet laureate, lived here from 1840 to 1841.

THACKERAY, WILLIAM MAKEPEACE (1811–63), novelist, stayed at Rock Villa, London Road, Aug–Sept 1860, and wrote and illustrated the essay 'Tunbridge Toys' as a result.

WALEY, ARTHUR DAVID (1889–1966), poet and translator, born here. His many translations from Chinese and Japanese poetry have considerably influenced Western literature.

89 Walmer BRIDGES, ROBERT (1844–1930), poet laureate 1913, born at Roselands. His *Testament of Beauty* appeared in 1929. In the nearby village of Great Mongeham is an epitaph in the church composed by him for his old nurse, who had her cottage in the village.

YATES, DORNFORD (pseudonym of Cecil William Mercer, 1885–1960), author, born at Wellesley House. Many of his highly popular adventure novels feature the character Berry, who first appeared in *Berry & Co*, 1921.

90 Westerham CHURCHILL, SIR WINSTON LEONARD SPENCER (1874–1965), statesman and author, lived at Chartwell Manor nearby from 1922 until his death and wrote much of his most important work here, including the histories of World War II and his biography of the Duke of Marlborough. The house is preserved for the public to visit.

91 Westwell BARHAM, RICHARD HARRIS (1788–1845), author of the *Ingoldsby Legends*, was curate here for three years. His son RICHARD (1815–86), biographer, was born here. He published his father's *Life and Letters*, 1880.

92 Wye BEHN, MRS APHRA (1640–89), novelist and dramatist, baptised and probably born here. Her best known novel is *Oroonoko*, 1688; her best known play, *The Forced Marriage*, 1671.

CONRAD, JOSEPH (1857–1924), novelist, lived briefly at Spring Grove at the end of World War I.

MACAULAY, CATHERINE (1731–91), historian, born nearby. Her *History of England* from James I to the rise of the Hanoverians, 1763–83, was much respected in her time.

Northamptonshire and Soke of Peterborough (*Map 7*)

1 Abington WELSTED, LEONARD (1688–1747), poet and satirist, born here. He and Alexander Pope engaged in a bitter satirical duel.

2 Aldwinkle All Saints DRYDEN, JOHN (1631–1700), dramatist and poet laureate 1670, born at the rectory. His satirical works, such as *Absalom and Achitophel*, 1681–82, mark the peak of his powers. He lost his laureateship at the 1688 Revolution for refusing to take the oaths of allegiance.

3 Aston-le-Walls BUTLER, ALBAN (1711–73), compiler of *Lives of the Saints*, 1756–59, born here. BUTLER, CHARLES (1750–1832), writer on law, history and other subjects, born here.

4 Aynho MARMION, SHACKERLEY (1603–39), dramatist, born here. His works include *A Fine Companion*, 1633, and *The Antiquary*, published 1641.

5 Barnack KINGSLEY, HENRY (1830–76), novelist, born at the Old Rectory. *Ravenshoe*, 1861, is regarded as his best work. His brother, CHARLES KINGSLEY (1819–75), author of *The Water Babies*, spent his childhood at the Old Rectory.

6 Barton Seagrave BRIDGES, JOHN (1665–1724), topographer and county historian, born and buried here.

7 Blakesley DRYDEN, JOHN (1631–1700), dramatist and poet laureate, lived here before moving to London in 1657 (see **Aldwinkle All Saints**).

8 Blatherwycke RANDOLPH, THOMAS (1605–35), poet and dramatist, died while on a visit to Blatherwycke, and is buried here (see **Newnham**).

9 Boughton WHYTE-MELVILLE, GEORGE JOHN (1821–78), author of historical and sporting novels, lived at the inn now bearing his name.

10 Brington SIDNEY, LADY DOROTHY (1617–84), the 'Sacharissa' of EDMUND WALLER's poetry, lived at Althorp Park after her marriage to Henry, Lord Spencer, in 1639, and is buried in the church.

11 Catesby PARKHURST, JOHN (1728–97), lexicographer, born at the manor house. His *Hebrew and English Lexicon without Points*, 1762, was for long a standard work.

12 Cold Ashby KNOLLES, RICHARD (c1550–1610), historian, born here. His *General History of the Turks*, 1603, was praised by Dr Johnson.

13 Easton Maudit PERCY, THOMAS (1729–1811), antiquary and poet, vicar 1753.

14 Fawsley WILKINS, JOHN (1614–72), bishop of Chester, scientist and writer, born here. His works include *The Discovery of a World in the Moon*, 1638, and *Mercury, or the Secret and Swift Messenger*, which discusses long-distance communications.

15 Grafton Regis WOODVILLE, ANTHONY, 2ND EARL RIVERS (1442–83) born here. His translation of the *Dictes and Sayengis of the Philosophers* was the first book to be printed in this country, by Caxton in 1477.

16 Great Harrowden VAUX OF HARROWDEN, THOMAS, 2ND BARON (1510–56), poet, lived at Harrowden Hall.

17 Guilsborough BELCHIER, DAUBRIDGCOURT (c1580–1621), dramatist, born at Guilsborough Hall. He subsequently settled in the Low Countries.

18 Hannington GODWIN, FRANCIS (1562–1633), bishop and author, born here. His *Man in the Moone, or a Voyage Thither*, 1638, is said to have inspired Cyrano de Bergerac's speculations about life on the moon.

19 Hardingstone HERVEY, JAMES (1714–58), devotional writer, born here. His *Meditations and Contemplations*, 1745–47, includes his famous 'Meditations among the Tombs'.

20 Harringworth BLAYDES, FREDERICK HENRY MARVELL (1818–1908), translator and editor of Aristophanes, vicar 1843–86.

21 Helmdon HAYDEN, ELEANOR G. (1865–19 ?), author, born here. Most of her books concern Berkshire, where she went to live as a child: among them, *From a Thatched Cottage*, 1902, and *Turnpike Travellers*, 1903.

22 Helpston CLARE, JOHN (1793–1864), poet, born and buried here. His first book of verse, *Poems descriptive of Rural life*, 1820, attracted immediate attention, and was followed by *The Village Minstrel*, 1821, *The Shepherd's Calendar*, 1827, and *Rural Muse*, 1835.

23 Horton MONTAGU, CHARLES, 1ST EARL OF HALIFAX (1661–1715), born. Friend and patron of literary men, he collaborated with Matthew Prior on *The Town and Country Mouse*, 1687, his satire on Dryden.

24 Kettering GILL, JOHN (1697–1741), baptist minister and author of scriptural commentaries, born here.

25 King's Cliffe LAW, WILLIAM (1686–1761), born here and returned to live in 1740. His *Serious Call to a Devout and Holy Life*, 1729, influenced Dr Johnson, the Wesleys, and other notable contemporaries.

26 King's Sutton BOWLES, WILLIAM LISLE (1762–1850), poet, born at the vicarage. Most of his poems, widely admired, appeared in fourteen volumes, 1789–1837, and he was responsible for a controversial edition of the works of Alexander Pope, 1806.

27 Nether Heyford STANBRIDGE, JOHN (1463–1510) born here. His English grammars, published by Wynkyn de Worde, were among the first to be written.

28 Newnham RANDOLPH, THOMAS (1605–35), dramatist, born here. His plays include *The Jealous Lovers*, 1632, *Amyntas*, and *The Muses' Looking-glass*.

29 Northborough CLARE, JOHN (1793–1864) poet, lived here 1832–7. His wife, the 'Patty' of his poetry, is buried here (see **Helpston**).

30 Northampton BAKER, GEORGE (1781–1851), topographer, lived at Hazelrigg Mansion.
BRADSTREET, ANNE (c1612–72), America's first poet, born here. She emigrated in 1630. *The Tenth Muse Lately Sprung up in America* was published in 1650, but her *Works in Prose and Verse* did not appear until 1867.
CLARE, JOHN (1793–1864), poet, was an inmate of the asylum from 1837 until his death there.
COWPER, WILLIAM (1731–1800), poet, supplied verses for seven years to the parish clerk of All Saints church to accompany the Bills of Mortality registering local deaths.
RICE, JAMES (1843–82), novelist, born here. Most of his works were written in collaboration with Walter Besant, including *Ready Money Mortiboy*, 1872, *The Golden Butterfly*, 1876, and *The Seamy Side*, 1881.

31 Orlingbury MANNING, OWEN (1721–1801), historian, born here. He wrote on Saxon literature, and completed Edward Lye's Anglo-Saxon Dictionary. His celebrated history of Surrey, with additions by William Bray, was published 1736–1832 (see **Yardley Hastings**).

32 Paulerspury CAREY, WILLIAM (1761–1834), translator, born here. He made the first translations of the Bible into Hindi, Sanskrit, Bengali and other Indian languages.

33 Rockingham Castle DICKENS, CHARLES (1812–70) often stayed here with his friends the Honourable Richard Watson and his wife and partly used it as model for 'Chesney Wold' in *Bleak House*, 1852–53; the Sondes Arms Inn in the village street is the 'Dedlock Arms' of the story.

34 Twywell CHAPONE, HESTER (1727–1801), author and poet, born here. One of the original bluestockings, her *Works* and *Posthumous Works* appeared in 1807.

35 Wellingborough ASKHAM, JOHN (1825–94), poet, born, lived at Clare Cottage, and is buried here. He published five volumes of verse.

36 Weston Favell COLE, JOHN (1792–1848), antiquary, author of histories of Northampton and Lincoln, born here.

HERVEY, JAMES (1714–58), devotional writer, curate to his father 1743–44 and rector 1752 until his death. He is buried in the church (see **Hardingstone**).

37 Woodford COLE, JOHN (1792–1848), antiquary, died and is buried here (see **Weston Favell**).

38 Yardley Hastings COWPER, WILLIAM (1731–1800) is believed to have written his 'God moves in a mysterious way' after standing under the tree now known as 'Cowper's Oak' during a thunderstorm.

LYE, EDMUND (1694–1767), Anglo-Saxon scholar, rector from 1750 until his death and is buried here.

Buckinghamshire (*Map 7*)

1 **Amersham** MACHEN, ARTHUR (1863–1947), poet, author and essayist, lived for many years at Old Amersham.

2 **Aston Sandford** SCOTT, THOMAS (1747–1821), commentator on the Bible, rector from 1803 until his death and is buried here.

3 **Aylesbury** BICKERSTETH, EDWARD (1814–92), religious writer and antiquarian, rector 1853–75.
GIBBS, ROBERT (1816–93), antiquarian, curator of the Buckinghamshire Archaeological Museum.
HESSION, BRIAN (1901–6i), author and pioneer of religious films, vicar of Holy Trinity, Walton, 1937–50.
WILKES, JOHN (1727–97) author and politician, lived at intervals at Prebendal House, now a school, from the time of his marriage in 1749 to the Aylesbury heiress, Mary Mead.

4 **Beaconsfield** BLYTON, ENID (1900–68), children's author and creator of Little Noddy, lived at Green Hedges.
BURKE, EDMUND (1729–97), statesman and philosopher, lived at Gregories, an estate he purchased in 1768. He is buried in Beaconsfield church.
CHESTERTON, GILBERT KEITH (1874–1936), author, poet and essayist, lived at Overroads from 1909 until his death. Here he wrote much of his best work, including the *Father Brown* detective stories.
WALLER, EDMUND (1606–87), poet, lived and died at Hall Barn and is buried in Beaconsfield churchyard.

5 **Bourne End** D'ISRAELI, ISAAC (1766–1848), author, lived at Bourne End and is buried here. His son BENJAMIN DISRAELI, LORD BEACONSFIELD, spent his childhood at the Manor House; nearby Bradenham was the locality of his novel *Endymion*, 1880.
WALLACE, EDGAR (1875–1932), writer of thrillers, lived at Chalklands 1929–32; *The Devil Man* was written in one weekend here.

6 **Brill** BROOKS, CHARLES WILLIAM SHIRLEY (1816–74), journalist and novelist, born here. He became editor of *Punch* in 1870.

7 **Burnham** BOYLE, MRS ELEANOR VERE ('E.V.B.' 1825–1916), author, lived for more than thirty years at Huntercombe Manor and wrote many of her books there, including *Days and Hours in a Garden*, a record of her own garden between 1882 and 1883.
DAVIES, RICHARD (d1581), translator of the Bible into Welsh, vicar of Burnham from 1550.
DIX, DOM GREGORY (1901–52), liturgical scholar, was a monk of Anglican Benedictine community at Nashdown Abbey, Burnham, where he wrote *The Shape of the Liturgy*, 1945.
GRAY, THOMAS (1716–71), poet, describes the locality in parts of his *Elegy in a Country Churchyard*; he often visited Burnham Grove, his uncle's home.
GROTE, GEORGE (1794–1871), banker and historian, wrote his *History of Greece*, 1846–56, at Burnham Cottage. He later built and occupied East Burnham Park.
SHERIDAN, RICHARD BRINSLEY (1751–1816), dramatist, lived for a time at East Burnham Cottage after his marriage in 1773.

8 **Chalfont St Giles** BIRKETT, WILLIAM NORMAN, 1ST BARON BIRKETT (1883–1962), Lord Justice and writer, lived here.
MILTON, JOHN (1608–74), lived in a 'pretty box of a cottage' (now open to the public), and here wrote *Paradise Regained*, 1671, at the suggestion of THOMAS ELLWOOD (1639–1713), poet, who was tutor at The Grange for a time after 1654.

9 **Chalfont St Peter** GOOCH, GEORGE PEABODY (1873–1968), historian and author, lived here.

10 **Chesham** CRAB, ROGER (c1620–80), author, kept a hat shop here 1649–51, gave away his possessions to the poor and became a recluse. Known as the Mad Hatter of Chesham.
LAWRENCE, DAVID HERBERT (1835–1940), novelist and poet, lived in a cottage here from Aug 1914–Jan 1915.

11 **Chicheley** COWPER, WILLIAM (1731–1800), poet, composed the epitaph of one of the Chester family buried here.

12 **Chilton** CROKE, SIR JOHN (1553–1620), judge, author of *Select Cases*, lived, died and is buried here.
HIGGONS, THEOPHILUS (1578–1659), theologian, born here. A Puritan, Catholic and Anglican in turn, he wrote prolifically for each cause.
WADE, HENRY (pseudonym of Sir Henry Aubrey-Fletcher, 1888–1969), writer of detective fiction, lived at Townhill Farm.

13 **Coleshill** WALLER, EDMUND (1606–87), poet, born here. Much of his best verse, including 'Go, lovely rose', was addressed to Lady Dorothea Sidney ('Sacharissa', 1617–84), whom he courted in vain.

14 **Cuddington** WILMOT, CHESTER (1911–54), military historian, lived at Dadbrook House.

15 **Drayton Beauchamp** HOOKER, RICHARD (c1554–1600), theological writer, rector 1584–85.

16 **Dropmore** TOYNBEE, PAGET (1853–1932), authority on Dante, buried here.

17 **Edlesborough** TODD, HENRY (1763–1845), editor of works of Milton and Dr Johnson, vicar 1805–7.

18 **Eton** Distinguished literary figures on the staff have included OSCAR BROWNING (1837–1923), WILLIAM JOHNSON CORY (1823–92), NICHOLAS UDALL (1505–56) and SIR HENRY WOTTON (1568–1639). Among the many notable figures educated here were ROBERT BRIDGES (1844–1930), THOMAS GRAY (1716–71), CHARLES GREVILLE (1794–1865), WILLIAM HAYLEY (1745–1820), MONTAGUE RHODES JAMES (1862–1936), PERCY BYSSHE SHELLEY (1792–1822), ALGERNON CHARLES SWINBURNE (1837–1909), EDMUND WALLER (1606–87) and HORACE WALPOLE (1717–97).

19 **Fawley** WHITELOCKE, BULSTRODE (1605–75), lawyer, writer and Keeper of the Great Seal, lived here for a time.

20 **Fenny Stratford** WILLIS, BROWNE (1682–1760), antiquary and historian, buried here.

21 **Gayhurst** DIGBY, SIR KENELM (1603–65), author and diplomat, inherited the estate from his mother.

22 **Grandborough** JONES, HENRY ARTHUR (1851–1929), dramatist, born here. *The Silver King*, 1882, was the most popular melodrama of its time.

23 **Great Horwood** SPENCE, JOSEPH (1699–1768), poet and anecdotist, rector from 1742 until his death here.

24 **Great Kimble** OLLYFFE, GEORGE (d1752), pamphleteer, vicar 1707–52.

25 **Grendon Underwood** According to John Aubrey, SHAKESPEARE stayed here at the Ship Inn, where the rustic humour provided the basis of the rustics' scene in

A Midsummer Night's Dream. The inn is now a farmhouse, Shakespeare's Farm, and the inn sign is in the county museum, Aylesbury.

26 Grove The Grove was owned by LORD CHESTERFIELD (1694–1773), statesman and letter-writer. His *Letters* to his son were published in 1774.

27 Haddenham ROSE, WALTER (1871–1960), carpenter and author, lived here all his life and wrote several books about the village, including *The Village Carpenter*, 1937, and *Good Neighbours*, 1942.

28 Hardwick GRENVILLE, GEORGE NUGENT, BARON NUGENT OF CARLANSTOWN (1788–1850), author, lived at Lilies.

29 Hedsor HOOKE, NATHANIEL (d1763), historian, buried here.

30 High Wycombe ALLEY, WILLIAM (1510–70), theologian and author, born here. He wrote numerous religious works, and the *Poor Man's Library*, 1565 and 1570, a commentary on the first epistle of St Paul.

31 Holtspur REYNOLDS, CLIFTON (1892–1969), author, rented Glory Hill Farm 1940–44 and described his experiences in the *Glory Hill Farm*, a work in four volumes published 1941–45.

32 Hughenden DISRAELI, BENJAMIN, EARL OF BEACONSFIELD (1804–81), statesman and novelist, lived at Hughenden Manor from 1848 until his death and is buried here. The manor and its contents are on view to the public.
GILL, ERIC (1882–1940), sculptor, typographer and author, lived at Pigotts 1928–40, and is buried at Speen nearby.

33 Ickford PHILLIPS, THOMAS (1708–74), Jesuit writer, born here. His chief work, *The History of the Life of Cardinal Pole*, appeared in 1764.

34 Ivinghoe TODD, HENRY (1763–1845), editor of the works of Milton and Dr Johnson, appointed rector in 1803.

35 Jordans ELLWOOD, THOMAS (1639–1713), poet and Quaker, buried here.
FOX, GEORGE (1624–91), author and founder of the Society of Friends, buried here.
PENN, WILLIAM (1644–1718), writer and founder of Pennsylvania, buried here.

36 Lacey Green BROOKE, RUPERT CHAWNOR (1887–1915), poet, had close associations with the Pink and Lily public house.

37 Little Marlow MARTYN, THOMAS (1735–1825), botanical writer, vicar 1776–84.
WALLACE, EDGAR (1875–1932), writer of thrillers, buried here.

38 Long Crendon MASSINGHAM, HAROLD (1888–1952), author of many nature books, lived here.

39 Ludgershall MARTYN, THOMAS (1735–1825), botanical writer, rector 1774–76.
WYCLIFFE, JOHN (c1320–84), religious reformer and translator of the Gospels, vicar 1368–74.

40 Marlow JEROME, JEROME KLAPKA (1859–1927), humorist, spent the latter part of his life here, in territory described in his *Three Men in a Boat*, 1889.
PEACOCK, THOMAS LOVE (1795–1866), novelist and poet, lived many years in West Street and found Albion House nearby for his friend PERCY BYSSHE SHELLEY, who lived there with Mary Godwin in 1817. It was at Albion House that Shelley wrote *The Revolt of Islam*.
SMEDLEY, FRANK (1818–64), novelist, born here. His best-known work is *Frank Fairleigh, or Scenes from the Life of a Private Pupil*, 1850.

41 Medmenham Medmenham Abbey was the scene of the first meetings of the Hell-Fire Club, of which several notable literary men were members (see **West Wycombe**).
HART, SIR BASIL LIDDELL (1895–1970), military writer and historian, lived here from 1958 until his death.

42 Middle Claydon VERNEY, LADY PARTHENOPE (1819–90), novelist, lived at Claydon House and was often visited by her sister, Florence Nightingale, in whose memory a room of relics is now preserved. Margaret Maria (1844–1930), wife of Sir Edmund Verney, completed the *Verney Memoirs* begun by Parthenope; they were published in 1892, 1894 and 1899, with two supplementary volumes in 1930.

43 Milton Keynes ATTERBURY, FRANCIS (1662–1732), bishop of Rochester, theologian, born here. His publications include *Absalom and Achitophel Latinised*, 1682, *Considerations on the Spirit of Martin Luther*, 1687, and *Atterburyana*, 1727.
WOTTON, WILLIAM (1666–1727), vicar from 1693. The arguments provoked by his *Reflections on Ancient and Modern Learnings*, 1694, written here, caused Swift to write *The Battle of the Books*, 1704.

44 Newport Pagnell BUNYAN, JOHN (1628–88) a soldier in the Parliamentary garrison here 1644–46. His *Holy War*, 1682, reflects this experience.
HAILEY, WILLIAM MALCOLM, 1ST BARON HAILEY (1872–1969), administrator, born here. He was the author of a number of books on colonial affairs.
TERRY, CHARLES SANFORD (1864–1936), historian and Bach scholar, born here.

45 Oakley TYRRELL, JAMES (1642–1718), historian and scholar, buried here.

46 Olney COWPER, WILLIAM (1731–1800), poet, lived here 1767–86. His house is now the Cowper Museum. Among many other works, *The Task*, 1785, was written here.
NEWTON, JOHN (1725–1807), hymn writer, curate of Olney 1764–79. He collaborated with William Cowper in producing the *Olney Hymns*.
WRIGHT, THOMAS (1859–1936), novelist, poet and local historian, lived here and founded the Cowper Museum.

47 Quainton BRETT, RICHARD (1560–1637), a translator of the Authorised Version of the Bible, rector from 1595 and buried here.
LIPSCOMB, GEORGE (1773–1846), historian of Buckinghamshire, born at Magpie Cottage. His county history was published in eight parts, 1831–47.

48 Slough BENTLEY, RICHARD (fl1890), local historian, lived at Upton.
DICKENS, CHARLES (1812–70), kept the actress Ellen Ternan at Elizabeth Cottage, High Street, during 1866.
HERSCHEL, SIR JOHN FREDERICK WILLIAM (1792–1871), astronomer, born at Slough. He published numerous works on astronomy and other scientific subjects. His father, SIR WILLIAM HERSCHEL (1738–1822), astronomer, lived at Slough 1786–1822, where he built his famous telescope and wrote many papers on his discoveries.

49 Stantonbury MASON, JOHN (c1646–94), poet and hymn writer, vicar 1668–74.

50 Stoke Hammond KEACH, BENJAMIN (1646–1704), author, poet and dissenting minister, born here (see **Winslow**).

51 Stoke Poges COKE, SIR EDWARD (1552–1634), jurist, of Stoke Place, was the first Lord Chief Justice of England and an influential legal writer.
GRAY, THOMAS (1716–71) buried here, in the setting of his *Elegy in a Country Churchyard*.

52 Swanbourne FREMANTLE, ELIZABETH, *née* Wynne (1779–1857), diarist, settled here in 1798.

53 Taplow DE LA MARE, WALTER JOHN (1890–1956), poet and novelist, lived here throughout the 1930s.

54 Wendover ROGER OF WENDOVER (d1236) born here. He was the author of *Flowers of History*, one of the first English historical works.

55 West Wycombe After its foundation at Medmenham in 1755, the Hell-Fire Club met for many years at West Wycombe Park, owned by their founder, SIR FRANCIS DASHWOOD (1708–81). Other notable literary members included CHARLES CHURCHILL (1731–64), poet and satirist, ROBERT LLOYD (1733–64), poet and dramatist, JOHN WILKES (1727–97), politician and satirist, and PAUL WHITEHEAD (1710–74), poet, who bequeathed his heart to West Wycombe where it remained on show for many years. Dashwood compiled a revised *Book of Common Prayer* in 1773, printed on his private press here.

56 Weston Underwood COWPER, WILLIAM (1731–1800), poet, lived here 1786–95 (see **Olney**).

57 Whaddon WILLIS, BROWNE (1682–1760), historian and antiquary, lived here.

58 Whiteleaf BRAILSFORD, HENRY NOEL (1873–1958), novelist and political writer, had a cottage here in the 1930s.

59 Winslow KEACH, BENJAMIN (1640–1704), author, poet and dissenting minister, pilloried at Winslow in 1664. His book *The Child's Instructor* or *A New and Easy Primer*, which had displeased the authorities, was burnt in front of him (see **Stoke Hammond**).

60 Woburn Sands HOW, RICHARD (d1800), editor of the letters of Lady Rachel Russell, buried here.
WIFFEN, JEREMIAH HOLMES (1792–1836), Quaker author, buried here.

61 Wolverton HART, SIR BASIL LIDDELL (1895–1970), military writer and historian, lived here 1947–58 (see **Medmenham**).

62 Worminghall KING, HENRY (1592–1669), poet and friend of John Donne and Ben Jonson, born here. He was appointed bishop of Chichester in 1642.

Bedfordshire (*Map 7*)

1 **Ampthill** BUNYAN, JOHN (1628–88) was first arrested in November 1660 while preaching at a local farmhouse. Houghton House nearby is the 'House Beautiful' of *Pilgrim's Progress*, 1678 and 1684.

2 **Bedford** BUNYAN, JOHN (1628–88) came to live here in 1655, and was imprisoned in Bedford County Gaol 1660–72. He spent a further six months in the prison in 1675, during which ·time he wrote the first part of *Pilgrim's Progress*.

RUTHERFORD, MARK (pseudonym of William Hale White, 1831–1913), novelist, born here. His best known works are *The Autobiography of Mark Rutherford*, 1881, and *Mark Rutherford's Deliverance*, 1885.

3 **Campton** BLOOMFIELD, ROBERT (1766–1823), poet, buried here.

4 **Cardington** GASCOIGNE, GEORGE (c1525–77), poet and dramatist, born here. His translation from Ariosto, *The Supposes*, 1566, is the earliest extant prose comedy in English.

5 **Chicksands** OSBORNE, DOROTHY (1627–95), letter-writer, born here. Her letters to her future husband Sir William Temple, over a period of seven years, have been described as the most exquisite of their kind.

6 **Cockayne Hatley** HENLEY, WILLIAM ERNEST (1849–1903), poet and critic, lived here. His ashes were brought to Cockayne Hatley after his death in Woking. His daughter, MARGARET HENLEY (1889–94), buried here, was the original of J. M. Barrie's Wendy in *Peter Pan* and of Reddy in his *Sentimental Tom*.

7 **Dunstable** SETTLE, ELKANAH (1648–1724), dramatist, born here. His plays, among them *Cambyses, King of Persia: a Tragedy*, 1666, for a time rivalled Dryden's in popularity and provoked a literary feud between the two.

8 **Elstow** BUNYAN, JOHN (1628–88) born at Harrowden. He returned to live in Elstow after his army service, married here in 1649 and remained until about 1655. The green and the market hall were settings for the Vanity Fair of *Pilgrim's Progress*, 1678 and 1654.

9 **Everton** TIPTOFT, JOHN, EARL OF WORCESTER (c1427–70), translator, lived here.

10 **Great Barford** FOSTER, WILLIAM, the original of Bunyan's Mr By-Ends in *Pilgrim's Progress*, buried here.

11 **Higham Gobion** CASTELL, EDMUND (1606–86), co-editor of the Polyglot Bible, 1657, rector during his last years, and buried here.

12 **Hockliffe** DODD, WILLIAM (1729–77), author hanged for forgery, rector, 1772.

13 **Houghton Conquest** GREY, ZACHARY (1688–1766), antiquary, rector from 1725 and buried here.

14 **Leighton Buzzard** CAMERON, VERNEY LOVETT (1844–94), explorer and writer, died here after a hunting accident.

15 **Lidlington** The hill here is BUNYAN's Hill Difficulty in *Pilgrim's Progress*.

16 **Little Barford** ROWE, NICHOLAS (1674–1718), poet laureate 1715, born here. He was also the author of several plays and edited the works of Shakespeare.

17 **Luton** POMFRET, JOHN (1667–1702), poet, born here. His chief work was *The Choice*, 1701.

18 **Millbrook** POMFRET, JOHN (1667–1702), poet, rector here from 1702 until his death (see **Luton**). At the same time he was vicar of Maulden (inducted in 1695), and is buried at Maulden.

19 **Shefford** BLOOMFIELD, ROBERT (1766–1823), poet, died here (see **Campton**).

20 **Shillington** The probable setting of BUNYAN's Delectable Mountains in *Pilgrim's Progress*.

21 **Silsoe** BUTLER, SAMUEL (1612–80), satirist, clerk for a time to Sir Samuel Luke of Cople Hoo, who appears as a character in *Hudibras*, 1663–68.

22 **Streatley** NORTON, THOMAS (1532–84), poet and playwright, died at Sharpenhoe nearby and is buried at Streatley.

23 **Toddington** REYNOLDS, JOHN (1581–1614), epigrammatist, born here. His series of distiches on British kings and queens appeared in 1611.

24 **Turvey** RICHMOND, LEGH (1772–1827), evangelical writer, rector from 1805.

25 **Wilden** DILLINGHAM, FRANCIS (fl1611), theological writer, rector from c1600 until his death.

FISHER, JASPER (fl1639), dramatist, rector from 1631 until his death.

26 **Woburn** WIFFEN, BENJAMIN BARRON (1794–1867), biographer, born here. He edited the writings of early Spanish reformers; his collection is in Wadham College, Oxford.

WIFFEN, JEREMIAH HOLMES (1792–1836), translator of Tasso, born here. He wrote a history of the house of Russell and was a minor poet. Brother of Benjamin Barron Wiffen (above).

27 **Wootton** This area was used by JOHN BUNYAN for many of the *Pilgrim's Progress* settings.

Hertfordshire (*Maps 7 & 8*)

1 Aldbury DUNCOMBE, JOHN (1729–86), writer on miscellaneous subjects including archaeology, born here.

WARD, MRS HUMPHREY (*née* Mary Augusta Arnold, 1851–1920), novelist, lived at Stocks 1892–1920 and is buried here.

2 Aldenham FAWCETT, JOSEPH (c1758–1804), poet, born here. His *War Elegies* appeared in 1801.

GIBBS, HENRY HUCKS, LORD ALDENHAM (1819–1907), author and bibliophile, lived at Aldenham House and is buried here.

3 Amwell SCOTT, JOHN (1730–83), poet, born here. His *Poetical Works* were issued in 1782; *Critical Essays* appeared posthumously in 1785.

SCOTT, JOHN (1819–1907), poet, lived here.

WARNER, WILLIAM (1558–1609), poet, born and buried here. He wrote a metrical history, *Albion's England*, extending from Noah to James I, published complete in 1612.

4 Anstey CAMPION, THOMAS (1567–1619), poet, composer and musician, born here. 'Cherry Ripe' is one of his most widely known songs.

5 Ardeley CHAUNCY, HENRY (1632–1719), antiquary, born and buried here. His *Antiquities of Hertfordshire* appeared in 1700.

6 Ayot St Lawrence SHAW, GEORGE BERNARD (1856–1950), playwright, lived at Shaw's Corner 1910–50, and died here. Many of his most notable works were written at this house, which is preserved with its contents for the public to visit.

7 Baldock SMITH, JOHN (d1870), translator of Pepys's *Diary* from shorthand code (1825), was rector here from 1832 and is buried here.

8 Barley WILLET, ANDREW (1562–1621), biblical commentator, rector 1599–1621.

9 Bayford YARRELL, WILLIAM (1784–1856), naturalist, buried here.

10 Berkhamsted BARRIE, SIR JAMES MATTHEW (1860–1937) was a constant visitor to the home here of Llewellyn Davis and his family, and is said to have based the character of Peter Pan on one of the children.

CHAUCER, GEOFFREY (c1340–1400) was clerk of the works at the castle in 1389.

COWPER, WILLIAM (1731–1800), poet, born at Great Berkhamsted rectory. *The Task*, 1785, marked the beginning of a new school of nature poetry.

11 Bishop's Stortford GILBEY, SIR WALTER (1831–1914), author of books on horses and riding, born here. His works include *History of the War Horse*, 1888, *The Life of George Stubbs*, 1898, and *Horses Past and Present*, 1900.

HILLS, WILLIAM (1813–94), poet, died here.

SALMON, NATHANIEL (1675–1742), Hertfordshire historian and antiquary, practised medicine here.

12 Brookmans Park MORE, SIR THOMAS (1478–1535) may have written *Utopia* here c1515 at his father's house, Gobion.

13 Buntingford BENSON, ROBERT HUGH (1871–1914), novelist, lived in Hare Street, and is buried here.

14 Bushey PAIN, BARRY ERIC ODELL (1864–1928), humorous novelist, buried here.

VIVIAN, EDWARD (1808–93), poet, born here.

15 Bygrave SMYTH, JOHN (1828–97), poet, born here.

16 Cheshunt GREW, NEHEMIAH (1641–1712), writer on botany, buried here.

JAY, WILLIAM, poet, born here c1845.

MEDLEY, SAMUEL (1738–99), devotional writer, born here.

WATTS, ISAAC (1674–1748), hymn writer, lived at Theobalds with Sir Thomas and Lady Abney from 1712.

17 Clothall STANLEY, THOMAS (1625–78), classical scholar, born here. He made many translations from Latin and Greek and published works of reference, including a *History of Philosophy*, 1655–62.

18 Datchworth YOUNG, EDWARD (1683–1765), poet, wrote some of his *Night Thoughts*, 1742, here.

19 Digswell WELLS, HERBERT GEORGE (1866–1946), novelist and sociologist, owned the Mill House for some time.

20 Elstree BURTON, SIR RICHARD FRANCIS (1821–90), travel writer and translator, born at Barham House. His translation of the *Arabian Nights* appeared 1885–88.

21 Essendon TOOKE, GEORGE (1595–1675), soldier and writer, lived at Pope's Farm, and is buried here.

22 Gorhambury BACON, SIR FRANCIS, 1ST BARON VERULAM (1561–1626), statesman, philosopher and author, lived here for many years.

23 Hadley DAY LEWIS, CECIL (1904–72), poet laureate and novelist, died at Lemmons, Hadley Common, during a visit. He was Professor of Poetry at Oxford from 1950–54, and wrote successful detective novels under the pseudonym Nicholas Blake. His last poem, written a few weeks before his death, was 'At Lemmons'.

TROLLOPE, ANTHONY (1815–82), novelist, set *The Bertrams*, 1859, here. His mother, FRANCES TROLLOPE (1780–1863), novelist and travel writer, had a house here for a year from January 1836, during which time he often visited her.

24 Harpenden CRAIG, GORDON (Edward Gordon Terry, 1872–1966), theatrical designer and director, born here. The son of Ellen Terry and Edward Godwin, he wrote several books about his influential work in the theatre and about personalities, including *Index to the Story of my Days*, 1957.

25 Hatfield LEE, NATHANIEL (c1653–92), dramatist, probably born here. His best known play is *The Rival Queens*, 1677.

WEST, RICHARD (1716–42), poet, born here. His letters and poems were published posthumously.

26 Hemel Hempstead SALTER, JOHN HENRY, Quaker poet, born here 1810.

27 Hertford CARR, JOHN (1732–1807), translator of Lucian, born here and headmaster of the grammar school. His translations appeared 1773–98.

JOHNS, CAPTAIN WILLIAM EARL (1893–1968), boys' novelist, born here. *The Camels are Coming*, 1932, was the first book-length appearance of his character Biggles, hero of some 70 subsequent novels.

MAURICE, THOMAS (1754–1824), oriental scholar and historian, born here. Dr Johnson wrote the preface for his translation of *Oedipus Tyrranus*. He was the first writer to bring Eastern religions to popular notice.

PENNINGTON, MARIANNE, poet, born here c1147.

SWAN, ANNIE S. (1859–1943), novelist, lived here during World War I.

WESTALL, RICHARD (1765–1836), book illustrator, born here.

28 Hinxworth CLUTTERBUCK, ROBERT (1772–1831), Hertfordshire historian, lived at Hinxworth Place where he spent eighteen years writing his *History of Hertfordshire*, 1827.

29 **Hitchin** BRAGGE, FRANCIS (1664–1728), poet, born here.

CHAPMAN, GEORGE (c1559–1634), dramatist and poet, born at Mount Pleasant. His name lives as the translator of Homer, eulogised by Keats in a sonnet.

LUCAS, ELIZABETH and FRANCIS, poets, born here c1816.

ORWELL, GEORGE (pseudonym of Eric Blair, 1903–50), novelist, owned 'The Stores' at Wallington nearby from 1936–47 but did not live there continuously.

SCOTT, JOSEPH NICOLL (c1703–69), theological writer, born here and minister here 1725–38. His brother, THOMAS (1705–75), clergyman and hymn writer, and sister, ELIZABETH (c1708–76), poet, were also born here.

30 **Hoddesdon** RAWDON, MARMADUKE (1610–69), traveller and writer, lived and died at St Monica's Priory.

ELLIS, MRS SARAH STICKNEY (1799–1872), novelist, lived at Rose Hill, Lord Street, from 1841 until her death.

31 **King's Langley** HOWARD, HENRY NEWMAN, poet, born here c1861.

32 **Knebworth** LYTTON, EDWARD GEORGE EARLE LYTTON BULWER-, 1ST BARON LYTTON (1803–73), statesman and novelist, lived here. Knebworth House, where Dickens, his family and circle used to present theatrical performances, is open to the public.

LYTTON, EDWARD ROBERT BULWER-, 1ST EARL OF LYTTON (1831–91), statesman and poet, born and lived at Knebworth. He used the pseudonym Owen Meredith for his poetry, which includes *Clytemnestra*, 1855, *Chronicles and Characters*, 1868, and *Fables in Song*, 1874.

33 **Lemsford** LAMB, LADY CAROLINE (1785–1828), novelist, lived at Brocket Hall from 1805 and wrote *Glenarvon*, 1816, caricaturing Byron.

34 **Lilley** JANEWAY, JAMES (c1636–74), nonconformist clergyman and author, born here. His *Token for Children*, 1671, was long popular.

35 **Little Berkhamsted** KEN, THOMAS (1637–1711), bishop of Bath and Wells, devotional writer, born here. His *Morning, Evening and Midnight Hymns*, originally part of a larger collection, were published separately in 1862.

36 **Much Hadham** NOWELL, ALEXANDER (c1507–1602), author of a Latin catechism, later translated and used in the Book of Common Prayer 1662.

37 **North Mimms** HEYWOOD, JOHN (c1497–c1580), 'the old English epigrammatist', born here. He wrote dramatic interludes, ballads, etc, some of which he performed, singing and playing the virginals, as entertainer to Queen Mary I.

PEACHAM, HENRY (c1576–c1643), author, born here. The best known of his varied works was *The Compleat Gentleman*, 1622.

YOUNG, ARTHUR (1741–1820), agriculturalist and author, lived at Bradmore Farm 1768–76 and wrote here *A Six Months' Tour through the North of England*.

38 **Redbourne** TATHAM, EMMA (1829–55), poet, born here.

39 **Ridge** BLOUNT, SIR HENRY POPE (1602–82), traveller and author, lived at Tittenhanger Park, and is buried here. His son, THOMAS (1649–97), author and poet, is also buried here.

40 **Royston** BELDAM, JOSEPH (1795–1866), poet, born here.

WRIGHT, THOMAS, poet, born here c1736.

41 **St Albans** BACON, FRANCIS, 1ST BARON VERULAM (1561–1626), statesman, philosopher and author, buried here.

BERNERS, JULIANA (1388–1460) lived at Sopwell Priory, where she may have been prioress. Her *Boke of St Albans*, containing treatises on hunting and hawking, was printed at St Albans in 1486.

COWPER, WILLIAM (1731–1800), poet, was an inmate 1763–65 of the private asylum kept in College Street by NATHANIEL COTTON (1705–88), verse writer (see **Berkhamsted**).

FERRERS, GEORGE (1512–79), poet and politician, born here. He contributed to *The Mirror for Magistrates*, 1559, which he and William Baldwin devised.

NECKHAM, ALEXANDER (1157–1217), churchman and scholar, born here. His works include *De Laudibus Divinae Sapientiae*, *De Contemptu Mundi*, and treatises on grammar.

PARIS, MATTHEW (d1259), historian, entered St Albans monastery in 1217 and succeeded to office of chronicler 1236.

ROGERS, HENRY (c1806–77), critic and author, born here. He was notable for his contributions to the *Edinburgh Review* from 1839.

SHIRLEY, JAMES (1596–1666), dramatic poet, master at the grammar school 1623–25.

TURNER, DANIEL (1710–98), writer of hymns and other works, born and lived at Blackwater Farm, near St Albans.

42 **Sandon** COBDEN, EDWARD (1684–1764), poet and author, born here. He issued poems and sermons 1718–58.

DOBELL, ELIZABETH (1828–1908), poet, born here.

43 **Sawbridgeworth** JOSCELYN, JOHN (1529–1603), Anglo-Saxon scholar, born at Hyde Hall. He contributed a collection of Anglo-Saxon pieces to Matthew Parker's *Homily of Aelfric Grammaticus*, c1567.

44 **Standon** VERNEDE, ROBERT (1875–1917), novelist and poet, lived at the Paper Mill, c1902–14.

45 **Stevenage** FORSTER, EDWARD MORGAN (1879–1970), author, lived at Rooks Nest House, between Weston and Stevenage, and described it in *Howard's End*, 1910.

46 **Therfield** DALE, THOMAS (1797–1870), dean of Rochester, theological writer, born here. He translated Sophocles, 1824.

47 **Tring** MASSEY, GERALD (1828–1907), poet, born at Gamble Wharf. A selection of his verse was published under the title *My Lyrical Life* in 1889. His prose writing includes *The Book of Beginnings*, 1881, and *Ancient Egypt: the Light of the World*, 1907.

48 **Walkern** WARD, NATHANIEL (c1578–1653), theological writer, rector 1645–48.

49 **Waltham Cross** TROLLOPE, ANTHONY (1815–82), novelist, lived at Waltham House 1859–71 and wrote many of his novels here.

50 **Ware** BARRAND, ELIZABETH (1804–89), poet, born here.

FANSHAWE, SIR RICHARD (1608–66), diplomat and author, born here. His published works include translations of Guarini's *Pastor Fido*, 1647, and of Camoens's *Lusiad*, 1655.

GODWIN, WILLIAM (1756–1836), philosopher and novelist, minister of the chapel here 1778–89.

GREENE, THOMAS (1742–88), poet, born here.

SCOTT, JOHN (1730–83), Quaker poet, lived in London Road (see **Amwell**).

VALLANS, WILLIAM (fl1578–90), poet, born here. His *A Tale of Two Swannes* describes places in Hertfordshire.

51 **Watford** CLUTTERBUCK, ROBERT (1772–1831), historian, buried here (see **Hinxworth**).

EXTON, RICHARD BRUDENELL, poet, born here c1839. He published *A Century of Sonnets on Sacred Subjects*, 1860.

FLETCHER, GILES the elder (1549–1611), ambassador and poet, born here. He wrote one of the earliest books on Russia (1591), which was suppressed at the time but published entire in 1856.

KENRICK, WILLIAM (c1725–79), miscellaneous writer, born here. He was remarkable for the number of his libels against contemporaries.

MASTERS, MARTIN KEDGEWIN, poet, born here c1807.

MEDLEY, SAMUEL (1738–99), devotional writer, baptist minister here 1767.

52 **Welwyn** CLINTON, HENRY FYNES (1781–1852), historian, lived here 1810–50.

YOUNG, EDWARD (1683–1765), poet, rector here. He lived at the Old Rectory in Mill Lane from 1730, then at Guessens, next to the church, from 1741 and died there. A curate, JOHN KIDGETT, believed that the housekeeper, Mrs Hallows, had an evil influence on Young, and wrote a novel, *The Card*, based on the situation.

53 **Welwyn Garden City** GIBBON, LEWIS GRASSIC (pseudonym of James Leslie Mitchell, 1901–35), novelist, lived and wrote here from 1928 until his death.

54 **Westmill** LAMB, CHARLES (1775–1834), essayist, owned Button Snap Cottage at Cherry's Green.

SALMON, NATHANIEL (1675–1742), historian and antiquary, curate here c1714.

55 **Wheathampstead** CHERRY-GARRARD, APSLEY (1886–1959), explorer and author of *The Worst Journey in the World*, 1937, lived here.

JOHN OF WHEATHAMPSTEAD (d1465), abbot of St Albans, wrote with others *The Chronicles of St Albans*.

LAMB, CHARLES (1775–1834), essayist, lived at Mackery End as a child, and wrote about it in *Essays of Elia*, 1823.

56 **Widford** ELIOT, JOHN (1604–90) born here. Styled 'the Indian Apostle', he translated the Bible for American Indians. Descendants of Eliot and his six brothers and six sisters have presented a memorial window in the church of St John the Baptist.

LAMB, CHARLES (1775–1834), essayist, addressed his first sonnets to Ann Simmons here, and frequently used the area for his settings.

57 **Willian** DENMAN, LEWIS WILLIAM (1820–1907), hymn writer, rector from 1861 until his death.

58 **Wormley** GOUGH, RICHARD (1735–1809), antiquary, died here.

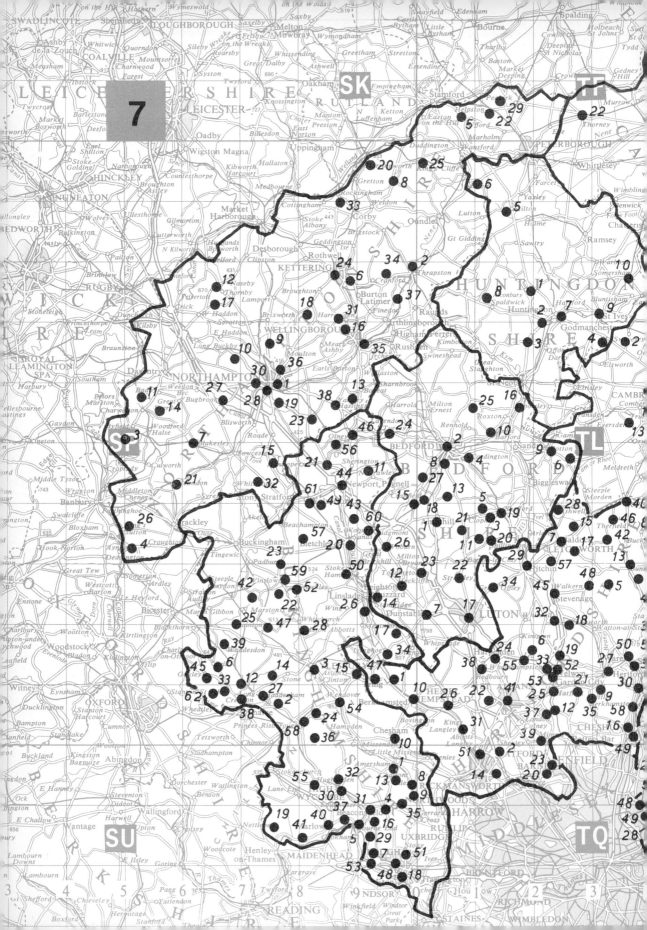

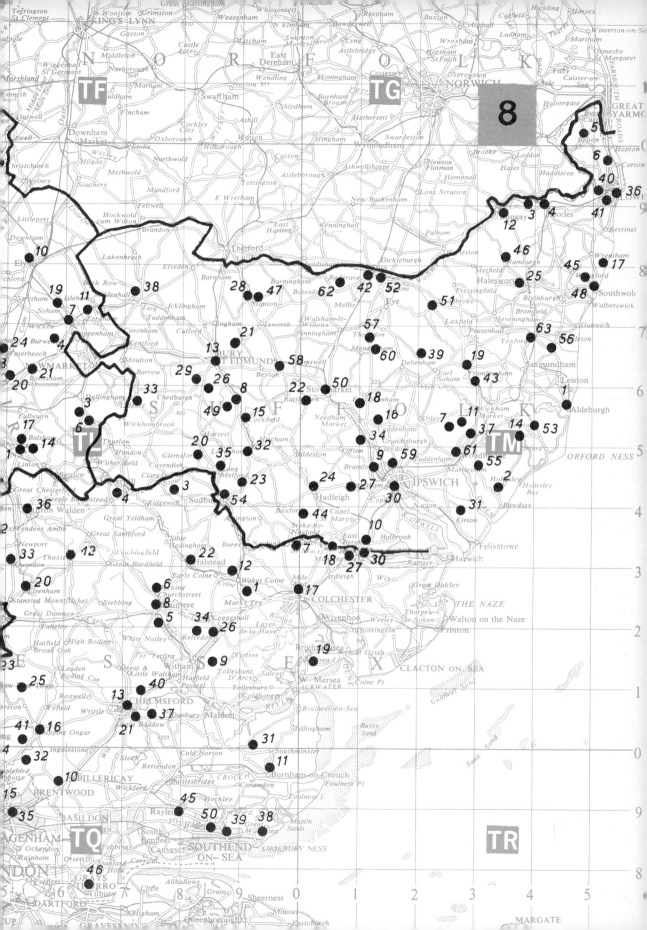

Huntingdonshire (*Map 7*)

1 **Alconbury** Jarvis Matcham was hanged on Alconbury Hill in 1796: RICHARD HARRIS BARHAM (1788–1845) included his story in the *Ingoldsby Legends*.

2 **Brampton** DRINKWATER, JOHN (1882–1937), poet and playwright, lived for some time at Pepys Farm, once the home of SAMUEL PEPYS's parents, who are buried at Brampton. Drinkwater wrote a life of Pepys, 1930.

3 **Buckden** STERNE, LAURENCE (1713–68), novelist, curate here in 1738.

4 **Conington** COTTON, SIR ROBERT BRUCE (1571–1631), antiquary, collector of MSS, historian, lived at Conington Castle until his death (see **Denton**).

5 **Denton** COTTON, SIR ROBERT BRUCE (1571–1631), antiquary, collector of MSS, historian, born here. He was the author of political tracts, and a history *The Reign of Henry III*, 1627. His library was made over to the nation and subsequently housed in The British Museum when it was founded in 1753.

6 **Elton** FABER, FREDERICK WILLIAM (1814–63), theologian and hymn writer, rector 1842–45, but was converted to the Roman church in 1848.

7 **Huntingdon** BEARD, THOMAS (fl1630), theological writer, master of the grammar school, where he taught Oliver Cromwell.

8 **Leighton Bromswold** HERBERT, GEORGE (1593–1633), poet, was prebendary 1626–30, and rebuilt the church.

9 **St Ives** WATTS-DUNTON, WALTER THEODORE (1832–1914), critic and novelist, born here. He is chiefly remembered for his long guardianship of Algernon Charles Swinburne at The Pines, Putney.

10 **Somersham** SAYERS, DOROTHY LEIGH (1893–1957), detective novelist and theological writer, lived here.

Cambridgeshire (*Maps 7 & 8*)

1 Abington MOORE, EDWARD (1712–57), dramatist, born here. His *Gil Blas* was produced in 1751, and *The Gamester* in 1753.

2 Boxworth BOYSE, JOHN (1560–1643), a translator of the Bible, rector 1596–1615.

3 Brinkley ANSTEY, CHRISTOPHER (1724–1805), versifier, born here. His satirical poem *The New Bath Guide* was published in 1766.

4 Burwell FITZBALL, EDWARD (1792–1873), dramatist and poet, born here. Achieved success with *Peveril of the Peak*, 1823. He also wrote romances and songs, including 'The Bloom is on the Rye', 1831.

5 Cambridge A great many literary men and women, notable and obscure, have studied or taught in the University of Cambridge down the centuries. Most of them appear elsewhere in this work and the entries under Cambridge have been limited to other associations.

BABINGTON, CHARLES CARDALE (1808–95), historian and naturalist, died and is buried at Cherry Hinton.

CHEKE, SIR JOHN (1514–57), classical scholar, born here. He edited many Greek texts and worked to reform English spelling. The pronunciation of Greek introduced by him is still in use.

CORNFORD, FRANCES CROFTS (1886–1960), poet, born in Cambridge. The best known of her poems is perhaps 'To a Fat Lady seen from the Train'. Her son, RUPERT JOHN CORNFORD (1915–36), poet and essayist, was largely inspired by the Spanish Civil War, in which he was killed.

CRASHAW, RICHARD (c1613–49), poet, vicar of St Mary the Less, 1639.

CUMBERLAND, RICHARD (1732–1811), dramatist, born in the lodge of Trinity College. He is alluded to in Goldsmith's *Retaliation* as 'the Terence of England', and is called 'Sir Fretful Plagiary' in Sheridan's *The Critic*.

GRAY, THOMAS (1716–71), poet, spent most of his life at Cambridge and died here.

HOUSMAN, ALFRED EDWARD (1859–1936), poet and classical scholar, died here.

LEWIS, CLIVE STAPLES (1898–1963), scholar and author of theological, literary and children's books, died here. He was born in Ireland.

MACAULAY, DAME ROSE (1881–1958), poet, essayist and novelist, born in Cambridge. Her principal novels are *The World My Wilderness*, 1950, and *The Towers of Trebizond*, 1956. She also wrote books of travel and published several collections of verse.

PALMER, EDWARD (1840–82), orientalist and writer, born here. His books include *The Desert of the Exodus*, 1871, and *Haroun Alraschid*, 1880.

POSTGATE, RAYMOND WILLIAM (1896–1971), novelist and historian, born here. His novels include *Verdict of Twelve*, 1940, and *Somebody at the Door*, 1943. He was editor of *The Good Food Guide* from its inception in 1951.

PRESTON, THOMAS (1537–98), dramatist, buried in the chapel of Trinity Hall.

TAYLOR, JEREMY (1613–67), theological writer, born in Cambridge. His *Holy Living*, 1650, and *Holy Dying*,

1651, remain notable expositions of the Christian duties.

WHITE, HENRY KIRKE (1785–1806), poet, was buried at All Saints, from where his memorial was transferred to St John's College chapel when All Saints was demolished in 1870.

WHITEHEAD, WILLIAM (1715–85), poet laureate 1757, born in Cambridge. His comedy *School for Lovers* was produced in 1762; his poems were collected in 1788.

6 Carlton ELYOT, SIR THOMAS (c1499–1546), diplomat and writer on education and politics, buried here.

7 Chippenham MAY, SIR THOMAS ERSKINE, 1ST BARON FARNBOROUGH (1815–86), writer of the authoritative work on Parliamentary procedure, buried here.

8 Christchurch SAYERS, DOROTHY LEIGH (1893–1950), detective novelist and author of religious drama, born here. Creator of Lord Peter Wimsey, hero of many best-selling novels. Her religious play sequence *The Man Born to be King* was produced in 1942.

9 Coton DOWNES, ANDREW (c1549–1628), a translator of the Apocrypha for the Authorised Version of the Bible, buried here.

10 Ely Setting for CHARLES KINGSLEY's *Hereward the Wake*, 1866.

11 Fordham WITHERS, JAMES (d1892), poet, buried here.

12 Grantchester BROOKE, RUPERT CHAWNOR (1887–1915), poet, lived at the Old Vicarage, subject of his most famous poem, 'The Old Vicarage, Grantchester', 1911. Other villages around Cambridge are mentioned in the poem.

BYRON's Pool here is named for the poet, a frequent visitor to it. The mill mentioned in CHAUCER's *Reeve's Tale* stood beside the pool, and TENNYSON made it the home of the heroine of his *Story of the Miller's Daughter*, 1830.

13 Great Eversden EVERSDEN, JOHN (fl c1300), chronicler, lived here.

14 Hildersham PARIS, MATTHEW (d1259), Latin chronicler and poet, believed to have lived here.

15 Ickleton HERBERT, ALGERNON (1792–1855), antiquary, buried here.

16 Landbeach RAWLEY, WILLIAM (c1588–1667), editor of Bacon's works and translator, was rector of Landbeach from 1616 until his death and is buried here.

17 Little Abingdon COLE, WILLIAM (1714–82), Cambridge antiquary, born here. His *Key to the Psalms* appeared in 1788.

18 Milton COLE, WILLIAM (1714–82), Cambridge antiquary, rector 1770–74 (see **Little Abingdon**).

19 Soham CHAMBERS, JAMES (1748–c1826), poet, born here. He wrote many of his verses in Soham workhouse.

20 Stow-Cum-Quy COLLIER, JEREMY (1650–1726), pamphleteer and historian, born here. His *Short View of the Immorality and Profaneness of the English Stage* appeared in 1698.

21 Swaffam Bulbeck BLOMEFIELD, LEONARD (1800–93), writer on natural history, vicar 1828–49.

22 Thorney PECOCK, REGINALD (c1395–c1460), bishop and author of controversial works, was incarcerated in Thorney Abbey from 1458 until his death.

23 Trumpington HENTY, GEORGE ALFRED (1832–1902), boys' novelist, born here. He was author of a great many immensely popular works, including *With Clive in India*, 1884, and *Redskin and Cowboy*, 1892.

24 Waterbeach COLE, WILLIAM (1714–82), Cambridge antiquary, rector 1767–70 (see **Little Abingdon**).

25 Wisbech CLARKSON, THOMAS (1760–1846), philanthropist and writer, born here. His works include pamphlets on slavery, theological tracts and a memoir of William Penn.

GODWIN, WILLIAM (1756–1836), philosopher and writer, born here. Author of *The Adventures of Caleb Williams*, 1794, and *Enquiry concerning Political Justice*, 1793. He was the father of Shelley's wife, Mary.

HILL, OCTAVIA (1838–1912), reformer and writer, born here. She described her work in the London slums in *Homes of the London Poor*, 1875.

Essex (*Maps 7 & 8*)

1 **Aldham** MORANT, PHILIP (1700–70), historian, rector from 1745 until his death. He wrote his *History and Antiquities of the County of Essex*, 1760–68, and other works about the county during his years here.

2 **Arkesden** CUTTS, JOHN (1661–1707), soldier and author, admired by Steele and Macaulay, born here. He published *La Muse de Cavalier* in 1685.

3 **Belchamp St Paul** GOLDING, ARTHUR (1536–1606), translator, born here. Shakespeare drew upon his translations from the classics, which included Caesar's *Commentaries*, 1565, and Ovid's *Metamorphoses*, 1565–67.

4 **Birdbrook** WALFORD, THOMAS (1752–1833), antiquary, buried here.

5 **Black Notley** RAY, JOHN (1628–1705), naturalist, born and buried here. He published several major works on his subject and is regarded as the 'father' of natural history in England.

6 **Bocking** GAUDEN, JOHN (1605–62), dean 1641 (see **Mayland**).

7 **Boxted** BLACKMORE, SIR RICHARD (d1729), poet and physician, died here.

8 **Braintree** UDALL, or UREDALE, NICHOLAS (1505–56), dramatist, vicar 1537–44.

9 **Braxted** LAWRENCE, GEORGE ALFRED (1827–76), novelist, born at the rectory. His *Guy Livingstone*, 1857, enjoyed wide popularity.

10 **Brentwood** JONES, EBENEZER (1820–60), poet, died here.

11 **Burnham** GATTY, MRS MARGARET (1809–73), children's author, born at the vicarage. Her *Parables from Nature* appeared in five parts, 1855–71, and she edited *Aunt Judy's Magazine* from 1866 until her death. She was mother of another children's author, Mrs Ewing (1841–85).

12 **Chapel** ROGERS, TIMOTHY (1589–1650), Puritan writer, ministered here.

13 **Chelmsford** STRUTT, JOSEPH (1749–1802), author and artist, born here. He published *Chronicle of England*, 1777–78, and two works on English pastimes. An unfinished novel of his, completed by Sir Walter Scott, gave the latter the idea for *Waverley*.

14 **Chigwell** The King's Head Inn is the Maypole Inn of CHARLES DICKENS's *Barnaby Rudge*, 1841.

15 **Chigwell Row** DAY, THOMAS (1748–89), poet and author, lived here.

16 **Chipping Ongar** TAYLOR, ISAAC (1759–1829), children's author, pastor from 1810 and buried here. His daughter JANE (1783–1824), who also wrote for children, lived here and is buried here. Her poem 'Twinkle, twinkle, little star' appeared in 1806 in one of the collections of children's poetry she published with her sister Ann.

17 **Colchester** TAYLOR, ISAAC (1759–1829), children's author, pastor here before 1810. The Taylor family lived in West Stockwell Street: ISAAC, the son (1787–1865), was artist, lay theologian and inventor; ANN (Mrs Gilbert, 1782–1866) wrote children's poetry; for JANE (1783–1824) see **Chipping Ongar**.

18 **Dedham** GIBSON, CHARLES (1878–1943), soldier and author of stories for boys, born here. He wrote prolifically for magazines and book publication (*The Realm of the Wizard King*, 1922, etc), and also wrote girls' adventure tales as Barbara Gilson.

19 **East Mersea** BARING-GOULD, SABINE (1834–1924), novelist, folklorist and hymn writer, rector 1871–81.

20 **Elsenham** GILBEY, SIR WALTER (1831–1914), author of books on horses and riding, lived here.

21 **Great Baddow** BARCLAY, ALEXANDER (c1475–1552), poet and translator, rector 1546.

22 **Halstead** BOURCHIER, JOHN, 2ND BARON BERNERS (1467–1533), statesman and author, lived at Stanstead Hall. He published a translation of Froissart's *Chronicles*, 1523–25.

23 **Harlow** ADAMS, SARAH FLOWER (1805–48), poet, born and buried here. She is remembered for the hymn 'Nearer, my God, to Thee'.

24 **High Beech** TENNYSON, ALFRED, LORD (1809–92), poet laureate, lived here 1837–40.

25 **High Laver** LOCKE, JOHN (1632–1704), philosopher and essayist, lived at Oates from 1691 and is buried here.

26 **Kelvedon** SPURGEON, CHARLES HADDON (1834–92), preacher and writer, born here. His works include *John Ploughman's Talks*, 1869. He edited *The Treasury of David*, 1870–85, a commentary on the Psalms.

27 **Lawford** MERIVALE, CHARLES (1808–93), poet and historian, rector here 1848–68, during which time he published his *History of the Romans under the Empire*, 1850–64.

28 **Leytonstone** DRINKWATER, JOHN (1882–1937), poet and playwright, born here. *Abraham Lincoln*, 1918, is perhaps the best known of his historical plays.
HORLER, SYDNEY (1888–1954), thriller writer, born here. His successful titles include *The Screaming Skull*, 1930, and *Tiger Standish*, 1932.

29 **Loughton** MARTIN, SARAH (1768–1826), author of the nursery rhyme 'Old Mother Hubbard', buried here.

30 **Manningtree** MACLAREN, IAN (pseudonym of John Watson, 1850–1907), clergyman and novelist, born here. His widely popular sketches of Scottish character include *Beside the Bonnie Brier Bush*, 1894.

31 **Mayland** GAUDEN, JOHN (1605–62), bishop of Exeter and of Worcester, born here. He was almost certainly the author of *Eikon Basilike*, 'the Pourtraicture of his Sacred Majesty in his Solitudes and Sufferings', 1649, at first attributed to Charles I himself.

32 **Navestock** STUBBS, WILLIAM (1825–1901), historian, vicar 1850–66.

33 **Quendon** WINSTANLEY, WILLIAM (1628–98), writer of chapbooks, buried here.

34 **Rivenhall** TUSSER, THOMAS (c1524–80), agricultural writer and poet, born here. He published *A Hundreth Goode Pointes of Husbandrie*, 1557. A number of popular proverbs had their origin in his writings.

35 **Romford** MORRIS, RICHARD (1833–94), etymologist, died at nearby Harold Wood, and is buried there.
QUARLES, FRANCIS (1592–1644), poet, born at Stewards nearby. His most popular work, *Divine Emblemes*, 1635, was a favourite book of Charles I.

36 **Saffron Walden** HARVEY, GABRIEL (c1545–1630), poet, born here. Lifelong friend of Edmund Spenser (c1552–99), he claimed to have been the originator of the English hexameter.
NEVILLE, RICHARD, 3RD BARON BRAYBROOKE (1783–1858), politician and first editor of Pepys's *Diary*, 1825, lived at Audley End.

SMITH, SIR THOMAS (1513–77), statesman and author, born here. His important work on the Tudor constitution, *De Republica Anglorum*, was published six years after his death.

37 Sandon WALTON, BRIAN (c1600–61), editor of the English Polyglot Bible, rector 1636–41.

38 Shoeburyness DENT, ARTHUR (c1607), whose *Plain Man's Pathway to Heaven* influenced Bunyan, was rector 1580–1607.

39 Southend DEEPING, GEORGE WARWICK (1877–1950), novelist, born here. His most popular work was *Sorrell and Son*, 1925.

40 Springfield, nr Chelmsford GOLDSMITH, OLIVER (1728–74), poet, dramatist and novelist, wrote much of *The Deserted Village*, 1770, while staying at a cottage near the church.

41 Stanford Rivers TAYLOR, ISAAC JNR (1787–1865), artist, author and inventor, lived at Stanford House from 1825 until his death.

42 Thaxted PURCHAS, SAMUEL (c1575–1626), clergyman and author, born here. From Hakluyt papers in his possession he compiled three works on man as a pilgrim, dealing with religions, history and discoveries, 1612, 1619 and 1625.

43 Theydon Bois BENT, JAMES THEODORE (1852–97), explorer and archaeological writer, buried here.

44 Theydon Mount SMITH, SIR THOMAS (1513–77), statesman and author, lived at Hill Hall and is buried here (see **Saffron Walden**).

45 Thundersley HUME, FERGUS (1859–1932), author of *The Mystery of a Hansom Cab*, 1887, one of the first detective stories, lived here from 1888.

46 Tilbury DEFOE, DANIEL (c1660–1731), journalist and novelist, was manager and part owner of a tile works here c1694–1703.

GERVASE OF TILBURY (fl1180), chronicler, probably born here.

47 Waltham Abbey TROLLOPE, ANTHONY (1815–82), novelist, lived at Waltham House, at nearby Waltham Cross, for eleven years from 1859, and wrote many of his books here. The house was demolished in 1936. The bells of Waltham Abbey inspired TENNYSON to write his New Year verses 'Ring out the old, ring in the new' while he was living at High Beech (qv).

48 Walthamstow MORRIS, WILLIAM (1834–96), poet, artist and socialist visionary, born here. His literary works included versions of the Icelandic epics, prose romances, and verse translations of the *Odyssey* and *Aeneid*. *The Dream of John Ball*, 1888, and *News from Nowhere*, 1891, were written as socialist propaganda. He was widely influential in the visual arts, and his birthplace is now an art gallery.

49 Wanstead HOOD, THOMAS junior (1835–74), son of the poet Thomas Hood (1799–1845), born here. His novels include the successful *Captain Master's Children*, 1865. He founded *Tom Hood's Magazine*, 1867.

50 Westcliffe-on-Sea BELL, ROBERT STANLEY WARREN (1871–1921), boys' author, lived here after World War I and died here.

51 Witham CAMPION, or CAMPIAN, THOMAS (1567–1619), musician and poet, born here. 'Cherry Ripe' was one of the many lyrics he wrote for masques he presented at court.

52 Woodford Green HOCKING, JOSEPH (1855–1937), novelist, pastor here c1889–1910.

53 Woodford PATMORE, COVENTRY KERSEY DIGHTON (1823–96), poet, born here. His *Angel in the House* consists of four poems, published between 1854–62, on the theme of love in marriage.

Suffolk (*Map 8*)

1 **Aldeburgh** CRABBE, GEORGE (1754–1832), poet, born here. He practised here as an apothecary 1777–80. One of his best known poems, *The Borough*, 1810, depicts life in the district.

2 **Alderton** FLETCHER, GILES THE YOUNGER (c1588–1623), poet and younger brother of the poet PHINEAS FLETCHER (1582–1650), was rector from c1618 until his death and is buried here.

3 **Barsham** SUCKLING, SIR JOHN (1609–42), poet and dramatist, raised a troop of horse for the Royalist cause at the old manor, where he lived.

4 **Beccles** CHATEAUBRIAND, FRANÇOIS RENÉ, VICOMTE DE (1768–1848), French writer and politician, taught French here for a time during his English sojourn of 1793–1800.

CRABBE, GEORGE (1754–1832), poet, married Sarah Elmy, the 'Mira' of his poems, here in 1783 (see **Aldeburgh**).

5 **Belton** IVES, JOHN (1751–76), historian, buried here. He published a history of Yarmouth, papers on English antiquities and other works.

6 **Blundeston** Features have been identified with the Blunderstone of CHARLES DICKENS's *David Copperfield*, 1849–50.

7 **Boulge** FITZGERALD, EDWARD (1809–93), translator of *The Rubaiyat of Omar Khayyam* and author, lived in a cottage in the Hall park for many years and is buried at Boulge (see **Bredfield**).

8 **Bradfield** YOUNG, ARTHUR (1741–1820), writer on agriculture, was the rector's son and lived here from childhood. He is buried here. Fanny Burney described his home in her novel *Camilla*, 1796. He published his *Annals of Agriculture* in 47 volumes, 1784–1809.

9 **Bramford** COWELL, EDWARD BYLES (1826–1903), translator from Sanskrit, buried here (see **Ipswich**).

10 **Brantham** TUSSER, THOMAS (c1524–80), agricultural writer, lived nearby at Cattawade for a time and here compiled his *Hundredth Goode Pointes of Husbandrie*, 1557.

11 **Bredfield** FITZGERALD, EDWARD (1809–83), author and translator, born at Bredfield House. His translation of the *Rubaiyat of Omar Khayyam*, one of the most widely sold publications of all time, appeared in 1859.

12 **Bungay** CHATEAUBRIAND, FRANÇOIS RENÉ, VICOMTE DE (1768–1848), French writer and politician, taught French here for a year during his English sojourn of 1793–1800.

HAGGARD, SIR HENRY RIDER (1856–1925), novelist, lived at Ditchingham House nearby from about 1885 until the end of his life, writing most of his books here.

13 **Bury St Edmunds** AUNGERVILLE, RICHARD (1281–1345), known as Richard de Bury, churchman and patron of literature, born here. His chief publication, *Philobiblon*, 1473, was a guide to the collection of books with which he founded the library of Durham College, Oxford (later dissolved).

COCKTON, HENRY (1807–53), novelist, lived and died here.

LYDGATE, JOHN (c1370–c1451), poet, spent most of his life at the monastery and is buried here.

OUIDA (pseudonym of Marie Louise de la Ramée, 1839–1908), novelist, born here. Her pseudonym is derived from her pronunciation of Louise when a child. Her colourful romances, such as *Under Two Flags*, 1867, enjoyed tremendous vogue.

ROBINSON, HENRY CRABB (1775–1867), journalist and diarist, born here. He was associated with *The Times* in various capacities. His *Diary* and *Letters* were published posthumously.

14 **Chillesford** PICKTHALL, MARMADUKE (1875–1936), novelist and orientalist, born here. His best known novel is *Said the Fisherman*, 1903.

15 **Cockfield** BABINGTON, CHURCHILL (1821–89), antiquary and naturalist, vicar for twenty-two years and buried here.

16 **Coddenham** BACON, NATHANIEL (1593–1660), statesman and constitutional historian, buried here.

17 **Covehithe** BALE, JOHN (1495–1563), religious polemicist and dramatist, born here. He wrote the first English historical play, *King John*, 1548.

18 **Creeting St Mary** AUSTIN, JOHN (1790–1859), writer on jurisprudence, born at Creeting Mill. His works include *The Province of Jurisprudence Determined*, 1832, which greatly influenced views on the subject in this country.

19 **Framlingham** HOWARD, HENRY, EARL OF SURREY (c1517–47), poet, buried here.

20 **Glemsford** CAVENDISH, GEORGE (1500–c1561), biographer of Wolsey, lived and is buried here.

21 **Great Barton** BUNBURY, SIR HENRY (1778–1860), author of works on the Peninsula War, lived and is buried here.

22 **Great Finborough** WOLLASTON, WILLIAM (1659–1724), author of *The Religion of Nature Delineated*, 1724, buried here.

23 **Great Waldingfield** HOPKINS, JOHN (d1570), versifier and compiler (with Thomas Sternhold (d1549)) of the 'Old Version' of the Psalms, was rector from 1561 until his death and is buried here.

24 **Hadleigh** ALABASTER, WILLIAM (1567–1640), poet, born here. He wrote the Latin tragedy *Roxana*, c1592.

BEAUMONT, JOSEPH (1616–99), poet and clergyman, born here. He returned to live here after 1644 and wrote his epic poem *Psyche*, 1648.

WOOLNER, THOMAS (1825–92), poet and sculptor and member of the Pre-Raphaelite brotherhood, born here. His work includes *My Beautiful Lady*, 1863, *Pygmalion*, 1881, and *Nelly Dale*, 1886.

25 **Halesworth** KIRBY, JOHN (1690–1753), topographer, born here. He compiled the much-reprinted *Suffolk Traveller*, 1735.

26 **Hawstead** DONNE, JOHN (1573–1631), poet and churchman, was inspired to write his elegy 'An Anatomy of the World', 1611, and a sequel 'Progress of the Soul', 1612, by the death of Elizabeth Drury, daughter of his friend Sir Robert Drury, of Hawstead. She is buried here.

MOORE, GILES (1617–79), diarist, born here. His important *Day Book*, 1656–79, was published complete in 1971.

27 **Hintlesham** ELLIS, HAVELOCK (1859–1939), psychologist and essayist, died here.

28 **Honington** BLOOMFIELD, ROBERT (1766–1823), poet, was born here and attended the village school kept by his mother. His best known poem is *The Farmer's Boy*, 1800.

29 **Ickworth** HERVEY, LADY MARY (1700–68), letter writer, buried here. She was eulogised by many writers; Voltaire's poem to her was the only verse he ever wrote in English, and Walpole composed the lines on her gravestone.

61

30 Ipswich COBBOLD, RICHARD (1797–1877), novelist, born here. He wrote *Margaret Catchpole*, 1845, based on the story of a local woman smuggler.

COWELL, EDWARD BYLES (1826–1903), translator and editor of Sanskrit texts, born here. He introduced Edward FitzGerald to the Omar Khayyam manuscript.

The Great White Horse Inn was used by CHARLES DICKENS for scenes in *The Pickwick Papers*, 1837–39.

KIRBY, JOHN (1690–1753), topographer, died here (see **Halesworth**).

REEVE, CLARA (1729–1807), novelist, born and is buried here. Her best known work was *The Champion of Virtue, a Gothic Story*, 1777, later re-titled *The Old English Baron*.

SIEVEKING, LANCELOT DE GIBERNE (1896–1972), author and radio playwright, died here. He lived nearby at Snape.

31 Kirton REEVE, CLARA (1729–1807), novelist, spent most of her life at the rectory (see **Ipswich**).

32 Lavenham TAYLOR, ANN (1782–1866) and JANE (1783–1824), sisters and poets, lived here 1786–1812, during which time they published *Original Poems for Infant Minds*, 1804, and similar collections. Jane Taylor wrote 'Twinkle, Twinkle, Little Star' here. Their brother ISAAC (1787–1865), philosopher, was born here. His works include *The Elements of Thought*, 1823, *The Natural History of Enthusiasm*, 1829, and *The World of the Mind*, 1857.

33 Lidgate LYDGATE, JOHN (c1370–c1451), the 'Monk of Bury', born here. His principal works are *Troy Book*, 1412–20, *The Falls of Princes*, 1430–38, and *The Story of Thebes*.

34 Little Blakenham CHARLESWORTH, MARIE LOUISA (1819–80), author of inspirational tales, born at the rectory. Her enormously successful *Ministering Children* was published 1854.

35 Long Melford STEED, HENRY WICKHAM (1871–1956), journalist and author, born here. He was editor of *The Times*, 1919–22, and owned and edited the *Review of Reviews*, 1925–38.

36 Lowestoft MAURICE, JOHN FREDERICK DENISON (1805–72), theological writer, born nearby. His views, radical for that time, are chiefly summarised in two collections of *Theological Essays*, 1853 and 1871.

NASH (or NASHE), THOMAS (1567–1601), satirist, born here. Much of his writing was directed against the Puritans. *The Unfortunate Traveller, or the Life of Jack Wilton*, 1594, has been described as probably the first adventure novel.

37 Melton MERRIMAN, HENRY SETON (pseudonym of Hugh Stowell Scott, 1862–1903), novelist, buried here.

38 Mildenhall HANMER, SIR THOMAS (1677–1746), editor of Shakespeare's works, buried here.

39 Monk Sohan GROOME, FRANCIS HINDES (1851–1902), author, born at the rectory. He published several books on gypsies, a novel *Kriegspiel*, 1896, and *Two Suffolk Friends*, a study of his father and the translator Edward FitzGerald.

40 Oulton BORROW, GEORGE (1803–81), author, lived from 1840 on his wife's estate and died there.

FASTOLF, SIR JOHN (c1378–1459), probably the original of SHAKESPEARE's Falstaff, buried here.

41 Oulton Broad, nr Lowestoft COLLINS, JOHN CHURTON (1848–1908), author and literary critic, drowned here.

42 Palgrave BARBAULD, MRS ANNA LAETITIA (1743–1825), poet, kept a boarding school here, 1774–85, with her husband.

MARTIN, THOMAS (1697–1771), 'honest Tom Martin of Palgrave', antiquary, buried here.

43 Parham CRABBE, GEORGE (1754–1832), poet, lived in the neighbourhood between 1792 and 1805.

44 Polstead MARTEN, MARIA (d1827) was murdered and is buried here: her murder in the Red Barn has been the subject of several books and the classic melodrama *Maria Marten*, 1840.

45 Reydon STRICKLAND, AGNES (1796–1874), biographer, lived at Reydon Hall with her sister Elizabeth, who sometimes assisted her.

46 Rumburgh DAVY, DAVID ELISHA (1769–1851), historian of Suffolk, born here.

47 Sapiston BLOOMFIELD, ROBERT (1766–1823), poet, worked as a boy on William Austin's farm and was probably recalling it in his poem *The Farmer's Boy*, 1800 (see **Honington**).

48 Southwold BELL, NEIL (pseudonym of Stephen Southwold, 1887–1964), novelist, born here. His prolific production includes *Precious Porcelain*, 1931, and *Flowers of the Forest*, 1932. He also wrote as PAUL MARTENS, and for children as STEPHEN SOUTHWOLD.

ORWELL, GEORGE (pseudonym of Eric Blair, 1903–50), novelist, lived here with his parents from 1930–33 at 3 Queen Street, and for subsequent short periods.

STRICKLAND, AGNES (1796–1874), biographer, and her sister Elizabeth both buried here.

49 Stanningfield INCHBALD, MRS ELIZABETH (1753–1821), novelist, dramatist and actress, born here. Her plays include *Such Things Are*, 1788, and *The Wedding Day*, 1794, but she is better remembered for her novels, *A Simple Story*, 1791, and *Nature and Art*, 1796.

50 Stowmarket MILTON, JOHN (1608–74), poet, is said to have planted the mulberry tree in the garden of the vicarage, then the home of his tutor, Thomas Young.

51 Stradbroke CHAMBERS, JAMES (1748–c1827), poet and author of ballads and acrostic verses, buried here.

GROSSETESTE, ROBERT (c1175–1253), theological and classical scholar and bishop of Lincoln, born here. He wrote an allegory, *Chasteau d'Amour*, in French, and *Compendium Scientiae*, a classification of contemporary knowledge.

52 Stuston BROOME, WILLIAM (1689–1745), translator of Homer and poet, rector here during his most productive years, and then of Eye and Oakley Magna nearby.

53 Sudbourne Lord Steyn in WILLIAM MAKEPEACE THACKERAY's *Vanity Fair*, 1847–48, and Lord Monmouth in BENJAMIN DISRAELI's *Coningsby*, 1844, were drawn from members of the Wallace family, buried here.

54 Sudbury Probably the Eatanswill of CHARLES DICKENS's *Pickwick Papers*, 1837–39.

55 Sutton SEWELL, MARY (1797–1884), poet and mother of the author Anna Sewell (1820–78), born here. Her works include *Homely Ballads*, 1858, *Mother's Last Words*, 1860, and *Our Father's Care*, 1861.

56 Theberton DOUGHTY, CHARLES MONTAGU (1843–1926), explorer and poet, born at Theberton Hall. His most celebrated work, *Travels in Arabia Deserta*, appeared in 1888.

57 Thwaite WHISTLECRAFT, ORLANDO (1810–83), poet, lived and is buried here.

58 Tostock NORTH, ROGER (1653–1734), lawyer and biographer of the North family, born here.

SIBBES, RICHARD (1577–1635), clergyman, poet and author, born here. His works include *The Saint's Cordials*, 1629, *The Bruised Reed and Smoking Flax*, 1630, and *The Church's Visitation*, 1634.

59 Westerfield EDWARDS, MATILDA BARBARA BETHAM (1836–1919), novelist and writer on French life, born here.

60 Wetheringsett HAKLUYT, RICHARD (c1553–1616), author of the *Voyages*, was rector from 1590 until his death, and compiled his great work here. His working room at the rectory has been restored to its 17th century appearance.

61 Woodbridge BARTON, BERNARD (1784–1849), poet and father-in-law of Edward FitzGerald (see **Bredfield**), spent most of his life at Woodbridge and is buried here.
FITZGERALD, EDWARD (1809–83), translator, lived on Market Hill 1861–74 (see **Bredfield**).

WADE, THOMAS (1805–75), poet and dramatist, born here. He published a translation of Dante's *Inferno*, volumes of verse, two tragedies and a farce.

62 Wortham COBBOLD, RICHARD (1797–1877), novelist, rector from 1825 until his death (see **Ipswich**).

63 Yoxford CANDLER, ANN (pseudonym of Ann More, 1740–1814), poet, born here. Known as the 'Suffolk Cottager', she published her collected verses in 1803.

Herefordshire (*Map 9*)

1 **Abbey Dore** HOSKINS, JOHN (1566–1638), lawyer and wit, buried here.

2 **Ashperton** GRANDISON, JOHN (c1292–1369), bishop of Exeter, christened here. He was the author of *Lessons from the Bible* and *Legends of the Saints*, both still extant.

3 **Bishopstone** The Roman pavement here is described in a poem which WORDSWORTH wrote while staying at Brinsop Court (qv).

4 **Bosbury** LYALL, EDNA (pseudonym of Ada Ellen Bayly, 1857–1903) set her novel *In Spite of All* here. Her ashes are in the churchyard.

5 **Brampton Bryan** HARLEY, LADY BRILLIANA (1600–43) lived here: 200 of her letters were published by the Camden Society in 1854. This was also the home of EDWARD HARLEY, 2ND EARL OF OXFORD (1689–1741), friend of Swift and Pope. His collection of books and MSS, with those of his father, Robert, 1st Earl of Oxford, form the Harleian Library, British Museum.

6 **Bredwardine** KILVERT, ROBERT FRANCIS (1840–79), clergyman and diarist, was vicar from 1877 until his death here. The years here are covered in his celebrated diary, published 1938–40.

7 **Brinsop** WORDSWORTH, WILLIAM (1770–1850), poet laureate, often stayed at Brinsop Court, home of his brother-in-law, Mr Hutchinson, and wrote some of his poems here.

8 **Bromyard** Presumed birthplace of JOHN OF BROMYARD (fl1390), Dominican friar and author of *Summa Praedicantium*, Nuremberg, 1485.

9 **Canon Frome** HOPTON, SUSANNA (1627–1709), devotional writer, lived here.

10 **Clehonger** MATTHEWS, JOHN (1755–1826), physician and poet, lived here.

11 **Credenhill** TRAHERNE, THOMAS (c1638–74), writer and poet, rector 1657–67 (see **Hereford**).

12 **Croft** CROFT, HERBERT (1603–91), bishop of Hereford, lived at Croft Castle. He was author of controversial anti-Roman Catholic works.

13 **Goodrich** SWIFT, JONATHAN (1667–1745), satirist, presented to Goodrich a chalice which is still in use. Newhouse Farm was built in 1636 by his grandfather, the vicar, who was buried here in 1658.

14 **Hereford** DAVIES, JOHN (c1565–1618), poet and writing master, born here. Some of his works are of interest for their picture of his famous contemporaries.

GARRICK, DAVID (1717–79), actor and playwright, born here. His best known original plays, as opposed to his adaptations of the plays of Shakespeare and other dramatists, are *The Lying Valet*, 1741, and *Miss in her Teens*, 1747.

MAPES, or MAP, WALTER (c1137–c1209), clergyman and wit, born here. His most important work for its light on his times is *De Nugis Curialium* ('Of Courtiers' Trifles'), edited by M. R. James in 1915.

MARTIN, BASIL KINGSLEY (1897–1969), editor and author, born here. As editor of the *New Statesman and Nation* from 1931 until his death, he was an influential figure in literature and socialism. He died in Cairo.

NICHOLAS OF HEREFORD (fl1390), translator of the Old Testament, was chancellor of Hereford cathedral, 1391, and treasurer of Hereford 1397–1417.

ROGER OF HEREFORD (fl1178), writer on mathematics and judicial astrology, presumed to have been born here.

SMITH, MILES (d1624), bishop of Gloucester, born here. He was a translator of the Authorised Version of the Bible.

TRAHERNE, THOMAS (c1638–74), writer and poet, born here. His poetry was not discovered and published until the early twentieth century.

15 **Hope-under-Dinmore** CONINGSBY, SIR THOMAS (d1625) born at Hampton Court. Close friend of Sir Philip Sidney, he wrote a *Diary of the Siege of Rouen*, 1591, published by the Camden Society in 1847.

16 **Holme Lacy** SCUDAMORE, SIR JAMES, and SIR JOHN (1601–71), buried here. The latter was friend and patron of Milton and Thomas Fuller. The former, his father, appears as Scudamour in Book 4 of SPENSER's *Faërie Queene*.

17 **Kinsham** ARKWRIGHT, SIR JOHN (b1872), poet, lived at Kinsham Court.

18 **Laysters** 'WORDSWORTH's Stone' bears the carved initials of the poet and his wife.

19 **Ledbury** BARRETT, EDWARD MOULTON, father of Elizabeth Barrett Browning, buried here in 1857.

MASEFIELD, JOHN (1878–1966), poet laureate 1930 and novelist, born here. His first collected verse, *Salt Water Ballads*, appeared in 1902, and his best-selling *Collected Poems* in 1923. He also wrote plays, including *The Tragedy of Nan*, 1909, and novels, including *Sard Harker*, 1924, and *The Midnight Folk*, 1927.

TONSON, JACOB (c1656–1736), first publisher of *The Spectator*, 1712, lived here 1720–36 and is buried here.

WORDSWORTH, WILLIAM (1770–1850), wrote of the legend of Katherine of Ledbury (Katherine Audley, c1300) while staying at Brinsop Court (qv).

20 **Leintwardine** TARLETON, GENERAL SIR BANASTRE (1754–1833), writer on the American War of Independence, buried here.

21 **Leominster** HAKLUYT, RICHARD (c1552–1616), compiler of the *Voyages*, 1598–1600, spent his childhood at Eaton Hall.

22 **Little Hereford** ADAM OF EASTON, cardinal and theological writer, died here in 1397.

23 **Monkland** BAKER, SIR HENRY (1821–77), hymn writer and editor of *Hymns Ancient and Modern*, 1861, vicar 1851–77 and buried here.

24 **Monnington** GLENDOWER, OWEN, died here c1416 and is thought to be buried here. He features in four of SHAKESPEARE's plays.

25 **Orleton** POPE, ALEXANDER (1688–1744), poet and satirist, stayed at Orleton Court, home of his lifelong friend Martha Blount, to whom he dedicated his *Epistle on Women*, 1735. It was also the home of THOMAS BLOUNT (1619–79), miscellaneous writer, who died here.

26 **Richard's Castle** Part of MILTON's *Comus* is set in the woods between here and Overton, Shropshire.

27 **Ross** KYRLE, JOHN (1637–1724), benefactor, lived here: the 'Man of Ross' eulogised by Pope in 1732. The Kyrle Society was founded in his memory in 1877.

NEWTON, JOHN (1622–78) born here. He was the author of numerous school textbooks on arithmetic, astronomy and geometry.

PRICHARD, JAMES (1786–1848) born here. He issued many works in his own field of physics and ethnology.

REID, THOMAS MAYNE (1818–83), Irish-born author of adventure stories, spent his last years in Ross.

28 Upton Bishop HAVERGAL, FRANCIS TEBBS (1829–90), author, prebendary of Hereford 1877–90, lived here. He published *Fasti Herefordenses*, 1869, and *Herefordshire Words and Phrases*, 1887.

29 Vowchurch VAUGHAN, ROWLAND (fl1629–58), Welsh author of devotional works and verse, lived here.

30 Whitbourne GODWIN, FRANCIS (1562–1633), bishop of Hereford and author of *Man in the Moone*, 1638, buried here.

31 Whitfield CLIVE, MRS CAROLINE ARCHER (1801–73), author and poet, died here.

32 Yazor PRICE, SIR UVEDALE (1747–1829), writer, born and died at Foxley Hall. His writings on 'the picturesque' were considered by Sir Walter Scott to have 'converted the age to his views'.

Worcestershire (*Maps 9 & 10*)

1 **Abberley** WALSH, WILLIAM (1663–1708), poet, critic and friend of Pope, born here. His works include *Dialogue Concerning Women*, 1691, for which Dryden wrote the preface, and *Poems*, 1716. His biography was written by Dr Johnson.

2 **Arley Regis** LAYAMON (fl1200), poetical historian, lived here during his priesthood. His epic poem *Brut d'Angleterre*, based on the *Roman de Brut* of Robert Wace, was the first major poem in Middle English.

3 **Bewdley** Tickenhall Manor was the home of the Sidney family. MARY SIDNEY, COUNTESS OF PEMBROKE (c1555–1621), was born here; she revised and edited *Arcadia*, the pastoral romance which her brother SIR PHILIP SIDNEY wrote for her amusement.

4 **Bredon Hill** The setting of A. E. HOUSMAN's poem 'In Summertime on Bredon' in *A Shropshire Lad*, 1896.

5 **Broadway** PHILLIPPS, SIR THOMAS (1792–1872), bibliophile, lived at Middle Hill House until 1862. He established a private printing press here and produced bibliographical works.

6 **Bromsgrove** HOUSMAN, LAURENCE (1865–1959), novelist and dramatist, born here. His works include the *Little Plays of St Francis*, 1922, and the once-banned plays about Queen Victoria, later published as *Victoria Regina*. He and his brother, A. E. HOUSMAN, attended Bromsgrove School (see **Fockbury**).

7 **Earl's Croome** BUTLER, SAMUEL (1612–80), author of *Hudibras*, was secretary to a Mr Jeffreys in his youth (see **Strensham**).

8 **Evesham** AVERY, HAROLD (1867–1943), boys' novelist, lived at Evesham for much of his life, and died here (see **Redditch**).

9 **Fockbury** HOUSMAN, ALFRED EDWARD (1859–1936), poet and classical scholar, born at Valley House, now called 'Housmans'. *A Shropshire Lad*, 1896, one of the most consistently sold volumes of English poetry, was rejected for commercial publication and Housman paid for it himself.

10 **Great Malvern** LANGLAND, WILLIAM (c1331–c1400), author of *The Vision of Piers the Plowman*, is believed to have been a monk of Malvern Priory.
ROGET, PETER (1779–1869), compiler of the *Thesaurus of English Words and Phrases*, 1852, died at West Malvern and is buried there.
TYTLER, PATRICK FRASER (1791–1849), historian and biographer, died here.

11 **Hagley** LYTTELTON, GEORGE, 1ST BARON LYTTELTON (1709–73), poet and statesman, born here. His works include *Monody*, 1747, written on the death of his wife, *Dialogues of the Dead*, 1760, and a *History of Henry II*, 1767–71. He is included in Dr Johnson's *Lives of the Poets*.

12 **Hampton Lovett** Pakington, Sir John (1671–1727), baronet and believed to be the original of ADDISON's Sir Roger de Coverley, is buried here.

13 **Halesowen** SHENSTONE, WILLIAM (1714–63), poet, born and lived here. His finest works are *The Schoolmistress*, 1742, and the four-part *Pastoral Ballad*, 1755.
YOUNG, FRANCIS BRETT (1884–1954), novelist and poet, born here. He gained wide recognition with *Deep Sea*, 1914, *Portrait of Clare*, 1927, *My Brother Jonathan*, 1928, and *The House under the Water*, 1932, and later again with *Portrait of a Village*, 1951.

14 **Hawford** PEARSON, HESKETH (1887–1964), author, born here. He was biographer of Oscar Wilde, Gilbert and Sullivan, Sydney Smith and many others, and collaborated with Hugh Kingsmill in lighthearted travel books.

15 **Hindlip** HABINGTON, WILLIAM (1605–54), poet, born here. Author of *Castara*, 1634, which immortalised Lucy Herbert. Other works include *The Queene of Aragon, a Tragi-comedie*, 1640.

16 **Kidderminster** BEDE, CUTHBERT (pseudonym of Edward Bradley, 1827–89), novelist, born here. His most successful work was his first novel, *The Adventures of Mr Verdant Green, an Oxford Freshman*, 1853–56.

17 **Lulsley** ALLIES, JABEZ (1787–1856) born here: author of *Antiquities and Folklore of Worcestershire*.

18 **Martley** CALVERLEY, CHARLES STUART (1831–84), born here. Regarded as 'the prince of parodists', he published his *Verses and Translations* in 1862, and *Fly Leaves* in 1872.

19 **Redditch** AVERY, HAROLD (1867–1943), boys' novelist, born here. He made his name in this field with *The Triple Alliance*, serialised in the *Boy's Own Paper* in 1896.

20 **Stanford** SHERWOOD, MRS MARY MARTHA (1775–1851), children's author, born here. She published *The Infant's Progress*, 1814, *Little Henry and his Bearer*, 1815, and a highly regarded family history, *The History of the Fairchild Family*, 1818–47.

21 **Stoulton** GARBET, SAMUEL (d c1751), historian, buried here.

22 **Stourbridge** MOSS, THOMAS (c1740–1808), poet, died here.
WOOD-SEYS, ROLAND, the novelist 'Paul Cushing', born here 1854. His books include *A Woman with a Secret*, 1885, and *The Shepherdess of Treva*, 1895.

23 **Strensham** BUTLER, SAMUEL (1612–80), satirist, born here. His *Hudibras*, ridiculing the Puritans, was published in parts, 1663, 1664 and 1678.

24 **Worcester** DOUGLAS, LORD ALFRED (1870–1945), poet and friend of Oscar Wilde, born at Ham Hill. He published several volumes of verse and two books on Wilde.
NECKAM, ALEXANDER (1157–1217), buried here. He was a chronicler, grammarian and author of *De Naturis Rerum*.
SHERWOOD, MRS MARY MARTHA (1775–1851), children's author, lived here from 1816 (see **Stanford**).
WOOD, MRS HENRY (1814–87), novelist, born here. Her famous *East Lynne* appeared in 1861.
Anne, the second wife of IZAAK WALTON, is buried at Worcester.

Gloucestershire (*Maps 9 & 10*)

1 Amberley CRAIK, MRS DINAH MARIA MULOCK (1826–87), novelist, wrote most of *John Halifax, Gentleman*, 1857, while living at Rose Cottage.

2 Bibury HYNE, CHARLES JOHN CUTCLIFFE WRIGHT (1865–1944), novelist, born here. He wrote a series of books around his character Captain Kettle.

3 Bourton-on-the-Hill OVERBURY, SIR THOMAS (1581–1613), poet, lived here.

4 Bourton-on-the-Water COLLINS, JOHN CHURTON (1848–1908), critic and editor of the English classics, born here. His works include *Studies in Shakespeare*, 1904, and *Studies in Poetry and Criticism*, 1905.

FOSTER, JOHN (1770–1843), essayist, lived here for a time.

5 Bristol ALLIES, THOMAS (1813–1903), theologian, born here. His *Formation of Christendom* appeared 1865–69.

BEDDOES, THOMAS LOVELL (1803–49), poet and author, born at 3 Rodney Place, Clifton. His first success was *The Bride's Tragedy*, 1822.

BROWN, THOMAS EDWARD (1830–97), Manx poet, was master at Clifton College 1864–93.

CHATTERTON, THOMAS (1752–70), poet, born and lived beside the church of St Mary Redcliffe. In 1770, after four months of penury in London he took poison. His Rowley poems, purporting to be by a medieval monk Thomas Rowley, briefly deceived the literary world but gained him a place in the history of the Romantic Revival.

COOMBE, WILLIAM (1741–1823), miscellaneous writer, born here. He is best remembered as the author of the Dr Syntax tours.

CONWAY, HUGH (pseudonym of Frederick John Fargus, 1847–85), novelist, lived here from 1868.

COTTLE, JOSEPH (1770–1853), poet and bookseller, lived here 1791–99. The first to publish Southey, Coleridge and Wordsworth, he wrote about his close association with the Lake Poets in his *Early Recollections*, 1837. Coleridge and Wordsworth frequently stayed at his home in the High Street.

DEFOE, DANIEL (c1660–1731), met the sailor Alexander Selkirk in Bristol around 1709, and based *Robinson Crusoe* on Selkirk's yarns.

EDWARDS, AMELIA ANN BLANFORD (1831–92), novelist, lived here towards the end of her life.

GREENWELL, DORA (1821–82), poet and writer, died at Clifton.

LEE, HARRIET (1757–1851), novelist, died at Clifton.

LOCKE, WILLIAM (1863–1930), novelist, was a master at Clifton College 1890–97.

MARRIOTT, CHARLES (1811–58), theological writer, born here. Editor with Pusey and Keble of *The Library of the Fathers*, *The Literary Churchman*, and other works.

MARSHALL, EMMA (d1899), children's author, lived at Clifton.

MORE, HANNAH (1745–1833), dramatist and religious author, born at Stapleton; her father was the schoolmaster there. She and her sisters ran a boarding school in Trinity Street, Bristol, c1757–68. *The Search after Happiness*, 1773, and *The Inflexible Captive*, 1774,

were among her plays, and she also wrote the popular novel *Coelebs in Search of a Wife*, 1809.

PENROSE, THOMAS (1742–79), poet, died in Bristol and is buried at Clifton.

PORTER, JANE (1776–1850), novelist, lived in Bristol for a time.

ROBINSON, MARY (1758–1800), actress, author and poet, born here. Known as 'Perdita', she lived by miscellaneous writing after leaving the stage through illness. Her work was popular, partly through her association with the Prince Regent, but she died in poverty.

ROSENBERG, ISAAC (1890–1918), poet, born here. Most of his life was spent in the East End of London, where his poems were obscurely published. He was one of the major poets of World War I and was killed in France.

SAVAGE, RICHARD (c1697–1743), poet, died in prison here.

SOUTHEY, ROBERT (1774–1843), poet laureate 1813, and biographer, born at 9 Wine Street. His *Thalaba* appeared in 1801, *A Vision of Judgement* in 1821, and his lives of Nelson, Wesley and Bunyan in 1813, 1820 and 1830.

SYMONDS, JOHN ADDINGTON (1840–93), poet and critic, born here. He published many studies of literary and historical figures and notable translations from the Italian.

TROLLOPE, FRANCES, *née* Milton (1780–1863), novelist and travel writer, born at Stapleton. The mother of Anthony Trollope, she published over a hundred works, including *Domestic Manners of the Americans*, 1832, *Paris and the Parisians*, etc.

WRAXALL, SIR NATHANIEL (1751–1831), historian, born here. He published works on the royal houses of Europe, but is best known for *Historical Memoirs of My Own Time, 1772–84*, 1815.

YEARSLEY, ANN (1756–1806), poet, born and lived here. Known as 'Lactilla', or 'the Bristol Milkwoman', she published *Poems on Several Occasions*, 1784, and the verse tragedy *Earl Goodwin*, 1791.

6 Cam TYNDALE, WILLIAM (c1484–1536), translator of the Bible, possibly born here (but see **Slymbridge**).

7 Charlton Kings CRAIK, MRS DINAH MARIA MULOCK (1826–87), novelist, wrote part of *John Halifax, Gentleman* at Detmore House (see **Amberley**). Charlton Kings is her Longfield.

DOBELL, SYDNEY THOMPSON (1824–74), poet, died at Barton End House.

8 Cheltenham BAYLY, THOMAS HAYNES (1797–1839), dramatist and song writer, buried here.

BRADLEY, ANDREW CECIL (1851–1935), critic, born here. His most notable work is *Shakespearian Tragedy*, 1904, a collection of his lectures as Professor of Poetry at Oxford.

DOBELL, SYDNEY THOMPSON (1824–74), poet, lived here most of his life (see **Charlton Kings**).

FLECKER, HERMAN JAMES ELROY (1884–1915), poet and playwright, buried here.

PAYN, JAMES (1830–98), novelist, born here. He published about sixty novels, among them *The Best of Husbands*, *By Proxy* and *Thicker than Water*.

TURNER, CHARLES TENNYSON (1808–79), poet and elder brother of Alfred, Lord Tennyson, died and buried here.

9 Cherrington TRAPP, JOSEPH (1679–1747), poet, born here. He is known chiefly for his blank verse rendering of Virgil, 1735.

10 Coleford HOWITT, MARY (1799–1888), author, born here. She produced many works, including *Wonderful Stories for Children*, 1846, some of her works being written in collaboration with her husband, William Howitt.

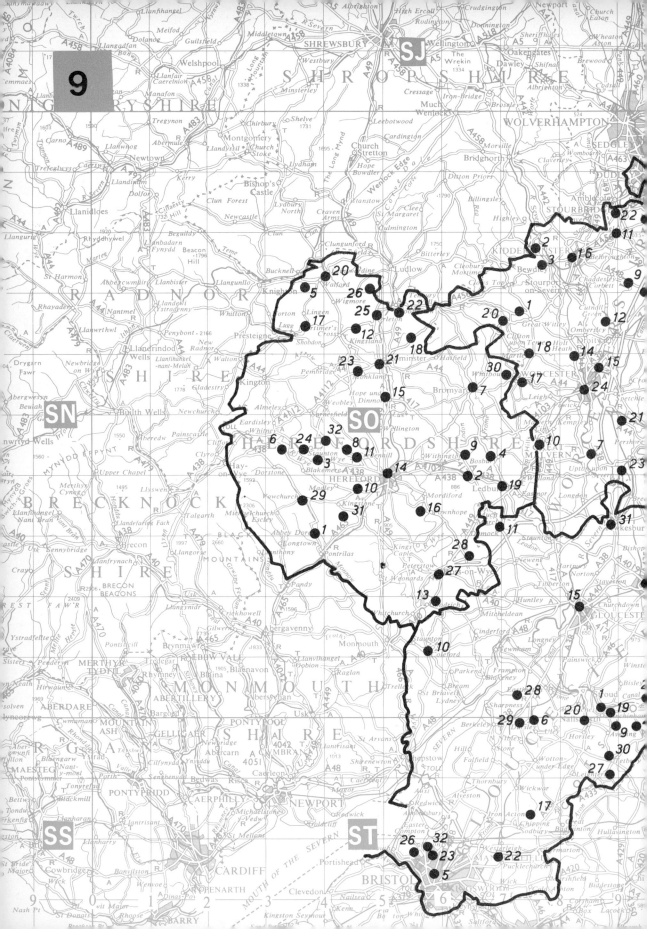

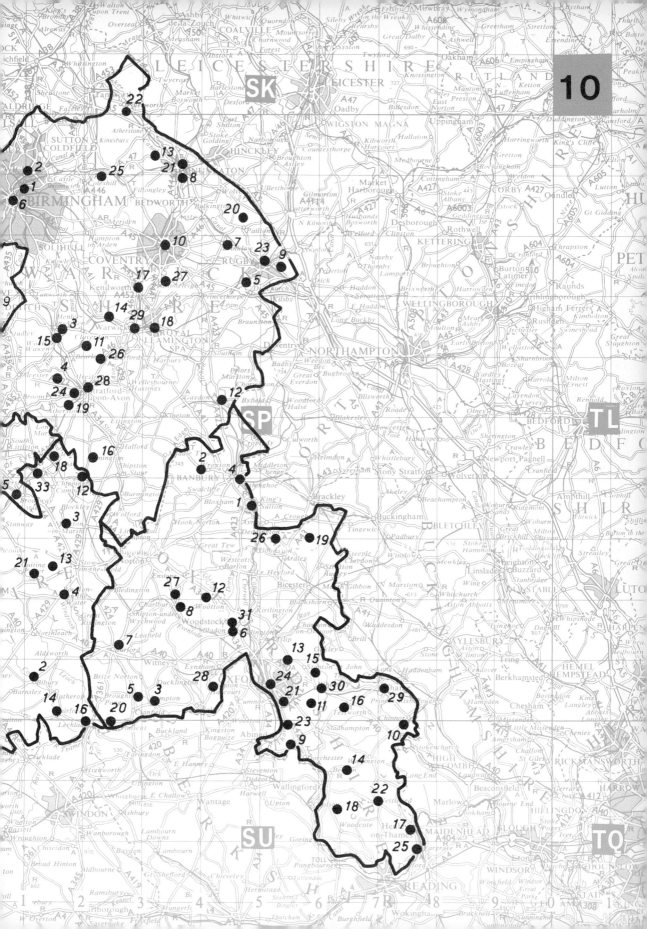

11 Dymock FROST, ROBERT (1875–1963), American poet, lived here for a time between 1912 and 1915.

12 Ebrington FORTESCUE, SIR JOHN (c1394–c1476), the first English legal writer, buried here.

13 Eyford MILTON, JOHN (1608–74) wrote part of *Paradise Lost* in Eyford Park during a visit sometime between 1658 and 1664.

14 Fairford KEBLE, JOHN (1792–1866), clergyman and poet, born here. His principal work apart from hymns was *The Christian Year*, a briefly successful collection of sacred poems which he published anonymously in 1827.

15 Gloucester HARKER, LIZZIE (1863–1933), novelist, born here. Her books include *Miss Esperance and Mr Wycherley*, 1908, and its sequel *Mr Wycherley's Wards*, 1912.

HENLEY, WILLIAM ERNEST (1849–1903), poet and critic, born in Eastgate Street. Besides producing volumes of verse, including *For England's Sake*, 1900, he edited several leading periodicals and collaborated with Robert Louis Stevenson on such plays as *Deacon Brodie*, 1890.

TAYLOR, JOHN (1580–1653), 'the Water Poet', born here. He wrote many doggerel pieces, composed pageants for Lord Mayors' shows in London, and published works about his travels.

16 Lechlade ARKELL, REGINALD (1882–1959), miscellaneous writer, born here. His work ranged from lyrics for stage reviews to books on country themes.

17 Little Sodbury TYNDALE, WILLIAM (c1484–1536), tutor and chaplain at the manor house 1521–22, where he began his translation of the Bible (see **Cam** and **Slymbridge**).

18 Mickleton GRAVES, RICHARD (1715–1804), writer, born here. His prose and verse works included *Spiritual Quixote*, 1772.

SHENSTONE, WILLIAM (1714–63), poet, landscaped the garden of the manor. Utrecia Smith, buried here in 1744, is recalled in his work *Ophelia's Urn*.

19 Minchinhampton RICARDO, DAVID (1772–1823), political economist and author of *The Principles of Political Economy and Taxation*, 1817, lived and died at Gatcombe Park.

20 Nailsworth DAVIES, WILLIAM HENRY (1871–1940), author of *Autobiography of a Super-Tramp*, 1907, lived and died here.

21 Naunton BARKSDALE, CLEMENT (1609–87), author of *The Cotswold Muse*, was rector here until his death.

22 Pucklechurch DENNYS, JOHN (d1609), poet, is buried here.

23 Redland HOBHOUSE, JOHN CAM, 1ST BARON BROUGHTON (1786–1869), politician and writer, born here. He was a close friend of Byron, who dedicated the fourth canto of *Childe Harold* to him; his works include *Historical Illustrations of the Fourth Canto of Childe Harold*, 1818.

24 Rodmarton LYSONS, SAMUEL (1763–1819) and DANIEL (1762–1834), brothers and co-authors of topographical works, lived here.

25 Sapperton MASEFIELD, JOHN (1878–1967), poet laureate, lived for a time at Pinbury Park.

26 Shirehampton SAYCE, ARCHIBALD (1845–1933), philologist, born here. His works include *An Introduction to the Science of Language*, 1880.

27 Shipton Moyne OLDHAM, JOHN (1653–83), poet, born here. His *Satire Against Virtue* appeared in 1679.

28 Slymbridge TYNDALE, WILLIAM (c1484–1536), translator of the Bible, may have been born here (but see **Cam**).

29 Stinchcombe WILLIAMS, ISAAC (1802–65), author of religious poetry, lived here from 1848 until his death.

30 Tetbury WHYTE-MELVILLE, GEORGE JOHN (1821–78), poet and author, buried here.

31 Tewkesbury Nortonbury in MRS DINAH CRAIK's *John Halifax, Gentleman*.

CARTWRIGHT, WILLIAM (1611–43), dramatist, born at nearby Northway. His plays included *The Royal Slave*, first performed before Charles I at Oxford in 1636; his poems appeared as *Comedies and Poems*, 1651.

MOORE, JOHN CECIL (1907–67), country writer, born here. He wrote both fictional and factual works, including *Country Men*, 1934, *The Countryman's England*, 1939, and *The Waters under the Earth*, 1965.

32 Westbury-on-Trym SOUTHEY, ROBERT (1774–1843), poet laureate and biographer, lived here while lecturing in Bristol in 1795 to raise money for the 'Pantisocrats' (Coleridge, Southey and Robert Lovell) (see **Bristol**).

33 Weston-sub-Edge LATIMER, WILLIAM (c1460–1545), classical scholar, spent most of his life at Latimer's House.

Warwickshire (*Map 10*)

1 Ashted MOGRIDGE, GEORGE (1787–1854), children's author, born here. He used many pseudonyms, including Old Humphrey and Ephraim Holding, but became most widely read as Peter Parley, writing such tales as *Peter Parley's Tales about Christmas*, 1839, in the style of the American originator of the name, Griswold Goodrich (1793–1860).

2 Aston FARNOL, JOHN JEFFREY (1878–1952), author of historical romances, born here. His best known novel, *The Amateur Gentleman*, appeared in 1913.
PARKES, WILLIAM KINETON (1865–1938), novelist, born here. His *Hardware*, 1914, is based on Birmingham (Meltingham), and *The Money Hunt*, 1914, on Macclesfield, Derbyshire (Weaverton).

3 Beaudesert JAGO, RICHARD (1715–81), poet, born at the rectory. His works include *Edgehill, or the Rural Prospect Delineated and Moralised*, 1767.

4 Billesley It is thought that SHAKESPEARE's *As You Like It* was written while he was staying at Billesley Manor in 1600.

5 Bilton ADDISON, JOSEPH (1672–1719), essayist and statesman, lived at Bilton Hall in the last year of his life.

6 Birmingham DRINKWATER, JOHN (1882–1937), poet and dramatist, lived here from 1901 and was manager and producer of the Pilgrim Players, later the Birmingham Repertory Company.
FIELD, MICHAEL (pseudonym of Katharine Harris Bradley, 1848–1914), poet and dramatist, born here. She published many volumes of verse and plays in collaboration with her niece Edith Emma Cooper (1862–1913).
FREEMAN, EDWARD AUGUSTUS (1823–92), historian, born at Harborne. His works include a *History of the Norman Conquest*, 1867–79, a *Historical Geography of Europe*, 1881–82, and a *History of Sicily*, 1891–92. He died in Alicante.
HUTTON, WILLIAM (1723–1815), Birmingham topographer, buried at Ward End church.
LLOYD, CHARLES (1775–1839), poet, born here. He lived with Samuel Taylor Coleridge from 1796–97 and his poems were published in an edition of Coleridge's.
MARTINEAU, HARRIET (1802–76), author and traveller, buried here.
NADEN, CONSTANCE (1858–89), author and poet, born at Edgbaston. Her poems were published 1881 and 1887.
NEWMAN, JOHN HENRY, Cardinal (1801–90), theologian, poet and author, died here.
PEMBERTON, SIR MAX (1863–1950), journalist and novelist, born here. He wrote many successful adventure stories for adults and boys and founded the London School of Journalism in 1920.
PRIESTLEY, JOSEPH (1733–1804), scientist and author, lived here 1780–91.
ROHMER, SAX (pseudonym of Arthur Sarsfield Ward, 1886–1959), novelist, born here. He created the character of Fu Manchu and wrote many thrillers round this oriental villain.
SHORTHOUSE, JOSEPH HENRY (1834–1903), novelist, born in Birmingham and buried at Edgbaston church. He is best known for *John Inglesant*, 1881.

WINN, GODFREY HERBERT (1908–71), author and journalist, born at Edgbaston. From shortly before World War II until his death he was outstanding as a feature journalist.

7 Brinklow MALORY, SIR THOMAS (d1471), poet, is said to have written *Le Morte d'Arthur* while living at Newbold Revel.

8 Chilvers Coton ELIOT, GEORGE (pseudonym of Mary Ann Evans, 1819–80), novelist, born on the Arbury estate. *The Mill on the Floss* was published in 1860, *Silas Marner* in 1861 and *Middlemarch* in 1871–72. Chilvers Coton is her Shepperton, and Arbury Hall is Cheveral Manor of her 'Mr Gilfil's Love Story' in *Scenes of Clerical Life*, 1857.

9 Clifton CARTE, THOMAS (1686–1754), historian, born here. His *History of England* appeared 1747–55.
HARVEY, CHRISTOPHER (1597–1663), poet, buried here.

10 Coventry BRAY, CHARLES (1811–84), philosophical writer, lived here. His wife Caroline (1814–1905) was George Eliot's intimate friend and sister to SARAH HENNELL (1812–99), writer on theology, who also lived in Coventry.
BRAZIL, ANGELA (1868–1947), author of school stories, lived here for some years.
ELIOT, GEORGE (pseudonym of Mary Ann Evans, 1819–80), novelist, lived for some years with her father at Bird Grove, Foleshill Road.
HOLLAND, PHILEMON (1552–1637), translator of the classics, master at the Free School 1608–28 and buried in Coventry.
MARSTON, JOHN WESTLAND (1819–90), dramatist, born here. His *Hard Struggle*, 1858, was much admired by Charles Dickens. *Our Recent Actors* which he published in 1888, is a useful source book.
WANLEY, NATHANIEL (1634–80), compiler of *The Wonders of the Little World*, 1678, was vicar of Holy Trinity 1662–80.
WILLIAMS, ELMA MARY (1913–71), author, born here. She wrote many books about the animals she kept in her Valley of Animals in Montgomeryshire.

11 Edstone SOMERVILLE, WILLIAM (1675–1742), poet, lived here from 1705 until his death here. He is buried in the chapel of Wootton-Wawen.

12 Fenny Compton DUDLEY, SIR HENRY BATE (1745–1824), satirist and journalist, born here. He edited the *Morning Post* and also wrote for the stage.

13 Hartshill DRAYTON, MICHAEL (1563–1631), poet, born here. His major work is *Polyolbion*, 1622, a verse description of England's topography and antiquities.

14 Hatton PARR, SAMUEL (1747–1825), literary conversationalist and book collector, perpetual curate here from 1785 until his death.

15 Henley-in-Arden BELL, ROBERT STANLEY WARREN (1871–1921), boys' author, born here. Many of his magazine serials about Greyhouse and Claverdon schools later appeared as books; he had a successful comedy, *A Companion for George*, produced in London in 1921.

16 Ilmington OVERBURY, SIR THOMAS (1581–1613), poet, born at Compton Scorpion. His poem *A Wife, now the Widow of Sir T. Overbury* appeared in 1614 after his death in the Tower of London: he was poisoned by agents of Lady Essex, whose marriage he had opposed.

17 Kenilworth BUTLER, SAMUEL (1774–1839), scholar and bishop of Lichfield, born here. He edited Aeschylus, 1809–26, and published geographical works.
FIELD, MICHAEL (pseudonym of Edith Emma Cooper, 1862–1913), poet and dramatist, born here. She shared

the pseudonym with her aunt and collaborator, Katharine Harris Bradley (1846–1914).

18 **Leamington** CROWLEY, ALEISTER (Edward Alexander, 1875–1947), magician, poet and autobiographer, born here. Self styled 'the Beast', he wrote *The Confessions of Aleister Crowley*, describing his beliefs, and *The Book of the Law*, which he claimed was dictated by his 'guardian angel'.

19 **Luddington** It is thought that WILLIAM SHAKESPEARE was married to Anne Hathaway here in 1582.

20 **Monks Kirby** GOODYER, SIR HENRY (1571–1627), patron of many literary men, born here. He wrote verse himself and figures in poems by Donne and Drayton, the latter having been his page in youth.

21 **Nuneaton** The town is Milby in GEORGE ELIOT's novel *Scenes of Clerical Life*, 1857. Bulkington nearby is Ravelo in her *Silas Marner*, 1861.
HAVERGAL, FRANCES RIDLEY (1836–79), poet and hymn writer, born at Astley rectory. Her *Ministry of Song* appeared 1870 and her poetical works in 1884.

22 **Polesworth** COKAYNE, SIR ASTON (1608–84), poet, born here. He published also plays and translations from the Italian.

23 **Rugby** Rugby School is the setting of THOMAS HUGHES's novel *Tom Brown's Schooldays*, 1856. Notable literary men educated here include MATTHEW ARNOLD (1822–88), poet and critic; RUPERT BROOKE (1887–1915), poet; LEWIS CARROLL (1832–1898), poet and author; and WALTER SAVAGE LANDOR (1775–1864), poet and author. The celebrated headmaster THOMAS ARNOLD (1795–1842), father of Matthew Arnold, published several works including the first three volumes of a *History of Rome*, 1838–43.
BROOKE, RUPERT CHAWNOR (1887–1915), poet, born here. His best known poem, 'The Old Vicarage, Grantchester', appeared in 1912, but the collection *1914 and Other Poems*, containing the body of work by which he is known, appeared posthumously.
CAVE, EDWARD (1691–1754), printer and publisher, born here. Under the name Sylvanus Urban he founded and edited the *Gentleman's Magazine*, 1731–54.
MOULTRIE, JOHN (1799–1874), poet, died at Rugby rectory.

SIDGWICK, ETHEL (1877–1970), novelist, born here. Her works include *Promise*, 1910, *The Accolade*, 1915, and *The Bells of Shoreditch*, 1928.
WOODS, MARGARET (1856–1945), novelist, born here. Her books included *A Village Tragedy*, 1887, and she wrote poems and plays.

24 **Shottery** HATHAWAY, ANNE (1556–1623), wife of WILLIAM SHAKESPEARE, lived at Hewlands Farm, preserved and open to the public as Anne Hathaway's Cottage.

25 **Shustoke** DUGDALE, SIR WILLIAM (1605–86), historian, antiquarian and later King-of-Arms, born and died here.

26 **Snitterfield** JAGO, RICHARD (1715–81), poet, vicar from 1754 until his death and is buried here (see **Beaudesert**).

27 **Stoneleigh** LEIGH, CHANDOS, 1ST BARON LEIGH (1791–1850), poet and author, lived here.

28 **Stratford-upon-Avon** CORELLI, MARIE (pseudonym of Mary Mackay, 1854–1924), novelist, spent her later years here.
SHAKESPEARE, WILLIAM (1564–1616), poet and playwright, was born, lived and is buried here. The house which was almost undoubtedly his birthplace and where he lived until the mid-1580s is open to the public. The garden and foundations of New Place, his own house, bought in 1597 and demolished in the 18th century, may be seen. Hall's Croft, open to the public, was the home of his daughter Susanna and her husband Dr John Hall. The rebuilt Shakespeare Memorial Theatre, devoted to the production of his plays, was opened here in 1932.
TREVELYAN, GEORGE MACAULAY (1876–1962), historian, born here. His *History of England* and *English Social History* appeared in 1926 and 1942 respectively.

29 **Warwick** GREVILLE, SIR FULKE, 1ST BARON BROOKE (1554–1628), poet and intimate of Sir Philip Sidney (1554–86), born at Beauchamp Court. His life of Sidney was published in 1652.
LANDOR, WALTER SAVAGE (1775–1864), poet and writer, born at Ipsley Court. He first gained attention with the drama *Don Juan*, 1811; the famous *Imaginary Conversations* appeared 1824–29.

Oxfordshire (*Map 10*)

1 Adderbury WILMOT, JOHN, EARL OF ROCHESTER (1647–80), poet and satirist, lived here (see **Ditchley**).

2 Alkerton LYDYAT, THOMAS (1572–1646), chronologer and cosmographer, rector from 1612 until his death and is buried in the church.

3 Bampton PHILIPS, JOHN (1676–1709), poet, born here. His chief work is *Cyder*, 1708, in imitation of Virgil.

4 Banbury SPRIGG, JOSHUA (1618–84), churchman, born here: author of *Anglia Rediviva*, 1647.

5 Blackbourton EDGEWORTH, MARIA (1767–1849), novelist, born here. Her many novels, which helped to pioneer 'regional' fiction and the family saga form, include *Castle Rackrent*, 1800. She died in Ireland, at Edgeworthstown, Co Longford.

6 Bladon CHURCHILL, SIR WINSTON LEONARD SPENCER (1874–1965), statesman and author, buried here.

7 Burford FALKNER, JOHN MEADE (1858–1932), scholar and novelist, buried here.
HEYLIN, PETER (1600–62), theological author, born here. He wrote *Ecclesia Restaurata, or History of the Reformation*, 1661, and a life of Archbishop Laud, 1668.

8 Charlbury MARCHANT, BESSIE (1862–1941), girls' novelist, died here.

9 Clifton Hampden The Barley Mow inn of JEROME K. JEROME's *Three Men in a Boat* is situated here.

10 Crowell ELLWOOD, THOMAS (1639–1713), poet, born here. Author of the sacred poem *Davideis*, 1712; it was he who moved Milton to write *Paradise Regained*.

11 Cuddesdon STUBBS, WILLIAM (1825–1901), bishop of Oxford, historian, buried here.

12 Ditchley WILMOT, JOHN, EARL OF ROCHESTER (1647–80), poet and satirist, born here. A collection of his complete works was issued posthumously 1731–32.

13 Elsfield BUCHAN, JOHN, 1ST BARON TWEEDSMUIR (1875–1940), novelist, lived at the manor house. His ashes are buried in the churchyard.

14 Ewelme JEROME, JEROME KLAPKA (1859–1927), author, buried here.

15 Forest Hill MICKLE, WILLIAM JULIUS (1735–88), poet and translator, was married and buried here.
MILTON, JOHN (1608–74) married his first wife, Mary Powell, here in 1643.

16 Great Haseley LELAND, JOHN (c1506–52), antiquary, rector from 1542 until his death.

17 Henley HAMILTON, PATRICK ANTHONY WALTER (1904–62), playwright and novelist, lived in Hart Street from 1930–37.
LATTER, MARY (1725–77), poet and dramatist, born here. Her *Siege of Jerusalem by Titus Vespasian*, 1763, was accepted by Rich for production at Covent Garden, but he died before it could be presented.

18 Ipsden READE, CHARLES (1814–84), novelist, born here. His most famous work, *The Cloister and the Hearth*, was published in 1861, and *Peg Woffington* in 1853.

19 Juniper Hill THOMPSON, FLORA (1877–1947), author, born here. It is the 'Lark Rise' of her *Lark Rise to Candleford*, 1945, comprising her three autobiographical novels.

20 Kelmscott MORRIS, WILLIAM (1834–96), poet, artist and socialist, lived from 1871 at Kelmscott Manor and produced much of his most important work here. The house is open to the public. Morris and his wife are buried in Kelmscott churchyard.

21 Littlemore NEWMAN, JOHN HENRY (1801–90), cardinal, was vicar here, 1842–45, before entering the Roman Catholic Church.

22 Nettlebed FLEMING, PETER (1907–71), writer and traveller, lived and died at Merrimoles House.
WILLMOTT, ROBERT (1809–63), poet, writer and anthologist, spent his last years and died here.

23 Nuneham Courtenay WHITEHEAD, WILLIAM (1715–85), poet laureate, wrote many of the inscriptions on the statues, tablets and urns in the park.

24 Oxford A great many literary men and women, notable and obscure, have studied or taught in the university of Oxford down the centuries. Most of them appear elsewhere in this work, and we have limited the entries under Oxford mainly to other associations.
ALINGTON, ADRIAN RICHARD (1895–1958), novelist, born here. His publications include *Slowbags and Arethusa*, 1930.
ARNOLD, SIR EDWIN (1832–1904), poet and journalist: his ashes are buried in University College Chapel.
BURTON, ROBERT (1577–1640), author of *The Anatomy of Melancholy*, came to live in Oxford in 1599 and held the living of St Thomas's from 1616 until his death.
CARROLL, LEWIS (pseudonym of Charles Lutwidge Dodgson, 1832–98) spent most of his working life in Oxford.
CARTWRIGHT, WILLIAM (1611–43), dramatist, buried in the cathedral.
D'AVENANT, SIR WILLIAM (1606–68), poet laureate 1638, born here. He was author of many plays and was responsible for important theatrical innovations.
FLECKNOE, RICHARD (c1620–c1678), poet and playwright, born here. He is best remembered for Dryden's satire on him, *MacFlecknoe*.
GRAHAME, KENNETH (1859–1932), author of *The Wind in the Willows*, is buried in Holywell churchyard.
GREEN, JOHN RICHARD (1837–83), historian, born here. His best known work is a *Short History of the English People*, first published in 1874 and often revised and reprinted.
MEADE, E. T. (Elizabeth Thomasina Meade, 1854–1914), Irish-born girls' novelist, lived and died here.
MURRAY, SIR JAMES AUGUSTUS HENRY (1837–1915), first editor of the *Oxford Dictionary*, buried here.
PATER, WALTER (1839–94), critic, spent most of his life here from 1864.
PHILLIPS, STEPHEN (1864–1915), poet and playwright, born here. He was once highly celebrated for his verse play *Paolo and Francesca*, 1900.
PUSEY, EDWARD BOUVERIE (1800–82), Hebrew scholar, author and leader of the Oxford Movement, buried in Oxford cathedral.
RAWLINSON, RICHARD (1690–1755), topographer, buried in St John's Chapel.
WOOD, ANTHONY A (1632–95), antiquary and historian, born here and buried in Merton College outer chapel. His *Historia et Antiquitates Universitatis Oxoniensis* first appeared in 1674, and *Athenae Oxonienses*, a biographical work of Oxford writers and bishops, in 1691–92.

25 Shiplake TENNYSON, ALFRED, LORD (1809–92), poet laureate, was married here to Emily Sellwood in 1850.
GRANGER, JAMES (1723–76), biographer, vicar from c1745 until his death and is buried here.

26 Souldern The parsonage is the subject of WORDSWORTH's sonnet 'On an Oxfordshire Parsonage', written after he had stayed there.

27 Spelsbury WILMOT, JOHN, EARL OF ROCHESTER (1647–80), poet and satirist, buried here (see **Ditchley**).

28 Stanton Harcourt POPE, ALEXANDER (1688–1744) stayed in Pope's Tower 1716–18 and completed Book V of his translation of the *Iliad*.

29 Thame BASSE, WILLIAM (c1583–c1653), poet, born here. His 'Angler's Song' is quoted by Izaak Walton in *The Compleat Angler*, 1653.

CRAIGIE, SIR WILLIAM (1867–1957), editor in chief of the *Oxford Dictionary*, lived here.

30 Wheatley MICKLE, WILLIAM JULIUS (1735–88), poet, lived in Crown Road and wrote here the poem which suggested *Kenilworth* to Sir Walter Scott.

31 Woodstock CHURCHILL, SIR WINSTON LEONARD SPENCER (1874–1965), statesman and author, born at Blenheim Palace. His many writings ranged from articles for newspapers and such popular periodicals as the *Strand Magazine*, reminiscences of his adventures in the Boer War, a novel, *Savrola*, 1900, and other minor pieces, to the outstanding works of biography and history which include *Marlborough*, 1933–38, *The World Crisis*, 1923–29, the six-volume account of the Second World War, 1948–54, and *History of the English Speaking Peoples*, 1956–58.

Pembrokeshire (*Map 11*)

1 Henllys, nr Newport OWEN, GEORGE (1552–1613), topographer, born here. His *Description of Pembrokeshire* appeared in 1603.

2 Milford NORRIS, CHARLES (1779–1858), antiquary, settled here in 1800.

3 Rosemarket WILLIAMS, ANNA (1706–83), poet and close friend of Dr Johnson, born here. Johnson and Mrs Thrale contributed to her *Miscellanies in Prose and Verse*, 1766.

4 St Davids ASSER (d c909), chronicler, a monk of St Davids and perhaps bishop here.

FENTON, RICHARD (1746–1821), topographer, born here. He published a *Historical Tour through Pembrokeshire*, 1811.

GERALD THE WELSHMAN (Giraldus Cambrensis, c1147–c1223), writer and churchman, died here (see **Tenby**).

PHAER or PHAYER, THOMAS (c1510–60), translator, born here. He translated nine books of the *Aeneid* into English verse between 1555 and 1560, and wrote on law and medicine.

5 Tenby GERALD THE WELSHMAN (Giraldus Cambrensis, c1147–c1223), writer and churchman, born at Manorbier Castle and rector of the Celtic church at Tenby. His *Itinerary through Wales* was written in 1188.

NORRIS, CHARLES (1779–1858), antiquary, lived here from 1810 and died here.

RECCORDE or RECORDE, ROBERT (c1510–58), scholar, born here. He was the first to write in English on arithmetic, geometry and astronomy.

Cardiganshire (*Maps 11 & 12*)

1 **Aberystwyth** BEBB, WILLIAM AMBROSE (1894–1955), novelist and historian, born at Goginan nearby. He wrote books on travel in Europe and was an authority on Breton history.

EVANS, CARADOC (1878–1945), author, died here (see **Llandyssul**).

JONES, DAVID JAMES (1899–1968), poet and critic, spent most of his life here and taught Welsh literature at University College.

JONES, THOMAS GWYNN (1871–1949), poet and critic, lived most of his life at Bow Street nearby.

NICHOLAS, THOMAS EVAN (1879–1971), poet, lecturer and communist, lived much of his life here.

2 **Cardigan** PHILIPS, KATHERINE (1631–64), poet and translator known as 'the matchless Orinda', lived at Cardigan Priory after her marriage in 1647.

3 **Cwmrheidol** RHYS, JOHN (1840–1915), scholar and philologist, born here. He published *Studies in the Arthurian Legend*, 1891, *Celtic Folklore, Welsh and Manx*, 1901, and *Lectures on Welsh Philology*, 1877.

4 **Hafod Uchtyd** JOHNES, THOMAS (1748–1816), landowner and man of letters, settled here in 1783 and printed, on his private press, his own translations of mediaeval chronicles.

5 **Llanbadarn** GWILYM, DAFYDD AP (c1325–70), poet, born at Bro-Gynin and buried at the Abbey of Strata Florida.

6 **Llandyssul** EVANS, CARADOC (1878–1945), author, born at Pantycroy Farm and educated at Rhydlewis, the centre of the country described in his stories. Publications include a collection of short stories, *My People: Stories of the Peasantry of West Wales*, 1915, a novel, *Nothing to Pay*, and a play, *Taffy*, 1925.

7 **Lledrod** EVANS, EVAN (1731–88), poet, born here. He played an important part in promoting the literary and antiquarian renaissance in Wales in the 18th century, and published *Some Specimens of the Poetry of the Ancient Welsh Bards*, 1764.

8 **Ponterwyd** BORROW, GEORGE (1803–81), author, stayed at the present George Borrow Inn during his tour of Wales in the summer and autumn of 1854. The resulting book *Wild Wales* appeared in 1862.

9 **Traethsaith** RAINE, ALLEN (pseudonym of Anne Puddicombe, 1836–1908), novelist, spent her last years at Traethsaith and died here.

Carmarthenshire
(*Maps 11 & 12*)

1 **Carmarthen** MORRIS, SIR LEWIS (1833–1907), poet, born here. His is best remembered for *The Epic of Hades*, 1876–77.

STEELE, SIR RICHARD (1672–1729), essayist and dramatist, lived at Ty-Gwyn, Llangunnor, near Carmarthen, died at the Ivy Bush Inn, Carmarthen, and is buried at St Peter's church. His second wife, Mary Scurlock, the 'Prue' of his works, was a native of the county.

2 **Laugharne** THOMAS, DYLAN (1914–53), poet, lived at The Boathouse after 1945 and is buried in the church-yard. The Boathouse is preserved as a memorial. Laugh-arne has been identified with Llaregubb of his most famous work, *Under Milk Wood*.

THOMAS, EDWARD (1878–1917), poet, lived here for a time around 1911.

3 **Llandilo** DYER, JOHN (1701–58), author, born at Aberglasney House, Llangathen, near Llandilo. His *Grongar Hill*, 1727, derives its title from the hill rising above his birthplace.

TAYLOR, JEREMY (1613–67), bishop and author, lived 1650–60 at Golden Grove, the seat of Lord Carbery, and wrote here his manual of devotion, *The Golden Grove*, 1655. For a time he kept a school at Newtonhall.

4 **Llandingat** PRICHARD, RHYS (d1644), poet and author of *The Welshman's Candle*, vicar here from 1594–1614.

5 **Llanfair-ar-y-Bryn** WILLIAMS, WILLIAM or PANTYCELYN (1717–91), poet and hymn writer, born here. His hymns achieved great popularity and he was a leading spokesman for the Welsh Methodist revival. After 1748, he lived at his mother's home, Pantycelyn, by which name he became known.

6 **Llansawel** WILLIAMS, DAVID JOHN (1885–1970), short-story writer and autobiographer, born at Penrhiw. His series of character sketches of rural Carmarthenshire, *Hen Wynebau*, appeared in 1934, and *The Old Farmhouse*, 1961, describes his boyhood in Llansawel.

7 **Newcastle-Emlyn** RAINE, ALLEN (pseudonym of Anne Puddicombe, 1836–1908), novelist, born here. Her works include *Torn Sails*, 1898, *A Welsh Witch*, 1902, and *Hearts of Wales*, 1905.

8 **Pibwr Lwyd, nr Carmarthen** WILLIAMS, ELIEZER (1754–1820), cleric and author, born here. He published historical and genealogical works and poetry.

Glamorganshire
(*Maps 11 & 12*)

1 **Aberdare** LEWIS, ALUN (1915–44), poet, born at Cwmaman nearby. His publications include *Raiders Dawn*, 1941, and *The Last Inspection*, 1942.

2 **Cardiff** CRADOCK, WALTER (c1610–59), theological writer, was curate at St John's church.

ERBURY, WILLIAM (1604–54), theological controversialist, was incumbent of St Mary's 1623–38.

NOVELLO, IVOR (1893–1951), playwright and actor, born here. He is best remembered for his musical plays, *Glamorous Night*, 1935, *The Dancing Years*, 1939, etc.

SPRING, HOWARD (1889–1965), novelist, born here. *My Son, My Son*, 1938, and *Fame is the Spur*, 1940, were the most successful of his widely read books.

3 **Cowbridge** MORGANWG, IOLO (pseudonym of Edward Williams, 1746–1826), poet and antiquary, kept a bookseller's shop here, 1797.

4 **Eglwysilan, nr Caerphilly** WILLIAMS, DAVID (1738–1816), writer and pamphleteer, born here. He was the founder of the Royal Literary Fund, 1788, he published numerous treatises on religious and educational questions.

5 **Llandaff** GEOFFREY OF MONMOUTH (c1090–1155), chronicler, archdeacon of Llandaff c1140 and died here. His *Historia Britonum*, with its stories of Arthur, Cymbeline, Lear and others, has been a profound literary influence down the ages.

6 **Mountain Ash** KEATING, JOSEPH (1871–1934), novelist, born here. His books, based on his experience as a miner, include *Son of Judith*, 1902, and *Maurice*, 1905.

7 **Swansea** BOWDLER, THOMAS (1754–1825), expurgator of Shakespeare, died at Rhyddings and is buried near Mumbles Head.

HAVERGAL, FRANCES RIDLEY (1836–79), hymn writer and poet, died nearby.

SAVAGE, RICHARD (1697–1743), poet, lived in Barber's Court, off Orchard Street, 1739–40.

THOMAS, DYLAN (1914–53), poet, born and spent his youth at 5 Cwmdonkin Drive. Much of his inspiration was derived from Swansea, and most of the poems were written during his 'Swansea period', 1930–34. The play *Under Milk Wood*, written for radio, was first broadcast in 1953.

8 **Tonypandy** JONES, LEWIS (1897–1939), miner–author, born nearby. Among his books is *Cwmardy. The Story of a Welsh Mining Village*, 1937.

Monmouthshire (*Map 12*)

1 **Caerleon** MACHEN, ARTHUR (1863–1947), novelist and essayist, born here. Many of his stories deal with the supernatural and include *The Great God Pan*, 1894, *The House of Souls*, 1906, and *The Terror*, 1917. He created the legend of 'the Angel of Mons' in his book *The Bowmen and other Legends of the War*, 1915.

TENNYSON, ALFRED, LORD (1809–92), poet laureate, stayed here while studying Arthurian legends for his *Idylls of the King*, the first part of which appeared in 1859. Caerleon is recognisable in *Geraint and Enid*.

2 **Coldbrook, nr Abergavenny** WILLIAMS, SIR CHARLES HANBURY (1708–59), political poet, born here. A collected edition of his writings appeared in 1822.

3 **Llanthony** LANDOR, WALTER SAVAGE (1775–1864), poet and writer, bought the estate of Llanthony Abbey in 1809, moved later to the village inn, and left the neighbourhood in 1814.

4 **Newport** DAVIES, WILLIAM HENRY (1871–1940), author and poet, born in Portland Street. His *Autobiography of a Super-Tramp* appeared 1907, and his *Collected Poems*, 1943.

5 **Penrhos** WILLIAMS, SIR ROGER (c1540–95), soldier and military writer, lived here.

6 **Raglan** SOMERSET, EDWARD, 2ND MARQUIS OF RAGLAN (1601–67), writer, lived at Raglan castle.

7 **Tintern Parva** WORDSWORTH, WILLIAM (1770–1850), poet laureate, visited Tintern Parva with his sister in 1798, and *Lines Composed a few Miles above Tintern Abbey* appeared soon after.

8 **Trelleck** RUSSELL, BERTRAND ARTHUR WILLIAM, 3RD EARL RUSSELL (1872–1970), philosopher and author, born here. He wrote many books on philosophy, education, morals and other subjects, including the *Principia Mathematica*, 1910–13, in collaboration with A. M. Whitehead.

9 **Usk** ADAM DE USK (1352–1430), lawyer and writer, born here. His Latin chronicle of English history is a valuable source book.

SOMERSET, FITZROY RICHARD, 4TH BARON RAGLAN (1885–1965), scholar and writer, lived at Cefu Tilla Court.

TRELAWNY, EDWARD JOHN (1792–1881), biographer, lived here while writing his *Records of Shelley, Byron, and the Author*, 1858, and other works.

WALLACE, ALFRED RUSSELL (1823–1913), naturalist and writer, born here. His publications include *Darwinism*, 1889, and *Man's Place in the Universe*, 1903.

10 **Ynysddu, nr Newport** THOMAS, WILLIAM (1832–78), poet, born here. Known as the Welsh Browning, he wrote philosophical poems, mostly in Welsh.

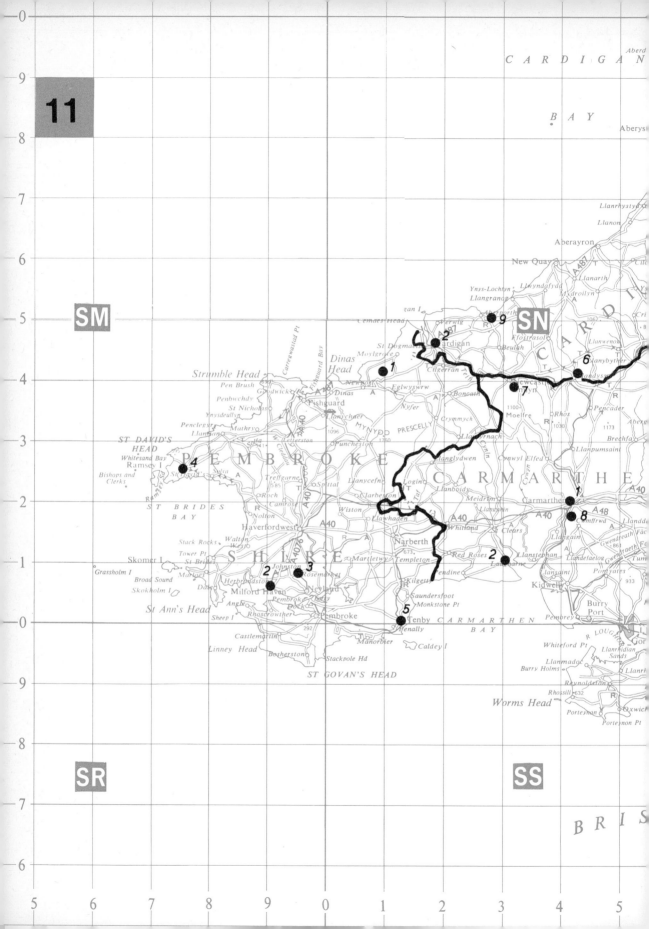

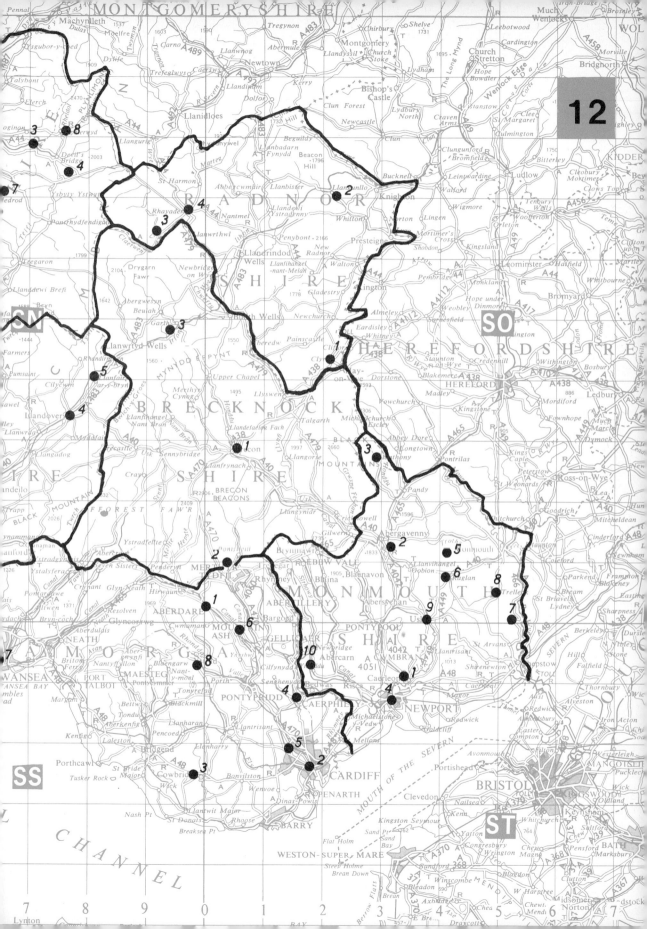

Brecknockshire (*Map 12*)

1 **Brecon** BULL, GEORGE (1634–1710), theological writer, died here.

VAUGHAN, HENRY (1621–95), poet, born at Newton Farm, Llansantffraed, and buried at Llansantffraed. Known as the 'Silurist' poet after the name of the ancient inhabitants of Brecknockshire. His best known work, the sacred poems *Silex Scintillans*, appeared in two parts, 1650 and 1655.

2 **Cefn Coed y Cymer** WILLIAMS, DAFFYD RHYS (1851–1931), author and journalist, born here.

3 **Llangammarch** HOWELL, JAMES (c1594–1666), author and letter writer, born here. His chief work is *Familar Letters*, 1655.

Radnorshire (*Map 12*)

1 Clyro, nr Hay-on-Wye KILVERT, ROBERT FRANCIS (1840–79), diarist, was curate here from 1864–76. The surrounding area is known as Kilvert Country, and much of his time here is covered by his celebrated diary, published 1938–40.

2 Llangunllo DAVIES, JONATHAN (1859–1932), traveller and folklorist, born here. His chief works are *Adventures in the Land of the Giants: a Patagonian Tale*, 1892, *Western Australia: its History and Progress*, 1902, and *Folk-lore of West and Mid-Wales*, 1911.

3 Nantgwyllt SHELLEY, PERCY BYSSHE (1792–1822), poet, lived here with his wife for a time from 1812.

4 Rhayader KILVERT, ROBERT FRANCIS (1840–79), diarist, was vicar of St Harmon's, 1876 (see **Clyro**).

SHELLEY, PERCY BYSSHE (1792–1822), poet, stayed at Cwm Elan nearby in 1811.

Anglesey (*Map 13*)

1 **Llandrygarn** MORRIS-JONES, SIR JOHN (1864–1929), poet and critic born here. He was professor of Welsh at University College of North Wales, Bangor, and wrote the standard work of Welsh Grammar, 1913.

2 **Llanfihangel Tre'r Beirdd** MORRIS, LEWIS (1701–65), poet and antiquary, born here. Also born here were his brothers, RICHARD (1703–79), founder of the Cymmrodorion Society, and WILLIAM (1705–63), antiquary, botanist and letter writer.

3 **Moelfre** OWEN, GORONWY (1723–69), poet, born at Rhos-fawr. He was curate of Llanfair-Mathafarn-Eithaf from 1746.

Caernarvonshire (*Map 13*)

1 **Aber** ROWLANDS, ROBERT JOHN (d1967), author and editor, lived here.

2 **Bangor** BEBB, WILLIAM AMBROSE (1894–1955), author, was lecturer at Bangor Training College.

JENKINS, ROBERT THOMAS (1881–1969), historian, was lecturer at University College of North Wales.

3 **Bethel** GRUFFYDD, WILLIAM JOHN (1881–1954), literary scholar, lived here.

4 **Bodvel** THRALE, MRS HESTER LYNCH (1741–1821), poet, born here. Her *Anecdotes of Dr Johnson* appeared in 1786, and four years later she returned to Wales and built Brynbella on the river Clwyd, where she lived until 1809.

5 **Caernarvon** GRUFFYDD, WILLIAM JOHN (1881–1954), scholar and literary figure, died here.

ROWLAND, ROBERT DAVID (c1853–1944), poet, editor and Methodist minister, lived here.

6 **Llanberis** HUGHES, THOMAS ROWLAND (1903–49), novelist and national poet, lived here.

7 **Llanllyfni** JONES, ALICE GRAY (1852–1943), author of Welsh books for children, lived here.

8 **Nantmor** GRIFFITH, RICHARD (1861–1947), bard and journalist, lived here.

9 **Pwllheli** JONES, ALBERT EVANS (1895–1970), national poet, playwright and actor, lived here.

JONES, THOMAS OWEN (1875–1942), short story writer, playwright and actor, lived here.

OWEN, JOHN (c1560–1622), epigrammist, born at Llanarmon. His Latin *Epigrammata* appeared 1606–13.

10 **Talyfan** EDWARDS, HUW THOMAS (1893–1970), poet, author and trade union leader, born in this district. His publications include *It Was My Privilege*, 1957.

11 **Talysarn** OWAIN, O LLEN (1878–1956), journalist and author, lived here.

PARRY, ROBERT WILLIAMS (1884–1956), poet, born here. One of the chief concerns of his work was the poet's place in modern society.

12 **Tremadoc** LAWRENCE, THOMAS EDWARD (1885–1935), 'Lawrence of Arabia', born at Gorphwysfa. His classic *Seven Pillars of Wisdom* appeared in 1926.

SHELLEY, PERCY BYSSHE (1792–1822), poet, lived here in 1812.

13 **Wybrnant, nr Penmachno** MORGAN, WILLIAM (c1545–1604), born here: translated the Bible into Welsh, 1588.

Merionethshire (*Map 13*)

1 **Aberdovey** ONIONS, OLIVER (1873–1961), novelist, lived nearby.

2 **Bala** EDWARDS, ROGER (1811–86), poet and writer, born here. He published *Canauon Roger Edwards*, 1855, and *Y Tri Brawd*, 1866.

3 **Blaenau Ffestiniog** POWYS, JOHN COWPER (1872–1963), poet and novelist, lived from 1955 at 1, Waterloo.

4 **Corwen** POWYS, JOHN COWPER (1872–1963), poet and novelist, lived here 1935–55.

5 **Cynfal** LLWYD, MORGAN (1619–59), minister and writer, born here. His most significant work is the *Book of the Three Birds*, 1653.

6 **Penrhyndeudraeth** RUSSELL, BERTRAND ARTHUR WILLIAM, 3RD EARL RUSSELL (1872–1970), philosopher and writer, lived at Plas Penrhyn from 1954 and died here.

Denbighshire (*Map 14*)

1 **Betws yn Rhos** JONES, THOMAS GWYNN (1871–1949), poet, novelist, biographer and scholar, lived here. He translated works into Welsh from several languages.

2 **Denbigh** BROUGHTON, RHODA (1840–1920), novelist, born nearby. Her first and best works were *Not Wisely But Too Well* and *Cometh Up as a Flower*, both published in 1867.
STANLEY, SIR HENRY MORTON (1841–1904), explorer and author, born within the castle precincts. His books of travel in Africa, America and Asia include *How I Found Livingstone*, 1872, and *In Darkest Africa*, 1890.

3 **Llanarmon-Dyffryn-Ceiriog** HUGHES, JOHN CEIRIOG (1832–87), most famous of the Welsh lyric poets, born here. His collected works were published in 1888. He was station master at Llanidloes and later manager of the Van Railway. He died at Caersws and is buried in Llanwnog church.

4 **Llanefydd** EDWARDS, THOMAS (1739–1810), poet, born here. His collected poems were published in 1790.

5 **Llanfair Talhaearn** JONES, JOHN (1810–69), architect and poet, born at the Harp Inn and died here. His works in Welsh appeared in 1849 and 1863.

6 **Llanferres** DAVIES, JOHN (1567–1644), scholar of the Welsh language, born here. Publications include *Antiquae Linguae Britannicae Rudimenta*, 1621, and *Dictionarium Duplex*, 1632.

7 **Llangollen** MORYS, HUW (1622–1709), poet, born here. A collection of his poems was published in 1823.

8 **Llanrhaeadr-ym-Mochnant** DAVIES, WALTER (1761–1849), poet and literary critic, lived here from 1837 until his death.

9 **Llansannan** SALESBURY, WILLIAM (c1520–c1584), author, lexicographer, translator, born here. Chief translator of the first Welsh New Testament, 1567.

10 **Llansilin** MORYS, HUW (1622–1709), poet, lived here from about 1647 (see **Llangollen**).

11 **Llanwrst** SALESBURY, WILLIAM (c1520–c1584), author, lexicographer, translator, spent most of his life at Plas Isa (see **Llansannan**).

12 **Nantglyn** DAVIES, ROBERT (1769–1835), poet and grammarian, born here. His poems, of which the best known is the satire 'Ewyllys Adda', were published in 1798 and 1803.
PUGHE, WILLIAM OWEN (1759–1835), poet, lexicographer and editor, lived here and is buried here.

13 **Wrexham** APPERLEY, CHARLES (1779–1843), the sporting writer 'Nimrod', born at Plas Gronow nearby. Author of *The Chase, the Road and the Turf*, 1837, and *The Life of a Sportsman*, 1842.
WARREN, SAMUEL (1807–77), novelist, born here. His most successful works were *Passages from the Diary of a Late Physician*, 1832–37, and *Ten Thousand a Year*, 1839.

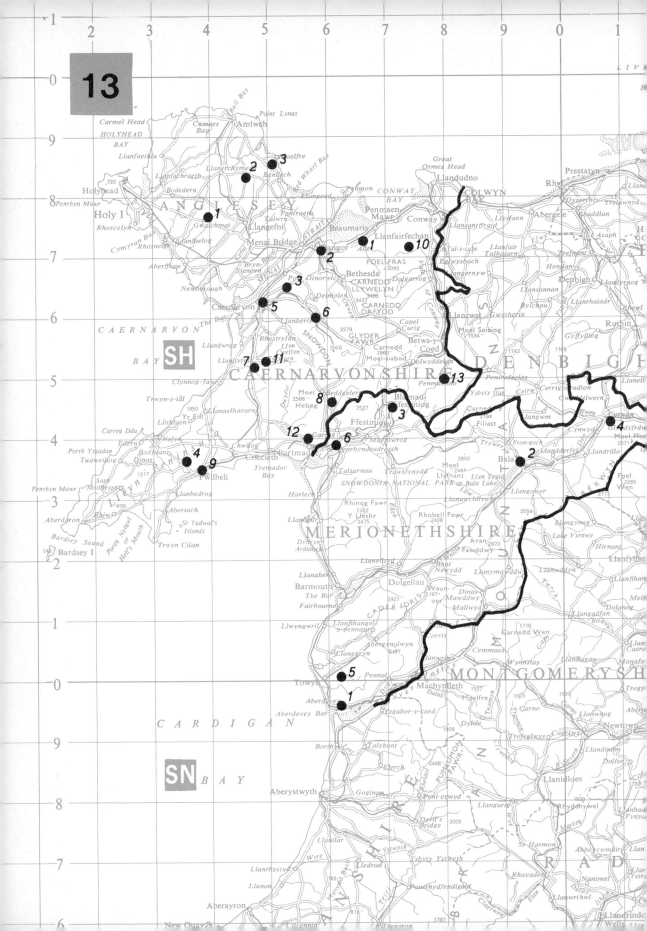

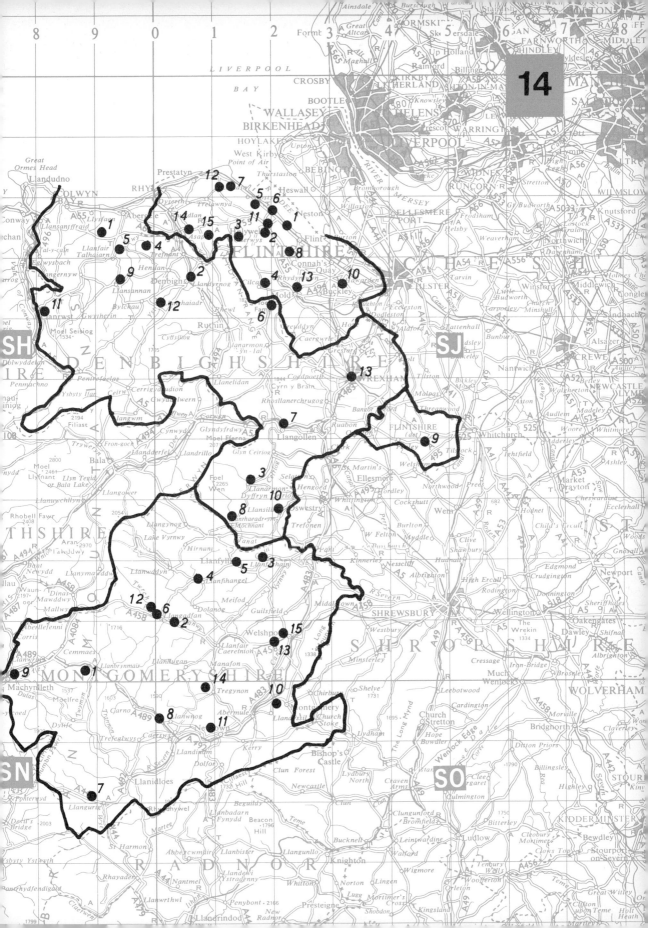

Flintshire (*Map 14*)

1 **Bagillt** SALISBURY, ENOCH ROBERT GIBBON (1819–90), book collector and writer, born here. Published *Border Counties Worthies*, 1880.

2 **Brynford** STANLEY, SIR HENRY MORTON (1841–1904), explorer and author, was assistant at a school here c1864.

3 **Caerwys** EDWARDS, WILLIAM (1790–1855), poet, born here. He published *Cell Callestr*, 1815.

LLWYD, ANGHARAD (1780–1866), antiquary, born here. Her publications include *The Castles of Flintshire*, 1824, *Genealogy and Antiquities of Wales*, 1824.

4 **Cilcain** JONES, EDWARD (1761–1836), poet and hymn writer, born here. He published *Caniadau Maes y Plwm*, 1857, and *Gwialen i gefn yr ynfyd*, 1831.

5 **Downing** PENNANT, THOMAS (1726–98), traveller and naturalist, born here. He published works on natural history and *Tour in Scotland*, 1771–75.

6 **Greenfield** PERRI, HENRY (1561–1617), scholar, born here. Publications included *Egluryn Phraethineb sebh Dosparth ar Retoreg*, 1595.

7 **Gwespyr** GRUFFYDD, ELIS (1490–1552), chronicler, born here. He published his *Chronicle of the History of the World* in 1548.

8 **Halklyn** WILLIAMS, ROWLAND (1817–70), essayist and author, born here. His *Essays and Reviews* appeared in 1860, and *Owen Glendower*, a dramatic biography, in 1870.

9 **Hanmer** EDMWND, DAFYDD AB (1450–90), poet, born here. His *Gwaith Dafydd ab Edmwnd*, edited by T. Toberts, appeared in 1914.

10 **Hawarden** GLADSTONE, WILLIAM EWART (1809–98), statesman and writer, lived at Hawarden for almost sixty years and died here.

11 **Holywell** ROLFE, FREDERICK (1860–1913), the novelist 'Baron Corvo', lived here for two years in the 1890s.

12 **Llansa** JONES, JOHN (1788–1858), poet, born here. His poems, published in 1856, were written in English.

13 **Mold** BLACKWELL, JOHN (1797–1840), poet, born here. His best known poems include 'Song to the Nightingale', 'Song of the Fisherman's Wife', and 'Tintern Abbey'.

EDWARDS, ROGER (1811–86), poet and writer, lived here.

JONES, THOMAS (1811–66), writer, born here. His publications include two volumes of Welsh versions of Aesop's *Fables*.

OWEN, DANIEL (1836–95), novelist, known as the Welsh Dickens, born here. His books include *Y Dreflan*, 1881, *Enoc Huws*, 1891, *Gwen Tomos*, 1894, *Rhys Lewis*, 1882, and *Y Siswrn*, 1888.

14 **St Asaph** GEOFFREY OF MONMOUTH (c1090–c1155), chronicler, was made Bishop of St Asaph in 1151.

MORGAN, WILLIAM (c1545–1604), translator, was made bishop of St Asaph in 1601.

STANLEY, SIR HENRY MORTON (1841–1904), explorer and author, lived in the workhouse from 1847–62.

15 **Tremeirchion** STANLEY, SIR HENRY MORTON (1841–1904), explorer and author, was christened and lived here for a time in his youth.

Montgomeryshire (*Map 14*)

1 Llanbrynmair DAVIES, RICHARD (1833–77), Welsh poet, born here. His works appeared in four volumes between 1866 and 1882.

REES, ABRAHAM (1743–1825), editor, born here: He edited *Chambers Encyclopaedia*, 1784–86, and the *New Cyclopaedia*, 1802–20.

2 Llanerfyl JONES, HUGH (1789–1858), poet and literary critic, born here. He was editor of the Welsh language magazine *Gwladgarwr*, 1835–40.

3 Llanfechain DAVIES, WALTER (1761–1849), poet, antiquary and clergyman, born here. His literary works were mainly in Welsh; his chief writings in English were two studies of the agriculture and domestic economy of North and South Wales.

THOMAS, DAVID (1880–1967), author, born here. He wrote the standard work on the Welsh poetic metres.

4 Llanfihangel yng Ngwynfa GRIFFITHS, ANN (1776–1805), one of finest Welsh hymn writers, born here.

5 Llanfyllin DAVIES, EDWARD (1819–87), poet, born here. A collection of his works, *Caneuon Iolo Trefaldwyn*, appeared shortly before his death.

EDWARDS, D. MIALL (1873–1941), writer and theologian, born here. He published *Philosophy of Religion* in 1929, and *Christianity and Philosophy* in 1932.

JONES, ROBERT (1810–79), author and clergyman, born here. He edited and published the works of Goronwy Owen, 1876, and was editor of *Y Cymmrodor* 1876–79.

6 Llangadfan DAVIES, JOHN CADVAN (1846–1923), poet, hymn writer and nonconformist minister, born here. His works appeared between 1878 and 1897.

7 Llangurig LLOYD, JACOB YONDE WILLIAM (1816–87), historian and antiquary known as Chevalier Lloyd of Llangurig, lived here.

8 Llanwnnog WORTHINGTON, WILLIAM (1704–78), author and cleric, born here. He was befriended by Dr Johnson and Thomas Pennant while vicar of Llanrhaeadr-ym-Mochnant.

9 Machynlleth WILLIAMS, ELMA MARY (1913–71), lived and died at Pant Glas, Tre-r-Ddol, where she cared for the many and varied animals about which several of her books were written.

10 Montgomery Castle HERBERT, GEORGE (1593–1633), poet, born here. His principal poetic work is *The Temple: Sacred Poems and Private Ejaculations*, 1634.

11 Newtown GOODWIN, GERAINT (1903–41), novelist and short-story writer, born here. Publications include *Come Michaelmas*, *Watch for the Morning*, *Heyday in the Blood*, and a volume of short stories, *The White Farm*. His works are all set in the Border country.

OWEN, ROBERT (1771–1858), social reformer and writer, born here. Author of *A New View of Society*.

12 Penybontfawr ELLIS, ROBERT ('Cynddelw' 1810–75), poet and Baptist minister, born here. Author of several books and a prolific contributor to journals.

13 Powys TALIESIN (c550), poet, lived in the neighbourhood: he is credited with the collection of poems known as *The Book of Taliesin*.

14 Tregynon OLIVERS, THOMAS (1725–99), hymn writer, born here. Author of the hymn that begins 'The God of Abraham praise'.

15 Welshpool DAVIES, RICHARD (1635–1708), Quaker writer, born here. His autobiography, *An account of the convincement, exercises, services and travels of that ancient servant of the Lord Richard Davies* ran into several editions and was published in a fine edition by the Gregynog Press in 1928.

Shropshire (*Map 15*)

1 **Atcham** VITALIS, ORDERICUS (1075–c1143), one of the earliest English historians, born here.

2 **Bishop's Castle** GIFFORD, RICHARD (1725–1807), poet, born here. His *Contemplation, a Poem*, 1753, was quoted in Dr Johnson's Dictionary.

3 **Bridgnorth** MOORE, FRANCIS (1657–c1715), astrologer and almanac compiler, born here. His *Vox Stellarum*, dubbed 'Old Moore's Almanac', first appeared in 1700.
PERCY, THOMAS (1729–1811), antiquary and anthologist, born here. His *Reliques of Ancient English Poetry*, culled from a 17th century manuscript, aroused interest in early poetry.

4 **Broseley** HARTSHORNE, CHARLES (1802–65), antiquary, born here. His *Ancient Metrical Tales* appeared in 1829.

5 **Cleobury Mortimer** LANGLAND, WILLIAM (c1330–c1399), poet, probably born here. The first version of his *Piers the Plowman* appeared in 1362.

6 **Clive** WYCHERLEY, WILLIAM (c1640–1716), dramatist, born here. He is best remembered for *The Country Wife*, which first appeared in 1672 or 1673.

7 **Culmington** DUPPA, RICHARD (1770–1831), author and artist, lived here.

8 **Earl's Ditton** BOTFIELD, BERIAH (1807–63), bibliographer, born here. His publications include *Notes on Cathedral Libraries of England*, 1849.

9 **Eaton Constantine** BAXTER, RICHARD (1615–91), presbyterian, divine and theological writer, born here. He was imprisoned by Judge Jeffreys for libelling the church in his *Paraphrase of New Testament*, 1685. He wrote an autobiography, *Reliquiae Baxterianae*.

10 **Eyton-on-Severn** HERBERT, EDWARD, 1ST BARON HERBERT OF CHERBURY (1583–1648), philosopher and historian, born here. His analysis of truth, *De Veritate*, published in Paris in 1625, was the first metaphysical work by an English thinker.

11 **Hodnet** CHOLMONDELEY, MARY (1859–1925), novelist, born here. Her *Red Pottage*, 1899, brought her a big public.
HEBER, REGINALD (1783–1826), bishop of Calcutta, poet, born here. He is best remembered for his hymns, especially 'From Greenland's icy mountains'.

12 **Ightfield** MAINWARING, ARTHUR (1668–1712), founder of *The Medley*, 1710, born here.

13 **Kenley** ALISON, SIR ARCHIBALD (1792–1867), historian, born here. His *History of Europe* appeared in 1833–42, and was extended 1852–59.

14 **Leighton** WEBB, MARY GLADYS (1881–1927), novelist, born here. Her works, which have many fine qualities, are mostly set in Shropshire. *Precious Bane*, 1924, is the best known.

15 **Ludlow** BUTLER, SAMUEL (1835–1902), author of *Erewhon*, lived here.
HOUSMAN, ALFRED EDWARD (1859–1936), poet and classical scholar, buried here. Ludlow is at the very heart of the country of his masterpiece *A Shropshire Lad*, 1896.
MILTON, JOHN (1608–74), poet, stayed here: the first performance of his *Comus*, a masque set to music by Henry Lawes, was given at Ludlow Castle in 1634.

WEYMAN, STANLEY (1855–1928), novelist, born here. His romances of adventure in foreign parts, such as *Under the Red Robe*, 1894, were widely popular.
WRIGHT, THOMAS (1810–77), antiquary, born nearby. The author of many works, including *Queen Elizabeth and her Times*, 1838, and *History of Domestic Manners and Sentiments in England During the Middle Ages*, 1862. He was a founder of the Camden and Shakespeare Societies.

16 **Lyth Hill** WEBB, MARY GLADYS (1881–1927), novelist, ran a market garden here with her husband, and wrote some of her novels. They themselves built the cottage in which they lived (see **Leighton**).

17 **Meole Brace** BARKER, THOMAS (fl1651), angling writer, born here. His work *The Art of Angling* appeared in 1651.
BATHER, LUCY ('Aunt Lucy', 1836–64), children's author, died here.
WEBB, MARY GLADYS (1881–1927), novelist, lived here before her marriage in 1912 (see **Leighton**).

18 **Minsterley** THYNNE, WILLIAM, first editor of Chaucer's works, died here in 1546.

19 **Morville** ACTON, JOHN, 1ST BARON ACTON (1834–1902), historian, lived here.

20 **Much Wenlock** BENSON, STELLA (1892–1933), author, born at Lutwyche Hall. *Tobit Transplanted*, 1931, is her most acclaimed work.

21 **Norbury** BARNFIELD, RICHARD (1574–1627), poet, born here. Some of his pieces were for a long time attributed to Shakespeare.

22 **Oswestry** OWEN, WILFRID (1893–1918), one of the foremost poets of World War I born here. He was killed a week before the armistice.

23 **Oteley** KYNASTON, SIR FRANCIS (1587–1642), poet, born here. The central figure of a literary coterie at court, he founded an academy of learning, the *Musaeum Minervae*, in 1635.

24 **Plaish** LEIGHTON, SIR WILLIAM (fl1603–14), poet and composer, lived here.

25 **Plowden** PLOWDEN, FRANCIS (1749–1829), author, born here. His *Historical View of the State of Ireland* appeared in 1803.

26 **Pontesbury** WEBB, MARY GLADYS (1881–1927), novelist, ran a market garden here with her husband shortly after their marriage, and wrote *The Golden Arrow*, 1916 (see **Leighton**).

27 **Shifnal** BROWN, THOMAS (1663–1704), satirical poet, born here. He was the author of 'I do not love thee, Dr Fell'.

28 **Shrewsbury** BLAKEWAY, JOHN (1765–1826), topographer, born here. His history of Shrewsbury appeared in 1825.
BURNEY, CHARLES (1726–1814), author and musician, born here. He wrote widely about music and published his *History of Music* 1776–89.
CHURCHYARD, THOMAS (c1520–1604), poet and miscellaneous writer, born here. *Shore's Wife*, 1563, and *The Worthiness of Wales*, 1587, are among his works; *Churchyard's Chips*, 1575, is autobiographical.
COSTARD, GEORGE (1710–82), writer on the history of astronomy, born here.
DARWIN, CHARLES ROBERT (1809–82), naturalist and author, born here. His great works, written in Kent after the voyage of the *Beagle*, 1831–36, include *Journal of Researches into the Geology and Natural History of the Countries Visited by HMS Beagle*, 1839, *Origin of Species by Means of Natural Selection*, 1859, and *The Descent of Man*, 1871.
FARMER, HUGH (1714–87), theological writer, born here.

FORREST, HERBERT EDWARD (1858–1942), natural history writer, lived at Bayston Hill.

OWEN, HUGH (1761–1827), topographer, born here. He published a work on Shrewsbury in 1808.

PHILIPS, AMBROSE (c1675–1749), poet, born here. He was viciously attacked by Alexander Pope after the publication of his *Pastorals*.

REYNOLDS, JOHN HAMILTON (1796–1852), poet, born here. He was a member of Keats's circle and produced several volumes of verse, including *The Naiad*, 1816, and *The Garden of Florence*, from Boccaccio, 1821.

WEBB, MARY GLADYS (1881–1927), novelist, buried here (see **Leighton**).

29 **Stanton** WEBB, MARY GLADYS (1881–1927), novelist, spent part of her childhood at the manor house (see **Leighton**).

30 **Stanwardine** ACHERLEY, ROGER (c1665–1740), writer on law, born here. His work *The Britannic Constitution* was published 1727.

31 **Uppington** ALLESTREE, RICHARD (1619–81), theological writer, born here. He was author of *The Whole Duty of Man*, and many tracts and sermons.

32 **Wem** IRELAND, JOHN (d1808), biographer of Hogarth, born here.

33 **Wellington** EYTON, ROBERT (1815–81), antiquary, born at the vicarage. *The Antiquities of Shropshire* appeared 1861.

STRETTON, HESBA (pseudonym of Sarah Smith, 1832–1911), author, born here. She contributed to Dickens's periodicals and wrote the immensely popular story, *Jessica's First Prayer*, 1866.

34 **West Felton** DOVASTON, JOHN FREEMAN MILWARD (1782–1854), miscellaneous writer, born here. He published *Lectures on Natural History and National Melody*, 1839, and poetical works.

WILLIAMS, SIR JOHN BICKERTON (1792–1855), nonconformist writer, born here. He published biographical and other writings on nonconformists and their beliefs.

35 **Whitchurch** COTTON, ROGER (fl1596), poet, born here. *An Armor of Proofe* and *A Spirituall Song*, devotional poems, appeared in 1596.

TURBERVILLE, GEORGE (c1540–c1610), poet, born here. He was one of the pioneers of blank verse.

Isle of Man (*Map 15*)

1 Douglas BROWN, THOMAS EDWARD (1830–97), poet, born here. Many of his narrative poems are written in Manx dialect.

GIBBON, CHARLES (1843–90), novelist, born here. His books are mainly set in Scotland, and include *By Mead and Stream*, 1884, and *A Princess of Jutedom*, 1886.

2 Greeba Castle CAINE, SIR THOMAS HENRY HALL (1853–1941), novelist, lived here.

Cheshire (*Maps 15 & 16*)

1 **Alderley** STANLEY, ARTHUR PENRHYN (1815–81), dean of Westminster, Dr Arnold's biographer, born at the rectory. His father, EDWARD STANLEY (1779–1849) was rector 1805–37 and author of *A Familiar History of Birds*, 1836.

2 **Arley** RAFFALD, ELIZABETH (1733–81), lived here from 1763 as wife of the head gardener at Arley Hall. She wrote on cookery and compiled the first Manchester directory, 1772.

WARBURTON, ROWLAND EYLES EGERTON (1804–91), poet, born and lived at Arley Hall. His *Hunting Songs* appeared in 1846.

3 **Audlem** WHITNEY, GEOFFREY (c1548–c1601), poet, born hereabouts. Shakespeare used his *Choice of Emblems*, 1586, as one of his sources.

4 **Ashton-upon-Mersey** ABERCROMBIE, LASCELLES (1881–1938), poet and critic, born here. His *Collected Poems*, 1930, include the verse plays *The Sale of St Thomas*, 1911, and *The End of the World*. His principal critical works are *The Idea of Great Poetry*, 1925, and *Principles of Literary Criticism*, 1932.

HOUGHTON, WILLIAM STANLEY (1881–1913), dramatist, born at Ashton. His best play, portraying Lancashire life, is *Hindle Wakes*, 1912. He died in Paris.

5 **Birkenhead** BROOKE, LEONARD LESLIE (1862–1940), book illustrator, born here. He illustrated many of the most successful children's books of his time, and wrote and illustrated a number of his own, including *Johnny Crow's Party*, 1907.

6 **Broxton** OWEN, WILFRED (1893–1918), said that his 'poethood was born' here during a visit in 1903.

7 **Chester** CALDECOTT, RANDOLPH (1846–86), book illustrator, born here. He made his reputation with his illustrations for Washington Irving's *Old Christmas* and *Bracebridge Hall*, both 1876, but his greatest success was his series of sixteen picture books, still in print, illustrating well known poems and rhymes.

HENRY, MATTHEW (1662–1714), known as 'the Commentator', wrote part of his *Exposition of the Old and New Testament*, 1708–10, while serving as non-conformist minister to Chester, 1687–1712. He is buried at Holy Trinity Church.

HIGDEN, RANULF (d1364), chronicler, became a Benedictine monk at St Werburg's in 1299, and is buried in the cathedral.

HOLME, RANDLE (1627–99), Cheshire antiquary and principal contributor to the Holme MSS, lived at the King's Head, Lower Bridge Street, and is buried at St Mary's-on-the-Hill.

HOWSON, JOHN SAUL (1816–85), dean of Chester, Bible commentator, buried beneath the cathedral cloister lawn.

PARNELL, THOMAS (1679–1718), Irish poet, buried at Holy Trinity church.

PEARSON, JOHN (1613–86), bishop of Chester, theological writer, buried in the cathedral.

8 **Congleton** WHITEHURST, JOHN (1713–88), horologer and writer, lived here.

9 **Daresbury** CARROLL, LEWIS (pseudonym of Charles Lutwidge Dodgson, 1832–98), author and mathematician, born at the vicarage, now demolished. *Alice's Adventures in Wonderland* appeared in 1865, and *Through the Looking-Glass*, 1871.

10 **Farndon** SPEED, JOHN (c1552–1629), historian and cartographer, born here. His *History of Great Britaine* appeared in 1611.

11 **Gawsworth** JOHNSON, SAMUEL (1691–1773), author of the burlesque *Hurlothrumbo*, 1729, buried here.

12 **Great Budworth** LEYCESTER, SIR PETER (1613–78), Cheshire historian, buried here.

13 **Haslington** BROOME, WILLIAM (1689–1745), translator of Homer, born here. Collaborated with Pope and Elijah Fenton in translating the *Odyssey*, 1722–26. Also published sermons and poems.

14 **Hyde** PRINCE, JOHN CRITCHLEY (1808–66), poet, lived at Hyde from 1827 and is buried here. Known as the Bard of Hyde.

15 **Knutsford** GASKELL, MRS ELIZABETH CLEGHORN (1810–65), novelist and biographer, was married here in 1832 and buried here. Knutsford is her Cranford and the Hollingford of *Wives and Daughters*.

16 **Lower Peover** WARREN, JOHN BYRNE LEICESTER, 3RD BARON DE TABLEY (1835–95), poet and naturalist, buried here (see **Nether Tabley**).

17 **Macclesfield** BROWNSWERD, JOHN (c1540–89), poet and grammarian, buried here. He is believed to have taught Shakespeare while a master at Stratford-upon-Avon.

HOLINSHED, RAPHAEL (d c1580), chronicler, born at Sutton. His *Chronicles* of England, Scotland and Ireland, upon which Shakespeare drew liberally, were written in collaboration with others and published in 1578.

18 **Malpas** HEBER, REGINALD (1783–1826), bishop of Calcutta, poet, born at the rectory. His *Poetical Works* appeared in 1812.

19 **Nantwich** MINSHULL, ELIZABETH (c1638–1727), Milton's third wife, died and is buried here.

20 **Nether Tabley** WARREN, JOHN BYRNE LEICESTER, 3RD BARON DE TABLEY (1835–95), poet and naturalist, born at Tabley House. He published volumes of verse under his own name and under the pseudonyms George F. Preston and William Lancaster.

21 **New Brighton** WAUGH, EDWIN (1817–90), 'the Lancashire Burns', spent his last years here.

22 **Parkgate** KING, EDWARD (1612–37), Milton's college friend, drowned here. *Lycidas*, 1638, was written to his memory.

23 **Rock Ferry** SINCLAIR, MAY (1870–1946), novelist, born here. Author of *Audrey Craven*, 1896, she became noted for her 'stream-of-consciousness' method.

24 **Runcorn** CAINE, SIR THOMAS HENRY HALL (1853–1931), novelist, born here. His novels enjoyed tremendous popularity and made him a fortune. They include *The Bondman*, 1890 and *The Manxman*, 1894.

25 **Shocklach** DOD, JOHN (c1549–1645), theologian, born here. He was called Decalogue Dod from his exposition of the Ten Commandments, 1604.

26 **Stockport** ASHE, THOMAS (1836–89), poet, born here. His collected poems were published in 1885.

27 **Wilmslow** EVENS, G. BRAMWELL (1884–1943), writer and broadcaster on country lore under the name of Romany, spent his last years here in his caravan, which is preserved.

28 **Wirral Peninsula** STAPLEDON, WILLIAM OLAF (1886–1950), novelist, born here. He was the author of prophetic fiction, including *Last and First Men*, 1931, and philosophical works.

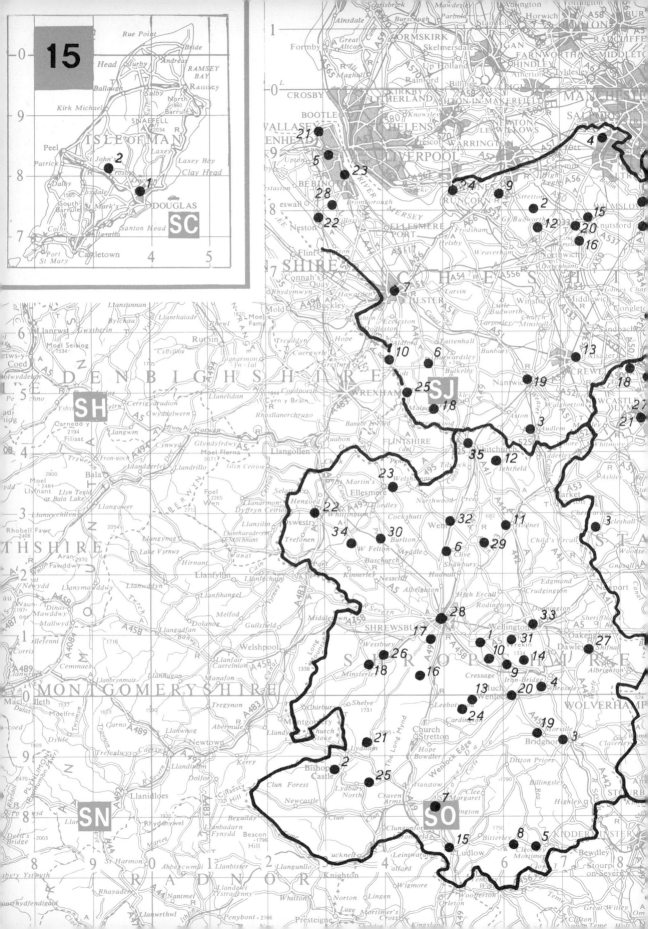

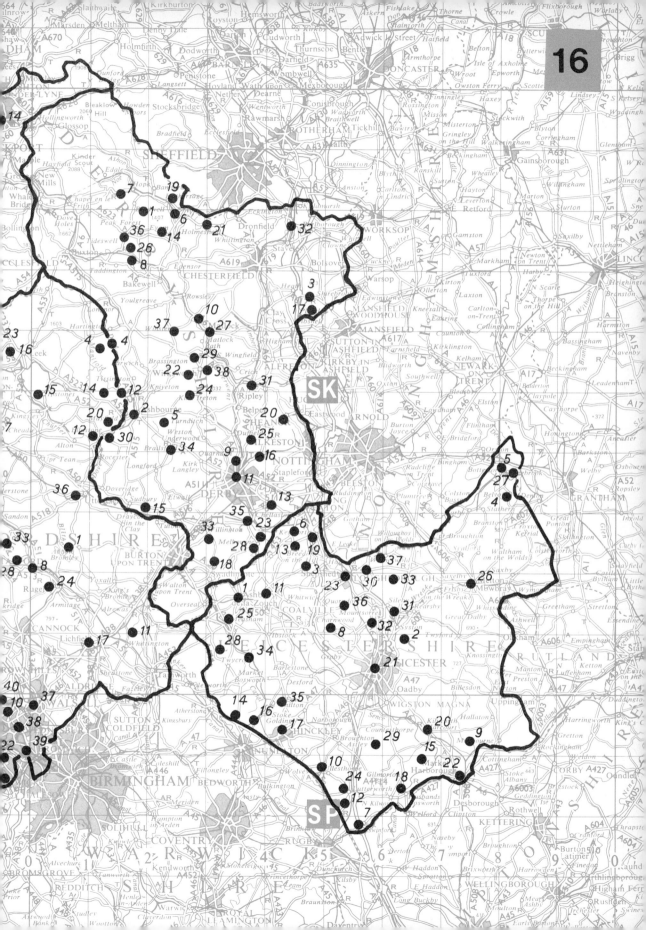

Staffordshire (*Maps 15 & 16*)

1 Abbot's Bromley CARY, HENRY FRANCIS (1772–1844), translator of Dante, vicar 1796–1800.

2 Acton Trussell ALSOP, JAMES (d1880), poet, vicar from 1867 until his death. His son, ARTHUR ALSOP, also a poet, was curate until 1880 and vicar from then until his death in 1928.

3 Adbaston ASH, CHARLES BOWKER, poet, born here in 1781.

4 Beresford COTTON, CHARLES (1630–87), poet and author, born and lived at Beresford Hall. He published burlesques of Virgil and a 'second part' of *The Compleat Angler* by his friend Izaak Walton.

5 Bilston MOSS, THOMAS (c1740–1808), poet, born here. His works include *Poems on Several Occasions*, 1769.
NEWBOLT, SIR HENRY (1862–1938), poet, born here. Best known for his sea poems, especially 'Drake's Drum', which brought him fame in 1896.

6 Burslem Bursley of ARNOLD BENNETT's *Anna of the Five Towns*, 1901. The Arnold Bennett Museum is in Waterloo Road.

7 Caverswall BUCHANAN, ROBERT (1841–1901), poet and novelist, born here. *God and the Man*, 1881, is his best known novel.

8 Colwich SOMERVILLE, WILLIAM (1675–1742), poet, born here. His predilection for field sport is reflected in *The Chace*, 1735, and a hawking poem, *Field Sports*, 1742.

9 Congreve HURD, RICHARD (1720–1808), bishop of Worcester, theological writer and poet, born here. His complete works appeared in 1811.

10 Darlaston BARNFIELD, RICHARD (1574–1627), poet, lived and died here.

11 Elford PAGET, FRANCIS EDWARD (1806–82), author of theological and children's works, was rector here from 1835 until his death. He wrote *The Hope of the Katzekopfs*, 1844, sometimes termed the first English fairy tale.

12 Ellastone Hayslope, and the setting for parts of GEORGE ELIOT's *Adam Bede*. She wrote about the village inn, and used either Calwich Abbey or Wootton Lodge as the original of Donnithorne Chase.
ROUSSEAU, JEAN-JACQUES (1712–78), French philosopher and writer, wrote much of his *Confessions* while a guest at Wootton Hall, 1766–68.

13 Hanley BENNETT, ENOCH ARNOLD (1867–1931), novelist and critic, born here. One of the most popular novelists and influential critics of his time, he set several of his works in his native county. His masterpiece is generally acknowledged to be *The Old Wives' Tale*, 1908. Hanley is the Hanbridge of his Five Towns novels.

14 Ilam CONGREVE, WILLIAM (1670–1729), dramatist, wrote his first comedy, *The Old Batchelor*, 1693, while staying at Ilam Hall.
The valley of Dovedale, near Ilam, was used by DR JOHNSON as a setting for *Rasselas*, 1759.

15 Ipstones COPE, ELIJAH (d1917), poet, born here.

16 Leek PARKES, WILLIAM KINETON (1865–1938), novelist, was for twenty years librarian of the Nicholson Institute here.

17 Lichfield ASHMOLE, ELIAS (1617–92), writer on astrology and antiquarian subjects, born here. His library is now the Ashmolean collection, Oxford University.
GARNETT, RICHARD (1835–1906), poet and biographer, born here. His series of pleasantly satirical fables, *Twilight of the Gods*, appeared in 1888.
JOHNSON, SAMUEL (1709–84), the most quoted English man of letters after Shakespeare, born and lived here until 1728. His *English Dictionary* appeared in 1755. From 1735–37 he kept a school at Edial Hall, near Lichfield, where one of his three pupils was the actor and dramatist, David Garrick.
LISTER, THOMAS HENRY (1800–42), novelist, born here. His works include *Granby*, 1826, and *Epicharis*, a tragedy, 1829.
SEWARD, ANNA (1747–1809), poet, known as the Swan of Lichfield, lived here from 1754 and is buried in the cathedral.

18 Linley Wood MARSH-CALDWELL, ANNE (1791–1874), novelist, born here. She wrote some twenty novels, including *Two Old Men's Tales*, *Emilia Wyndham*, 1846, and *Norman's Bridge*.

19 Longton Longshaw of ARNOLD BENNETT's Five Towns novels.

20 Mayfield MOORE, THOMAS (1779–1852), poet, lived here after his marriage in 1811 and wrote much of *Lalla Rookh*, 1817.

21 Newcastle-under-Lyme BRITTAIN, VERA MARY (1896–1970), novelist, born here. Her novels include *The Dark Tide*, 1923, and *Account Rendered*, 1945. Among her autobiographical works are *Testament of Youth*, 1933, about her wartime experiences, and *Testament of Friendship*, 1940, celebrating her friendship with Winifred Holtby.

22 Rowley Regis WOODHOUSE, JAMES (1735–1820), 'the poetical shoemaker', born here. He gained recognition with *Poems on Sundry Occasions*, 1764.

23 Rudyard The lake here provided RUDYARD KIPLING's christian name: his parents visited it soon after their marriage.

24 Rugeley PORTER, JOHN (1838–1922), racehorse trainer and novelist, born here. He wrote a popular novel, *Kingsclere*, 1896.

25 Sedgley CORNFIELD, JOHN (c1827–78), poet, born here. He lived in Can Lane, Hurst Hill, and published *A Round Unvarnished Tale of the Vicar of Sedgley*, 1862, and *Allan Chace and other Poems*, 1877.

26 Shallowford WALTON, IZAAK (1593–1683), author of *The Compleat Angler*, lived at Halfhead Farm from about 1644 until near the end of his life. The house is now a museum.

27 Shelton FENTON, ELIJAH (1683–1730), poet, born here. He translated parts of the *Odyssey* for Pope.

28 Shugborough Park ANSON, GEORGE, LORD (1697–1762), admiral and author, born here. His *Voyage Round the World* appeared in 1748.

29 Smethwick PETTITT, HENRY (1848–93), author of melodramas and dramatic pieces, born here.

30 Stafford COOPER, THOMAS (1805–92), Chartist poet, imprisoned in the county gaol in 1842 and wrote several of his works here.
TALFOURD, SIR THOMAS NOON (1795–1854), judge and dramatist, died here.
WALTON, IZAAK (1593–1683), born here. Beside his celebrated work *The Compleat Angler*, 1653, he published verse and several biographies.

31 Stoke-on-Trent Knype-on-Trent of ARNOLD BENNETT's *Anna of the Five Towns*.
CRAIK, MRS DINAH MARIA (1826–87), novelist, born here. Her most successful work was *John Halifax, Gentleman*, 1857.

32 Stone BAKEWELL, THOMAS (d1835), poet, buried here.
BARNFIELD, RICHARD (1574–1627), poet, buried here.

33 Tixall FULLERTON, LADY GEORGIANA (1812–85), novelist, born at Tixall Hall. Her most successful work was *Too Strange not to be True*, 1852.

34 Trentham MOSS, THOMAS (c1740–1808), poet, minister here during the 1760s (see **Bilston**).

35 Tunstall Turnhill of ARNOLD BENNETT's *Anna of the Five Towns*.

36 Uttoxeter The scene of DR JOHNSON's penance in 1779, when he stood bareheaded in the rain to atone for his refusal to work at his father's market bookstall sixty years earlier. The American novelist NATHANIEL HAWTHORNE describes his own pilgrimage here in *English Notebooks*, 1870.
HOWITT, WILLIAM (1792–1879) and MARY (1799–1888), authors, married here in 1821.

37 Walsall ANDREW, STEPHEN (pseudonym of Frank G. Layton, 1872–1941), novelist, lived here from 1898 until his death.

JEROME, JEROME KLAPKA (1859–1927), author, born at Belsize House, Bradford Street. His celebrated humorous work *Three Men in a Boat* appeared in 1889.

38 Wednesbury TREECE, HENRY (1911–66), poet and children's novelist, born here. He is particularly associated with tales of Roman and Viking times.

39 West Bromwich MURRAY, DAVID CHRISTIE (1847–1907), novelist and journalist, born here. He published many novels, and two books on the writer's craft, *A Novelist's Note-Book*, 1887, and *The Making of a Novelist*, 1894.

40 Willenhall The original of Mumpers Dingle in GEORGE BORROW's *Romany Rye*.

41 Wolverhampton FORREST, HERBERT EDWARD (1858–1942), natural history writer, born here. He published works on the fauna of Shropshire and North Wales.
NOYES, ALFRED (1880–1958), poet, born here. His best works include the sea epic *Drake*, 1906–8, and *The Torchbearers*, 1922–30.

Derbyshire (*Map 16*)

1 Abney NEWTON, WILLIAM (1750–1830), poet, born here. He was dubbed by Anna Seward 'the Minstrel of the Peak'.

2 Ashbourne Oakbourne in GEORGE ELIOT's *Adam Bede*.
COKAYNE, SIR ASTON (1608–84), dramatist and poet, lived on his estate here 1664–71 (see **Elvaston**).
MOORE, THOMAS (1779–1852), poet, wrote his series of poems *Lalla Rookh* while living here at Mayfield c1813–17.
MORRIS, FRANCIS ST VINCENT (1896–1917), war poet, lived here from 1898.

3 Ault Hucknall HOBBES, THOMAS (1588–1679), philosopher and writer, buried here (see **Hardwick Hall**).

4 Beresford Dale COTTON, CHARLES (1630–87), translator of Montaigne and contributor to Izaak Walton's *Compleat Angler*, lived here.

5 Bradley BANCROFT, THOMAS (fl1633–58), poet and epigrammist, lived here towards the end of his life and probably died here (see **Swarkestone**).

6 Breadsall DARWIN, ERASMUS (1731–1802), physician, poet and philosopher, lived and died at Breadsall Priory.

7 Castleton Site of the Castle of the Peak, the setting for SIR WALTER SCOTT's *Peveril of the Peak*.

8 Cressbrook NEWTON, WILLIAM (1750–1830), poet, became part-owner of the mills here through the interest of Anna Seward (see **Abney**).

9 Darley Abbey AINGER, ALFRED (1837–1904), biographer and editor of the works of Charles Lamb and Thomas Hood, died here and is buried in the abbey churchyard.
BAGE, ROBERT (1728–1801), novelist, born here. Much admired by Sir Walter Scott, his most successful novel was *Hermsprong, or, The Man as he is not*, 1796.

10 Darley Dale GISBORNE, JOHN (1770–1851), poet, lived here 1818–35 (see **Derby**).

11 Derby Stoniton in GEORGE ELIOT's *Adam Bede*.
COKAYNE, SIR ASTON (1608–84), dramatist and poet, died here (see **Elvaston**).
GISBORNE, JOHN (1770–1851), poet, born at St Helen's. His principal works are *The Vales of Wever*, 1797, and *Reflections*.
HUTTON, WILLIAM (1723–1815), historian, born here. His topographical works included *History of Derby*, 1791.
SPENCER, HERBERT (1820–1903), philosopher and sociologist, born here. His numerous works include *Principles of Psychology*, 1855, *Political Institutions*, 1882, and *Man versus the State*, 1884.

12 Dovedale Eagledale in GEORGE ELIOT's *Adam Bede*.

13 Elvaston COKAYNE, SIR ASTON (1608–84), dramatist and poet, born here. Collections of his poems appeared in 1658 and 1669.

14 Eyam CUNNINGHAM, PETER (d1805), poet, curate here 1775–88.
FURNESS, RICHARD (1791–1857), poet and author, born and buried here. His work *The Rag Bag* appeared in 1832.

SEWARD, ANNA (1747–1809), poet, 'the Swan of Lichfield', born here. Her poetry was edited by Sir Walter Scott, who used some of it in his work *Minstrelsy of the Scottish Border*, 1802–3. Her father, Thomas Seward (1708–90) was rector here until the family left for Lichfield in 1754.

15 Foston AGARD, ARTHUR (1540–1615), antiquary and historian of Westminster Abbey, born at the old Hall. He was a founder member of the Society of Antiquaries.

16 Grindleford Whitecross in CHARLOTTE BRONTË's *Jane Eyre*.

17 Hardwick Hall HOBBES, THOMAS (1588–1679), philosopher and writer, lived at Hardwick Hall from 1675 and died here (see **Ault Hucknall**).

18 Hartshorne SHAW, STEBBING (1762–1802), topographer, rector from 1799 and is buried here.

19 Hathersage The Morton of *Jane Eyre*. CHARLOTTE BRONTË took her heroine's name from that of a local family.

20 Heanor HOWITT, WILLIAM (1792–1879), author and poet, born at the Dene. He published numerous works, popularising history, literature and travel, many in collaboration with his wife MARY (1799–1888).

21 Holmesfield CARPENTER, EDWARD (1844–1929), social reformer and author, lived at Millthorpe until 1919.
GILCHRIST, ROBERT MURRAY (1868–1917), novelist, lived and died at Cartledge Hall and is buried here.

22 Hopton GELL, WILLIAM (1777–1836), classical scholar, born at Hopton Hall. He published topographical works on ancient cities, and itineraries of southern Europe.

23 King's Newton BRIGGS, JOHN (1819–76), naturalist and historian, born here. He published several works on Derbyshire history and antiquities, and has been called the Gilbert White of King's Newton.

24 Kirk Ireton BLACKWALL, ANTHONY (1674–1730), classical scholar, born here. He is best remembered for his *Introduction to the Classics*, 1718.

25 Little Eaton WILSON, THEODORE (d1918), war poet, born at the vicarage. His collected poems were published under the title *Magpie in Picardy*. His sister, MARJORIE WILSON, also born here, published some verse.

26 Litton, nr Tideswell The textile mill here was the setting of JOHN BROWN's *A Memoir of Robert Blincoe: an Orphan Boy*, 1832: an account of child labour in the nineteenth century.

27 Matlock WOLLEY, ADAM, county historian, buried here in 1827.

28 Melbourne BAXTER, RICHARD (1615–91), presbyterian minister and author, wrote part of his *Saint's Everlasting Rest*, 1650, here.

29 Middleton by Wirksworth BATEMAN, THOMAS (1821–61), antiquary, lived at Lomberdale House and is buried here.
LAWRENCE, DAVID HERBERT (1885–1930), novelist and poet, lived in a cottage here from May 1918 until April 1919.

30 Norbury Norbourne in GEORGE ELIOT's *Adam Bede*.

31 Pentrich GISBORNE, JOHN (1770–1851), poet, died here (see **Derby**).

32 Renishaw Family seat of the Sitwell family, much referred to in the autobiographical sequence of Sir Osbert Sitwell (1892–1969).

33 Repton STEVENS, WILLIAM BAGSHAW (1756–1800), poet and diarist, lived here.

34 Shirley POWYS, JOHN COWPER (1892–1963), novelist and essayist, born here. His most praised works are

A Glastonbury Romance, 1932, and *Weymouth Sands*, 1934. His brother, THEODORE FRANCIS POWYS (1875–1953), was also born here. He is best known for the humorous and allegorical novel *Mr Weston's Good Wine*, 1927.

35 **Swarkestone** BANCROFT, THOMAS (fl1633–58), poet and epigrammist, born here. His works include *The Glutton's Feauer*, 1633, *Two Bookes of Epigrammes and Epitaphs*, 1639, and *The Heroical Lover*, 1658.

36 **Tideswell** NEWTON, WILLIAM (1750–1830), poet, buried here (see **Abney**).

37 **Winster** JEWITT, LLEWELLYN (1816–86), county historian and antiquary, lived at Winster Hall from 1868 and is buried here.

38 **Wirksworth** Snowfield in GEORGE ELIOT's *Adam Bede*. Her aunt Elizabeth Evans, portrayed as Dinah Morris in that novel, is buried here.

Leicestershire (*Map 16*)

1 **Ashby-de-la-Zouch** HILDERSHAM, ARTHUR (1563–1632), puritan churchman and author of religious works, vicar here 1593.

2 **Barksby** MARSHALL, THOMAS (1621–85), dean of Gloucester and author of Saxon grammars and dictionaries, born here.

3 **Belton** BEAUMONT, FRANCIS (1584–1616), dramatist, born at Grace Dieu Manor. He wrote *The Knight of the Burning Pestle*, 1609, and collaborated with John Fletcher in other plays. His brother JOHN BEAUMONT (1582–1627), poet, was also born here.
BOOTH, CHARLES (1840–1916), social reformer and author, lived at the modern manor house.

4 **Belvoir Castle** CRABBE, GEORGE (1754–1832), poet, domestic chaplain here c1782–85.

5 **Bottesford** Elizabeth, Countess of Rutland, only child of SIR PHILIP SIDNEY, poet, shares a monument in the church with her husband, Roger, 5th Earl (1576–1612), for whom Bacon is thought to have written his *Profitable Instructions*.

6 **Castle Donington** MOORE, THOMAS (1779–1852), poet, was a frequent visitor here when it was the residence of his patron, Lord Moira, and probably wrote some of his Irish Melodies here (see **Kegworth**).

7 **Catthorpe** DYER, JOHN (c1700–58), nature poet, was vicar here after 1741.

8 **Charnwood Forest** Described in MICHAEL DRAYTON'S *Polyolbion*, 1622.

9 **Church Langton** VERGIL, POLYDORE (c1470–1555), Italian historian, rector 1503–35. At the invitation of Henry VII he wrote a history of England which was published 1534–55.

10 **Claybrooke** JENNER, CHARLES (1736–74), novelist and poet, rector from 1769 until his death.

11 **Coleorton** WORDSWORTH, WILLIAM (1770–1850), poet laureate, lived at Coleorton Farm 1806–7 with his wife and sister DOROTHY, where they were visited by SAMUEL and HARTLEY COLERIDGE, SIR WALTER SCOTT, LORD BYRON, ROBERT SOUTHEY and SAMUEL ROGERS.

12 **Cotesbach** MARRIOTT, JOHN (1780–1825), clergyman and poet, born at the rectory. Sir Walter Scott addressed the second canto of *Marmion*, 1808, to him.

13 **Diseworth** LILLY, WILLIAM (1602–81), astrologer and historian, born near the church. He published his almanac every year from 1644 until his death, and wrote a *True History of King James I and King Charles I*, 1651.

14 **Fenny Drayton** FOX, GEORGE (1624–91), founder of the Society of Friends, born here. His *Journal*, edited by William Penn and others, has become a religious literary classic.

15 **Gumley** CRADOCK, JOSEPH (1742–1826), dramatist and author, built Gumley Hall and lived here.

16 **Higham-on-the-Hill** BURTON, ROBERT (1577–1640), born at Lindley Hall. Known as 'Democritus Junior', he published his *Anatomy of Melancholy* in 1621. His brother, WILLIAM (1575–1645), historian and author of a *Description of Leicestershire*, 1622, was also born here.

17 **Hinckley** NICHOLS, JOHN (1745–1826), printer and author, lived here from 1778 and had a bookshop in Red Lion Court. He published the *Gentleman's Magazine* 1792–1826, and wrote, among other works, a history of Leicestershire.

18 **Husbands Bosworth** DUPORT, JOHN (d1617), biblical scholar and a translator of the Authorised Version, rector from c1580 until his death.

19 **Kegworth** MOORE, THOMAS (1779–1852), poet, lived at The Cedars during 1812 and wrote here some of his Irish Melodies.

20 **Kibworth** BARBAULD, MRS ANNA LETITIA, *née* Aikin (1743–1825), poet, born here. Her poem 'Eighteen Eleven' inspired Macaulay's 'New Zealander'. She published prose essays, among them *Evenings at Home*, 1792–95, in collaboration with her brother, JOHN AIKIN (1747–1822), also born here. His own chief work is a *General Biography* in ten volumes, 1799–1815.
DODDRIDGE, PHILIP (1702–51), hymn writer and religious author, ministered here from 1723.

21 **Leicester** COOPER, THOMAS (1805–92), Chartist poet and author, born here. He wrote novels, poems and politically-motivated tales such as *The Purgatory of Suicides*, 1845.
DICKINSON, WILLIAM CROFT (1897–1964), children's novelist, born here. His *Borrobil*, 1944, had two sequels: *The Eildon Tree*, 1947, and *The Flag from the Isles*, 1951.
GARDINER, WILLIAM (1770–1853), composer and writer on music, born here.
ORTON, JOSEPH (1933–67), playwright, author of the play *Loot*, born here.
PHILLIPS, SIR RICHARD (1767–1840), author and publisher, born here. He founded the *Leicester Herald*, 1792, and the London *Monthly Magazine*, 1796.
STONE, LOUIS (1871–1935), novelist, born here. His works, eg *Jonah*, 1911, are mostly associated with Australia, where he lived as a child.

22 **Little Bowden** WEST, MRS JANE (1758–1852), poet and author of 'improving' tales, lived here.

23 **Loughborough** CLEVELAND, JOHN (1613–58), Cavalier poet, born here. His verses were highly popular in royalist circles, but earned him imprisonment under Cromwell for a time. His *Poems* were published in 1656.

24 **Lutterworth** WYCLIFFE, JOHN (c1320–84), rector here from 1365. He spent his last years translating the Bible, and is buried here.

25 **Measham** JEWSBURY, GERALDINE ENDSOR (1812–80), novelist, born here. Friend of Thomas Carlyle and his wife. She published several novels between 1845 and 1859, and children's stories. Her sister, MARIA JANE (1800–33) wrote poetry and some prose pieces.

26 **Melton Mowbray** HENLEY, JOHN (1692–1756), 'Orator Henley' born here. He contributed to *The Spectator* as Dr Quir, wrote for the Whig journal *Hyp Doctor* 1730–39, was caricatured by Hogarth, and ridiculed by Pope in the *Dunciad*.

27 **Muston** CRABBE, GEORGE (1754–1832), poet, vicar 1789–1813.

28 **Norton-Juxta-Twycross** WHISTON, WILLIAM (1667–1752), writer and lecturer on theology, mathematics, science and other subjects, born at the rectory. Among more than fifty publications on religious and other subjects was his translation of *Josephus*, 1737, which became the recognised version.

29 **Peatling Magna** PORTER, ELIZABETH (Tetty), wife of DR SAMUEL JOHNSON, was born here in 1689.

30 **Prestwold** The epitaph for the church monument to Sir William Skipwith was written by JOHN BEAUMONT (see **Belton**).

31 **Ratcliffe-on-the-Wreake** KILBYE, RICHARD (c1561–1620), biblical scholar and a translator of the Authorised Version, born here.

32 **Rothley** MACAULAY, THOMAS BABINGTON, 1ST BARON MACAULAY (1800–59), statesman, historian and poet, born at Rothley Temple, where his aunt was the wife of the owner, Thomas Babington. He spent many holidays here. His most important work is the *History of England from the Accession of James II*, the first part of which appeared in 1849. His *Essays* were collected in 1843. The best known of his poems, 'Horatius', appeared in his *Lays of Ancient Rome*, 1842.

TREVELYAN, SIR GEORGE OTTO (1838–1928), historian and statesman, born at Rothley Temple. His most notable works include the six-volume *American Revolution*, 1899–1914.

33 **Segrave** BURTON, ROBERT (1577–1640), rector 1630–40 (see **Higham-on-the-Hill**).

34 **Shackerstone** JENNENS, CHARLES (1700–73), friend of Handel, wrote the words for *Saul*, 1735, *Messiah*, 1742, and *Belshazzar*, 1745: lived at the former Gopsall Hall where Handel also stayed. Jennens was nicknamed Solyman the Magnificent.

35 **Stapleton** DAWES, RICHARD (1708–66), Greek scholar, born here. He published his *Miscellanea Principia* in 1745.

36 **Woodhouse** HERRICK, ROBERT (1591–1674), poet, apprenticed for ten years to his uncle and guardian Sir William Herrick, goldsmith, who lived at Beaumanor.

37 **Wymeswold** POTTER, THOMAS RUSSELL (1799–1873), antiquary, kept a school at Wymeswold and is buried here. He was author of the *History and Antiquities of Charnwood Forest*.

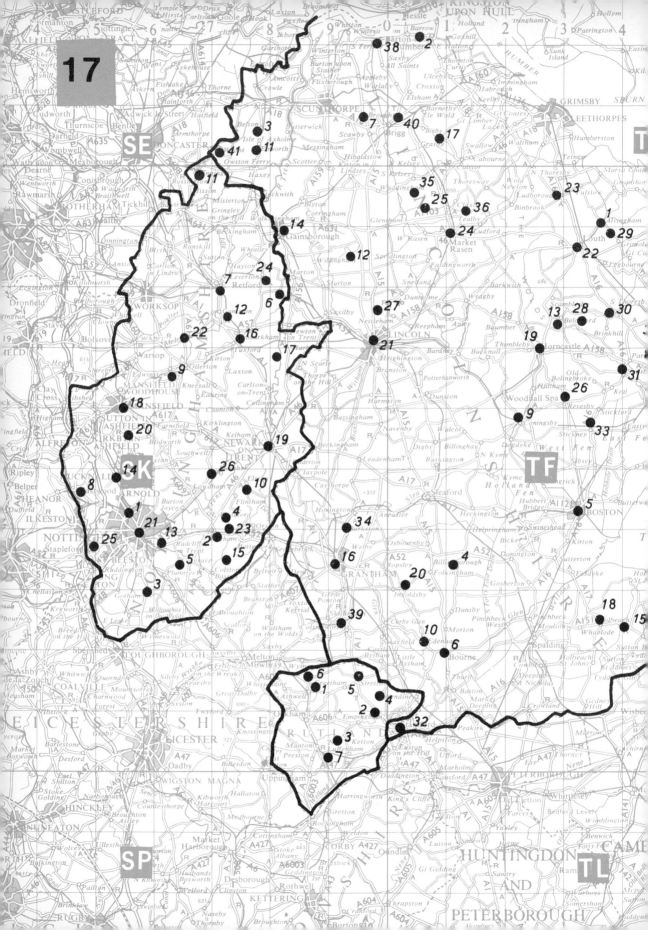

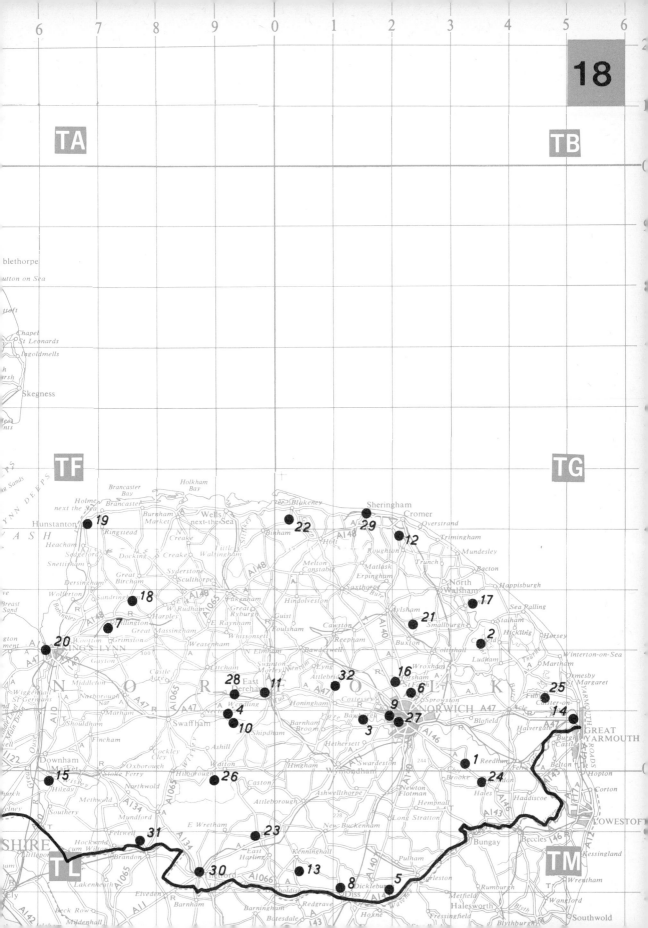

Lincolnshire (*Map 17*)

1 **Alvingham** GOOGE, BARNABE (1540–94), poet, born here. He is best known for a series of eight eclogues and *Cupido Conquered.*

2 **Barton-on-Humber** TREECE, HENRY (1911–66), poet and children's novelist, died here.

3 **Belton** Claims to be the Willingham of SIR WALTER SCOTT's work *The Heart of Midlothian* (but see **Syston**).

4 **Billingborough** LATHAM, ROBERT (1812–88) born at the vicarage. He published many ethnological works and a new edition of Johnson's *Dictionary*, 1870.

5 **Boston** CONINGTON, JOHN (1825–69), classical scholar, born and died here. His annotated edition of Virgil's works is still considered the best English commentary.
INGELOW, JEAN (1820–97), poet and novelist, born here. Of her poetry, 'High Tide on the Coast of Lincolnshire', 1863, is best known. Her works for children include *Mopsa the Fairy*, 1869.
MARSTON, JOHN WESTLAND (1820–90), dramatic poet, born here. His most successful play was *Hard Struggle*, 1858, and he was influential in maintaining the integrity of poetical drama in his time.
MERES, FRANCIS (c1565–1647), author, born at nearby Kirton. He produced *God's Arithmeticke*, 1597, *Palladis Tamia*, 1598, and *Wits Treasury*, 1598.

6 **Bourne** MANNING, or MANNYNG, ROBERT (c1264–c1340), poet, known as Robert de Brunne, born here. His work includes *Handlyng Synne* and a *Chronicle of England* in verse.

7 **Broughton** PRYME, ABRAHAM DE LA (1672–1704), antiquary and diarist, was curate here from 1695–98.

8 **Candlesby** ALINGTON, CYRIL ARGENTINE (1872–1955), novelist and biographer, born here. His works range from theological studies to detective stories.

9 **Coningsby** DYER, JOHN (c1700–1758), poet, rector from 1752 until his death here.
EUSDEN, LAURENCE (1688–1730), poet laureate, rector from c1725 until his death here.

10 **Edenham** KINGSLEY, CHARLES (1819–75), novelist and historian, is said to have written much of *Hereward the Wake*, 1866, while staying at the rectory.

11 **Epworth** WESLEY, JOHN (1703–91) and CHARLES (1707–88) born here. As well as hymns, the brothers wrote journals, published in 1827 and 1849 respectively, and other works. John Wesley was the founder of Methodism, which dates its beginning from May 1738. Their father, SAMUEL WESLEY (1662–1735) was rector at Epworth 1695–1735 and published verse and prose. The house is open to the public.

12 **Fillingham** WYCLIFFE, JOHN (c1320–84), religious reformer and translator, rector c1360–68.

13 **Fulletby** WINN, HENRY (d1914), poet and antiquary, buried here.

14 **Gainsborough** The town is the original of St Oggs in GEORGE ELIOT's novel *The Mill on the Floss.*
MILLER, THOMAS (1807–74), poet and novelist, born here. *Songs of the Sea Nymphs* was published in 1832, *A Tale of Old England* in 1849, and *Original Poems for My Children*, 1852.

PATRICK, JOHN (1632–95), author of controversial theological works, born here.

15 **Gedney** HAKLUYT, RICHARD (c1553–1616), author of the *Voyages*, rector from 1612.

16 **Grantham** MORE, HENRY (1614–87), poet and philosopher, born here. His views are expressed in Spenserian stanzas in *Psychozoia Platonica: or, A Platonical Song of the Soul*, 1642.
STILL, JOHN (c1543–1608), bishop of Bath and Wells, born here. To him is attributed the authorship of *Gammer Gurton's Needle* (first published 1575), the second extant English comedy.

17 **Grasby** TURNER, CHARLES TENNYSON (1808–79), poet, vicar from 1834 (see **Somersby**).

18 **Holbeach** ANGELL, SIR NORMAN (baptised Ralph Norman Angell Lane, 1872–1967), writer on international questions, born here. *The Great Illusion*, 1910, had an enormous sale throughout the world.
CENTLIVRE, SUSANNAH (c1667–1723), actress and playwright, probably born here. She wrote many comedies, including *The Perjured Husband*, 1700, and *A Bold Stroke for a Wife*, 1717.
STUKELEY, WILLIAM (1687–1765), antiquary, born here. A founder-member of the Society of Antiquaries, he published works on Druidism which earned him the name of 'Arch-Druid'.

19 **Horncastle** A setting for GEORGE BORROW's novel *Romany Rye*, 1857.

20 **Lavington** BEDE, CUTHBERT (pseudonym of Edward Bradley, 1827–89), novelist, vicar here 1883.

21 **Lincoln** Lindum in GEORGE ELIOT's writings.
MARKHAM, MRS (pseudonym of Elizabeth Penrose, *née* Cartwright, 1780–1837), historian, died here.

22 **Louth** TENNYSON, FREDERICK (1807–98), poet and elder brother of Alfred and Charles, born here. His works include *Days and Hours*, 1854, and *Isles of Greece*, 1890. The Tennyson brothers were educated at Louth.

23 **Ludborough** MORYSON, FYNES (1566–c1617), travel writer, born here. His *Itinerary* was published in 1617.

24 **Market Rasen** PALMER, HERBERT (1880–1961), poet and critic, born here. His *Collected Poems* appeared in 1932, but further volumes of verse were published subsequently.

25 **Owersby** HADATH, GUNBY (1880–1954), boys' novelist, born here. He wrote more than sixty novels, several featuring a schoolboy hero, Sparrow.

26 **Revesby** BANKS, SIR JOSEPH (1743–1820), president of the Royal Society, traveller and diarist, lived here.

27 **Riseholme** WORDSWORTH, CHRISTOPHER (1807–85), biographer of his uncle, William Wordsworth, is buried here.

28 **Somersby** TENNYSON, ALFRED, LORD (1809–92), poet laureate, born at the rectory, now Somersby House. His brother, Charles Tennyson (1808–79), with whom he collaborated in 1827 to produced *Poems of Two Brothers*, also born here. Alfred lived at Somersby until 1837, writing many of his poems here, including *The Lotus Eaters* and *The Lady of Shalott.*

29 **South Cockerington** SCROPE, SIR CARR (1649–80), poet, born here. He was a popular versifier at the court of Charles II.

30 **South Ormsby** WESLEY, SAMUEL (1662–1735), poet and father of John and Charles Wesley, rector 1690.
JOHN WESLEY was later rector here (see **Epworth**).

31 **Spilsby** The memorial here to Sir John Franklin, the Arctic explorer, was composed by ALFRED, LORD TENNYSON.

32 **Stamford** HORRABIN, JAMES FRANCIS (1884–1962), book illustrator, born here. He is best remembered by

many for the *Happy* and *Japhet Annuals*, 1921–51, arising from his cartoon series in the *News Chronicle* newspaper, 1919–50.

33 **Stickney** VERLAINE, PAUL (1844–96), French poet, taught here c1876–77.

34 **Syston** Claims to be the Willingham of SIR WALTER SCOTT's work *The Heart of Midlothian* (but see **Belton**).

35 **Thornton-le-Moor** LE NEVE, JOHN (1679–1741), antiquary, rector from 1722.

36 **Walesby** BURTON, ROBERT (1577–1640), author of *The Anatomy of Melancholy*, 1621, rector here.

37 **Willoughby** SMITH, CAPTAIN JOHN (1580–1631), adventurer and explorer, born here. He published several works about his experiences in the Americas, and is said to have been rescued from the Indians by their princess, Pocahontas.

38 **Winteringham** WHITE, HENRY KIRKE (1785–1806), poet, lived at the old rectory house during 1804.

39 **Woolsthorpe-by-Colsterworth** NEWTON, SIR ISAAC (1642–1727) born at Woolsthorpe Manor. He wrote extensively about his scientific theories in such famous treatises as *Light and Colours*, 1672, and *Principia*, 1687, and also on theology.

40 **Wrawby** NICHOLSON, JOSEPH (1850–1927), writer on economics, born here. He also published three romances.

41 **Wroot** WESLEY, SAMUEL (1662–1735), poet and father of John and Charles Wesley, was rector 1722–35. JOHN WESLEY was assistant curate to him 1727–29 (see **Epworth**).

Rutland (*Map 17*)

1 **Barrow** BEVERIDGE, WILLIAM (1637–1708), theological writer, bishop of St Asaph, born here. He was author of *Private Thoughts upon Religion*, 1709.

2 **Great Casterton** CLARE, JOHN (1793–1864), poet, lived here 1817–20. He married Martha Turner ('Sweet Patty of the Vale') here in 1820.

3 **Lyndon** BARKER, THOMAS (1721–1809), naturalist, theologian and diarist, brother-in-law of Gilbert White of Selborne, lived here all his life and is buried here.
WHISTON, WILLIAM (1667–1752), writer on theology, mathematics and science, is buried here.

4 **Pickworth** CLARE, JOHN (1793–1864), poet, lived here for a short time before 1817.

5 **Stretton** BEDE, CUTHBERT (pseudonym of Edward Bradley, 1827–89), novelist, was rector here for many years and wrote his humorous classic *The Adventures of Mr Verdant Green, an Oxford Freshman*, 1853–57.

6 **Teigh** BENTON, JOHN (d1848), poet and grammarian, kept the village school and is buried here.

7 **Wing** MERES, FRANCIS (1565–1647), author, rector from 1602 until his death.

Nottinghamshire (*Map 17*)

1 **Basford** BAILEY, PHILIP JAMES (1816–1902), poet, born at the home of his father, THOMAS BAILEY (1785–1856), Nottinghamshire historian and miscellaneous writer. Philip Bailey's poem *Festus*, 1839, enjoyed tremendous popularity on both sides of the Atlantic.

2 **Bingham** PRIOR, JAMES (pseudonym of James Prior Kirk, 1851–1922), novelist, spent his last thirty years at Bingham, and is buried here (see **Nottingham**).

3 **Bunny** PARKYNS, SIR THOMAS (1664–1741), wrestling enthusiast and author of *The Inn-play; or: Cornish-hugg Wrestler*, 1714, lived at Bunny Hall.

4 **Car Colston** THOROTON, ROBERT (1623–78), antiquary, lived and is buried here.

5 **Cotgrave** MORDAUNT, ELINOR (Evelyn May Mordaunt, 1877–1942), novelist and traveller, born at Cotgrave Place. Letters which she wrote while living in Mauritius were published as *The Garden of Contentment* in 1902.

6 **Cottam** MARKHAM, GERVASE (c1568–1637), miscellaneous writer, born here. He has been termed 'the earliest English hackney writer'.

7 **East Retford** GORE, CATHERINE GRACE FRANCES (1799–1861), novelist and dramatist, born here. Several of her plays were produced at the Haymarket and Drury Lane theatres, and her novels enjoyed great vogue in the circulating libraries.

8 **Eastwood** LAWRENCE, DAVID HERBERT (1885–1930), novelist and poet, born at 8A Victoria Street. His father was a collier here. *Sons and Lovers* appeared in 1913, *The Rainbow*, 1915, *Women in Love*, 1920, and *Lady Chatterley's Lover*, 1928.

9 **Edwinstowe** BREWER, EBENEZER COBHAM (1810–97), author of *The Dictionary of Phrase and Fable*, died while staying at the vicarage, and is buried here.

10 **Elston** DARWIN, ERASMUS (1731–1802), physician, poet and botanical writer, born at Elston Hall. His varied interests are reflected in: *The Loves of the Plants*, 1789, and *Economy of Vegetation*, 1791, poetic works which make up the *Botanic Garden*, a much-ridiculed publication. He was the grandfather of Charles Darwin.

11 **Finningley** BIGLAND, JOHN (1750–1823), author of standard educational works, was master at the school here.

12 **Gamston** CLINTON, HENRY FYNES (1781–1852), chronologist, born here. He wrote notable works of Greek and Roman chronology.

13 **Holme Pierrepont** OLDHAM, JOHN (1653–83), poet, died and is buried here.

14 **Hucknall-Torkard** BYRON, GEORGE GORDON NOEL, 6TH LORD BYRON (1788–1824), poet, buried here.

15 **Langar** BUTLER, SAMUEL (1835–1902), satirist and novelist, born here. *The Way of All Flesh*, published posthumously in 1903, is an autobiographical novel, while *Erewhon: or Over the Range*, 1872, satirically compares life in a utopian New Zealand, where Butler farmed sheep 1860–64, with English ways.

16 **Markham** MARKHAM, MRS (pseudonym of Elizabeth Penrose, *née* Cartwright, 1780–1837), children's author, lived here with her aunts and adopted the name of the village as her pseudonym (see **Marnham**).

17 **Marnham** MARKHAM, MRS (pseudonym of Elizabeth Penrose, *née* Cartwright, 1780–1837), children's author, born here. Her works include school histories of England, 1823, and of France, 1828.

18 **Mansfield** DODSLEY, ROBERT (1703–64), poet, dramatist and bookseller, born here. His best known work is *Select Collection of Old Plays*, 1744. He founded the *Annual Register*, 1758, in conjunction with Edmund Burke.

19 **Newark** CLEVELAND, JOHN (1613–58), Cavalier poet, wrote many of his verses while helping defend the town during the Civil War.

CONSTABLE, HENRY (1562–1613), poet, born here. His volume of sonnets, *Diana*, appeared in 1592.

ROBERTSON, THOMAS WILLIAM (1829–71), dramatist, born here. *Caste*, 1867, was a highly successful play in the then new naturalistic style.

20 **Newstead Abbey** BYRON, GEORGE GORDON NOEL, 6TH LORD BYRON (1788–1824), poet, lived here 1808–14.

21 **Nottingham** ATHERSTONE, EDWIN (1788–1872), poet, born here. His epic *The Fall of Nineveh* appeared in instalments from 1828 for some forty years.

CAVENDISH, WILLIAM, DUKE OF NEWCASTLE (1592–1676), poet and dramatist, lived at the castle.

FYLEMAN, ROSE (1877–1957), children's poet, born here. She published many collections of fairy poems following the appearance of her first, and most famous, poem, 'There are Fairies at the Bottom of our Garden', 1917.

HOOTON, CHARLES (c1813–47), American novelist, died and is buried here.

HOWITT, WILLIAM (1792–1879) and MARY (1799–1888), authors of popular non-fiction, lived here 1822–36.

JACKS, LAWRENCE PEARSALL (1860–1955), author and philosopher, born here. He wrote widely on education, creating for the purpose an imaginary city, 'Smokeover', and was first editor of the *Hibbert Journal*, 1902.

MILLER, THOMAS (1807–74), poet, worked as a basket maker here.

MILLHOUSE, ROBERT (1788–1839), weaver and poet, born and buried here. His first verses appeared in 1810.

PRIOR, JAMES (pseudonym of James Prior Kirk, 1851–1922), novelist, born here. His publications include *Forest Folk*, 1901, and *Fortuna Chance*, 1910. He has been called the 'Thomas Hardy of Nottinghamshire'.

TAYLOR, ANN (1782–1866), children's poet, lived here.

WAKEFIELD, GILBERT (1756–1801), classical scholar, born at St Nicholas's rectory. He edited the *Georgics*, 1788, and a number of Greek plays, and violently attacked Richard Porson's editing of the *Hecuba of Euripides*, 1797, in his *Diatribe Extemporalis*.

WHITE, HENRY KIRKE (1785–1806), poet, born in the old Shambles. He came to public notice with *Clifton Grove . . . with other Poems*, 1803.

22 **Perlethorpe** MONTAGU, LADY MARY WORTLEY (1689–1762), letter writer, born here. She also composed *Town Eclogues*, which were privately published as *Court Poems* in 1716.

23 **Scarrington** SHIPMAN, THOMAS (1632–80), poet, born and died here. He was the author of *Carolina, or Loyal Poems*, 1683.

24 **South Leverton** SAMPSON, WILLIAM (c1590–c1636), dramatist, lived here.

25 **Stapleford** MEE, ARTHUR (1875–1943), journalist and author, born here. He compiled many reference works, founded and edited the *Children's Newspaper*, and wrote the 38 volume guide to the English counties, *The King's England*, 1936–43.

26 **Thurgarton Priory** HILTON, WALTER (d1396), religious writer, Augustinian canon here.

Norfolk (*Map 18*)

1 **Ashby** WORDSWORTH, CHRISTOPHER (1774–1846), author and brother of William Wordsworth, rector 1804–08.

2 **Barton Broad** PIKE, MARTIN (pseudonym of David Herbert Parry, 1868–1950), boys' author and writer on militaria, lived most of his life in Ben Gunn's Cottage nearby, and died here.

3 **Bawburgh** WAGSTAFFE, JOHN (d 1813), verse writer, died here.

4 **Bradenham** HAGGARD, SIR HENRY RIDER (1856–1925), novelist, born at Bradenham Hall. *She* appeared in 1887 and *King Solomon's Mines* in 1885.

5 **Brockdish** BLOMEFIELD, FRANCIS (1705–52), topographer, rector here (see **Fersfield**).

6 **Catton** SEWELL, MARY (1797–1884), poet and mother of the novelist ANNA SEWELL (1820–78), spent her last years here.

7 **Congham** SPELMAN, SIR HENRY (1564–1641), historian, born here. He wrote a *History of Sacrilege*, 1698, and a *History of the English Councils*, 1639.

8 **Diss** SKELTON, JOHN (1460–1529), poet, probably born here. Poet laureate at both Oxford and Cambridge, he was tutor to Henry VIII, and later became rector of Diss. His satirical poetry includes *Colin Clout* and *Why Come Ye not to Court?*, both appearing in 1522 and directed at Cardinal Wolsey.

9 **Earlham** GURNEY, JOSEPH (1788–1847), Quaker writer, born and died at Earlham Hall. Among his works are *Religious Peculiarities of the Society of Friends*, 1824, and *A Winter in the West Indies*, 1840.

10 **East Bradenham** STRODE, WILLIAM (1602–45), poet, rector 1633–38.

11 **East Dereham** BORROW, GEORGE (1803–81), author, born at Dumpling Green nearby. His *Lavengro* appeared in 1851 and *Romany Rye* in 1857.
COWPER, WILLIAM (1731–1800), poet, lived here with Mrs Unwin from 1795 until his death, and is buried in St Thomas's chapel.

12 **Felbrigg** WINDHAM, WILLIAM (1750–1810), politician and diarist, lived here.

13 **Fersfield** BLOMEFIELD, FRANCIS (1705–52), topographer, born here. He later became rector of Hargham and Fersfield. His *History of Norfolk* was uncompleted at his death and was finished by others.

14 **Great Yarmouth** AMES, JOSEPH (1689–1759), antiquary and historian of printing, born here. His chief work was *Typographical Antiquities*, 1749.
DICKENS, CHARLES (1812–70), visited Great Yarmouth in 1848 and called it 'the strangest place in the world'. He set Peggotty's hut in *David Copperfield*, 1849–50, on the seafront, near the Nelson column.
GIBBON, CHARLES (1843–90), novelist, died here.
PALGRAVE, FRANCIS TURNER (1824–97), poet, born here. He compiled *The Golden Treasury of Songs and Lyrics*, 1861, and published several collections of his own verse, including *Visions of England*, 1881.
SEWELL, ANNA (1820–78), author, born here. Her *Black Beauty*, 1877, the story of a horse, remains one of the most popular children's books in Great Britain.

SWINDEN, HENRY (1716–72), author of *The History of Great Yarmouth*, lived and is buried here.

15 **Hilgay** FLETCHER, PHINEAS (1582–1650), poet, rector here from 1621 until his death.

16 **Horsham St Faith** SOUTHWELL, ROBERT (c1562–95), poet and Jesuit martyr, born here: best known for his poem 'The Burning Babe', contained in *Maeoniae*, 1895.

17 **East Ruston** PORSON, RICHARD (1759–1808), classical scholar, born here. He was editor of Aeschylus, 1795, Euripides and others.

18 **Houghton** WALPOLE, HORACE, 4TH EARL OF ORFORD (1717–97), politician and author, is buried in Houghton Hall church.

19 **Hunstanton** LE STRANGE, SIR NICHOLAS (d1655), collector of anecdotes and compiler of *Merry Passages and Jests*, lived and died here.
L'ESTRANGE, SIR ROGER (1616–1704), pamphleteer and journalist, born here. He founded periodicals, campaigned for the royalist cause, and published classical works and Aesop's *Fables*, 1692.

20 **King's Lynn** ARAM, EUGENE (1704–59), usher at the grammar school at the time that his murder of Daniel Clarke was discovered. Bulwer-Lytton wrote a popular novel and Thomas Hood a poem on the subject.
BURNEY, FANNY (Francis, Madame d'Arblay, 1752–1840), diarist and novelist born, probably in Chapel Street, and lived here until 1760. She had great success with *Evelina, or The History of a Young Lady's Entry into the World*, 1778, and *Cecilia*, 1782. Her *Early Diary*, published 1889, covers the years 1768–78 and includes sketches of famous contemporaries.
KEMPE, MARGERIE (b1364), born here: author of the first known autobiography in English.

21 **Lammas** SEWELL, ANNA (1820–78), author of *Black Beauty*, and her mother MARY SEWELL (1797–1884), poet, are buried in the Quaker burial ground.

22 **Langham** MARRYAT, CAPTAIN FREDERICK (1792–1848), novelist, farmed at Langham Manor from 1843, died and is buried here.

23 **Larling** MURRY, JOHN MIDDLETON (1889–1957), author and critic, lived here.

24 **Loddon** BARTHOLOMEW, ANN (d1862), author and miniaturist, born here. Her *Songs of Azrael* appeared in 1840, and a domestic comedy, *The Ring*, in 1845.

25 **Mautby** Many of the Paston Letters, 1422–1509, originated here and in neighbouring parts of the county, written by members of the Paston family.

26 **Merton** FITZGERALD, EDWARD (1809–83), translator of *The Rubaiyat of Omar Khayyam*, 1859, died while on his annual visit to his friend George Crabbe at the rectory.

27 **Norwich** ASHFORD, DAISY (1881–1972), author of *The Young Visiters*, 1919, died at Hellesdon.
BORROW, GEORGE (1803–81), lived during his youth at Borrow House, Willow Lane. Mousehold Heath, near Norwich, is one of his *Lavengro* settings (see **East Dereham**).
BROWNE, SIR THOMAS (1605–82), physician and author, lived here from 1637, wrote his great *Religio Medici*, 1642, and is buried in St Peter Mancroft church.
DELONEY, THOMAS (c1543–1600), novelist and ballad writer, called by Thomas Nash 'the Balletting Silk-Weaver of Norwich', worked here as a silk-weaver before 1586.
GREENE, ROBERT (1558–92), dramatist, probably born here. He was a prolific writer of plays, prose romance, pamphlets and author of an autobiography in which he termed Shakespeare an 'upstart crow'.

110

JULIANA OF NORWICH (c1342–1413), anchoress and mystic, lived here. Author of *XVI Revelations of Divine Love*, her work has been termed the most perfect expression of mediaeval mysticism.

KEMP, WILLIAM (fl1580–1605), actor, danced from London to Norwich in 1599 and described it in *Kemps Nine Daies Wonder*.

MANN, MARY E. (1848–1929), novelist, born here. Her stories, set in Norfolk, include *Gran Ma's Jane*, 1903, and *A Sheaf of Corn*, 1908.

MARSHALL, EMMA (1830–99), historical novelist, born here.

MARTINEAU, HARRIET (1802–76), born here. Her writings deal mostly with travel and economics, the greatest being her *History of England during the Thirty Years' Peace*, 1849. Her brother, JAMES MARTINEAU (1805–1900), theological writer and author of hymns, was also born here. He published a *Study in Religion* in 1888.

MOTTRAM, RALPH HALE (1883–1971), novelist and biographer, born and lived here most of his life. Norwich is the Easthampton of several of his works. His most celebrated publication is *The Spanish Farm* trilogy of novels, 1924–26.

OPIE, MRS AMELIA (1769–1853), novelist, born here. Friend of Sidney Smith and Sheridan, her works include *Father and Daughter*, 1801, and *Tales from Real Life*, 1813.

28 Scarning JESSOPP, AUGUSTUS (1823–1914), author and essayist, rector 1879–1911.

29 Sheringham HAMILTON, PATRICK ANTHONY WALTER (1904–62), playwright and novelist, lived at 3 Martincross from 1959 until his death here. He had had a home at Overy Staithe, on this coast, from 1930–37.

MANN, MARY E. (1848–1929), novelist, lived here (see **Norwich**).

MORTIMER, MRS FLAVELL (1802–78), children's author, buried in St Peter's church.

30 Thetford PAINE, THOMAS (1737–1809), radical writer, born in White Hart Street. His influential work *The Rights of Man* appeared 1791–92.

31 Weeting SHADWELL, THOMAS (c1642–92), poet and dramatist, possibly born at Broomhill House, Brandon. He became poet laureate 1688, after Dryden, with whom he had conducted a feud in print for a number of years. Some accounts favour Brandon, Durham, as his birthplace.

32 Weston Longville WOODFORDE, JAMES (1740–1803), diarist, was rector from 1774 until his death here.

Lancashire (*Map 19*)

1 **Aldingham** HAYMAN, HENRY (1823–1904), translator of Homer, rector from 1874 until his death.

2 **Blackburn** MORLEY, JOHN, 1ST VISCOUNT MORLEY OF BLACKBURN (1838–1923), biographer, journalist and statesman, born here. He was editor of the *Fortnightly Review* from 1867 and the *Pall Mall Gazette* from 1880. He wrote several political biographies, including one of Gladstone, 1903.
WESTALL, WILLIAM BURY (1834–1903), novelist and journalist, born here. He edited the *Swiss Times* in Geneva. His novel *The Old Factory*, 1881, is set in Lancashire.

3 **Blackpool** CLARKE, CHARLES ALLEN (1863–1935), novelist, lived here (see **Bolton**).

4 **Bolton** AINSWORTH, ROBERT (1660–1743), lexicographer, was master of the grammar school.
CLARKE, CHARLES ALLEN (1863–1935), novelist, born here. He wrote impressions of his county in *Windmill Land*, 1916, and the sequels to it.
LEMPRIERE, JOHN (c 1765–1824), classical scholar, was master of the grammar school.
TANNAHILL, ROBERT (1774–1810), Scottish poet, worked several years as a weaver here.

5 **Broughton** BYROM, JOHN (1692–1763), poet, born here. Most of his verse championed the Jacobite cause, but he is best remembered for the hymn 'Christians, awake!' He also invented a system of shorthand.

6 **Bury** CROMPTON, RICHMAL (Richmal Crompton Lamburn, 1890–1969), novelist, born here. She created her schoolboy character William in a short story. He first appeared in book form in *Just William*, 1922. This and its sequels have sold millions of copies in many languages.

7 **Cartmel Fell** COLLINGWOOD, ROBIN GEORGE (1889–1943), historian and philosopher, born here. His *Essay on Philosophical Method* appeared in 1933, and *Idea of History* in 1946.

8 **Chadderton** CHADDERTON, LAURENCE (c1536–1640), theological writer, born at Chadderton Hall. He was a translator of the Authorised Version of the Bible, 1607–11.

9 **Clitheroe** WILSON, THOMAS (1747–1813), compiler of an archaeological dictionary, was master of the grammar school.

10 **Coniston** RUSKIN, JOHN (1819–1900), writer on art and sociology, lived at Brantwood 1871 until his death and is buried in the churchyard.

11 **Didsbury** FARINGTON, JOSEPH (1747–1821), diarist and artist, buried here.

12 **Dragley Beck** BARROW, SIR JOHN (1764–1848), traveller and author, born here. He wrote widely of his travels, especially to the Arctic, and founded the Royal Geographical Society in 1830.

13 **Grassendale** BROSTER, DOROTHY KATHLEEN (d1950), novelist, born here. Her works include *The Flight of the Heron*, 1925, and its sequel, *The Gleam in the North*, 1927.

14 **Great Crosby** FRANCIS, M. E. (pseudonym of Mrs Mary Francis Blundell, 1859–1930), novelist, lived here and set many of her stories in nearby Liverpool.

15 **Hawkshead** BECK, THOMAS ALCOCK (1795–1846), Lancashire historian, buried here.
SMITH, ELIZABETH (1776–1806), poet and oriental scholar, lived at Tent Lodge.
WORDSWORTH, WILLIAM (1770–1850), poet laureate, lived at the present Wordsworth Cottage while attending the school here, 1778–86.

16 **Hazlehurst** HODSON, JAMES LANSDALE (1891–1956), novelist, born here. His works, mostly with Lancashire settings, include *Grey Dawn, Red Night*, 1929, and *Harvest in the North*, 1934.

17 **Holme** WHITAKER, THOMAS DUNHAM (1759–1821), author of topographical works on Lancashire, lived and is buried here.

18 **Hornby** LINGARD, JOHN (1771–1851), historian, lived here from 1811 until his death.

19 **Hurstwood** SPENSER, EDMUND (c1552–99), poet, was here for a year in 1576, at his family's home, after leaving Cambridge.

20 **Kersal (Broughton)** WAUGH, EDWIN (1817–90), poet, buried here (see **Rochdale**).

21 **Lancaster** BELLEW, JOHN (1823–74), preacher and poet, born. His novel *Blount Tempest* appeared in 1864.
BINYON, LAURENCE (1869–1943), poet, born here. His poem for the dead of the World War I, 'For the Fallen', appeared in the volume *The Four Years*, 1918.
WHEWELL, WILLIAM (1794–1866), philosopher, born here. He wrote many distinguished works on science and morality.

22 **Leigh** FARINGTON, JOSEPH (1747–1821), artist and diarist, born here. His diary was found in an attic in 1921.
HILTON, JAMES (1900–54), novelist, born here. His popular novels, made into films, include *Lost Horizon*, 1933, *Goodbye, Mr Chips*, 1934, and *Random Harvest*, 1941.

23 **Liverpool** ARNOLD, MATTHEW (1822–88), poet, collapsed and died in Dingle Lane while staying with his sister at Dingle Bank, now demolished.
BIRRELL, AUGUSTINE (1850–1933), statesman and essayist, born at Wavertree. He published miscellaneous literary criticism and works on Hazlitt, 1902, and Marvell, 1905.
CLOUGH, ARTHUR HUGH (1819–61), poet, born at 9 Rodney Street. His works include *The Bothie*, 1848, *Amours de Voyage*, 1849, and *Dipsychus*, 1849.
CRANE, WALTER (1845–1915), book illustrator, born here. He did the pictures for his sister Lucy's books of rhymes and for many of Mrs Molesworth's books.
GLADSTONE, WILLIAM EWART (1809–98), statesman and author born at 62 Rodney Street. He wrote books on religion and the classics, and translated a number of classical authors.
GUNTER, ARCHIBALD (1847–1907), novelist, born in Liverpool and lived here until 1853. He wrote and dramatised *Mr Barnes of New York*, 1887, and *Mr Potter of Texas*, 1888.
HAWTHORNE, NATHANIEL (1804–64), American novelist, was US Consul here 1853–57 and lived in Duke Street and at Rock Park. *Our Old Home*, 1863, is a collection of essays about his impressions of England.
HEMANS, MRS FELICIA DOROTHEA (1793–1835), poet, born 118 Duke Street and lived from 1827 at High Street, Wavertree. Her works include 'Casabianca' ('The boy stood on the burning deck').
HOCKING, SILAS (1850–1935), novelist, wrote *Her Benny*, 1879, set in the Liverpool slums, while a pastor at Grove Street.
JACKSON, HOLBROOK (1874–1948), literary historian, born here. He wrote the first study of G. Bernard Shaw, 1907.

IRVING, WASHINGTON (1793–1859), essayist and historian, had a merchant business here until its failure in 1818. This led to his writing *The Sketch-Book*, 1819–20, which contains the story of Rip Van Winkle.

LEAR, EDWARD (1812–88), poet and artist, wrote his *Book of Nonsense*, 1846, for the Earl of Derby's children while staying at the Earl's seat at Knowsley where he was working on a series of lithographs of the private zoo.

LE GALLIENNE, RICHARD (1866–1947), poet and essayist, born here. His most popular work was *Quest of the Golden Girl*, 1896.

LOWRY, CLARENCE MALCOLM (1909–57), novelist and poet, born here. His principal work, *Under the Volcano*, was published in 1947.

OLIPHANT, MRS MARGARET (1828–97), novelist, lived here from early childhood until the appearance of her first book, *Mrs Margaret Maitland*, 1849.

PICTON, SIR JAMES ALLANSON (1805–89), historian and founder of the Picton Library here, 1879, was born and died in Liverpool. His publications include *Memorials of Liverpool*, 1873.

RICHMOND, LEGH (1772–1827), novelist, born here. His novelettes, *Dairyman's Daughter*, *Negro Servant* and *Young Cottager*, were published together as *Annals of the Poor*, 1814.

ROSCOE, WILLIAM (1753–1831), poet and historian, born at Mount Pleasant. His works include a *Life of Lorenzo de' Medici*, 1795, and a life of Leo X, 1805.

STANLEY, FERDINANDO, 5TH EARL OF DERBY (c1559–94), poet and patron of the arts, lived at Knowsley Hall. He was Amyntas in Edmund Spenser's *Colin Clout*, 1595.

TIREBUCK, WILLIAM EDWARDS (1854–1900), novelist, born here. His works include *Miss Grace of All Souls*, 1895, and the posthumous *Twixt God and Mammon*, 1903.

TRESSELL, ROBERT (pseudonym of Robert Noonan, 1868–1911), author of *The Ragged Trousered Philanthropists*, 1910, lodged at 35 Erskine Street and died in Liverpool Royal Infirmary.

WATSON, SIR WILLIAM (1858–1935), poet, is buried at Childwall.

WHITE, JOSEPH BLANCO (1775–1841), poet, buried here.

24 Manchester AGATE, JAMES EVERSHED (1877–1947), novelist and dramatic critic, born here. His best known work is his diary, published in nine volumes under the general title *Ego*.

AINSWORTH, WILLIAM HARRISON (1805–82), novelist, born here. His many popular historical novels include *The Tower of London*, 1840, *Old St Paul's*, 1841, and *The Lancashire Witches*, 1848.

BAMFORD, SAMUEL (1788–1872), poet, known as the Bard of Middleton, born there. A weaver, he published poems and *Passages in the Life of a Radical* and *Early Days*, 1840–59.

BANKS, MRS LINNAEUS (1821–97), novelist, born here. Her works include the novel *The Manchester Man*, 1872. She was married to George Linnaeus (1821–81), poet and journalist.

BILLINGTON, WILLIAM (1827–84), dialect poet and writer, born at Salmesbury.

BRIERLEY, BENJAMIN (1825–96), dialect writer, born at Failsworth. He helped to found Manchester Literary Club, 1864, and edited *Ben Brierley's Journal*, 1869–91.

BURNETT, FRANCES ELIZA HODGSON (1849–1924), novelist, born here. Her *Little Lord Fauntleroy* appeared in 1886. She died in America.

BYROM, JOHN (1692–1763), poet, lived in St John's Street and is buried in the cathedral.

BYRON, HENRY JAMES (1834–84), dramatist, born here. His most popular play was *Our Boys*, 1875.

COLLIER, JOHN (1708–86), poet, known as Tim Bobbin, born at Urmston. He was best known for his *View of the Lancashire Dialect*, 1775.

DE QUINCEY, THOMAS (1785–1859), essayist, born at Greenheys and baptised at St Anne's church. *Confessions of an English Opium-Eater* appeared in 1821 in the *London Magazine*.

DIXON, WILLIAM HEPWORTH (1821–79), historian and traveller, born here. He edited the *Athenaeum* 1853–69.

GASKELL, MRS ELIZABETH CLEGHORN (1810–65), novelist and biographer, lived at several addresses in Manchester after her marriage to William Gaskell, a Unitarian minister. Manchester working-class life is much featured in her books.

GOLDING, LOUIS (1895–1958), novelist, born here. Manchester is the Doomington of many of his books, the best known of which is *Magnolia Street*, 1931.

GOULD, NAT (Nathaniel, 1857–1919), novelist and journalist, born here. His first book about racing, *The Double Event*, 1891, was followed by over 130 more novels of the turf.

HAMILTON, MARY AGNES (1884–1966), novelist, biographer and historian, born here. Her works include *Less than the Dust*, 1912, and *Dead Yesterdays*, 1916.

MONKHOUSE, ALLAN (1858–1936), dramatist and novelist, worked on the *Manchester Guardian* 1902–32.

OXENHAM, JOHN (pseudonym of William Dunkerley, 1852–1941), novelist and religious poet, born here. He wrote many novels and collections of verse. His volume of verse *Bees in Amber*, rejected by publishers, sold over a quarter of a million copies when published privately in 1913.

SWAIN, CHARLES (1801–74), poet, born at Every Street, lived and died at Prestwich Park and is buried in Prestwich churchyard. Many of his verses were set to music and became very popular, among them 'I cannot mind my wheel, mother' and 'Somebody's waiting for somebody'.

25 Oldham HAMERTON, PHILIP (1834–94), writer on art, born at Shaw.

26 Preston BRAZIL, ANGELA (1868–1947), writer of school stories, born here. Her schoolgirl tales enjoyed great popularity, beginning with *The Fortunes of Philippa*, 1906.

SERVICE, ROBERT WILLIAM (1874–1958), poet, born here. Termed the Canadian Kipling, he spent eight years in the Yukon. Among his published collections are *Songs of a Sourdough*, 1907, and *Bar Room Ballads*, 1940.

THOMPSON, FRANCIS (1859–1907), poet, born here. His famous 'Hound of Heaven' was included in his first collection of verse, 1893.

27 Rochdale COLLIER, JOHN (1708–86), poet, was master of the school 1739 until his death and is buried here (see **Manchester**).

WAUGH, EDWIN (1817–90), poet and novelist, born here. He was known as the Lancashire Burns for his *Poems and Songs*, 1859.

28 Salford BRIGHOUSE, HAROLD (1882–1958), dramatist, born here. *Hobson's Choice* was first produced in 1916.

29 Sawrey POTTER, BEATRIX (1866–1943), children's writer and artist, owned Hill Top 1905 until her death. The house, preserved for the public to visit, is the setting for several of her best known stories of animal characters, among them *The Tale of Mr Jeremy Fisher*, *The Tale of Tom Kitten* and *The Tale of Jemima Puddle-Duck*. Most of the stories were written and illustrated here. In 1909 she bought nearby Castle Farm and used Hill Top as a writing retreat.

30 Silverdale RILEY, WILLIAM (b1866), Pennine novelist, lived here.

31 **Singleton** LEIGH, CHARLES (1662–c1701), physician and naturalist, born at The Grange. He published a natural history of Lancashire 1700.

32 **Southport** JEANS, SIR JAMES HOPWOOD (1877–1946), astronomer and author, born here. His popular books on astronomy include *The Universe Around Us*, 1929, and *The Mysterious Universe*, 1930.

33 **Walton-le-Dale** BAINES, EDWARD (1774–1848), historian, topographer and journalist, born here.

34 **Warrington** AIKIN, LUCY (1781–1864), essayist and historian, born here. Daughter of JOHN AIKIN (1747–1822), author, and niece of MRS ANNA LETITIA BARBAULD (1743–1825), author, both of whose lives she wrote. She was chiefly known for *Memoirs of the Courts of Elizabeth, James I, and Charles I*, 1818–33.

35 **Wigan** LINACRE, THOMAS (c1460–1524), physician and classical scholar, rector for a time between 1509–20.

WINSTANLEY, GERRARD (c1609–c1660), reformer and pamphleteer, born here. Known as the 'digger' or 'leveller', he advocated common people's rights to waste land.

Yorkshire: West Riding
(*Maps 19 & 20*)

1 **Aldborough** THOMAS, ANNIE (1838–1918), novelist, born here. She wrote more than a hundred books, including *Denis Donne*, 1864, and *Essentially Human*, 1897.

2 **Appleton Roebuck** THOMAS, LORD FAIRFAX (1612–71), soldier and poet, lived at Nun Appleton Hall and died here (see **Denton**).

3 **Aston** MASON, WILLIAM (1724–97), poet, rector from 1754 and buried here.

4 **Bardsey** CONGREVE, WILLIAM (1670–1729), dramatist, born here. His classic comedies include *The Double Dealer*, 1693, *Love for Love*, 1695, and *The Way of the World*, 1700.

5 **Barnsley** ELLIOTT, EBENEZER (1781–1849), the 'Corn Law Rhymer', lived from 1841 at Great Houghton nearby and died there (see **Rotherham**).
GOODYEAR, ROBERT ARTHUR HANSON (1877–1948), boys' author, born here. His many school stories were widely popular in their time.

6 **Bilbrough** THOMAS, LORD FAIRFAX (1612–71), soldier and poet, buried here (see **Denton**).

7 **Bilton** KEARY, ANNIE (1825–79), novelist, born at Bilton Hall. Her *Castle Daly*, 1875, set in Ireland, was highly praised.

8 **Bingley** NICHOLSON, JOHN (d1843), the Airedale poet, buried here (see **Harewood**).
SUTCLIFFE, HALLIWELL (1870–1932), novelist, born at Castlefield House. His many novels, mostly set in Yorkshire, include *Under the White Cockade*.

9 **Birtall** BRONTË, CHARLOTTE (1816–55), novelist, often visited the home of her friend Ellen Nussey here and mentioned Birtall in her works.

10 **Bishopthorpe** SANDYS, GEORGE (1578–1644), travel writer and translator, born here. He wrote a notable book, *A Relation of a Journey begun An. Dom. 1610*, about his travels in Turkey, Egypt, the Holy Land and Italy. He also translated Ovid's *Metamorphoses*, 1621–26.

11 **Bolton Abbey** CLIFFORD, HENRY DE (c1455–1523), buried here. He is celebrated in WORDSWORTH's 'Brougham Castle' and 'White Doe of Rylstone'.

12 **Bowland Forest** GARTH, SIR SAMUEL (1661–1719), poet, born here. He wrote the satirical poem 'The Dispensary', 1699, and the topographical 'Claremont', 1715. In 1700 he ensured burial for the neglected John Dryden in Westminster Abbey.

13 **Bradford** ONIONS, OLIVER (1873–1961), novelist, born here. He was first successful with a trilogy: *In Accordance with the Evidence*, 1912, *The Debit Account*, 1913, and *The Story of Louie*, 1913.
RILEY, WILLIAM (1866–1937), novelist, born here. Most of his many novels are set in the West Riding, including *Windyridge*, 1912, *Old Obbut*, 1933, and *Common Clay*, 1941.

14 **Brotherton** DAUBUZ, CHARLES (1673–1717), writer on religious subjects, was vicar from 1699 and is buried here.

15 **Burley-in-Wharfedale** WATSON, SIR WILLIAM (1858–1935), poet, born here. His 'Lachrymae Musarum', 1892, was the official elegy on Tennyson.

16 **Calverley** FABER, FREDERICK WILLIAM (1814–63), hymn writer, born here. His compositions include 'The Pilgrims of the Night' and 'The Land beyond the Sea'.

17 **Conisborough** The setting for parts of SIR WALTER SCOTT's *Ivanhoe*, 1819.

18 **Crofton** MAGNALL, RICHMAL (d1820), author of the once standard history book for children, *Magnall's Questions*, taught for most of her life at Crofton Hall School and is buried here.

19 **Dacre** ORAGE, ALFRED RICHARD (1873–1934), journalist and editor, born here. As editor of the *New Age*, 1907–22, he made an important contribution to the literature of the time, and also published critical writings of his own, including *Readers and Writers*, 1922, and *The Art of Reading*, 1930.

20 **Darfield** ELLIOTT, EBENEZER (1781–1849), the 'Corn Law Rhymer', buried here (see **Rotherham**).

21 **Denton** THOMAS, LORD FAIRFAX (1612–71), soldier and poet, born here. His publications include two memoirs of the Civil War.

22 **Ecclesfield** EWING, MRS JULIANA HORATIA (1841–85), children's author, born at the vicarage. Her works include *A Flat Iron for a Farthing*, 1872, *Jan of the Windmill*, 1876, and *Jackanapes*, 1883.
GATTY, MRS MARGARET (1809–73), children's author and mother of Mrs Ewing, lived here 1840–73 and founded *Aunt Judy's Magazine*, 1865. Her husband, Alfred Gatty, a clergyman, wrote historical books. Both are buried here.
HUNTER, JOSEPH (1783–1861), historian and Shakespearean scholar, buried here.

23 **Gomersal** The home of Hiram Yorke in CHARLOTTE BRONTË's *Shirley*, 1849.
KNOWLES, HERBERT (1798–1817), poet, born here. His works include 'Stanzas in Richmond Churchyard'.

24 **Halifax** ASPINALL, ARTHUR (1901–72), historian, was born at Stainland nearby. He published many works, including series of the letters of George III, 1962–70, and of George, Prince of Wales, 1963–69.
FAVOUR, JOHN (d1624), churchman and author, buried here.
FLETCHER, JOSEPH SMITH (1863–1935), novelist, born here. He also wrote non-fiction, including a history of Yorkshire, 1901, but was best known for such detective novels as *Middle Temple Murder*, 1918.
SAVILE, SIR HENRY (1549–1622), classical scholar and mathematician, born here. His principal work is *Rerum Anglicarum Scriptores*, 1596, a collection of the chronicles of William of Malmesbury, Henry of Huntingdon, Roger Hovedon and Ingulf.

25 **Harewood** NICHOLSON, JOHN (1790–1843), the Airedale poet, born here. A wool-sorter, he published *Airedale in Ancient Times*, 1825. His poems were collected after his death.

26 **Harrogate** HAMILTON, ELIZABETH (1758–1816), novelist, died here.

27 **Haworth** The parsonage was the home of the BRONTË FAMILY from 1821 and the scene of the composition of such masterpieces as *Jane Eyre*, 1847, and *Wuthering Heights*, 1847. All except Anne are buried here, and the parsonage is a Brontë museum.

28 **Heckmondwike** KNOWLES, HERBERT (1798–1817), poet, buried here (see **Gomersal**).

29 **Horbury** BARING-GOULD, SABINE (1834–1924), novelist, folklorist and hymn writer, curate in 1864.

30 **Idle** WRIGHT, JOSEPH (1855–1930), philologist, born here. He taught himself to read and write and eventually became professor of philology at Oxford. He compiled

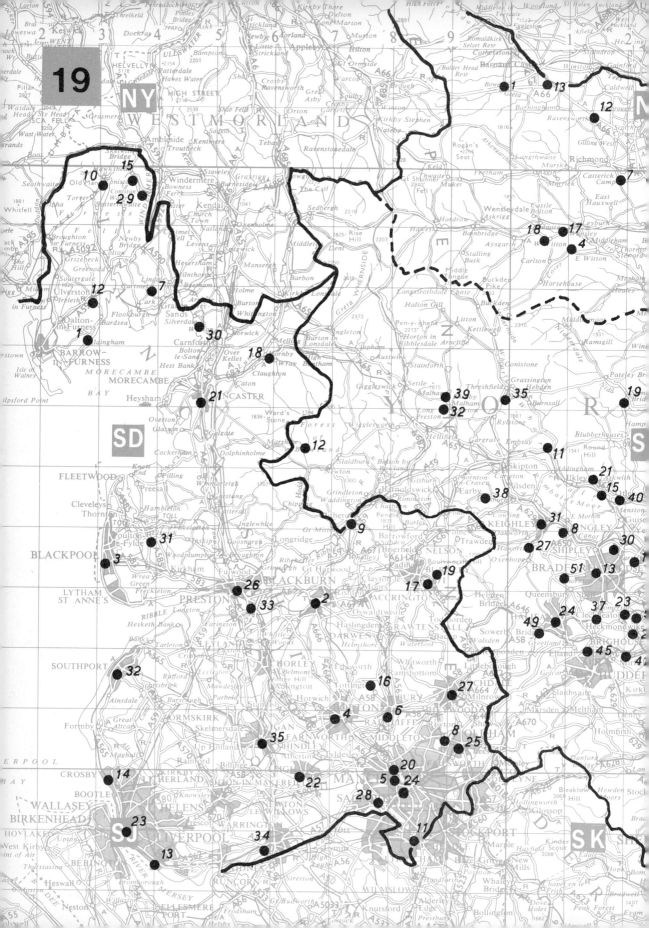

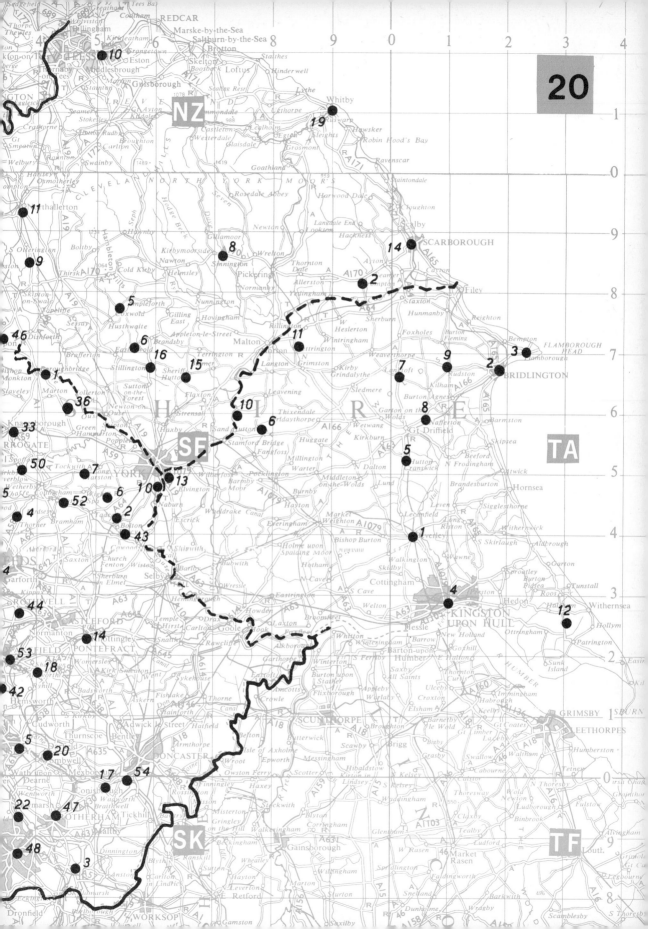

The English Dialect Dictionary, 1896–1905, among other works.

31 Keighley BOTTOMLEY, GORDON (1874–1948), poet and dramatist, born here. He revived English verse drama with such plays as *The Crier by Night*, 1902, and *The Riding to Lithend*, 1909, and published volumes of verse including two series of *Chambers of Imagery*, 1907 and 1912.

SNOWDEN, JAMES KEIGHLEY (1860–1947), novelist, born here. His stories, mostly set in Yorkshire, include *The Plunder Pit*, 1898, and *Barbara West*, 1901.

32 Kirkby Malham The setting of CHARLES KINGSLEY's novel *The Water Babies*, 1863.

33 Knaresborough The scene of Eugene Aram's murder of Daniel Clark in 1745, the subject of a romance by BULWER LYTTON and of a ballad by THOMAS HOOD.

STUBBS, WILLIAM (1825–1901), bishop and historian, born here. His chief work is the *Constitutional History of England* (to 1485), published 1874–78. He was bishop of Chester and of Oxford.

34 Leeds AUSTIN, ALFRED (1835–1913), poet laureate 1896, born at Headingley. He published many volumes of lyrical verse and several novels, but was much criticised as laureate.

AYSCOUGH, JOHN (pseudonym of Francis Browning Drew Bickerstaffe-Drew, 1858–1928), Catholic priest and novelist, born here. His works include *Dromina*, 1909, and *Monksbridge*, 1914.

CORNWALL, BARRY (pseudonym of Bryan Waller Procter, 1787–1874), poet and playwright, born here. His most successful play was *Mirandola*, 1821, and the best of his poetry is in *English Songs*, 1832.

FAIRBROTHER, NAN (1915–71), writer on the environment, born here. Her works on landscape and architecture include *Men and Gardens*, *The House* and *New Lives, New Landscapes*.

HAKE, THOMAS (1809–95), the 'Parable Poet', born here. His works include *Madeline*, 1871, and *Parables and Tales*, 1873.

NICOLL, ROBERT (1814–37), poet, died here.

PRIESTLEY, JOSEPH (1733–1804), scientist and author, born here. His best known theological writing is *History of the Corruptions of Christianity*, 1782. His *History of Electricity*, 1767, won him election as Fellow of the Royal Society. He died in Pennsylvania.

RANSOME, ARTHUR (1884–1967), critic and children's novelist, born here. He was first recognised for literary studies, but gained wide fame with *Peter Duck*, 1932, and such other children's stories as *Swallows and Amazons*, 1930.

SMILES, SAMUEL (1812–1904), author of *Self-Help*, 1859, was a surgeon here and then editor of the *Leeds Times*.

SUDDABY, DONALD (1900–64), boys' novelist, born here. His books include *Lost Men in the Grass*, 1940, and *The Star Raiders*, 1950.

THORESBY, RALPH (1685–1725), antiquary and topographer, buried here.

35 Linton SUTCLIFFE, HALLIWELL (1870–1932), novelist, lived at White Abbey House and died here.

36 Little Ouseburn BRONTË ANNE (1820–49), novelist, was governess to the Robinson children at Thorp Green, 1841–45.

37 Liversedge Healds Hall was the home of Hammond Roberson, portrayed by CHARLOTTE BRONTË as the Reverend Matthewman Helstone in *Shirley*, 1849.

38 Lothersdale Stonegappe House is the original Gateshead of CHARLOTTE BRONTË's *Jane Eyre*, 1847.

39 Malham KINGSLEY, CHARLES (1819–75), novelist, began to write *The Water Babies*, 1863, while staying here c1862. With **Kirkby Malham** it is the story's setting.

40 Menston KNIGHT, ERIC (1897–1943), author and cartoonist, born here. He wrote the immensely popular dog story *Lassie Come Home*, first published in 1942 in the USA, where Knight spent most of his life.

41 Mirfield BRONTË, CHARLOTTE, EMILY and ANNE were pupils at Miss Margaret Wooler's school at Roe Head 1831–32. Charlotte returned for a short time in 1835 to teach. Anne was governess at Blake Hall 1839–41 and wrote much of *Agnes Grey*, 1847, there.

42 Newmillerdam NORTON, CAROLINE ELIZABETH SARAH (1808–77), poet and novelist, lived at Kettlethorpe Hall.

43 Nunappleton DOYLE, SIR FRANCIS HASTINGS CHARLES (1810–88), poet, born here. His works include *Return of the Guards*, 1866, and *The Private of the Buffs*.

44 Oulton BENTLEY, RICHARD (1662–1742), classical scholar, born here. His *Dissertation on the Letters of Phalaris*, 1699, has long been regarded as a masterpiece of literary exposition.

45 Rastrick FAIRLESS, MICHAEL (pseudonym of Margaret Fairless Barber, 1869–1901), essayist, born at Castle Hill. Her book of essays, poems and reflections, *The Roadmender*, appeared posthumously in 1902.

46 Ripon JACOB, NAOMI ELLINGTON (1884–1964), novelist, born here. Her first novel, *Jacob Usher*, 1926, was one of her most successful. She also enjoyed a large readership for her autobiographical series, beginning with *Me: A Chronicle about Other People*, 1933.

47 Rotherham ELLIOTT, EBENEZER (1781–1849), the 'Corn Law Rhymer', born at Masborough nearby. Besides *Corn-Law Rhymes and the Ranter*, 1831, he published *Night*, 1818, and *The Village Patriarch*, 1829.

48 Sheffield BAILEY, SAMUEL (1791–1870), philosophical writer, born here. He published *Letters on the Philosophy of the Human Mind*, 1855–63.

CHATTERTON, EDWARD KEBLE (1878–1944), writer about the sea, born here. He wrote on all aspects of ships and the sea for adults and young readers.

GILCHRIST, ROBERT MURRAY (1868–1917), novelist, born here. Most of his books are set in Derbyshire's High Peak district, and include *A Peakland Faggot*, 1897, and *Willowbrake*, 1898.

GREEN, MARY ANNE EVERETT (1818–95), historian, born here. She wrote *Lives of the Princesses of England*, 1849–55, and *Letters of Royal and Illustrious Ladies*, 1846, among other works.

HOLLAND, JOHN (1794–1872), poet and writer, born here. He edited Sheffield newspapers, wrote *Sheffield Park*, 1820, and completed the *Poets of Yorkshire*, 1845.

MONTGOMERY, JAMES (1771–1854), poet, died here.

RUSKIN, JOHN (1819–1900), writer on art and sociology, founded the Ruskin Museum, Walkley, in 1875.

WILSON, ROMER (pseudonym of Florence Roma Muir Wilson, 1891–1930), novelist, born here. Her most acclaimed work was *The Death of Society*, 1921. She also published collections of fairy stories.

49 Sowerby Bridge FOSTER, JOHN (1770–1843), essayist, born here. His four *Essays, in a Series of Letters* appeared 1805.

50 Spofforth EUSDEN, LAURENCE (1688–1730), poet laureate 1718, born here. He was satirised in Pope's *Dunciad* as a drunken parson.

51 Thornton BRONTË, CHARLOTTE (1816–55), BRANWELL (1817–48), EMILY (1818–48) and ANNE (1820–49) all born here. The family moved to Haworth (qv) in 1820.

ROLLE, RICHARD (c1290–1349), the 'Hermit of Hampole', near Doncaster, born here. His main work was *The Pricke of Conscience*, a poem in English and Latin.

52 Thorp Arch ATKINSON, WILLIAM (1757–1846), poet, born and buried here. He published *Political Essays*, 1786.

53 Wakefield BURTON, JOHN (1710–71), antiquary, born here. Author of *Monasticon Eboracense*, he was immortalised by Laurence Sterne as Dr Slop in *Tristram Shandy*, 1759.

GISSING, GEORGE ROBERT (1857–1903), novelist, born here. His publications include *The Nether World*, 1889, *The Odd Women*, 1893, and *New Grub Street*, 1891.

WATERTON, CHARLES (1782–1865), naturalist, born and lived at Walton Hall. His travels are vividly recounted in *Wanderings in South America, the Northwest of the United States, and the Antilles*, 1825.

54 Warmsworth FAWKES, FRANCIS (1720–77), poet and clergyman, born at the rectory. Translator of many classic authors, he is best remembered as author of the comic song 'The Brown Jug'.

Yorkshire: North Riding
(*Maps 19 & 20*)

1 Bowes What remains of William Shaw's school, the original of Dotheboys Hall in CHARLES DICKENS's *Nicholas Nickleby*, 1838–39, is now a café. A pupil's tombstone in Bowes churchyard inspired Dickens to create the character Smike.

2 Brompton WORDSWORTH, WILLIAM (1770–1850), poet laureate, married Mary Hutchinson (1770–1859) here in 1802.

3 Catterick BRAITHWAITE, or BRATHWAITE, RICHARD (c1588–1673), poet, spent his last years at Catterick and is buried here.

4 Coverham COVERDALE, MILES (1488–1568), born here. He was a translator of the Bible, 1535, and bishop of Exeter 1551–53.

5 Coxwold STERNE, LAURENCE (1713–68), novelist, lived at Shandy Hall from 1760 until his death, finishing *Tristram Shandy*, 1759–67, and writing *A Sentimental Journey*, 1768, and *Journal to Eliza*, 1773. His house has been restored for the public to visit, and in 1969 his remains were brought from London to Coxwold graveyard.

6 Crayke INGE, WILLIAM (1860–1954), dean of St Paul's and author, born here. His most popular publications were *Lay Thoughts of a Dean*, 1926 and 1931, and *Outspoken Essays*, 1919 and 1922.

7 Hipswell WYCLIFFE, JOHN (c1320–84), religious reformer and writer, born here. He instituted the first translation of the whole Bible into English and performed much of the task himself.

8 Kirbymoorside READ, SIR HERBERT EDWARD (1893–1968), poet and critic, born here. He wrote and lectured widely on art and literature and published several collections of verse.

9 Kirby Wiske ASCHAM, ROGER (1515–68), classical scholar, born here. He wrote *The Scholemaster*, 1570, an unfinished treatise on classical education and also *Toxophilus*, 1545, a work on archery at which he was skilled. Dr Samuel Johnson wrote his biography.

10 Middlesborough HORNUNG, ERNEST WILLIAM (1866–1921), novelist, born here. His best known work was *The Amateur Cracksman*, 1899, which introduced the gentleman-burglar Raffles.

11 Northallerton RYMER, THOMAS (1641–1713), critic and historiographer, born at Yafforth Hall. He stirred up much controversy with *Tragedies of the Last Age Considered*, 1678, disapproving of Shakespeare's method of dealing with history.

12 Ravensworth SHAW, CUTHBERT (1739–71), poet, born here. His works include *The Race* 'by Mercurius Spur', 1766, satirising other poets.

13 Rokeby SCOTT, SIR WALTER (1771–1832), novelist and poet, stayed at the hall with John Morritt in 1809 and wrote much of his poem *Rokeby*, 1813.

14 Scarborough BRONTË, ANNE (1820–49), youngest of the Brontë sisters and author of *Agnes Grey*, 1847, and *The Tenant of Wildfell Hall*, 1848, died and is buried here.

GOODYEAR, ROBERT ARTHUR HANSON (1877–1948), boys' author, spent his last years at Wintergleam, Wheatcroft, and died here.

MARTIN, JOHN PERCIVAL (c1880–1966), Methodist minister and children's author, born here. He achieved considerable success late in life with *Uncle*, 1964, and other books about Uncle the learned elephant.

15 Sheriff Hutton SKELTON, JOHN (c1460–1529), poet laureate, lived at the castle with his patron the Duke of Norfolk from 1513 until a few years before his death, writing here his *Garlande of Laurell*, 1523.

SMITH, SYDNEY (1771–1845), author and wit, a founder of the *Edinburgh Review*, rector at Foston nearby, 1808–29, where he built his own parsonage house in 1814.

16 Stillington and Sutton-on-the-Forest STERNE, LAURENCE (1713–68), novelist, was vicar of Sutton 1738 and of Stillington 1743.

17 Wensley MAUDE, THOMAS (1718–98), poet, buried here. He wrote principally of the Yorkshire dales.

18 West Witton JAMES, JOHN (1811–67), antiquary, born and buried here. His *History and Topography of Bradford* appeared 1841.

19 Whitby CAEDMON (d c670–680), the first English poet, is believed to have been a cowherd here before entering the monastery, where he spent the rest of his life.

LINSKILL, MARY (1840–91), novelist, born here. Her works include *Tales from the North Riding*, 1871, under the pseudonym Stephen Yorke, and *The Haven under the Hill*, 1886.

Yorkshire: East Riding
(Map 20)

1 **Beverley** ALFRED OF BEVERLEY (12th century), chronicler, was treasurer of the church.

DANIEL, GEORGE (1616–57), Cavalier poet, lived at Beswick nearby.

PARDOE, JULIA (1806–62), travel writer, historian and novelist, born at Beverley. Her many works include *The Hungarian Castle*, 1842, *Louis XIV and the Court of France*, 1847, and *The Confessions of a Pretty Woman*.

2 **Bridlington** KENT, WILLIAM (1684–1748), book illustrator, painter, architect and landscape gardener, born here. Illustrated Spenser's *Faerie Queene*, Gray's *Fables* and poems of Alexander Pope. *The Designs of Inigo Jones*, which he published in 1727 with the help of his patron Lord Burlington, had an important effect not only on architecture but on taste in general in the eighteenth century.

3 **Flamborough** The coast line is the setting for R. D. Blackmore's novel *Mary Anerley*, 1880.

4 **Hull** DYKES, JOHN BACCHUS (1823–76), hymn writer, born here. He was joint editor of *Hymns Ancient and Modern*, his own compositions including 'Lead, Kindly Light' and 'Nearer my God to Thee'.

EVENS, GEORGE BRAMWELL (1884–1943), writer and broadcaster on country lore known as Romany, born here. He wrote many books, beginning with *A Romany in the Country*, 1932.

MASON, WILLIAM (1724–97), poet and author, born here. His works include *Musaeus*, a monody on Pope's death, 1747.

SMITH, STEVIE (Florence Margaret, 1902–71), poet and novelist. She first gained acclaim with *Novel on Yellow Paper*, 1936, and was awarded the Queen's Medal for Poetry 1969.

5 **Hutton Cranswick** JESSE, EDWARD (1780–1868), naturalist and author, born here. His publications include *Scenes and Tales of Country Life*, 1844, and *Anecdotes of Dogs*, 1846.

6 **Kirby Underdale** THIRLWALL, CONNOP (1797–1875), prelate and historian, rector 1834–40.

7 **Langtoft** PETER OF LANGTOFT (d c1307), rhyming chronicler, probably born here.

8 **Nafferton** MORRIS, FRANCIS ORPEN (1810–93), naturalist, vicar 1844–54 and wrote his *History of British Birds* here.

9 **Rudston** HOLTBY, WINIFRED (1898–1935), novelist, born and buried here. Her *South Riding*, 1935, is set in an imaginary Yorkshire riding. Other works include *The Land of Green Ginger*, 1927. A Winifred Holtby Award is presented for the best regional novel of each year.

10 **Scrayingham** COX, SIR GEORGE (1827–1902), mythologist, born here. His works include *Tales of Ancient Greece*, 1868, and *Comparative Mythology and Folklore*, 1881.

11 **Settrington** TAYLOR, ISAAC jnr (1829–1901), author, rector from 1875 until his death.

12 **Winestead** MARVELL, ANDREW (1621–78), poet and satirist, born at the rectory. A powerful political writer, he is now chiefly remembered for his poetry, including 'Horatian Ode upon Cromwell's Return from Ireland', 1650, and 'Thoughts in a Garden'.

13 **York** ALCUIN, OR ALBINUS (735–804), theologian and philosopher, born here. His complete works appeared in 1617 and again in 1777.

MUNBY, ARTHUR JOSEPH (1828–1910), poet, barrister and diarist, born in The Terrace, Clifton. *Verses Old and New* appeared in 1865, *Vestigia Retrorsum* in 1891, *Poems* in 1901, and *Relicta* in 1909. His diaries were first published in 1972.

MURRAY, LINDLEY (1745–1826), grammarian, lived at Holgate from 1785 until his death and is buried in the Quaker graveyard.

SMITH, SYDNEY (1771–1845), clergyman and wit, lived at Heslington 1809–14.

WINTER, JOHN (pseudonym of Henrietta Vaughan Palmer, 1856–1911), born here. Her publications include *Regimental Legends* and *Bootles' Baby*.

WOOLMAN, JOHN (1720–72), diarist, buried here.

Cumberland (*Map 21*)

1 **Bassenthwaite** SPEDDING, JAMES (1808–81), essayist and editor, born at Mirehouse nearby. He edited Bacon's *Works*, 1857–59, and his *Life and Letters*, 1861–74.

2 **Bridekirk** TICKELL, THOMAS (1686–1740), poet, born at the vicarage. He was a close associate of Joseph Addison, who made him his Under-Secretary of State, 1717. His works include a notable elegy on Addison's death.

3 **Caldbeck** GRAVES, JOHN WOODCOCK (1795–1886), wool weaver, lived here. He wrote 'D'ye ken John Peel', 1832, about his huntsman friend who also lived here (see **Wigton**).

4 **Carlisle** ANDERSON, ROBERT (1770–1833), poet, born and buried here. He published the *Cumbrian Ballads*, 1805, written in dialect.
BARTON, BERNARD (1784–1849), Quaker poet and close friend of Charles Lamb, born here. His works include *The Convict's Appeal*, 1818, and *Household Verses*, 1845.
BLAMIRE, SUSAN (1747–94), poet, died here (see **Dalston**).
BROWN, JOHN (1715–66), 'Estimate Brown', poet and dramatist, a minor canon here.
CREIGHTON, MANDELL (1843–1901), prelate and historian, born here. He was appointed bishop of London, 1897. He published theological and biographical works, and edited the *English Historical Review* 1886–91.
HACK, MARIA (1777–1844), writer of stories for children, Bernard Barton's sister and also born in Carlisle.

5 **Cockermouth** WORDSWORTH, CHRISTOPHER (1774–1846), churchman and scholar, born here. He was brother of William and Dorothy, and published various works.
WORDSWORTH, DOROTHY (1771–1855), diarist, born here. Sister of William, she was his lifelong companion. Her *Grasmere Journal* inspired several of his best poems, and is valued in its own right for its descriptive qualities.
WORDSWORTH, WILLIAM (1770–1850), born here. Most eminent of the 'Lake Poets', he was created poet laureate in 1843.

6 **Crosthwaite** SOUTHEY, ROBERT (1774–1843), poet laureate and biographer, buried in the churchyard.

7 **Dalston** BLAMIRE, SUSAN (1747–94), poet, known as the Muse of Cumberland, born here. The county character is well reflected in her poems, collected in 1842.

8 **Keswick** COLERIDGE, SAMUEL TAYLOR (1772–1834), poet, philosopher and critic, lived here 1800–9. His daughter SARA (1802–52) was born at Greta Hall; she published translations and stories for children and edited her father's works.
LINTON, ELIZA LYNN (1822–98), novelist, born here. She wrote some twenty novels and was widely popular in her day; the 'new woman' was her particular target for criticism.
MYERS, FREDERIC HENRY (1843–1901), poet and psychic investigator, born here. He published several volumes of verse, and the first accounts of the work of the Society for Psychical Research, of which he was a founder.
SOUTHEY, ROBERT (1774–1843), poet laureate and biographer, lived at Keswick from 1803 and died here.
WALPOLE, SIR HUGH SEYMOUR (1884–1941), novelist, had his country home nearby.

9 **Muncaster Castle** LINDSAY, ALEXANDER WILLIAM CRAWFORD, 25TH EARL OF CRAWFORD and 8TH EARL OF BALCARRES (1812–80), historian and genealogist, born here. His works include *Sketches of the History of Christian Art*, 1847.

10 **Mungrisdale** CALVERT, RAISLEY (d1794), sculptor, lived here. His legacy of £900 enabled William Wordsworth to devote himself to poetry.

11 **Naworth** HOWARD, LORD WILLIAM (1563–1640), lived here. Sir Walter Scott's 'Belted Will' of *The Lay of the Last Minstrel*, he assisted William Camden in the compilation of *Britannia*, 1586.

12 **Netherby** Featured in SIR WALTER SCOTT's *Marmion*.

13 **Penrith** WORDSWORTH, WILLIAM and DOROTHY, attended school here for a time. Their mother is buried here.

14 **St John's-in-the-Vale** RICHARDSON, JOHN (1817–86), Cumberland dialect poet, buried here.

15 **Scaleby** GILPIN, WILLIAM (1724–1804), author, born here. He published biographies and works on the picturesque and romantic aspects of the scenery of Britain, illustrated with his own engravings.

16 **Sebergham** DENTON, THOMAS (1724–77), poet, born here. His work includes *Immortality*, 1754, and *The House of Superstition*, 1762.
RELPH, JOSEPH (1712–43), poet, born and lived here. His works were issued as *A Miscellany of Poems*, 1747.

17 **Wigton** GRAVES, JOHN WOODCOCK (1795–1886), wool weaver and author of the song 'D'ye Ken John Peel', born here.

Westmorland (*Map 21*)

1 Ambleside ARNOLD, MATTHEW (1822–88), poet and critic, lived at Fox How during the last years of his life.
COLERIDGE, HARTLEY (1796–1849), poet and biographer, son of Samuel Taylor Coleridge, was educated here as a child and later kept a school in Ambleside.
MARTINEAU, HARRIET (1802–76), journalist, reformer and novelist, lived at the Knole from 1845 until her death.

2 Crossthwaite SOUTHEY, ROBERT (1774–1843), poet laureate and biographer, buried here.

3 Grasmere COLERIDGE, SAMUEL TAYLOR (1772–1834), poet, spent long periods at Dove Cottage with the Wordsworths and de Quincey. His eldest son, HARTLEY (1796–1849), poet, lived in Grasmere after 1828 and is buried here.
DE QUINCEY, THOMAS (1785–1859), essayist, lived at Townend, moving to Dove Cottage in 1808 after the Wordsworths left. Apart from a break in 1821, when he moved to London and published *Confessions of an English Opium-Eater*, de Quincey lived at Grasmere until 1828, having married here in 1816.
WORDSWORTH, WILLIAM (1770–1850), poet laureate, lived at Dove Cottage from 1799, at first with his sister Dorothy (1804–47). In 1802 he married, and the three of them remained at the cottage until 1808. Wordsworth is buried at Grasmere. Dove Cottage is preserved for public view and there is a Wordsworth museum nearby.

4 Kendal BRAITHWAITE, or BRATHWAITE, RICHARD (1588–1673), poet, born here. His most notable work is a verse account of travel in England, in Latin, *Barnabae Itinerarium*, 1638.

5 Kirkby Lonsdale BICKERSTETH, EDWARD (1786–1850), author of the *Christian Psalmody*, born here.

6 Kirkby Stephen BURN, RICHARD (1709–85), antiquary and historian, born nearby at Winton, and was vicar of Orton from 1736 until his death there. His publications include a *History of Westmorland and Cumberland*, 1771.
CLOSE, JOHN (1816–91), termed by many contemporaries the worst poet in England, lived here.
LANGHORNE, JOHN (1735–79), poet, born nearby at Winton. His *Poetical Works* appeared in 1766, but he is best remembered as translator of Plutarch's *Lives*, 1770, in collaboration with his brother WILLIAM (1721–72), also born at Winton.

7 Long Sleddale WARD, MRS HUMPHREY (Mary Augusta Arnold, 1851–1920), novelist, wrote *Robert Elsmere*, 1888, here.

8 Rydal Mount WORDSWORTH, WILLIAM (1770–1850), poet laureate, lived here from 1813 and died here.

9 Milnthorpe HOLME, CONSTANCE (1881–1955), novelist, born here. Most of her books are set in Westmorland, and include *The Lonely Plough*, 1914, and *The Trumpet in the Dust*, 1921.

10 Windermere RANSOME, ARTHUR (1884–1967), critic and children's novelist, lived here until his death.
NORTH, CHRISTOPHER (pseudonym of John Wilson, 1785–1854), poet, essayist and journalist, lived at Elleray 1807–15.

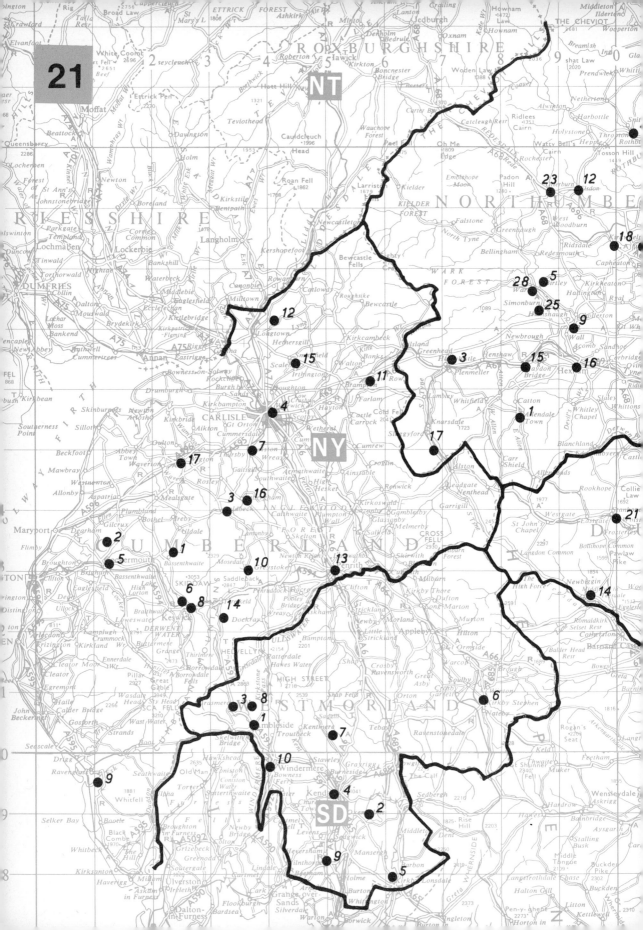

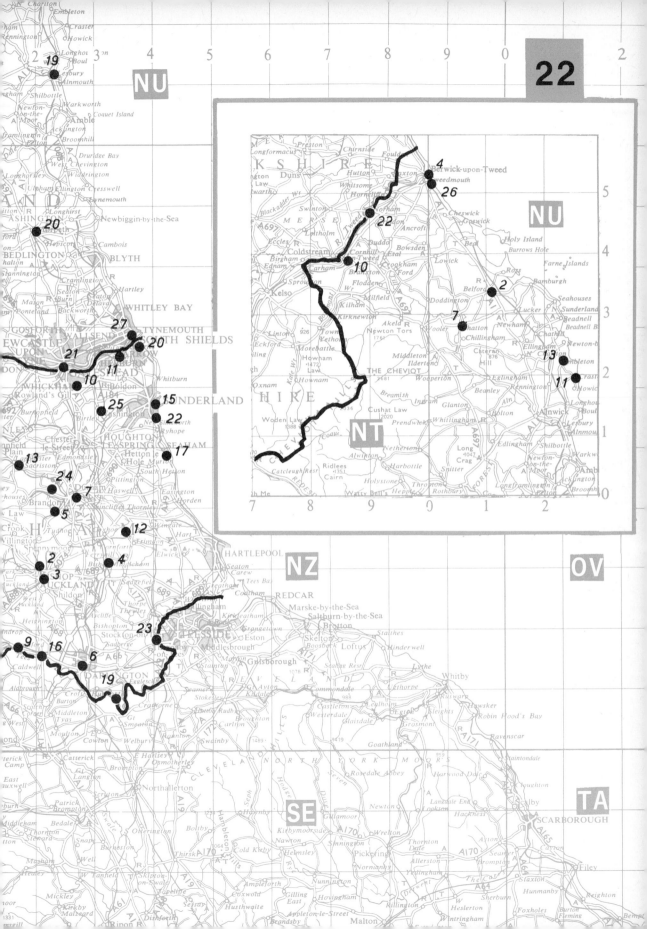

Durham (*Maps 21 & 22*)

1 Barnard Castle DICKENS, CHARLES (1812–70), novelist, stayed at the King's Head Inn in 1838 and is said to have derived the idea for *Master Humphrey's Clock*, 1840, from contemplating a clockmaker's sign across the road.

HUTCHINSON, WILLIAM (1732–1814), topographer of Durham and Cumberland, lived here.

MONKHOUSE, ALLAN (1858–1936), dramatist and novelist, born here. His novels are mostly set in Manchester, including *Man and Ghosts*, 1918, and *Alfred the Great*, 1927.

SCOTT, SIR WALTER (1771–1832), poet and novelist, frequently visited Rokeby, home of his friends the Morritts, and wrote some of his poems here, including 'Brignall Banks'.

2 Binchester LIDDELL, HENRY GEORGE (1811–98), lexicographer and dean of Christ Church, Oxford, born here. He was a friend of LEWIS CARROLL (1832–98), who wrote *Alice's Adventures in Wonderland*, 1865, for Liddell's daughter Alice.

3 Bishop Auckland LIGHTFOOT, JOSEPH BARBER (1828–89), theological scholar, writer and bishop of Durham, buried in the chapel of Auckland Castle.

WESTCOTT, BROOKE FOSS (1825–1901), theological historian and bishop of Durham, buried in the chapel of Auckland Castle.

4 Bishop Middleham SURTEES, ROBERT (1779–1834), historian, lived at Mainsforth and is buried in Bishop Middleham churchyard (see **Durham**).

5 Brandon SHADWELL, THOMAS (c1642–92), dramatist and poet, possibly born at Broomhill House, though some accounts favour Weeting, Norfolk. He conducted a lengthy literary feud with Dryden, whom he succeeded as poet laureate at the Revolution of 1688.

6 Darlington HODGSON, RALPH (1871–1962), poet, born here. Among the few collections of his verse—mostly dealing with nature—are *The Skylark and Other Poems*, 1961, and *Collected Poems*, 1961.

MATHER, JAMES MARSHALL (1851–1916), novelist, born here. His books include *By Roaring Loom*, 1898, and *The Sign of the Wooden Shoon*, 1896, set in Lancashire where he settled.

STEAD, WILLIAM THOMAS (1849–1912), journalist and social reformer, edited the *Northern Echo* here 1871–80 and lived at Grainey Hill.

7 Durham AUNGERVILLE, RICHARD (1281–1345), known as Richard de Bury, patron of literature and bishop of Durham, buried in the cathedral chapel.

BELL, GERTRUDE (1868–1926), travel writer, born at Washington Hall. Her posthumously published *Letters* are her best known writings.

BUTLER, JOSEPH (1692–1752), theological writer and bishop of Durham, died here.

DYKES, JOHN BACCHUS (1823–76), joint editor of *Hymns Ancient and Modern* and hymn writer, vicar of St Oswald's 1864–76 and buried here.

FALKNER, JOHN MEADE (1858–1932), scholar and novelist, died here.

HUNT, VIOLET (1866–1942), novelist, born here. Her books include *Unkist, Unkind!*, 1897, and *The House of Many Mirrors*, 1910.

MORTON, THOMAS (1764–1838), dramatist, born here. His *Speed the Plough*, 1798, created 'Mrs Grundy', the symbol of censorious society, though she appears only by reference, eg 'What would Mrs Grundy say if . . .'.

PORTER, JANE (1776–1850) and ANNA MARIA (1780–1832), novelist sisters, born here. Their most popular works, respectively, were *The Scottish Chiefs*, 1810, and *Don Sebastian*, 1809, and they collaborated on *Tales Round a Winter's Hearth*, 1824. Jane also wrote tragedies but had no success with them.

SURTEES, ROBERT (1779–1834), historian, born here. His *History of the County of Durham* appeared 1816–40. Sir Walter Scott included two of his ballads in his *Minstrelsy of the Scottish Border*. The Surtees Society was founded in 1834 to publish his unedited works.

SURTEES, ROBERT SMITH (1803–64), novelist, born and lived at Hamsterley Hall. His *Jorrocks's Jaunts and Jollities* first appeared in book form in 1838.

8 Ebchester SURTEES, ROBERT SMITH (1803–64), novelist, buried here.

9 Gainford DENHAM, MICHAEL AISLABIE (d1859), collector of folklore, buried here.

10 Heworth HODGSON, JOHN (1779–1845), historian of Northumberland, perpetual curate here and lived at High Heworth Farm 1808–23.

11 Jarrow BEDE ('the Venerable', 675–735), historian and learned in classics and the sciences, spent most of his life at the monastery of Jarrow and was buried here, his remains being removed to Durham in the eleventh century (see **Monkwearmouth**).

12 Kelloe BROWNING, ELIZABETH BARRETT (1806–61), poet, born at Coxhoe Hall. The family moved soon afterwards to Herefordshire.

13 Lanchester GREENWELL, DORA (1821–82), poet and essayist, born here. Her *Carmina Crucis* appeared 1869.

HODGSON, JOHN (1779–1845), historian of Northumberland, schoolmaster and curate here.

14 Middleton-in-Teesdale WATSON, RICHARD (b1833), wrote *Poems and Songs of Teesdale*.

15 Monkwearmouth BEDE ('the Venerable', 673–735), historian and learned in classics and the sciences, born in the district and spent part of his youth in the monastery. He wrote many works, including *The Ecclesiastical History of the English People* and the scientific treatise *De Natura Rerum*.

16 Piercebridge DENHAM, MICHAEL AISLABIE (d1859), collector of folklore, died here.

17 Seaham BYRON, GEORGE GORDON, 6TH LORD (1788–1824), poet, married Anne Isabella Milbanke in the drawing room of Seaham Hall in 1815.

18 Shotley Bridge ARMSTRONG, TOMMY (1848–1919), 'the pitman poet', born here. He wrote many Durham songs.

19 Sockburn WORDSWORTH, WILLIAM (1770–1850), poet laureate, and his sister DOROTHY (1771–1855), diarist, stayed at Sockburn Farm in 1799. It was here that he met Mary Hutchinson, whom he married three years later.

20 South Shields THOMPSON, ERNEST SETON (1860–1946), naturalist and author, born here. He wrote about animals of all parts of the world, beginning with the immensely successful *Wild Animals I Have Known*, 1898. He died in New Mexico.

21 Stanhope BUTLER, JOSEPH (1692–1752), theological writer and bishop of Durham, rector 1725–33.

22 Sunderland TAYLOR, TOM (1817–80), dramatist, born here. He wrote over a hundred plays, including *Still Waters Run Deep*, 1855, and contributed prolifically to *Punch*.

23 Stockton-on-Tees RITSON, JOSEPH (1752–1803), critic

and antiquary, born here. He made notable collections of songs and poems.

24 Ushaw LINGARD, JOHN (1771–1851), Roman Catholic historian of England, was vice-president of Ushaw College c1795–1811 and is buried here.

25 Washington BRAND, JOHN (1744–1806), antiquary, born here. He was resident secretary to the Society of Antiquaries, 1784–1806, and published a history of Newcastle-upon-Tyne.

Northumberland
(*Maps 21 & 22*)

1 **Allendale Town** PATTEN, ROBERT (fl1715–17), historian of the Jacobite rebellion, was curate here c1715.

2 **Belford** The source of many of the hunting characters in the Jorrocks sketches by ROBERT SMITH SURTEES (1803–64).
DODS, MARCUS (1786–1838), theological writer, minister 1810–38 and is buried here.

3 **Beltingham** HEDLEY, ANTHONY (1777–1835), historian, buried here.

4 **Berwick-upon-Tweed** MELVILL, JAMES (1556–1614), Scottish poet and diarist, buried here.
WILSON, JOHN MACKAY (1804–35), journalist and author, born and buried here. He edited the *Berwick Advertiser*, 1832, and issued *Tales of the Borders* 1834–35.

5 **Birtley** HALL, GEORGE ROME (1835–95), writer on Celtic antiquities, rector from 1860 until his death and is buried here.

6 **Cambo** ROBSON, WILLIAM (1785–1863), author and translator, was headmaster of the school.
TREVELYAN, GEORGE MACAULAY (1876–1962), historian and biographer, lived here.

7 **Chatton** WIDDRINGTON, SAMUEL EDWARD (c1791–1856), writer on Spain, born at the vicarage. He published his *Sketches in Spain during 1829–32* in 1834.

8 **Cherryburn, nr Newcastle-upon-Tyne** BEWICK, THOMAS (1753–1828), book illustrator, born here. He also created some notable books of his own, including *A General History of Quadrupeds*, 1790, and *A Natural History of British Birds*, 1797–1804. He was responsible for many innovations in the art of wood-engraving.

9 **Chollerford** CLAYTON, JOHN (1792–1890), classical scholar, lived at Chesters.

10 **Cornhill** STOCKDALE, PERCIVAL (1736–1811), author and critic, buried here.

11 **Craster** Claims (with Maxton, Roxburghshire) to be the birthplace of the philosopher and writer JOANNES SCOTUS DUNS (c1265–c1308).

12 **Elsdon** DUTENS, LOUIS (1730–1812), writer on literary and philosophical topics, was rector from 1765 until his death.

13 **Embleton** CREIGHTON, MANDELL (1843–1901), theological writer, bishop of London, and co-founder of the Northumberland County History, was vicar 1875–84.
STEAD, WILLIAM THOMAS (1849–1912), journalist and reformer, born at the Presbyterian manse. He was founder of the *Review of Reviews*, 1890, and instigator, while editor of the *Pall Mall Gazette*, 1883–90, of the 'Maiden Tribute' sensation, exposing the sale of girl children into prostitution. He drowned in the *Titanic* disaster.
TOVEY, DE BLOSSIERS (1692–1745), historian of the Jews in England, vicar here from 1727–32.

14 **Hartburn** HODGSON, JOHN (1779–1845), Northumberland historian, vicar 1833–45 and is buried here.
WHITTLE, THOMAS (d1731), poet, buried here.

15 **Haydon Bridge** TWEDDELL, JOHN (1769–99), classical scholar, born at Threepwood Hall. His *Prolusiones Juveniles* appeared in 1792.

16 **Hexham** GIBSON, WILFRED WILSON (1878–1962), poet of World Wars I and II, born here. He also wrote widely of ordinary workers and their lives, in town and country.

17 **Kirkhaugh** WALLIS, JOHN (1714–93), county historian, born at Castle Nook Farm. His *Natural History and Antiquities of Northumberland* appeared 1769.

18 **Kirkwhelpington** HEDLEY, ANTHONY (1777–1835), historian, curate here 1814–19.
HODGSON, JOHN (1779–1845), was vicar here 1823–32, writing most of his *History of Northumberland* in this time.

19 **Lesbury** STOCKDALE, PERCIVAL (1736–1811), author and critic, was vicar until his death here.

20 **Morpeth** HORSLEY, JOHN (1686–1732), archaeologist and author, minister and schoolmaster 1709–32, and buried here.

21 **Newcastle-upon-Tyne** AKENSIDE, MARK (1721–70), poet and physician, born here. His *Pleasures of the Imagination* was published in 1744.
BRUCE, JOHN COLLINGWOOD (1805–92), antiquary, buried here.
CUNNINGHAM, JOHN (1729–73), poet, buried here.
FORSTER, JOHN (1812–76), Charles Dickens's closest friend and biographer, born here. Besides his great life of Dickens (1872–74), he wrote on Walter Savage Landor and Oliver Goldsmith, and was author of many other works.
LANDELLS, EBENEZER (1818–60), founder of *Punch*, 1841, born here.
MERRIMAN, HENRY SETON (pseudonym of Hugh Stowell Scott, 1862–1903), novelist, born here. Of his many popular novels the best known is *Barlasch of the Guard*, 1902.
MONTAGU, LADY MARY WORTLEY (1689–1762), letter writer, lived at Denton Hall in the 1750s.
REID, SIR THOMAS WEMYSS (1842–1905), biographer, novelist and journalist, born here. Editor of the *Leeds Mercury* 1870–87, manager of the publishing house of Cassell & Co from 1887 until his death, and author of works of fiction and biography.

22 **Norham** GILLY, WILLIAM (1789–1855), author, vicar 1831–55 and buried here.

23 **Otterburn** HEDLEY, ANTHONY (1777–1835), historian, born here.

24 **Rothbury** BROWN, JOHN (1715–66), poet, playwright and author, born here. He became noted for his *Estimate of the Manners and Principles of the Times*, 1757.

25 **Simonburn** WALLIS, JOHN (1714–93), county historian, was curate here c1746–72.

26 **Tweedmouth** WILSON, JOHN MACKAY (1804–35), author and poet, born here. He founded the series *Tales of the Borders* with six volumes, published 1834–40. It was continued by others after his death.

27 **Tynemouth** SKIPSEY, JOSEPH (1832–1903), the 'collier poet', born here.

28 **Wark** STORY, ROBERT (1795–1860), Northumbrian poet, born here. His *Poetical Works* were issued by the Duke of Northumberland in 1857.

Scotland

Ayrshire (*Map 23*)

1 Airdmoss HYSLOP, JAMES (1798–1827), poet, wrote *Cameronian's Dream*, 1821, while farming at Airdmoss, the place where Richard Cameron, the outlawed covenanter, had been killed in 1680.

2 Alloway BURNS, ROBERT (1759–96), poet, born here. *Poems Chiefly in the Scottish Dialect* was published in 1786 in an attempt to raise money for him to emigrate, after failure in several trades, but it led instead to his becoming famous and remaining in Scotland.

3 Auchinleck BOSWELL, JAMES (1740–95), Dr Johnson's biographer, became laird on the death of his father in 1782.
BOYD, ANDREW KENNEDY HUTCHINSON (1825–99), essayist, born at the manse. Publications include *Recreations of a Country Parson* in three series, 1859–78.

4 Ayr RAMSAY, ANDREW MICHAEL (1686–1743), writer, born here. Known as the 'Chevalier de Ramsay', he published *Vie de Fenelon*, 1723, and *Les Voyages de Cyrus*, 1727.

5 Beith MONTGOMERIE, ALEXANDER (c1556–c1610), poet, born at Hasilhead Castle nearby. Laureate at the court of James VI, his main work was *The Cherry and the Slae*, 1597.

6 Dailly AINSLIE, HEW (1792–1878), poet, born here. His best known works are *A Pilgrimage to the Land of Burns*, 1822, and *Scottish Songs, Ballads and Poems*, 1855.

7 Dundonald MACPHAIL, MARION (1817–84), blind poet, born here. Her chief work was *Religious Poems*, 1882.

8 Irvine GALT, JOHN (1779–1839), novelist, born here. He published *The Ayrshire Legatees*, 1820, and *Annals of the Parish*, 1821.
MONTGOMERY, JAMES (1771–1854), poet, born here. Publications include *The Wanderer of Switzerland*, 1806, *The World Before the Flood*, 1812, and *The Pelican Island*, 1828.

9 Kilmarnock AITON, WILLIAM (1760–1847), agricultural writer, born at Silverwood. His *Agricultural Report for Ayrshire*, 1811, is a valuable source of 18th–19th century history.
PATERSON, JAMES (1805–76), journalist and antiquary, born at Struthers Farm. Author of a *History of the County of Ayr*, 1863–66, and editor of *Contemporaries of Burns*, 1840.
SMITH, ALEXANDER (1830–67), poet and essayist, born here. Publications include *A Life Drama*, 1853, *City Poems*, 1857, *Edwin of Deira*, 1861, and—in collaboration with Sidney Dobell—*Sonnets on the War*, 1855.

10 Kirkmichael KENNEDY, WALTER (c1460–c1508), poet, born here. He is best known for his *Flyting of Dunbar and Kennedy*, 1508.

11 Ladyland HAMILTON OF GILBERTFIELD, WILLIAM (c1665–1751), poet, born here. He corresponded in verse with Allan Ramsay in *Seven Familiar Epistles*, 1719, and translated Blind Harry's *Wallace* into English verse, 1722.

12 Lochgoin HOWIE, JOHN (1735–93), biographer, farmed here.

13 Lochlea BURNS, ROBERT (1759–96), poet, lived here for some years.

14 Mauchline BURNS, ROBERT (1759–96), poet, farmed at Mossgiel nearby with his brother Gilbert, and married Jean Armour at Mauchline in 1788.
TODD, ADAM BROWN (1822–1915), poet and journalist, born at Craighall nearby. Published *The Circling Year*, 1880, and *Homes, Haunts and Battlefields of the Covenanters*, 1886.

15 Muirkirk LAPRAIK, JOHN (1727–1807), poet and friend of Burns, born at Dalfram nearby. He published his *Poems* in 1788.

16 Ochiltree DOUGLAS, GEORGE (pseudonym of George Douglas Brown, 1869–1902), novelist, born here. He is best known for *The House with the Green Shutters*, 1901.

17 Pinmore KENNEDY, GRACE (1782–1824), novelist, born here. Her works include *Father Clement* and *Anna Ross*.

Galloway (Wigtown and Kirkcudbrightshire)
(*Map 23*)

1 **Borgue** NICHOLSON, WILLIAM (1783–1849), poet, born and died here. His *Tales in Verse and Miscellaneous Poems* appeared in 1814.

2 **Elrig** MAXWELL, GAVIN (1914–70), naturalist, artist and author, born here. *Ring of Bright Water* appeared in 1960 and *House of Elrig* in 1965.

3 **Kirkcudbright** BLACKLOCK, THOMAS (1721–91), poet, minister 1762–64.

4 **Lauriston** CROCKETT, SAMUEL RUTHERFORD (1860–1914), novelist, born here. *The Raiders*, 1894, a smuggling adventure, is set in Galloway, as is his equally successful tale *The Stickit Minister*, 1893.

Renfrewshire (*Map 23*)

1 Barrhead DAVIDSON, JOHN (1857–1909), poet, born here. His works include the chronicle play *Bruce*, 1886, *In a Music Hall*, 1891, and *Fleet Street Eclogues*, 1893 and 1896.

2 Eaglesham POLLOCK, ROBERT (1798–1827), poet, born here. *The Tales of the Covenanters* appeared in 1824 and *The Course of Time* in 1827.

3 Elderslie HAY, JOHN MACDOUGALL (1881–1919), author and poet, was minister of Elderslie West Church.

4 Greenock ADAM, JEAN (1710–65), poet, born here. A volume of her religious poems was published in 1734.

BLAKE, GEORGE (1893–1961), novelist, critic and historian, born here. He made his name with *The Shipbuilders*, 1926, but is better remembered for the series *The Westering Sun*, 1946, *The Five Arches*, and *The Voyage Home*, 1952.

CAIRD, EDWARD (1835–1908), philosopher, and JOHN (1820–98), theologian, born here. The latter became widely known for his *Introduction to the Philosophy of Religion*, 1880.

GALT, JOHN (1779–1839), novelist, came to live here in 1789 and again in 1834, and died here.

WEIR, DANIEL (1796–1831), poet, born here. He contributed songs to the *Scottish Minstrel* collection and edited the volumes of songs *The National Minstrel*, etc.

5 Lochwinnoch SEMPILL, FRANCIS (1616–82), poet, born here. He wrote *The Banishment of Poverty* and ballads, including 'Maggie Lauder'.

SEMPILL, SIR JAMES (1566–1625), satirist, lived here. Grandfather of Francis (above), his works include a satire on the Roman Catholic Church, *A Picktooth for the Pope, or the Packman's Paternoster*, 1600.

SEMPILL, ROBERT (c1595–1665), poet, son of James and father of Francis (above), probably born here. The metre of his *Life and Death of Habbie Simpson, the Piper of Kilbarchan*, 1640, became the standard metre for Scottish elegiac verse.

6 Paisley CARLILE, ALEXANDER (1788–1860), poet, born here. His poems were published in volume form in 1855.

FINLAY, WILLIAM (1792–1847), poet, born here. His *Poems, Humorous and Sentimental*, appeared in 1846.

HERVEY, THOMAS KIBBLE (1799–1859), poet, born here. He achieved recognition with his poem 'Australia' in 1824.

KENNEDY, WILLIAM (1799–1849), poet and writer, born here. His first volume of poems was *Fitful Fancies*, 1827.

LYLE, THOMAS (1792–1859), poet and surgeon, born here. His collection *Ancient Ballads and Songs, Chiefly from Tradition, Manuscripts and Scarce Works*, 1827, included several of his own compositions.

MOTHERWELL, WILLIAM (1797–1835), poet, was deputy-sheriff-clerk here 1819–29 and edited the *Paisley Advertiser* 1828–30.

NORTH, CHRISTOPHER (pseudonym of John Wilson, 1785–1854), journalist and essayist, born here. He was closely connected with *Blackwood's Magazine*, and published *The City and the Plague*, 1816, *Noctes Ambrosianae*, 1822–35, and *Lights and Shades of Scottish Life*, 1822.

PICKEN, ANDREW (1788–1833), novelist, born here. His publications include *The Dominie's Legacy*, 1830, and *The Black Watch*, 1833.

PICKEN, EBENEZER (1769–1816), poet, born here. He published several volumes of Scottish poems and a *Pocket Dictionary of the Scottish Dialects*, 1818.

SCADLOCK, JAMES (1775–1818), poet, born here. His 'October Winds' and some of his other lyrics were widely popular in his day.

SEMPLE, DAVID (1808–78), antiquary, practised as a conveyancer here.

SHARP, WILLIAM (1855–1905), novelist, born here. He published *Earth's Voices*, 1884, and novels under the pseudonym Fiona Macleod, including *The Mountain Lovers*, 1895.

TANNAHILL, ROBERT (1774–1810), poet, born here. His poems include 'Bonnie Woods o' Craigilea', 'Braes o' Gleniffer' and 'Jessie the Flower o' Dumblane'. He drowned himself in Paisley canal.

WILSON, ALEXANDER (1766–1813), poet and ornithologist, born here. His volume of poems published in 1791 included the well-known 'Watty and Meg'. His *American Ornithology*, 1808–14, was a pioneer study.

Dumfriesshire (*Maps 23 & 24*)

1 **Annan** BLACKLOCK, THOMAS (1721–91), poet, born here. He published translations and religious works also, and encouraged Burns in the early days of his career.
CARLYLE, THOMAS (1795–1881), historian, taught mathematics here in 1814.
CLAPPERTON, CAPTAIN HUGH (1788–1827), traveller and writer, born here. Publications include *Journal of a Second Expedition into the Interior of Africa, from the Bight of Benin to Soccatoo*, 1827.
IRVING, EDWARD (1792–1834), author and founder of the Catholic Apostolic Church, born here.

2 **Burnfoot** MALCOLM, SIR JOHN (1769–1833), diplomat and author, born here. He wrote a *History of Persia*, 1815, and books on Clive and India.

3 **Caerlaverock** PATERSON, ROBERT (1715–1801), SCOTT's 'Old Mortality', died at Bankend and is buried in the churchyard of the parish, where Scott's publishers erected a memorial to him.

4 **Craigenputtock** CARLYLE, THOMAS (1795–1881), historian, lived here 1828–31 and 1832–34.

5 **Dalswinton** CUNNINGHAM, ALLAN (1784–1842), poet and man of letters, born nearby. His works include *Traditional Tales of the English and Scottish Peasantry*, 1822, and *The Songs of Scotland, Ancient and Modern*, 1825, which contains 'A Wet Sheet and a Flowing Sea'.

6 **Dumfries** AIRD, THOMAS (1802–76), poet and editor of the *Dumfries Herald* 1835–63, died here.
BURNS, ROBERT (1759–96), poet, farmed at Ellisland nearby 1788–91, then moved to a house in the Wee Vennel, now Bank Street, and subsequently to a cottage in Burns Street (now a museum) where he died. At the Globe Inn are two verses which he scratched on a window.
CARRUTHERS, ROBERT (1799–1878), journalist and editor, born here. He edited the works of Pope, and, with Robert Chambers, the first edition of *Chambers's Cyclopaedia of English Literature*, 1842–44.
HANNAY, JAMES (1827–73), novelist and journalist, born here. His novels include *Singleton Fontenoy*, 1850, and *Eustace Conyers*, 1855.
MCKENNA, ROBERT WILLIAM (1874–1930), novelist, born here. His publications include *Flower of the Heather*, 1922, and *Bracken and Thistledown*, 1924.

7 **Ecclefechan** CARLYLE, THOMAS (1795–1881), historian, born and buried here. Ecclefechan school appears in *Sartor Resartus* as Entephfuhl.
LITTLE, JANET (1759–1813), poet, born here. *The Poetical Works of Janet Little, the Scottish Milkmaid* appeared in 1792.

8 **Hoddom** SHARPE, CHARLES KIRKPATRICK (1781–1851), poet, born here. He edited border ballads for Sir Walter Scott and contributed two of his own, 'The Lord Herries his Complaint' and 'The Murder of Caerlaveroc'.

9 **Irongray** WALKER, HELEN (c1710–91), the original of SCOTT's Jeanie Deans in *Heart of Midlothian*, is buried in the churchyard, where Scott erected a memorial to her.

10 **Kirkconnel** ANDERSON, ALEXANDER (1845–1909), poet, born here. Writing under the name 'Surfaceman', he published *A Song of Labour and Other Poems*, 1873, *Two Angels*, 1875, *Songs of the Rail*, 1878, and *Ballads and Sonnets*, 1879.
HYSLOP, JAMES (1798–1827), poet, born here. His poems, including *The Cameronian's Dream*, were collected in 1887.

11 **Langholm** IRVING, DAVID (1778–1860), historian and biographer, born here. He published *Lives of the Scottish Poets*, 1804, and a *History of Scottish Poetry*, 1861.
MICKLE, WILLIAM JULIUS (1735–88), poet and translator, born here. His ballad 'Cumnor Hall', 1784, suggested to Scott the idea for *Kenilworth*. He wrote the poem 'There's nae luck aboot the hoose'.
RUSSELL, WILLIAM (1741–93), historian, died nearby.

12 **Maxwelltown** MCDOWALL, WILLIAM (1815–88), writer and editor, born here. He edited the *Dumfries Standard* from 1846 until his death and wrote books about the county.

13 **Mouswold** REID, ROBERT CORSANE (1882–1963), genealogist and antiquarian, lived at Cleughbrae.

14 **Penpont** GLADSTONE, SIR HUGH STEUART (1877–1949), writer on natural history, lived here.
THOMSON, JOSEPH (1858–95), explorer and author, born here. Publications include *Mungo Park and the Niger*, 1890, and *Through Masai Land*, 1885.

15 **Sanquhar** GRIERSON, SIR ROBERT, LAIRD OF LAG (c1655–1733), born here. He lived at Dunscore and was the infamous persecutor of Scottish covenanters immortalised by SCOTT as Sir Robert Redgauntlet.

16 **Tinwald** PATERSON, WILLIAM (1658–1719), financier and writer, born here. Founder of the Bank of England, his publications include *An Inquiry into the Reasonableness and Consequences of an Union with Scotland*, 1706.

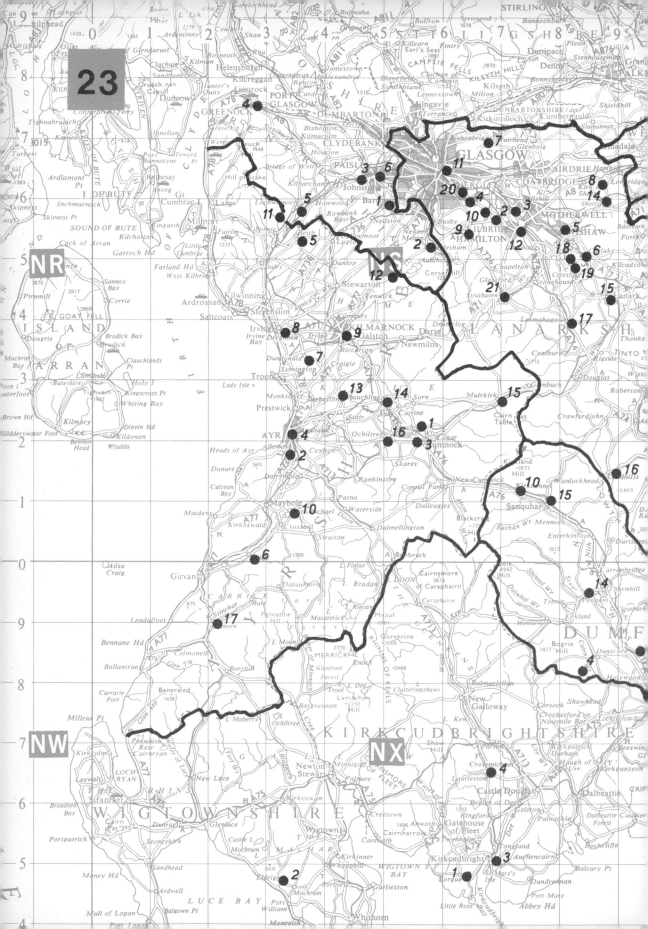

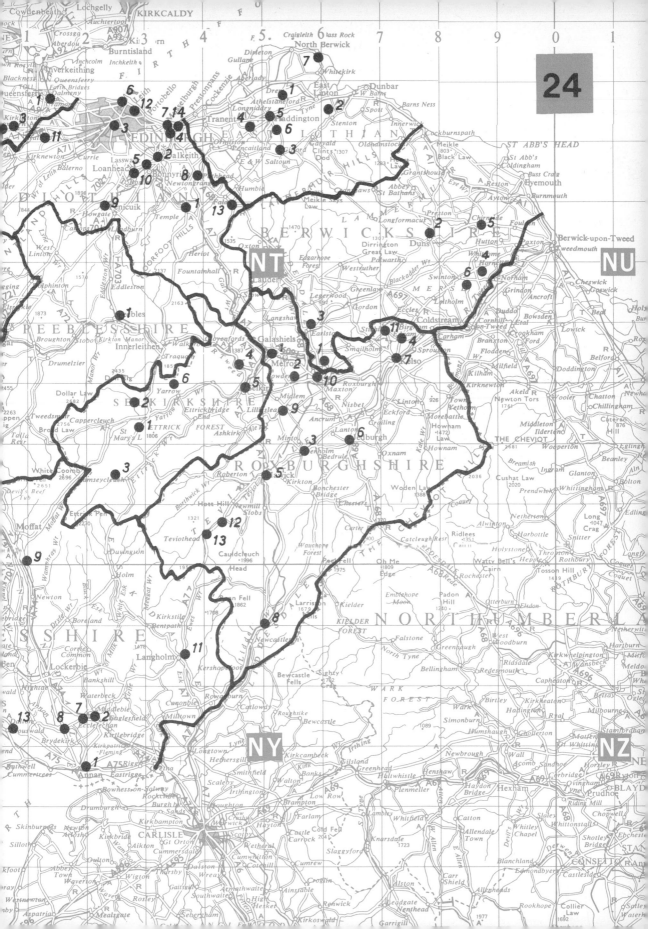

Lanarkshire (*Maps 23 & 24*)

1 Biggar BROWN, JOHN (1810–82), essayist, born here. His three-volume collection of essays, *Horae Subsecivae*, appeared in 1858.

RAE, GILBERT, poet and novelist, born here 1875. Volumes of verse include *Tween Clyde and Tweed*, 1919, and *'Mang Lowland Hills*, 1923; the novel *Where Falcons Fly* appeared 1927.

2 Blantyre LIVINGSTONE, DAVID (1813–73), explorer and author, born here. He published *Missionary Travels*, 1857, and *The Zambesi and its Tributaries*, 1865. His diary appeared in 1874 as *Last Journals of David Livingstone in Central Africa*.

3 Bothwell BAILLIE, JOANNA (1762–1851), dramatist and poet, born here. She published *Plays on the Passions*, 1798, 1802 and 1812, *Miscellaneous Plays*, 1804, and three volumes of dramatic poetry, 1836.

BAIN, FRANCIS WILLIAM (1863–1940), historian, born here. Publications include *Queen Christina of Sweden*, 1890, and *The English Monarchy and its Revolutions*, 1894.

4 Cambuslang BUCHANAN, CLAUDIUS (1766–1815), miscellaneous writer, born here. He translated the scriptures into various oriental languages.

LOUDON, JOHN CLAUDIUS (1783–1843), author, born here. He wrote mainly on gardening and county architecture.

WHITEHEAD, MRS SARAH R., novelist, born here 1817. Her publications include *The Two Families*, 1852, *Nelly Armstrong*, 1853, and *Rose Douglas*, 1862.

5 Cambusnethan LOCKHART, JOHN GIBSON (1794–1854), biographer and novelist, born here. He was Sir Walter Scott's son-in-law, and published his *Life of Scott* in 1838.

6 Carluke CROSS, JOHN KEIR (1914–67), children's author and radio dramatist, born here. His first books concerned a group of children known as 'The J's' (*Detectives in Greasepaint*, 1944, etc). Later successes include *The Angry Planet*, 1945, and *The Owl and the Pussycat*, 1946.

7 Chryston WATSON, WALTER (1780–1854), poet and song writer, born here. His *Select Poems* appeared 1853.

8 Carshill HAMILTON, MRS JANET (1795–1873), poet, born here. She published four volumes of verse between 1863 and 1871.

9 East Kilbride HUNTER, JOHN (1728–93), and WILLIAM (1718–83), authors of medical works, born at Long Calderwood.

STRUTHERS, JOHN (1776–1853), poet, born here. He published *The Poor Man's Sabbath*, 1804, and other religious verse.

10 Gilbertfield HAMILTON OF GILBERTFIELD, WILLIAM (c1665–1751), poet, lived here.

11 Glasgow ADAM, JEAN (1710–65), poet, died in the poorhouse.

BARR, ROBERT (1850–1912), novelist, born here. He wrote the detective series *The Triumphs of Eugene Valmont*, 1906, and collaborated with Jerome K. Jerome in founding *The Idler*.

BELL, JOHN JOY (1871–1934), novelist, born here. The best known of his books, mostly set in and around Glasgow, is *Wee MacGregor*, 1903.

BLACK, WILLIAM (1841–98), novelist, born in the Trongate. Publications include *A Daughter of Heth*, 1871, and *A Princess of Thule*, 1873.

BLACKIE, JOHN STUART (1809–95), translator and author, born here. His many translations include *Faust*, 1834, and he published *Self-Culture*, 1873, and *Horae Hellenicae*, 1874.

BRIDIE, JAMES (pseudonym of Osborne Henry Mavor, 1888–1951), playwright, born here. He practised here as a doctor until 1938. Plays include *The Sunlight Sonata*, 1928, *Tobias and the Angel*, 1930, *The Anatomist*, 1930, and *Mr Bolfry*, 1943.

CAMERON, JOHN (c1579–1625), theological scholar. born here. Known as 'the walking library', he published eight works between 1616 and 1642.

CAMPBELL, THOMAS (1777–1844), poet, born here. His principal poem was 'The Pleasures of Hope', 1799, but he is best remembered for 'Ye Mariners of England' and the ballad 'Lord Ullin's Daughter'.

CARSWELL, CATHERINE ROXBURGH (1870–1946), novelist and biographer, born here. She championed D. H. Lawrence, especially in *The Savage Pilgrimage*, 1932, and published a controversial biography of Burns, 1930.

DE QUINCEY, THOMAS (1785–1859), essayist, lived here 1841–43.

FRAZER, SIR JAMES (1854–1941), anthropologist, born here. His classic *The Golden Bough* appeared in twelve volumes, 1890 and 1915.

GLEN, WILLIAM (1789–1826), poet, born and died here. He published *Poems, Chiefly Lyrical* in 1815.

GRAHAME, JAMES (1765–1811), poet, born and died here. His best known poem is 'The Sabbath', 1804.

GRANT, ANNE (1755–1838), poet and essayist, born here. She published *Poems*, 1803, *Letters from the Mountains*, 1806, and *Superstitions of the Highlanders*, 1811.

HARTE, FRANCIS BRETT (Bret Harte, 1836–1902), American novelist, was US consul here for some years and lived at 35 Burnbank Gardens.

JAMIESON, JOHN (1759–1838), minister and lexicographer, born here. He is best known for his *Etymological Dictionary of the Scottish Language*, 1808–9.

MACLEOD, NORMAN (1812–72), author, minister of the Barony church from 1851 until his death.

MAXWELL, WILLIAM STERLING- (1818–78), historian, born at Kenmure House. His works include *Cloister Life of Charles V*, 1852, *Velazquez*, 1855, and *Don John of Austria*, 1883.

MOORE, JOHN (1729–1802), novelist and travel writer, practised medicine here.

MOTHERWELL, WILLIAM (1797–1835), poet, born and died here. Editor of the *Glasgow Courier* from 1830, he published *Minstrelsy, Ancient and Modern*, 1827, and *Poems, Narrative and Lyrical*, 1832.

MUIR, EDWIN (1887–1959), novelist, poet and critic, lived here 1901–19.

MUNRO, NEIL (1864–1930), novelist, edited the *Glasgow Evening News*, 1918–27.

NIVEN, FREDERICK (1878–1944), novelist, lived here for many years before making his home in British Columbia. Here he wrote some of the novels he set in Scotland, among them *Ellen Adair*, 1913, and *Justice of the Peace*, 1914.

SCOTT, MICHAEL (1789–1835), novelist, born at Cowlairs and returned to live here in 1822. His stories include *Tom Cringle's Log* and *The Cruise of the Midge*, both published in 1836.

SMITH, ADAM (1723–90), author of *The Wealth of Nations*, became professor of moral philosophy at the university in 1752, and lord rector, 1787.

SMITH, ALEXANDER (1830–67), poet and essayist, was a pattern designer here.

STRUTHERS, JOHN (1776–1853), poet, was county librarian here from 1832 (see **East Kilbride**).

THOMSON, JAMES (1834–82), poet, born at Port Glasgow. His best known poem is 'The City of Dreadful Night', 1874.

WINGATE, DAVID (1828–92), poet, born at Cowglen. He published *Poems and Songs*, 1862, *Annie Weir*, 1866, *Lily Neil*, 1879, and *Selected Poems*, 1890.

12 Hamilton CULLEN, WILLIAM (1710–90), author of medical and scientific works, born here.

JOHNSTON, HELEN (d1873), poet, known as 'The Factory Girl', born here. Her *Poems and Songs* were published in 1869.

13 Haywood WELSH, JAMES C. (1880–1954), politician and novelist, born here. His novels include *The Underworld*, 1920, *The Morlocks*, 1924, and *Norman Dale, MP*, 1928. He also published a volume of verse, *Songs of a Miner*, 1917.

14 Kirk of Shotts JEFFREY, WILLIAM (1896–1946), poet and journalist, born here. Volumes of verse published by him include *Prometheus Returns*, 1921, *The Lamb of Lomond*, 1926, *Mountain Songs*, 1928, and *Sea Glimmer*, 1947.

15 Lanark LITHGOW, WILLIAM (1582–c1645), traveller, born and died here. He described his travels in *Rare Adventures and Painful Peregrinations*, 1632, and wrote other works.

16 Leadhills RAMSAY, ALLAN THE ELDER (1686–1758), poet, born here. His best known work, *The Gentle Shepherd*, appeared in 1725.

17 Lesmahgow WILSON, JOHN (1720–89), poet, born here. Parish schoolmaster in 1746. He is best remembered for his dramatic descriptive poem 'The Clyde', 1764.

18 Milton Head ROY, WILLIAM (1726–90), antiquary, born here. Author of *Military Antiquities of the Romans in Britain*, 1793.

19 Milton Lockhart LOCKHART, LAURENCE WILLIAM MAXWELL (1832–82), novelist, born here. Nephew of John Gibson Lockhart (see **Cambusnethan**). Publications include *Doubles and Quits*, 1869, *Fair to See*, 1871, *Mine is Thine*, 1878.

20 Rutherglen COCKER, WILLIAM DIXON, poet and dramatist, born here 1882. He published *Poems, Scots and English*, 1932.

21 Strathaven AITON, WILLIAM (1731–93), botanist, born here. He was responsible for the catalogue of the plants cultivated in the Royal Gardens, Kew, 1789.

West Lothian (Linlithgow)
(*Maps 23 & 24*)

1 Dalmeny WILKIE, WILLIAM (1721–72), poet, born here. His epic *Epigoniad* appeared in 1757, and *Moral Fables in Verse* in 1768.

2 Houston House SHAIRP, JOHN CAMPBELL (1818–85), poet and critic, born here. Publications include *Studies in Poetry and Philosophy*, 1868, *The Poetic Interpretation of Nature*, 1877, *Aspects of Poetry*, 1881, and *Sketches in History and Poetry*, 1887.

3 Uphall HAMILTON, WILLIAM (1704–54), poet, was probably born at his father's estate of Bangour nearby. He contributed to Ramsay's *Tea-Table Miscellany*, 1724, and made the earliest Homeric translation into English blank verse.

Berwickshire (*Map 24*)

1 **Dryburgh** LOCKHART, JOHN GIBSON (1794–1854), biographer, buried here.

SCOTT, SIR WALTER (1771–1832), author and poet, buried at the abbey.

2 **Duns** BOSTON, THOMAS (1676–1732), author and minister of independent Presbyterian sect, born here. He wrote the religious classic *The Fourfold State*, 1720.

DUNS, JOANNES SCOTUS (c1265–1308), philosopher, born here. Known as the 'Subtle Doctor', he is recognised as Britain's greatest medieval philosopher. His writings include a philosophic grammar and works on logic and metaphysics.

M'CRIE, THOMAS (1772–1835), church historian, born here. His works on Scottish ecclesiastical history include lives of Knox, 1811, and other figures of the Reformation period.

3 **Earlston** THOMAS THE RHYMER (c1220–c1297), seer and poet, lived here.

4 **Ladykirk** RIDPATH, GEORGE (c1717–72), historian, born at the manse. He published *The Border History of England and Scotland*, 1776.

5 **Ninewells** HUME, DAVID (1711–76), philosopher and historian, wrote his *Essays, Moral and Political*, 1741–42, here.

6 **Simprin** BOSTON, THOMAS (1676–1732), theological author, minister here 1699–1707.

East Lothian (*Map 24*)

1 **Athelstaneford** BLAIR, ROBERT (1699–1746), poet, minister from 1731 and is buried here.

2 **Biel** DUNBAR, WILLIAM (c1465–c1520), poet, probably born here. His allegorical poetry included *The Thistle and the Rose*, 1503, *The Dance of the Seven Deadly Sins*, and *Lament for the Makaris*.

3 **Gifford** KNOX, JOHN (1505–72), minister and writer, probably born here. His most important writings are *The First Blast of the Trumpet against the Monstrous Regiment of Women*, 1558, and a *History of the Reformation in Scotland*, 1586.

4 **Gladsmuir** ROBERTSON, WILLIAM (1721–93), historian, minister here 1743–56.

5 **Haddington** CARLYLE, JANE BAILLIE WELSH (1801–66), wife of Thomas Carlyle, born here, daughter of the local physician. Her verses were published in 1815 and her *Letters* in 1883.

LAUDER, SIR THOMAS DICK (1784–1848), novelist and journalist, born at Fountainhall. His novels include *Lochandhu*, 1825, and *The Great Wolf of Badenoch*, 1827, but he is best known for his *Account of the Great Floods in Morayshire in 1829*.

SMILES, SAMUEL (1812–1904), biographer and social reformer, born here. His influential *Self-Help*, 1859, has had one of the biggest sales of any book in English.

6 **Lethington** MAITLAND, SIR RICHARD (1496–1586), lawyer and poet, born here. His important collection of ancient Scots poetry passed via Samuel Pepys to Magdalene College, Cambridge. The Maitland Club was founded in 1828 in recognition of his services to literature.

7 **Tantallon Castle** DOUGLAS, GAVIN (c1474–1522), poet, born here. His chief works are the allegorical poems *The Palace of Honour*, c1553, and *King Hart*, first printed in 1786. His translation of the *Aeneid*, 1553, was the first rendering into English of a classical work.

Midlothian (*Map 24*)

1 Borthwick ROBERTSON, WILLIAM (1721–93), historian, born here. Publications include a *History of Scotland*, 1759, and a *History of America*, 1777.

2 Dalkeith CALDERWOOD, DAVID (1575–1650), historian and minister, born here. His most notable work is the *Historie of the Kirk of Scotland*, 1646.

3 Edinburgh ADAM, ALEXANDER (1741–1809), author of *Roman Antiquities*, 1791, came here in 1757, was headmaster of Watson's Hospital from 1761 and rector of the High School from 1768. He died here.

ALBERT, EDWARD (1888–1944), novelist, born here. All his work is set in Scotland, including *Man's Chief End*, 1928, *The Grey Wind*, 1929, and *Herrin' Jennie*, 1931.

ALISON, ARCHIBALD (1757–1839), clergyman, born here. He wrote a notable *Essay on the Nature and Principles of Taste*, 1790.

ANDERSON, ALEXANDER (1845–1909), known as 'the Surfaceman-poet', came here in 1880, was appointed chief university librarian, 1905.

ANDERSON, JOSEPH (1832–1916), antiquary, keeper of the National Museum of Antiquities 1870–1913.

AYTOUN, WILLIAM EDMONDSTONE (1813–65), poet, born here. He was appointed professor of rhetoric and belles-lettres at the university in 1845. His works include *Lays of the Scottish Cavaliers*, 1848.

BALLANTINE, JAMES (1808–77), artist and author, born and died here. Publications include *The Gaberlunzie's Wallet*, 1843, *Ornamental Art*, 1847, and *Poems*, 1856.

BALLANTYNE, ROBERT MICHAEL (1825–94), author, born here. His many novels for boys include *The Young Fur Traders* and *The Coral Island*. He died in Rome.

BANNATYNE, GEORGE (1545–1608), compiler of the *Bannatyne Manuscript* of the plague year of 1568, lived here and was made a burgess in 1587. The Bannatyne Club was founded in 1823, with Sir Walter Scott as president.

BANNERMAN, HELEN BRODIE COWAN (1863–1946), children's author, born and died here. She wrote and illustrated *The Story of Little Black Sambo*, 1899, and its tremendous success resulted in several further stories: *Little Black Mingo*, 1901, and *Little Black Quibba*, 1902, etc.

BIRD, ISABELLA (Mrs Isabella Bishop, 1832–1904), travel writer, born here. Publications include *The Englishwoman in America*, 1858, *Unbeaten Tracks in Japan*, 1880, and *Persia and Kurdistan*, 1891.

BLACKIE, JOHN STUART (1809–95), professor of Greek at the university 1852–82 and established the chair of Celtic languages and literature in 1876. He died here.

BLACKLOCK, THOMAS (1721–91), poet, lived here from 1764 until his death.

BLAIR, ROBERT (1699–1746), poet and author, born here. His best known work, 'The Grave', 1743, was illustrated later by Blake.

BONAR, HORATIUS (1808–89), minister and poet, born here. His many works include the hymn 'I heard the voice of Jesus say'.

BOSWELL, JAMES (1740–95), biographer, born at Blair's Land, Parliament Close, and lived in St Mary's Wynd, Canongate. His classic *Life of Samuel Johnson* appeared in 1791.

BROUGHAM, HENRY PETER, BARON BROUGHAM AND VAUX (1778–1868), lawyer, politician and writer, born here. He wrote not only on legal subjects but also on metaphysics, mathematics, history, science and many other matters.

BURNS, ROBERT (1759–96), poet, arrived here in 1786 upon the success of his first volume of poems. He was fêted on every hand, but could only afford to share a humble lodging with a writer's apprentice in Baxter's Close, Lawnmarket. His favourite Edinburgh inn was the White Hart, Grassmarket.

BURTON, JOHN HILL (1809–81), historian, lived here most of his life and died nearby.

CAMPBELL, JOHN (1708–75), compiler, born here. He published *Lives of the Admirals* and similar works.

CHAMBERS, ROBERT (1802–71), and WILLIAM (1800–83), authors and publishers, founded *Chambers's Edinburgh Journal* in 1832 and the printing house of W. & R. Chambers here.

COCKBURN, ALISON (1713–95), poet, lived in Edinburgh for more than sixty years and died here.

CROWE, CATHERINE (1800–76), novelist, lived here for many years.

DE QUINCEY, THOMAS (1785–1859), essayist, moved to Edinburgh in 1830 to live in Great King Street. Apart from short absences, he lived and worked here until his death.

DOUGLAS, GAVIN (1474–1522), poet, appointed provost of St Giles in 1501.

DOYLE, SIR ARTHUR CONAN (1859–1930), novelist, born at 11 Picardy Place. His first Sherlock Holmes story, *A Study in Scarlet*, appeared in 1887, and his best known historical novel, *The White Company*, in 1890. The scientific basis of Sherlock Holmes's deductive methods derived from the diagnostic skill of Doyle's tutor in surgery at Edinburgh University, Dr Joseph Bell.

DYCE, ALEXANDER (1798–1869), editor and critic, born here. He edited the works of notable authors including Beaumont and Fletcher, 1843–46, Marlowe, 1850, and Shakespeare, 1857. His own writings include *Recollections of the Table-talk of Samuel Rogers*, 1856.

ELLIOT, JEAN (1727–1805), poet and song writer, author of 'The Flowers of the Forest', lived here 1756–1804.

FALCONER, WILLIAM (1732–69), poet, born here. His celebrated *Shipwreck* appeared in 1764 and he compiled a *Universal Marine Dictionary*, 1769.

FERGUSSON, ROBERT (1750–74), poet, born and lived here. His collected poems were published in 1773.

FERRIER, SUSAN EDMONSTONE (1782–1854), novelist, born and died here. Her works include *Marriage*, 1818, *The Inheritance*, 1824, and *Destiny*, 1831.

FINDLATER, JANE HELEN (1866–1946), novelist, born here. She collaborated with her sister Mary Findlater, her own works including *The Green Graves of Balgowrie*, 1896, and *A Daughter of Strife*, 1897.

GRAHAME, KENNETH (1859–1932), essayist and children's author, born here. His children's classic, *The Wind in the Willows*, was published in 1908.

GRANT, ANNE (1755–1838), poet and essayist, lived here from 1811.

HALL, BASIL (1788–1844), travel writer, born here. Among his works are *Fragments of Voyages and Travels*, 1831–40, and *Patchwork*, 1841, a collection of tales and sketches.

HAMILTON, ELIZABETH (1758–1816), novelist, lived here from 1804.

HENLEY, WILLIAM ERNEST (1849–1903), poet and critic, wrote *Hospital Verses* while a patient in the infirmary 1873–75. It was here that he met ROBERT LOUIS STEVENSON, with whom he collaborated on three plays, *Deacon Brodie*, *Beau Austin* and *Admiral Guinea*.

HOME, JOHN (1722–1808), dramatist, lived in Edin-

141

burgh from 1778 and died here. His drama *Douglas* was first produced here in 1756.

HUME, DAVID (1711–76), philosopher and historian, born here. He lived in St James's Court, off the Lawnmarket, and was in Edinburgh from 1769 until his death. His *Philosophical Essays concerning Human Understanding*, 1748, reissued as *An Enquiry concerning Human Understanding*, 1758, are his most celebrated philosophical writings, but his six-volume *History of England*, 1754–62, enjoyed considerable vogue.

IRVING, DAVID (1778–1860), historian, was librarian of the faculty of advocates 1820–48.

JAMES VI & I (1566–1625), born in Edinburgh Castle. His literary works include *Daemonology*, 1599, and *Counterblast against Tobacco*, 1604.

JAMIESON, JOHN (1759–1838), lexicographer, was a pastor here from 1797 until his death.

JEFFREY, FRANCIS, LORD (1773–1850), critic and writer, born here. He lived at Craigcrook from 1815 until his death there. He helped establish the *Edinburgh Review* and was its editor 1802–29.

KENNEDY, GRACE (1782–1825), novelist, lived and died here.

KNOX, JOHN (1505–72), ministered at St Giles and was buried in the churchyard.

LAING, DAVID (1793–1878), antiquary, born and lived here. He was librarian of the Signet Library from 1837 until his death, a prolific contributor to the transactions of the Bannatyne Club, and a collector of rare MSS and books, which he left to Edinburgh university.

LAUDER, SIR THOMAS DICK (1784–1848), novelist, lived at the Grange, near Edinburgh, from 1832 until his death.

MCGONAGALL, WILLIAM (1830–1902), poet, born and died here. His fame rests upon the badness of his verse.

MACKENZIE, AGNES MURE (1891–1955), historian and novelist, was a lecturer at the university for some years and returned later in life to live in Edinburgh.

MACKENZIE, HENRY (1745–1831), novelist and essayist, born and died here. His home was at 6 Heriot Row. *The Man of Feeling*, after which he was nicknamed, appeared 1771, and *The Man of the World*, 1773.

MACRITCHIE, DAVID (1851–1925), historian, born here. Publications include *Fians, Fairies and Picts*, 1893, and *Scottish Gypsies under the Stewarts*, 1894.

MARTIN, SIR THEODORE (1816–1909), poet and biographer, born here. His *Bon Gaultier Ballads*, written with W. E. Aytoun, appeared in 1855. Other works include *Life of the Prince Consort*, 1874–80, and *Queen Victoria as I Knew Her*, 1908.

MITCHISON, NAOMI MARGARET (1897–1964), novelist, born here. Her novels, chiefly set in ancient times, include *When the Bough Breaks*, 1924, *Cloud Cuckoo Land*, 1925, and *Black Sparta*, 1928.

NORTH, CHRISTOPHER (pseudonym of John Wilson, 1785–1854), journalist and essayist, came to Edinburgh in 1816 and was professor of moral philosophy at the university 1820–51.

PICKEN, EBENEZER (1769–1816), poet, taught and died here.

PINKERTON, JOHN (1758–1826), historian, born here. Publications include *Ancient Scottish Poems*, 1786, a *Medallic History of England*, 1790, and a *Treatise on Rocks*, 1811.

RAMSAY, ALLAN, the elder (1686–1758), poet, came to Edinburgh in 1701; started the first circulating library in Scotland from his bookshop in the High Street; died in his house (which he called 'the goose-pie') on Castle Hill.

ROBERTSON, WILLIAM (1721–93), historian, joint-minister of Greyfriars from 1761 until his death, and principal of the university from 1762.

RORIE, DAVID (1867–1946), poet, born here. Among his poems 'Lum Hat wantin' a Croon' has become a classic.

SCOTT, ALEXANDER (c1530–84), poet, lived in or near Edinburgh; his work is preserved in the Bannatyne MS.

SCOTT, SIR WALTER (1771–1832), novelist, was born in College Wynd near the university. He lived during childhood in George Square, then from 1802–26 at 39 Castle Street, where many of the Waverley novels were written.

SCOTT, WILLIAM BELL (1811–90), poet and artist, born and lived here until 1837. He published five volumes of poetry and several works on painting.

SINCLAIR, CATHERINE (1800–64), children's author, born here. Her *Holiday House*, 1839, was one of the first collections of stories aimed at giving children sheer entertainment.

SKELTON, SIR JOHN (1831–97), novelist, born here. Using the pseudonym 'Shirley', he wrote *The Crookit Meg*, 1880, *Essays of Shirley*, 1882, and *The Table Talk of Shirley*, 1895.

SMART, ALEXANDER (1798–1866), poet, died here.

SMITH, ADAM (1723–90), author of *The Wealth of Nations*, came to Edinburgh for a time in 1748 and again in 1778. He died in the Canongate.

SMITH, ALEXANDER (1830–67), poet and novelist, was secretary of the university.

SMITH, WALTER CHALMERS (1824–1908), poet, was a Free Church minister here 1873–94.

STEVENSON, ROBERT LOUIS (1850–94), poet and novelist, born at 8 Howard Place (now the Stevenson Memorial House), moving as a child to 17 Heriot Row, where he lived for thirty years. *Treasure Island* first appeared in book form in 1882, and *A Child's Garden of Verses* in 1885.

SWAN, ANNIE S. (1859–1943), novelist, born here. Her numerous books include *Alderayde*, 1883, *Carlowrie*, 1884, and *Ursula Vivian*, 1927.

TENNANT, WILLIAM (1784–1848), poet, became parish schoolmaster of Lasswade nearby in 1813.

THOMSON, GEORGE (1757–1851), compiler of the *Collection of Scottish Songs and Airs*, 1799–1818, was clerk to the Board of Trustees in Edinburgh for sixty years.

TYTLER, PATRICK FRASER (1791–1849), historian and biographer, born here. Among his publications are a *Life of the Admirable Crichton*, 1819, *The Scottish Worthies*, 1832, and a *History of Scotland*, 1828–43.

VEDDER, DAVID (1790–1854), writer, died here.

WALFORD, LUCY (1845–1915), novelist, born at Portobello. She wrote numerous books, including *Recollections of a Scottish Novelist*, 1910.

YATES, EDMUND HODGSON (1831–94), novelist and journalist, born here. His novels include *Running the Gauntlet*, 1866, *Black Sheep*, 1867, and *The Silent Witness*, 1875.

4 Inveresk CARLYLE, ALEXANDER (1722–1805), autobiographer, was minister here from 1748 until his death. He was known in literary circles as 'Jupiter Carlyle'.

5 Lasswade BELLENDEN, WILLIAM (c1555–1633), author, probably born here. He published *De Statu Libri Tres*, 1616, and *De Tribus Luminibus Romanorum*, 1634.

DRUMMOND, WILLIAM 'OF HAWTHORNDEN' (1585–1649), poet, buried here.

6 Leith HOME, JOHN (1722–1808), dramatist, born here. His most successful play was *Douglas*, 1756. His *History of the Rebellion of 1745* appeared in 1802.

7 Musselburgh HANNAN, THOMAS (1870–1938), historian, rector of St Peter's Episcopal Church for forty-six years. He wrote books on the Scottish islands and famous Scottish houses.

MOIR, DAVID MACBETH (1798–1851), poet and humorist, born here. He practised as a doctor here from 1817

142

until his death. Publications include *Mansie Wauch*, 1828, *The Legend of Genevieve*, 1824, and *Domestic Verses*, 1843.

8 Pathhead DODDS, ANDREW (b1872), poet, lived here from 1880.

9 Penicuik CROCKETT, SAMUEL RUTHERFORD (1860–1914), novelist, was Free Church minister here 1886–95.

10 Polton DE QUINCEY, THOMAS (1785–1859), essayist, stayed here 1843–54.

11 Ratho WILKIE, WILLIAM (1721–72), poet, minister here 1756–59.

12 South Leith LOGAN, JOHN (1748–88), poet, minister here 1773–86.

13 Soutra LOGAN, JOHN (1748–88), poet, born here. His tragedy *Runnamede* was first performed in 1783. 'Ode to the Cuckoo', which Burke termed the most beautiful lyric in the language, has been credited both to Logan and to Bruce, whose poems he edited in 1770.

14 Wallyford, nr Musselburgh OLIPHANT, MRS MARGARET (1828–97), novelist and biographer, born here. She gained immediate success with her first novel, *Mrs Margaret Maitland*, 1849, and produced many more, all of which appeared in *Blackwood's Magazine*.

Peeblesshire (*Map 24*)

1 Peebles BUCHAN, ANNA (d1948), novelist, who used the pseudonym Olive Douglas, lived most of her life at Bank House, the Priorsford of her novels, one of them having the title *Priorsford*, published in 1932.

CHAMBERS, ROBERT (1802–71) and WILLIAM (1800–83), authors and publishers, born here. They established the publishing house of W. & R. Chambers and founded *Chambers's Journal* in 1832, besides writing a number of books on various subjects.

VEITCH, JOHN (1829–94), philosopher and historian, born here. Publications include *History and Poetry of the Scottish Border*, 1877, *Feeling for Nature in Scottish Poetry*, 1887, and *Border Essays*, 1896.

Roxburghshire (*Map 24*)

1 Abbotsford LAIDLAW, WILLIAM (1780–1845), poet, became steward on the Abbotsford estate in 1817 and eventually Sir Walter Scott's secretary: he is remembered for his ballad 'Lucy's Flittin' '.

LOCKHART, JOHN GIBSON (1794–1854), biographer, died here. He was son-in-law and biographer of Sir Walter Scott.

SCOTT, SIR WALTER (1771–1832), author and poet, bought the house and estate in 1812 and lived here until his death.

2 Bowden AIRD, THOMAS (1802–76), poet, born here. His chief work is *The Captive of Fez*, 1830.

3 Denholm LEYDEN, JOHN (1775–1811), poet and orientalist, born here. He contributed to Scott's *Minstrelsy of the Border*, 1802–3, and to 'Monk' Lewis's *Tales of Wonder*, 1801.

MURRAY, SIR JAMES AUGUSTUS HENRY (1837–1915), Scottish philologist and lexicographer, born here. He made his name with *Dialects of the Southern Counties of Scotland*, 1873, and edited the *New Oxford English Dictionary*.

4 Ednam, nr Kelso LYTE, HENRY (1793–1847), hymn writer, born here. He composed 'Abide with Me' and published *Poems: Chiefly Religious*, 1833.

THOMSON, JAMES (1700–48), poet, born here. His most famous work, *The Seasons*, appeared in 1730.

5 Hawick PATERSON, ROBERT (1715–1801), the original of Scott's Old Mortality, born at Haggisha nearby (see **Caerlaverock** in Dumfriesshire).

6 Jedburgh BREWSTER, SIR DAVID (1781–1868), author, editor and physician, born here. He edited the *Edinburgh Magazine* and *Edinburgh Encyclopaedia* and was a founder of the British Association for the Advancement of Science.

SOMERVILLE, MRS MARY (1780–1872), writer on science, born here. Her works include *The Connection of the Physical Sciences*, 1834.

7 Kelso BONAR, HORATIUS (1808–89), poet, minister of the new North Church, 1837–66.

DOUGLAS, SIR GEORGE (1856–1935), poet and miscellaneous writer, lived here.

OGILVIE, WILLIAM HENRY (1869–1963), poet, born here. He published mostly sporting verse, as Will H. Ogilvie.

8 Liddesdale OLIVER, JANE (pseudonym of Helen Rees, 1903–70), novelist, born here. She wrote for adults and children, and her last novel appeared posthumously, *The Blue Heaven Bends Over All*, 1971.

9 Lilliesleaf JEFFREY, ALEXANDER (1806–74), historian and antiquarian, born here. He described the history and antiquities of Roxburghshire in four volumes, 1864.

10 St Boswells BOYD, HALBERT JOHNSTON (1872–1957), novelist and clergyman, born at Whiterigg. His works are mostly set in his native country.

11 Stitchell RIDPATH, GEORGE (c1717–72), historian, minister 1742–72.

12 Teviotdale ELLIOT, JEAN (1727–1805), poet, born at Minto House, where she is believed also to have died. She composed the Flodden lament 'Flowers of the Forest'.

PRINGLE, THOMAS (1789–1834), poet, born at Blaiklaw. Obtaining a grant of land in South Africa through Scott's influence, he became one of the first poets to use the scenery and vocabulary of that country.

13 Teviothead RIDDELL, HENRY SCOTT (1798–1870), poet, minister here 1831–41 and lived here again after his release from an asylum in 1844.

Selkirkshire (*Map 24*)

1 **Altrive** HOGG, JAMES (1770–1835), poet, known as the Ettrick Shepherd, spent his later years here.

2 **Blackhouse** LAIDLAW, WILLIAM (1780–1845), poet, born here. Friend of James Hogg and secretary to Sir Walter Scott, he is remembered for his ballad 'Lucy's Flittin' '.

3 **Ettrick** BOSTON, THOMAS (1677–1732), writer, was minister from 1707 until his death here. His *Four-fold State* appeared in 1720 and his autobiography in 1776.

HOGG, JAMES (1770–1835), poet, known as the Ettrick Shepherd, born here. *The Forest Minstrels* appeared in 1810 and *Confessions of a Justified Sinner* in 1824. He is buried here.

4 **Fairnilee** COCKBURN, ALISON (1713–94), poet, born here. She is chiefly remembered for her poem 'The Flowers of the Forest'.

5 **Selkirk** LANG, ANDREW (1844–1912), folklorist, historian and poet, born at Viewfield. He published many works of poetry, translation, history and literary criticism, but may be remembered chiefly for his series of *Fairy Books* for children.

6 **Yarrow** RUSSELL, WILLIAM (1741–93), historian, born nearby at Windydoors Farm. His *History of Modern Europe* appeared in five volumes 1779–84.

Dunbartonshire (*Map 25*)

1 **Cardross** GRAHAM, ROBERT BONTINE CUNNINGHAME- (1852–1936), author, traveller and Scottish nationalist, lived here for some years.

2 **Craigendoran** MUNRO, NEIL (1864–1930), novelist, lived here towards the end of his life, and died here.

3 **Dalquhurn, nr Bonhill** SMOLLETT, TOBIAS (1721–71), novelist, born here. His *Roderick Random* appeared in 1748, *Peregrine Pickle* in 1751, and *Humphrey Clinker* in 1770.

4 **Helensburgh** BELL, JOHN JOY (1871–1934), novelist, lived here for some time.
MUNRO, NEIL (1864–1930), novelist, spent most of his life here.

5 **Kirkintilloch** GRAY, DAVID (1838–61), poet, born and died here. His chief poem, 'The Luggie', and a series of sonnets under the title *In the Shadows*, appeared in 1862.

Perthshire (*Maps 25 & 26*)

1 **Auchterarder** LORIMER, NORMA (1864–1948), author, born here. Her works include *By the Waters of Egypt, By the Waters of Sicily*, etc.

2 **Balquhidder** BUCHANAN, DUGALD (1716–68), poet, born here. Known as the Cowper of the Highlands, he dictated in Gaelic his autobiography *The Life and Conversion of Dugald Buchanan*.

3 **Buchanty** PAE, DAVID (1828–84), author and editor, born here. He edited *The People's Friend*, and wrote *Eustace, the Outcast: or the Smugglers of St Abb's*.

4 **Callander** FERGUSON, JOHN ALEXANDER, novelist, born here 1873. He wrote chiefly mystery novels, including *Death Comes to Périgord*, 1931, and *Man in the Dark*, 1928, and many Scottish one-act plays.

5 **Cargill** FORD, ROBERT (1846–1923), author and editor, born here. His publications include *Ballads of Babyhood, Ballads of Bairnhood, Thistledown*, etc.

6 **Comrie** GILFILLAN, GEORGE (1813–78), minister and writer, born here. He published several collections of biographies of literary figures.

7 **Crieff** MALLET, DAVID (c1703–65), poet, born here. He is chiefly remembered for his ballad 'William and Margaret', 1724. He collaborated with James Thomson in writing the masque *Alfred*, 1740, in which 'Rule Britannia' was first heard, and claimed that he was the author of the song, though this has been disputed.

8 **Dunkeld** CARLYLE, THOMAS (1795–1881), historian, was tutor to Charles Buller here 1822–24.

9 **Errol** BEATTIE, JAMES (1735–1803), the 'Gowrie poet', lived here.

10 **Fortingall** FERGUSSON, ROBERT MENZIES (1859–1921), poet and writer, born here. His publications include *The Ochil Fairy Book, My Village, A Village Poet, The Silver Shoe Buckle*, etc.

MACGREGOR, SIR JAMES (d1551), compiler of the first collection of Gaelic heroic verse, ministered here from c1530. He is buried in Inchordian church.

11 **Gask** OLIPHANT, CAROLINA, Baroness Nairne (1776–1845), Jacobite song writer, born here. Her eighty-seven songs were published in *The Scottish Minstrel* 1821–24, and include 'Caller Herrin' ' and 'Charlie is my Darling'.

12 **Kinnaird** STEVENSON, ROBERT LOUIS (1850–94), poet and novelist, wrote *Thrawn Janet*, 1881, and *The Merry Men*, 1882, while staying here.

13 **Lochearnhead** FINDLATER, MARY, novelist, born here 1865. She wrote with her sister, Jane Helen Findlater (1866–1946), and alone, her own works including *Over the Hills*, 1897, *Betty Musgrove*, 1899, and *Penny Moneypenny*, 1911.

14 **Logiealmond** WATSON, JOHN (1850–1907), novelist under the name Ian Maclaren, was Free Church pastor here from 1878.

15 **Menteith, Lake of** GRAHAM, ROBERT BONTINE CUNNINGHAME- (1852–1936), author and politician, is buried on the Isle of Inchmahome.

16 **Perth** ARCHER, WILLIAM (1856–1924), dramatic critic and author, born here. His translation of Ibsen's *Pillars of Society* brought the playwright's work into the English theatre for the first time (1880).

BUCHAN, JOHN, 1ST BARON TWEEDSMUIR (1875–1940), statesman and novelist, born here. His best known adventure story, *The Thirty-nine Steps*, appeared in 1915, and *The Three Hostages* in 1924. He also wrote biographies and verse.

FITTIS, ROBERT SCOTT (1824–1903), historian and novelist, born here. He wrote numerous books on Scottish history, and a novel, *The Mosstrooper*.

JAMES I, KING OF SCOTLAND (1394–1437), author of plays and poems, was assassinated here at the monastery of the Black Friars.

MACKAY, CHARLES (1814–89), poet and journalist, born here. He published *Songs and Poems*, 1834, including the songs 'There's a good time coming' and 'Cheer, boys, cheer'. He was the father of the novelist Marie Corelli.

SOUTAR, WILLIAM (1898–1943), poet, born here, spent his life in Perth, and is buried here. His published works include *Seeds in the Wind*, 1933, *Riddles in Scots*, 1937, *The Expectant Silence*, 1944, and *Diaries of a Dying Man*, 1954.

Stirlingshire (*Maps 25 & 26*)

1 Bannockburn BRYCE, JAMES (pseudonym of Alexander Anderson, 1862–1949), novelist, died here (see **Denny**).

2 Denny ALLAN, DOT (1892–1964), novelist, dramatist and journalist, born here. Her novels, centred on Glasgow and the Clyde, include *The Syrens*, 1921, *The Deans*, 1929, *Deepening River*, 1932, and *Hunger March*, 1934.

BRYCE, JAMES (pseudonym of Alexander Anderson, 1862–1949), novelist, born here. His publications include *Story of a Ploughboy*, 1912, *The Double Journey*, 1925, and *Apollo in Exile*, 1926.

3 Drymen BRIDIE, JAMES (pseudonym of Osborne Henry Mavor, 1888–1951), dramatist, lived at Finnich Malise nearby for a number of years.

SCOTT, SIR WALTER (1771–1832), novelist, lived at Ross Priory nearby while writing *Rob Roy*, 1817.

4 Killearn BUCHANAN, GEORGE (1506–82), historian, born here. Claimed as Scotland's greatest humanist, he published *De Jure Regni*, 1579, and *Rerum Scoticarum Historia*, 1582. He also wrote two tragedies, *Baptistes*, 1578, and *Jepthes*, 1554.

5 Raploch GRAHAM, DOUGAL (c1724–79), poet, born here. He was the author of prose chapbooks and numerous ballads, of which 'John Hielandman's Remarks on Glasgow' and 'Turnimspike' are the best known.

6 Slamannan CORRIE, JOE (1894–1968), dramatist, novelist and poet, born here. His one-act plays contributed to the development of modern Scottish drama.

7 Stirling CAMPBELL, HARRIETTE (1817–41), novelist, born here. She published *The Only Daughter*, 1839, *The Cardinal Virtue*, 1841, and *Katherine Randolph or Self Devotion*, 1842.

GLEIG, GEORGE ROBERT (1796–1888), novelist, biographer and historian, born here. He was chaplain-general to the forces and most of his works reflect military life, among them *The Subaltern*, 1830, *Life of Arthur, First Duke of Wellington*, 1862, and *History of India*, 1830–35.

HAMILTON, ELIZABETH (1758–1816), novelist, was brought up on a farm on the Carse of Gowrie, four miles from Stirling.

HARVEY, WILLIAM (1874–1936), novelist, biographer and historian, born here. His publications include *Scottish Life and Character in Anecdote and Story*, 1899, *Robert Burns in Stirlingshire*, and *Scottish Chapbook Literature*, 1903.

MOORE, JOHN (1729–1802), novelist, physician and traveller, born here. His works include a novel, *Zeluco*, 1786, *Journal During a Residence in France*, 1793–94, and *Progress of the French Revolution*, 1795.

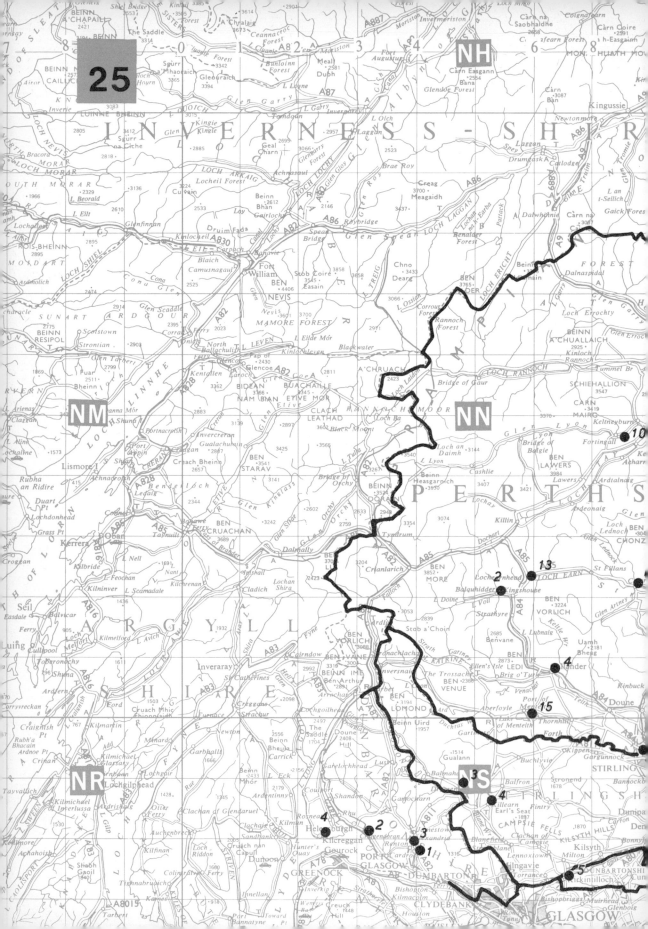

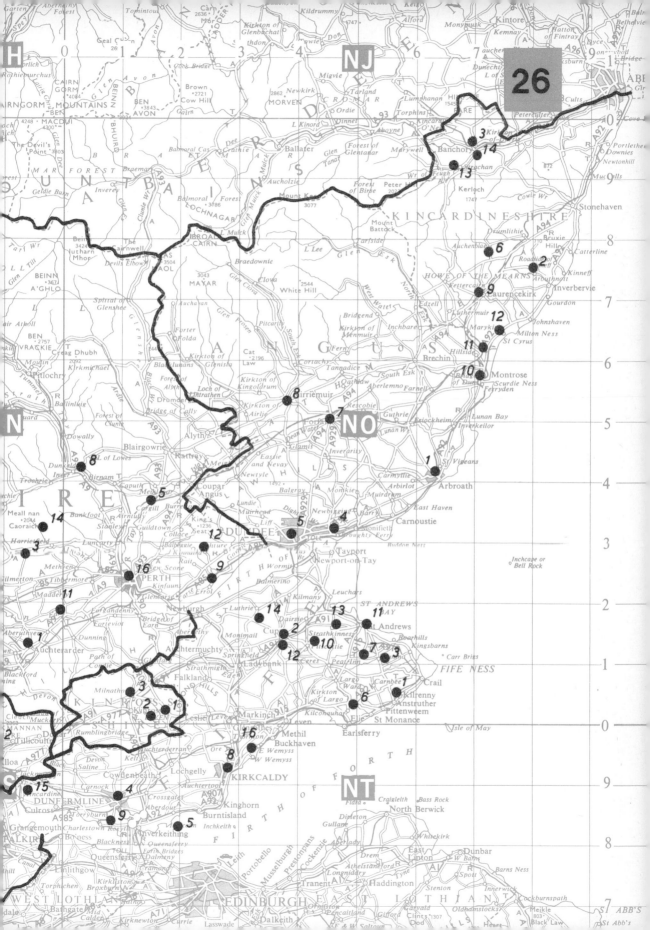

Angus and Kincardineshire
(*Map 26*)

1 Arbroath ANGUS, MARION (1866–1946), poet, born here. Her *Selected Poems* were published in 1950.

SALMOND, JAMES BELL (1891–1958), poet and writer, born here. Dundee editor of the *Scots Magazine* for twenty years, he wrote poetry under the pseudonym 'Wayfarer' and published a standard work *Wade in Scotland*.

2 Arbuthnott ARBUTHNOT, JOHN (1667–1735), satirist and medical writer, born here. He was principal author of *Memoirs of Martinus Scriblerus*, 1741, to which his friend Pope contributed, and also published a *History of John Bull*, 1712, and *The Art of Political Lying*.

GIBBON, LEWIS GRASSIC (pseudonym of James Leslie Mitchell, 1901–35), novelist, moved in 1909 to a farm near here and used this district as the setting for his trilogy *Sunset Song*, 1932, *Cloud Howe*, 1933, and *Grey Granite*, 1934, published collectively as *A Scots Quair*, 1946.

3 Banchory GRANT, DAVID (1823–86), poet, born nearby. His publications include *Metrical Tales*, 1880, and *Lays and Legends of the North*, 1884.

LANG, ANDREW (1844–1912), poet and folklorist, died here.

MURRAY, CHARLES (1864–1941), poet, spent his last years here.

4 Broughty Ferry SPENCE, JAMES (1874–1955), poet and mythologist, born here. His works include *Songs, Satanic and Celestial*, 1913, and *An Encyclopaedia of Occultism*, 1920.

5 Dundee BOECE, OR BOETHIUS, HECTOR (c1456–1536), historian, educated, and probably born here. He published a Latin *History of Scotland*, 1527.

BOWER, ARCHIBALD (1686–1766), historian, born here. Publications include a *History of Rome*, 1735–44, and a *History of the Popes*, 1748–66.

GARDINER, WILLIAM (1809–52), poet and botanist, born and died here. His *Botanical Rambles in Braemar*, 1848, contains a number of his poems.

GILFILLAN, GEORGE (1813–78), writer, was minister of School Wynd church for many years.

GRAHAM, CLEMENTINA STIRLING (1782–1877), author, lived at Duntrune nearby.

HONEYMAN, WILLIAM (1845–1919), journalist and early writer on the work of detectives, was on the staff of John Leng & Co from 1872.

MACKENZIE, SIR GEORGE (1636–91), historian and writer on law, born here. He published treatises on the law of Scotland and was the author of moral essays.

MCGONAGALL, WILLIAM (1830–1902), poet notorious for the badness of his verse, spent most of his life here.

NICOLL, ROBERT (1814–37), poet, spent most of his life here.

SMART, ALEXANDER (1798–1866), poet, lived here for some years.

THOM, WILLIAM (c1798–1848), poet, died at Hawkhill.

THOMSON, JAMES (1799–1864), poet and historian, lived here.

VEDDER, DAVID (1790–1854), writer and man of letters, spent much of his life here.

WEDDERBURN, JAMES (c1495–1553), JOHN (c1500–56) and ROBERT (c1510–c1557), poets and brothers, born here. They were joint authors of *Ane compendious Booke of Godly and Spirituall Sangs*, the ballads that were an important influence in the Reformation.

6 Fordun FORDUN, JOHN OF (d1384), chronicler, born here. The most important authority on Scottish history before 1400, he completed five books of the *Scotichronicon*, to 1153.

7 Forfar JAMIESON, JOHN (1759–1838), compiler of the *Etymological Dictionary of the Scottish Language*, 1808–9, was pastor of a secessionist congregation here 1781–97.

8 Kirriemuir BARRIE, SIR JAMES MATTHEW (1860–1937), novelist and playwright, born at 9 The Tenements, Brechin Road. His birthplace is famous as the 'Thrums' of his early novels and *A Window in Thrums*, 1889.

9 Laurencekirk BEATTIE, JAMES (1735–1803), poet, born here. His chief work was *The Minstrel*, 1771 and 1774.

10 Montrose BEATTIE, GEORGE (1786–1823), poet, practised here as an attorney and contributed his principal poems to the *Montrose Review*.

JACOB, VIOLET (1863–1946), poet and novelist, born here. Many of her poems are in the Angus dialect: her Scottish poems were collected in 1944.

SMART, ALEXANDER (1798–1866), poet, born here. His *Songs of Labour* were popular in his day.

11 Northwater Bridge MILL, JAMES (1773–1836), historian, born here. Publications include a *History of British India*, 1817.

12 St Cyrus BEATTIE, GEORGE (1786–1823), poet, born here (see **Montrose**).

13 Strachan REID, THOMAS (1710–96), philosopher, born here. The leading representative of the 'common sense' school of philosophers, he published *Inquiry into the Human Mind*, 1764, and *Philosophy of the Intellectual Powers*, 1785.

14 Tilquhillie DOUGLAS, NORMAN (1868–1952), novelist, born here. His most celebrated book is *South Wind*, 1917.

Clackmannanshire (*Map 26*)

1 **Alloa** CRAWFORD, JOHN (1816–73), poet, settled here in 1834.

WATT, LAUCHLAN MACLEAN (1867–1957), historian and biographer, became minister here in 1900.

2 **Alva** STIRLING, WILLIAM ALEXANDER, EARL OF (1567–1640), statesman and poet, born at Menstrie House. His love lyrics and moral verse are contained in *Aurora*, 1604, and *Recreations with the Muses*, 1637. He also composed four tragedies and an epic, *Doomsday*, 1614–37.

Fife (*Map 26*)

1 **Anstruther** CHALMERS, THOMAS (1780–1847), minister and theological writer, born here. First moderator of the Free Church of Scotland (1843), he published *Lectures on the Epistle of Paul the Apostle to the Romans*, 1842, and many other works.

TENNANT, WILLIAM (1784–1848), poet and linguistic scholar, born here. His *Anster Fair* appeared in 1812 and his tragedies *Cardinal Beaton*, 1823, and *John Baliol*, 1825.

2 **Cupar** TYTLER, SARAH (pseudonym of Henrietta Keddie, 1827–1914), novelist, born here. Author of *Citoyenne Jacqueline*, 1865, and many other books.

3 **Dunino** ROGERS, CHARLES (1825–90), historian and genealogist, born here. He wrote widely on Scottish history and literature.

4 **Dunfermline** CARNEGIE, ANDREW (1835–1919), author and patron of letters, born here. The family emigrated to the USA in 1848, where Carnegie made a fortune in railways and steel, using much of it to provide for libraries and educational foundations in Great Britain. His works include *The Empire of Business*, 1902, *The Gospel of Wealth and Other Timely Essays*, 1901.

GILFILLAN, ROBERT (1798–1850), poet, born here. His works include the Scottish emigrant's song, 'Why I left my hame'.

HENRYSON, ROBERT (c1430–1506), poet, attached to Dunfermline Abbey as a schoolmaster from c1477 until his death.

JAMES I, KING OF SCOTLAND (1394–1437), born here. His poetry includes *The Kingis Quair*, printed 1783, and probably *Peeblis to the Play* and *Christis Kirke on the Greene*.

PATON, SIR JOSEPH NOEL (1821–1901), poet and painter, born here. He published *Poems by a Painter*, 1861, and *Spindrift*, 1867.

5 **Inchcolm** BOWER, WALTER (1385–1449), historian, was abbot here.

6 **Kilconquhar, nr Colinsburgh** LINDSAY, ALEXANDER WILLIAM CRAWFORD, 25TH EARL OF CRAWFORD and 8TH EARL OF BALCARRES (1812–80), genealogist and historian, lived at the Balcarres mansion here.

LINDSAY, LADY ANNE (1750–1825), poet, born here. She wrote the ballad 'Auld Robin Gray', 1771, anonymously and only acknowledged it as her own two years before her death.

7 **Kinaldie** AYTON, or AYTOUN, SIR ROBERT (1570–1638), poet, born here. He was one of the first Scotsmen to write in English; his chief work is *Diophantus and Charidora*.

8 **Kirkcaldy** BUCHAN, ANNA (d1948), novelist sister of John Buchan, born here. Her works, under the pseudonym Olive Douglas, include *The Setons*, 1917, *Priorsford*, 1932, and *The House that is Our Own*, 1940.

CARLYLE, THOMAS (1795–1881), historian, was mathematics and classics master at the Burgh School 1816–19.

FLEMING, MARGARET (1803–11), poet, born here. Known as 'Pet Marjorie', she wrote humorous poems of precocious quality, but died at the age of eight.

MELDRUM, DAVID STORRAR (1864–1940), novelist, born here. His novels, such as *Grey Mantle and Gold Fringe*, 1896, realistically depict life in his native county.

SMITH, ADAM (1723–90), author of *The Wealth of Nations*, 1776, born here. He also lived here with his mother 1767–73 while working on the book, and at other times during his life.

9 **Limekilns** THOMSON, GEORGE (1757–1851), poet, born here. Friend of Burns, he contributed to his *Collection of Scottish Songs and Airs*, 1799–1818.

10 **Pitscottie, nr Cupar** LINDSAY OF PITSCOTTIE, ROBERT (c1500–65), chronicler of Scotland, lived here.

11 **St Andrews** ANDREW OF WYNTOUN (c1350–c1420), chronicler, was a canon regular of St Andrews.

BOYD, ANDREW KENNEDY HUTCHISON (1825–99), essayist and clergyman, minister here in 1865.

BUCHANAN, GEORGE (1506–82), historian, was appointed principal of the college of St Leonards in 1566.

CHAMBERS, ROBERT (1802–71), publisher and author, died here.

FLEMING, DAVID HAY (1849–1931), historian and critic, born here. His writing made him known as the champion of the Scottish Reformation and of the Covenanters.

DOUGLAS, GAVIN (c1474–1522), first translator of the *Aeneid*, 1553, was created archbishop of St Andrews in 1514.

KNOX, JOHN (1505–72), minister and writer, preached his first public sermon in the parish church in 1547.

LANG, ANDREW (1844–1912), poet and author, spent much of his life here.

MUIR, EDWIN (1887–1959), novelist, poet and critic, lived here 1938–41.

SHAIRP, JOHN CAMPBELL (1819–85), author, became principal of the United College in 1868.

SPOTTISWOOD, JOHN (1565–1639), Scots historian, was archbishop of St Andrews.

12 **Scotstarvit** SCOTT, SIR JOHN (1585–1670), patron of literature, acquired Tarvit and other lands and gave them the name Scotstarvit.

13 **Strathkiness** WHYTE-MELVILLE, GEORGE JOHN (1821–78), novelist and poet, born here. His sporting and historical novels include *Kate Coventry*, 1856, *The Queen's Maries*, 1862, and *The Gladiators*, 1863.

14 **The Mount** LINDSAY, SIR DAVID (1490–1555), poet and satirist, died here and may have been born here. His principal writings are *The Dreme*, 1528, *Ane Pleasant Satyre of the Three Estaitis*, 1540, and *The History of Squyer Meldrum*.

15 **Tulliallan** JOHNSTON, SIR CHRISTOPHER NICOLSON, LORD SANDS (1857–1934), lawyer and miscellaneous writer, born here. His fiction includes *Kinlochmoidart's Dirk, and Other Tales*, 1931.

16 **West Wemyss** SETOUN, GABRIEL (pseudonym of Thomas Nicoll Hepburn, 1861–1930), novelist, born here. His novels describing local life include *Barncraig: Episodes in the Life of a Scottish Village*.

Kinross-shire (*Map 26*)

1 **Kinnesswood** BRUCE, MICHAEL (1746–67), poet, born here. *Poems on Several Occasions*, a posthumous publication, appeared in 1770.

2 **Loch Leven** ANDREW OF WYNTOUN (c1350–c1425), chronicler, became prior of St Serf's monastery, where he probably wrote his chronicles, about 1395.

3 **Milnathort** GUTHRIE, JOHN, poet, born here 1814. His works include *Sacred Lyrics*, *Heroes of Faith*, etc.

HALIBURTON, HUGH (pseudonym of James Logie Robertson, 1846–1922), poet, born here. Publications include *Horace in Homespun: a Series of Scottish Pastorals*, 1886, and *Ochil Idylls*, 1891.

Argyllshire (*Map 27*)

1 **Campbeltown** MACLEOD, NORMAN (1812–72), author, born here. The first editor of *Good Words*, 1860–72, he published many novels including *The Earnest Student*, 1854, *The Old Lieutenant*, 1862, and *Reminiscences of a Highland Parish*, 1867.

2 **Glenorchy** MACINTYRE, DUNCAN BEN (1724–1812), poet-gamekeeper, born here. He was gamekeeper at Beinndorain. The first edition of his poems was published in 1786.

3 **Inverary** MUNRO, NEIL (1864–1930), novelist, born here. He is remembered by many for his Para Handy series of tales, the first of which, *The Vital Spark*, appeared in 1906.

4 **Islay** CAMPBELL, JOHN FRANCIS (1822–85), folklorist, born here. He is chiefly remembered for *Popular Tales of the West Highlands*, 1860–62.

5 **Lochfyne** HAY, JOHN MACDOUGALL (1880–1919), novelist, born at Tarbert. His publications include *Gillespie*, 1914, and *Barnacles*, 1916.
MACCOLL, EVAN (1808–c1901), Gaelic and English poet, lived here. He was known as the Lochfyneside Bard.

6 **Oronsay** SHAIRP, JOHN CAMPBELL (1819–85), poet and critic, died here.

Aberdeenshire (*Map 28*)

1 Aberdeen ALEXANDER, WILLIAM (1826–94), miscellaneous writer, born at Rescivat. His best known work is *Johnnie Gibb of Gushetneuk*, 1871, a series of sketches of country people in north-east Scotland.

ANGUS, MARION (1866–1946), poet, lived here.

ARBUTHNOT, ALEXANDER (1538–83), poet, was principal of King's College from 1569 until his death, and is buried here.

BAIN, ALEXANDER (1818–1903), philosopher and writer, born here. He was professor of logic at Aberdeen University 1860–81, and later rector. Publications include *The Senses and the Intellect*, 1855, *The Emotions and the Will*, 1859, and an autobiography, 1904.

BARBOUR, JOHN (1316–95), poet, probably born nearby: he was archdeacon of Aberdeen from 1357 until his death. His chief work was the *Brus*, 1375, an epic celebrating Robert the Bruce and James Douglas.

BARCLAY, JOHN (1652–91), poet, born here. He translated Arthur Johnston's Latin *Epigrams*, 1685, and wrote a verse satire on the Roman Catholic faith, 1689.

BEATTIE, JAMES (1735–1803), poet, was a master at the grammar school 1758–60. He is chiefly remembered for his poem 'The Minstrel'.

BEATTIE, WILLIAM (1760–1815), poet, born here. Well known poems of his include 'The Winter's Night', 'The Ale House' and 'The Ale Wife'.

BLACKIE, JOHN STUART (1809–95), translator and poet, was professor of humanity at Marischal College 1841–52.

BLACKWELL, THOMAS (1701–57), classical historian, born here; he was professor of Greek at Marischal College 1723–57 and principal 1748–57. Publications include *An Enquiry into the Life and Writings of Homer*, 1735, and *Memoirs of the Court of Augustus*, 1753–55.

BOECE, or BOETHIUS, HECTOR (c1465–1536), historian, was first principal of Aberdeen University, which he helped to found in 1505.

BULLOCH, JOHN MALCOLM (1867–1938), historian and journalist, born here. He was editor of several national periodicals, including the *Sketch*, *Sphere* and *Graphic*. He published a history of the university of Aberdeen, 1890.

BURTON, JOHN HILL (1809–81), historian, born here. Publications include *Life of Hume*, 1846, *The Scot Abroad*, 1864, and a *History of Scotland*, 1867–70.

CADENHEAD, WILLIAM (1819–1904), poet and journalist, born here. Publications include *Flights of Fancy*, 1853, and *Ingatherings*, 1905.

CRUDEN, ALEXANDER (1701–70), compiler of *The Biblical Concordance*, 1737, born here. He wrote pamphlets about contemporary events, believing himself divinely appointed to reform the nation.

DALGARNO, GEORGE (1626–87), philosophical scholar, born here. Publications include the *Ars Signorum, vulgo Character Universalis*, 1661, and *Didascalocophus*, 1682.

DOUGLAS, FRANCIS (1710–90), miscellaneous writer and journalist, founded the *Aberdeen Intelligence*, a Jacobite organ, in 1750.

IMLAH, JOHN (1799–1846), poet and song writer, born here. His works include *May Flowers*, 1827, and *Poems and Songs*, 1841.

JOHNSTON, ARTHUR (1587–1641), poet, was rector of King's College from 1637 (see **Caskieben**).

JOHNSTON, JOHN (1570–1611), poet, was professor of divinity at Aberdeen University 1593–1611.

LEATHAM, JAMES (1865–1945), poet, critic and journalist, born here. He founded and edited *The Gateway*, 1912–42, and wrote many works, including *The Season of Hope* (poems) and *The Blight of Ibsenism*.

MACDONELL, ARCHIBALD GORDON (1895–1941), novelist, born here. His works include *England, their England*, 1933, *Autobiography of a Cad*, 1939, and, as Neil Gordon, detective stories such as *The New Gun Runners*, 1928, and *The Shakespeare Murders*, 1933.

MASSON, DAVID (1822–1907), biographer, born here. His works include *Essays Biographical and Critical*, 1856, *British Novelists*, 1859, and a six-volume *Life of John Milton*, 1859–80.

RABAN, EDWARD (d1658), printer and publisher, introduced printing to Aberdeen in 1622, becoming printer to the university, and was responsible for the issue of many important Scottish works.

RAMSAY, EDWARD BANNERMAN (1793–1872), writer and clergyman, born here. Universally known as Deacon Ramsay, he is chiefly remembered for the classic *Reminiscences of Scottish Life and Character*, 1857.

ROBERTSON, JOSEPH (1810–66), historian, born here. He assisted in founding the Spalding Club in 1839.

RORIE, DAVID (1867–1946), poet and physician, lived most of his life here.

ROSS, ALEXANDER (1591–1654), poet and churchman, born here. He published poems in English and Latin.

SCOUGAL, HENRY (1650–78), writer and churchman, was a professor at King's College and a precentor in the cathedral, during which time he wrote the religious classic *The Life of God in the Soul of Man*.

SIMPSON, WILLIAM DOUGLAS (1896–1968), historian, was librarian of Aberdeen university.

SMITH, WALTER CHALMERS (1824–1908), poet, born here. Publications include *The Bishop's Walk*, 1861, *Raban*, 1880, and *Kildrostan*, 1884.

WEDDERBURN, DAVID (1580–1646), Latin poet, was a professor at Marischal College 1614–24 and official Latin poet to the city 1620–46.

2 Alford MINTO, WILLIAM (1845–93), critic and novelist, born here. He wrote three novels, as well as books on literature and logic, and edited Sir Walter Scott.

MURRAY, CHARLES (1864–1941), poet, born here. His volumes of verse include *Hamewith*, 1900, *A Sough o' War*, 1917, and *In the Country Places*, 1920.

3 Auchterless DEMPSTER, THOMAS (c1579–1625), biographer and miscellaneous writer, born on the estate of Cliftbog. He composed Latin poems and wrote *Historia Ecclesiastica Gentis Scotorum*, 1627, and *De Etruria Regali*, not published until 1723–4.

GIBBON, LEWIS GRASSIC (pseudonym of James Leslie Mitchell, 1901–35), novelist, born at Hillhead of Seggat. The trilogy of novels about his native countryside appeared under the title *A Scots Quair* in 1946 and comprises *Sunset Song*, 1932, *Cloud Howe*, 1933, and *Grey Granite*, 1934.

4 Birse SKINNER, JOHN (1721–1807), historian and song writer, born here. His poems, collected in 1809, include 'The Ewie wi' the Crookit Horn' and 'Tullochgorum'.

5 Caskieben JOHNSTON, ARTHUR (1587–1641), poet, born here. He published a Latin version of the psalms in 1637, and contributed poems to *Delitiae Poetarum Scotorum hujus Aevi*, 1637, which he helped to produce.

6 Fraserburgh STILL, PETER (1814–48), poet, born here.

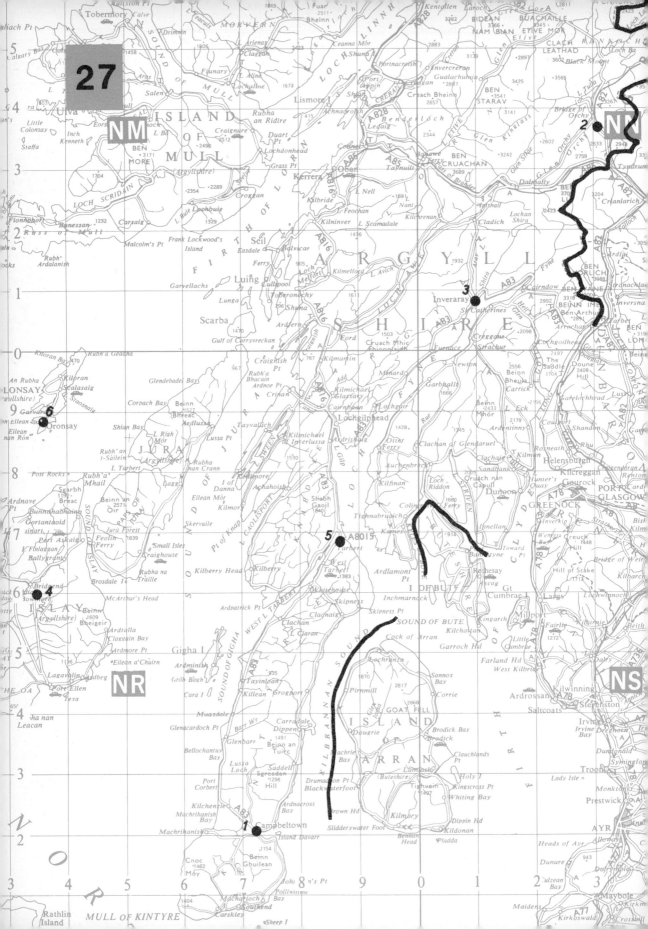

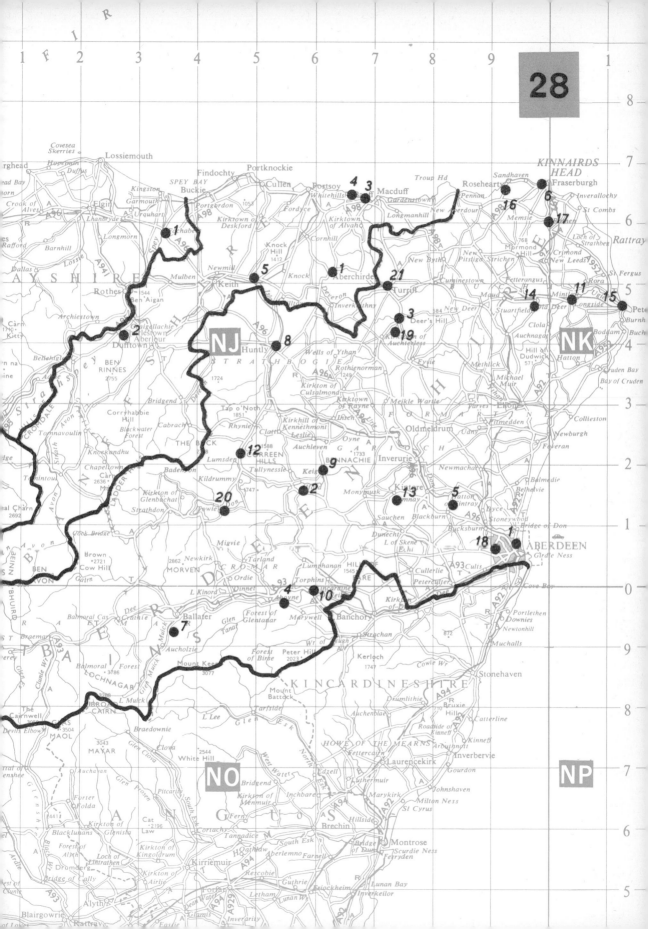

Publications include *Rustic Rhyme, Song and Sonnets*, 1842, *Poems and Songs*, 1844, and *The Cottar's Sunday Night*, 1845.

7 **Glenmuick** CAMERON, WILLIAM (1751–1811), poet, born here. Publications include *Poems of Various Subjects*, 1780, and *Poems of Various Occasions*, 1813.

8 **Huntly** GORDON, LORD GEORGE (1617–45), poet and song writer, born here. He wrote songs and poems in honour of the Marquis of Montrose, for whose army he was fighting when killed at the battle of Alford.
MACDONALD, GEORGE (1824–1905), poet and novelist, born here. Publications include *Poems*, 1857, *David Elginbrod*, 1862, and the largely autobiographical *Alec Forbes of Howglen*, 1865. He also wrote much for children, including *At the Back of the North Wind*, 1871.

9 **Keig** SMITH, WILLIAM ROBERTSON (1846–94), theological writer, born here. He was dismissed from a scholastic post in Aberdeen in 1881 for the allegedly heretical nature of his articles on the Bible in the *Encyclopaedia Britannica*, and became. joint editor of the *Britannica* the same year.

10 **Kincardine O'Neil** ROSS, ALEXANDER (1699–1784), poet, born here. His works include *The Fortunate Shepherdess*, 1768.

11 **Longside** SKINNER, JOHN (1721–1807), historian and song writer, was minister from 1742 until his death (see **Birse**).

12 **Lumsden** NICOLL, SIR WILLIAM ROBERTSON (1851–1923), journalist and minister, born here. He edited the *British Weekly* from 1886 until his death and founded *The Bookman* in 1891. His own contributions were published in book form as *The Daybook of Claudius Clear* and *A Bookman's Letters*.

13 **Midmar** MESTON, WILLIAM (c1688–1745), poet, born here. His chief work was *Knight of the Kirk*, 1723, in imitation of Butler's *Hudibras*.

OGILVIE, JOHN (1733–1813), writer, born here and Presbyterian minister here from 1759. He published poems and religious works and was a friend of Johnson and Boswell.

14 **Old Deer** SCOTT, WILLIAM (b1785), poet and song writer, born here. Published *Poems Chiefly in the Buchan Dialect*, 1832.

15 **Peterhead** BUCHAN, PETER (1790–1854), writer and publisher, born here. He set up a press here in 1816 and printed collections of Scottish ballads and his own poetry and historical writings.
BUCHAN, PATRICK (1814–81), song writer and doctor, son of Peter Buchan, born here. His most famous song is 'Watt o' the Hill'.

16 **Pitsligo** FORBES, SIR WILLIAM (1739–1806), writer and banker, born here. A member of Dr Johnson's literary club, his publications include *Memoirs of a Banking House*, 1803, and *Life of Beattie*, 1806.

17 **Rathen** HALKET, GEORGE (d1756), poet and song writer, born here and schoolmaster 1714–25. He published *Occasional Poems on Several Subjects*, 1727, and his most celebrated song is the ballad 'Logie o' Buchan'.

18 **Rubislaw** SKENE, JAMES (1775–1864), miscellaneous writer, born here. A close friend of Sir Walter Scott, he wrote *Sketches of Existing Localities Alluded to in the Waverley Novels*, 1829, and edited Spalding's *History of the Troubles*, 1828.

19 **Seggat of Auchterless** GIBBON, LEWIS GRASSIC (pseudonym of James Leslie Mitchell, 1901–35), novelist, lived here for some years (see **Auchterless**).

20 **Towie** BARCLAY, WILLIAM (c1570–c1630), miscellaneous writer, born here. He is remembered for *Nepenthes, or the Virtues of Tobacco*, 1614.

21 **Turriff** FORSYTH, WILLIAM (1818–79), poet and writer, born here. He edited the *Aberdeen Journal* and published *Idylls and Lyrics*, 1872.

160

Banffshire (*Map 28*)

1 **Aberchirder** STABLES, WILLIAM GORDON (1840–1910), boys' travel and adventure novelist, born here. Publications include *Wild Adventures in Wild Places*, 1881, *Kidnapped by Cannibals*, 1899, and *The Cruise of the Land Yacht Wanderer*, 1886.

2 **Aberlour** GRANT, ELIZABETH (c1745–1814), novelist, born nearby. Publications include *Roy's Wife of Aldivalloch*.

3 **Banff** CRAIG, ALEXANDER (c1567–1627), poet, born and died nearby. Among his works were *Poetical Essays*, 1604, *Amorose Songes*, 1606, and *Poetical Recreations*, 1609 and 1623.

4 **Boyndie** RUDDIMAN, THOMAS (1674–1757), philologist, born here. His works include a notable edition of George Buchanan's works, 1715, but he is best remembered for a Latin grammar *Grammaticae Latinae Institutiones*.

5 **Grange** HALLIDAY, ANDREW (1830–77), dramatist and essayist, born at the manse. He wrote *The Great City*, 1867, domestic dramas and adaptations of Dickens and Scott.

Moray (*Map 28*)

1 **Fochabers** CHALMERS, GEORGE (1742–1825), antiquary, born here. His publications include *Caledonia: An Account Historical and Topographical, of North Britain*, 1807–24.

2 **Forres** ADAM, ALEXANDER (1741–1809), antiquary, born here. His principal work is *Roman Antiquities*, 1791.

MACPHERSON, IAN (1905–44), writer on Highland life, born here. His works include *Land of our Fathers*, 1933, and *Pride in the Valley*, 1936.

Inverness-shire (*Map 29*)

1 Fort Augustus GRANT, ANNE (1755–1838), poet and author, lived here from 1773, was married in 1779, and left finally for Edinburgh in 1811. During her time here, she published a volume of poems, 1803, *Letters from the Mountains*, 1806, and *Superstitions of the Highlanders*, 1806.

2 Inverness DAVIOT, GORDON. See Tey, Josephine (below).

HUMPHREYS, ELIZA (d1938), novelist who used the pseudonym 'Rita', born near Inverness. The best known of some sixty novels is *Souls*, 1903.

TEY, JOSEPHINE (pseudonym of Elizabeth Mackintosh, 1897–1952), novelist and playwright, born here. Her books include *Miss Pym Disposes*, 1947, *The Franchise Affair*, 1949, and *The Man in the Queue*, 1929, in which her popular Inspector Grant first appeared. Her plays, written under the name Gordon Daviot, include *Richard of Bordeaux*, 1933.

3 Ruthven MACPHERSON, JAMES (1736–96), poet and translator, born here. His epic poems *Fingal*, 1762, and *Temora*, 1763, which he claimed to be translations from the Gaelic of one Ossian, were widely alleged to have been wholly his own work. He died at Bellville.

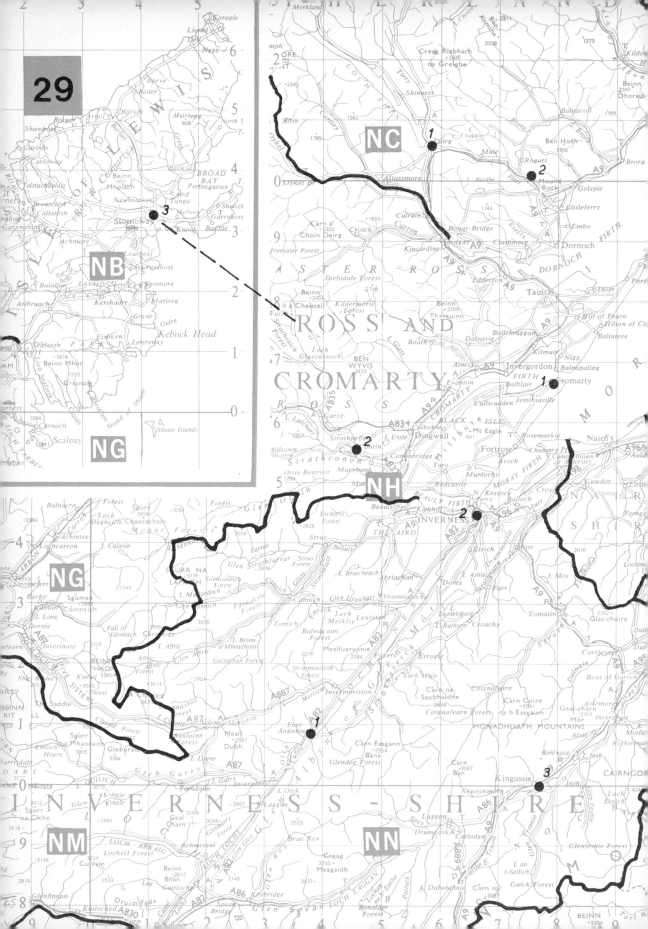

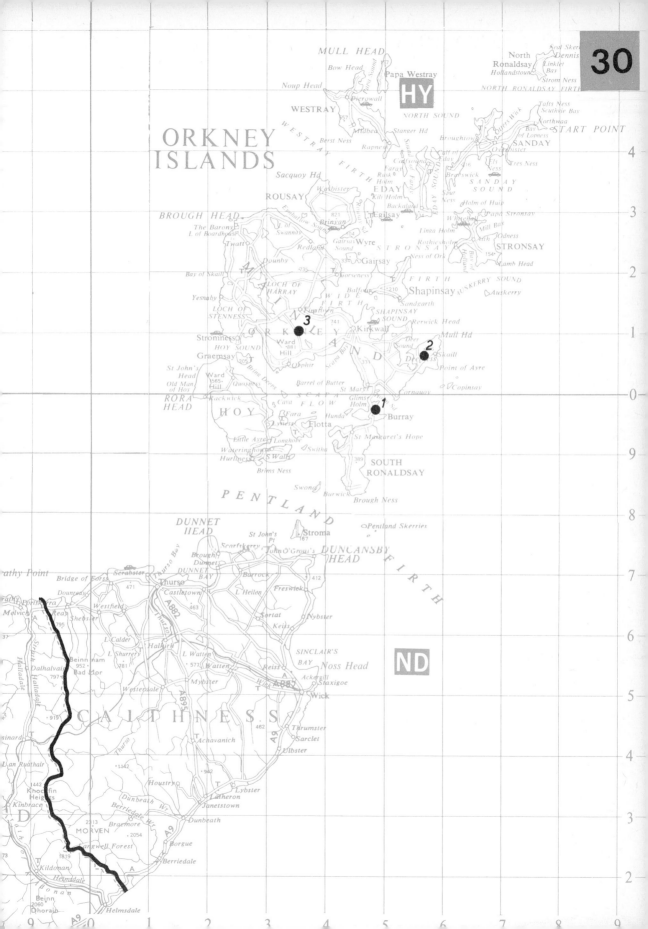

Ross and Cromarty (*Map 29*)

1 Cromarty MILLER, HUGH (1802–56), essayist and geologist, born here. Publications include *Old Red Sandstone*, 1841, and *My Schools and Schoolmasters*, 1852.

URQUHART, SIR THOMAS (1611–60), translator and writer, lived at Cromarty Tower 1645–50.

WATT, LAUCHLAN MACLEAN (1867–1957), historian and biographer, born here. Publications include *History of Britain from the Accession of George I*, 1912, and works on Carlyle, Burns and Gawain Douglas.

2 Ross LAIDLAW, WILLIAM (1780–1845), poet and secretary to Sir Walter Scott, became factor on two farms here in 1832 and died on his brother's farm at Contin.

3 Stornoway MACKENZIE, AGNES MURE (1891–1955), historian and novelist, born here. Her chief work is a *History of Scotland to 1939*, 1934–41. Novels include *Cypress in Moonlight*, 1931, and *Between Sun and Moon*, 1932.

Sutherland (*Map 29*)

1 **Lairg** MILLER, HUGH (1802–56), topographer and biographer, lived nearby for some years. Several of his works deal with Sutherland, among them *The Old Red Sandstone* and *My Schools and Schoolmasters*.

2 **Morvick** SELLAR, WILLIAM YOUNG (1825–90), classical scholar, born here. Publications include *The Roman Poets of the Republic*, 1863, *The Roman Poets of the Augustan Age*, 1877, and *Horace and the Elegiac Poets*, 1892.

Orkney (*Map 30*)

1 Burray BRUNTON, MRS MARY (1778–1818), novelist, born here. She wrote the two popular works *Self-Control*, 1811, and *Discipline*, 1814.

2 Deerness MUIR, EDWIN (1887–1959), novelist, poet and critic, born here. His essays were collected as *Latitudes*, 1924; *Collected Poems* appeared 1952; books of criticism included *The Structure of the Novel*, 1928, and *The Present Age*, 1939.

3 Orkney AYTOUN, WILLIAM EDMONSTOUNE (1813–65), poet, became sheriff of Orkney in 1852.

LAING, MALCOLM (1762–1818), historian, born here. He published his *History of Scotland, 1603–1707*, in 1802, and *Poems of Ossian* in 1805.

VEDDER, DAVID (1790–1854), writer and man of letters, born here. He was an influential member of the Dundee literary coterie, with Nicoll, Grant, McCosh, Thom and others.

London

London (*Letter and number reference system*)

The map of London (31–2) is based on the Ordnance Survey 1 inch to 1 mile map, outline edition, and has a grid reference system of letters and numbers superimposed in red. Where it is possible to locate a gazetteer entry on the map a grid reference is given in brackets. There are, however, a few entries which fall outside the area of the map, and also a number in which the location is given simply as 'London'.

A reference is obtained by reading off the letter in the eastern or western margin opposite the square in which the item is located, followed by the number directly above or below the square in the northern or southern margin. Westminster Abbey, for instance, has a reference of K15; the Tower of London, J18.

Because of the nature of the gazetteer entries there are necessarily two grades of accuracy in the grid references: (*a*) where a street or house name is provided this has been located precisely; (*b*) where only a general area or a district such as 'Kensington' is given, the reference serves only to provide the reader with a rough idea as to location.

In a number of cases the streets or buildings cited have long since disappeared—the reference then shows the former site of the entry.

London (*Maps 31 & 32*)

À BECKETT, Arthur William (1844–1909), author, born at Portland House, Hammersmith (?K7), and died in London. Third son of Gilbert Abbott À Beckett (qv), his works include *The Doom of St Querce*, 1875, with F. C. Burnand, and *The Ghost of Greystone Grange*, 1877.

À BECKETT, Gilbert Abbott (1811–56), comic writer, born on Haverstock Hill (D12). He produced over fifty plays and several humorous works, and was a member of the original staff of *Punch*.

À BECKETT, Gilbert Arthur (1837–91), comic writer, born at Portland House, Hammersmith (?K7), and buried in Mortlake cemetery (O6). Eldest son of Gilbert Abbott À Beckett (qv), he wrote plays and libretti, including *The Happy Land*, 1873, in collaboration with W. S. Gilbert.

ADDISON, Joseph (1672–1719), poet and essayist, died at Holland House, Kensington (K9) and is buried in Westminster Abbey (K15).

AIKIN, Lucy (1781–1864), essayist and historian, buried in Hampstead churchyard (C11).

AINGER, Alfred (1837–1904), author, born at 10 Doughty Street (G15) and buried in Hampstead churchyard (C11). He is chiefly remembered as the biographer and editor of Charles Lamb.

AINSWORTH, William Francis (1807–96), travel writer, died at 11 Wolverton Gardens, Hammersmith (L8).

AINSWORTH, William Harrison (1805–82), novelist, lived at 27a Old Bond Street 1834–41 (J14), and for twelve years at Kensal Manor House, Hammersmith (K7). He is buried in Kensal Green cemetery (G8).

AKENSIDE, Mark (1721–70), poet, settled as a doctor in Bloomsbury Square, 1749 (H15); lived in Craven Street, Strand 1759 (J15); died in Old Burlington Street (J14).

ALBERY, James (1838–89), dramatist, born in Swan Street, Trinity Square (K17); died at 8 Melina Place, St John's Wood (G11); is buried in Kensal Green cemetery (G8). He was the author of *Two Roses*, 1870, and *Dr Davy*, 1866.

ALCOCK, Sir Rutherford (1809–97), writer on oriental subjects, born at Ealing (H1); died at 14 Great Queen Street, WC2 (H15). He published numerous works on Japan, including *Elements of Japanese Grammar*, 1861, and *Art in Japan*, 1878.

ALDRICH, Henry (1647–1710), scholar, born at Westminster (K14). Published the *Artis Logicae Compendium*, 1691.

ALFORD, Henry (1810–71), author and poet, Dean of Canterbury, born at 25 Alfred Place, Bedford Square (H14). Minister of Quebec Chapel, Marylebone, 1853–57 (H13); first editor of the *Contemporary Review*.

ALLINGHAM, Margery Louise (1904–66), crime novelist, born in London. Her amateur detective, Albert Campion, first appeared in *The Crime at Black Dudley*, 1928.

AMORY, Thomas (c1691–1788), author, was living in Westminster (K14) around 1757.

ANDREWES, Lancelot (1555–1626), scholar, born in the parish of All Hallows, Barking; died in Winchester Palace, Southwark (J17), and is buried in Southwark cathedral (J17). His *Works* were issued in 1854 in eleven volumes.

ANSTEY, F. (pseudonym of Thomas Anstey Guthrie, 1856–1934), novelist, born at Kensington (K10). Best remembered for *Vice Versa*, 1882, and *The Brass Bottle*, 1900.

ARBUTHNOT, John (1667–1735), satirist and medical writer, died at Hampstead (D11).

ARNOLD, Sir Edwin (1832–1904), poet and journalist, lived and died at 31 Bolton Gardens, Kensington (L11).

ARNOLD, Matthew (1822–88), poet, lived at 2 Chester Square, Westminster (K13).

ASCHAM, Roger (1515–68), educationist and scholar, is buried in the church of St Sepulchre-without-Newgate (H16).

AUMONIER, Stacy (1887–1928), novelist, lived at 35 Marlborough Hill, St John's Wood (F11).

AUSTEN, Jane (1775–1817), novelist, lived for a time in Henrietta Street (J15).

BACON, Sir Francis 1st Baron Verulam (1561–1626), statesman and essayist, was born in the former York House, near Victoria Embankment (J15); lived in chambers in Gray's Inn (H15); died at Arundel House, Highgate (B13). Published *The Advancement of Learning*, 1605, *Novum Organum*, 1620. His *Essays* first appeared complete in 1625.

BAGEHOT, Walter (1826–77), writer, banker and economist, lived at 12 Upper Belgrave Street, Westminister (K13).

BAILEY, Henry Christopher (1878–1961), novelist, born in London. Author of the Mr Fortune series of detective stories. Other works are historical novels, *The Lonely Queen*, and *Knight at Arms*. He lived in Highgate in later years (B13).

BAILEY, Nathan (d1742), compiler, kept a boarding house at Stepney, where he died (H20).

BAILLIE, Joanna (1762–1851), Scottish dramatist and poet, lived at Hampstead from 1806, dying at Bolton House, Windmill Hill (D11); she is buried in Hampstead churchyard (D11).

BAKER, Sir Richard (c1568–1644), religious and historical writer, died in the Fleet prison (H16) and is buried in St Brides church, Fleet Street (H16).

BANKS, John (fl1696), dramatist, was probably born in London; he is buried at St James's, Westminster (K14). Among his productions are *The Rival Kings*, 1677, *The Unhappy Favourite*, 1682, and *Cyrus the Great*, 1696.

BANKS, Sir Joseph (1744–1820), naturalist, born Argyle Street, Gray's Inn Road (G15). He wrote valuable journals of his voyage round the world with Captain Cook in the *Endeavour*, 1768–71.

BARBAULD, Mrs Anna Letitia (1743–1825), poet, lived in Church Street, Stoke Newington, from 1802 (C18).

BARING, Maurice (1874–1945), poet and novelist, born in Mayfair (J13). He produced several volumes of poems, parodies and critical essays, *An Outline of Russian Literature*, 1914, and the anthology *Have You anything to Declare?*, 1936.

BARKER, Harley Granville (1877–1946), dramatist and critic, born in Kensington (K10). His plays include *The Voysey Inheritance*, 1905, and *Waste*, 1907.

BARRIE, Sir James Matthew (1860–1937), novelist and playwright, lived at 3 Robert Street, Adelphi, from 1911 (J15); he had previously lodged at 100 Bayswater Road (J11).

BEAUMONT, Francis (1584–1616), poet, lived with John Fletcher in a house on the Bankside (J16); he is buried in Poets' Corner, Westminster Abbey (K15).

BEERBOHM, Sir Max (1872–1956), novelist, essayist and caricaturist, born 57 Palace Gardens Terrace, Kensington (**J10**). His caricatures and witty satires were much prized by his contemporaries, many of whom he parodied brilliantly. From 1910 he lived in Italy and died there.

BEHN, Mrs Aphra (1640–89), novelist and dramatist, the first woman writer and the only female writer to be buried in Westminster Abbey (**K15**).

BENNETT, Arnold (1867–1931), novelist, lived at 75 Cadogan Square 1923–30 (**K12**); he went to live at 97 Chiltern Court Mansions, off Baker Street (**H13**), in the following year and died there.

BENNETT, William Cox (1820–95), poet, born at Greenwich (**M23**); died at Eliot Cottages, Blackheath (**N24**), and is buried in Nunhead cemetery (**O20**). His *War Songs* appeared in 1855 and *Collected Poems* in 1862.

BENTHAM, Jeremy (1748–1832), philosopher, born in Red Lion Street, Houndsditch (**H18**); died at Queen Square, Bloomsbury (**G15**). He wrote mostly on legal matters, his most influential work being *Introduction to the Principles of Morals and Legislation*, 1789. His skeleton, fully clothed, is preserved in a glass case at University College (**G14**), of which he was a founder.

BENTLEY, Edmund Clerihew (1875–1956), novelist and journalist, born at Shepherds Bush (**J7**). His nonsense verse was published in *Biography for Beginners*, 1905, *More Biography*, 1929, and *Baseless Biography*, 1939: his novels include the detective stories *Trent's Last Case*, 1913, and *Trent Intervenes*, 1938.

BESANT, Sir Walter (1836–1901), novelist, lived at 18 Frognal Gardens, Hampstead (**D11**), from 1892 until his death; he is buried in Church Row cemetery (**D11**).

BICKERSTETH, Edward (1786–1850), minister and hymn writer, worked as a clerk in the London Post Office (**H17**) and in a solicitor's office, 1801–16.

BICKERSTETH, Edward (1825–1906), poet, son of Edward Bickersteth senior, was born in Barnsbury Park, Islington (**E16**), and died in Westbourne Terrace (**H11**). He was vicar of Christ Church, Hampstead (**C11**), from 1855, and is best remembered for *Yesterday, Today, and For Ever*.

BIRCH, Thomas (1705–66), compiler, born at Clerkenwell (**G16**); died at Hampstead Road (**G14**). He published the lives of several eminent men.

BLADES, William (1824–90), author and printer, born at Clapham (**O14**). His works include a *Life of Caxton*, 1861–63, and *The Pentateuch of Printing*, 1891.

BLAKE, William (1757–1827), poet and artist, born at 74 Broadwick Street, Golden Square (**H14**); lived at 23 Green Street, Leicester Fields, from 1782 (**J13**), later at 17 South Molton Street (**J13**); moved in 1821 to 3 Fountain Court, Strand (**J15**), where he died. He is buried in Bunhill Fields (**J17**). *Songs of Innocence* appeared in 1789, *Songs of Experience* in 1794, and *The Marriage of Heaven and Hell* in 1790.

BLANCHARD, Edward Laman (1820–89), pantomime writer and journalist, born at 31 Great Queen Street (**J15**); died at Albert Mansions, Victoria Street (**K14**). He produced pantomime for Drury Lane for thirty-seven years (**H15**).

BLANCHARD, Samuel Laman (1804–45), poet and essayist, journalist in London from 1831, died by suicide at 20 Air Street, Piccadilly (**J14**).

BLOOMFIELD, Robert (1766–1823), poet, came to London in 1781, first living at Fisher Court, Bell Alley (**H17**), and later at Blue Hart Court, Great Bell Alley, off Coleman Street (**H17**); after 1790 he lived at 14 Great Bell Yard, Telegraph Street (**H17**), moving to the City Road in 1800 (**G17**).

BLYTON, Enid (1900–68), children's author, born at Dulwich (**P18**). She wrote hundreds of books. many featuring her enormously popular Little Noddy.

BOLDREWOOD, Ralph (pseudonym of Thomas Alexander Browne, 1826–1915), author, born in London. He wrote stories set in Australia, including *Robbery Under Arms*, 1888.

BOORDE, Andrew (c1490–1549), physician, traveller and writer, died in the Fleet prison (**H16**).

BORROW, George (1803–81), author, worked as a hack writer in London 1824; lived at 22 Hereford Square (**L11**), off the Gloucester Road, for fourteen years. In *Lavengro*, 1851, he describes the London of his youth.

BOSWELL, James (1740–95), biographer, had lodgings in Old Bond Street in 1769 (**J14**); first met Dr Johnson at 8 Russell Street in 1763 (**H15**); lived in Devonshire Street, off Bishopsgate (**H18**); died at 122 Great Portland Street (**H13**).

BOWER, Archibald (1686–1766), author, buried in Marylebone churchyard (**G13**).

BRADDON, Mary Elizabeth (1837–1915), novelist, born in Soho Square (**H14**). Her best-seller, *Lady Audley's Secret*, appeared in 1862.

BRAY, Anna (1790–1883), author, born at Newington (**K17**); died at 40 Brompton Crescent (**L12**). *The Borders of the Tamar and the Tavy*, 1836, and *A Peep at the Pixies*, 1854, are among her works.

BRETON, Nicholas (c1545–c1626), poet and satirist, born in the parish of St Giles-without-Cripplegate (**G17**). His poetry includes *The Soul's Heavenly Exercise*, 1601, *The Passionate Shepherd*, 1604; prose works include *Strange News out of Divers Countries*, 1622.

BREWER, Ebenezer Cobham (1810–97), compiler, born in Russell Square (**G15**). The best known of his works is the *Dictionary of Phrase and Fable*, which first appeared in 1870.

BROOKS, Charles Shirley (1816–74), writer, born at 52 Doughty Street (**G14**). He succeeded Mark Lemon as editor of *Punch* in 1870; among his novels are *Aspen Court*, 1855, and *The Silver Cord*, 1861.

BROWN, George (1869–1902), novelist, died at Muswell Hill.

BROWN, Oliver Madox (1855–74), author and artist, son of Ford Madox Brown, born at Finchley. His books include *The Black Swan*, 1873.

BROWNE, Frances (1816–?79), children's author, settled in London in 1852 and wrote *Granny's Wonderful Chair and Its Tales of Fairy Times*, 1857.

BROWNE, Hablôt Knight (1815–82), the illustrator Phiz, born at Kennington (**M15**). He illustrated the works of Charles Dickens from 1836, and of Harrison Ainsworth and Surtees.

BROWNE, Sir Thomas (1605–82), writer, born in the parish of St Michael, Cheapside (**H17**). His best known work, *Religio Medici*, appeared in 1642.

BROWNING, Elizabeth Barrett (1806–62), poet, lived first at 99 Gloucester Place, Portman Square (**H12**); moved to 50 Wimpole Street in 1838 (**H13**); married Robert Browning at St Marylebone parish church, 1846 (**G13**).

BROWNING, Robert (1812–89), poet, born in Southampton Street, Camberwell (**L17**); lived here and at nearby Hanover Cottage until 1840; resided at 19 Warwick Crescent, Paddington (**H11**), after 1861, and is buried in Westminster Abbey (**K15**).

BUCHANAN, Robert (1841–1901), poet and novelist, died at Streatham.

BUCKLE, Henry Thomas (1821–62), historian, born at Lee (**P24**). As a result of wide travels he commenced a vast *History of Civilisation in England*. Only two volumes were published in 1857 and 1861, but his approach considerably influenced the writing of history.

BUCKSTONE, John (1802–79), comedian and dramatic writer, born at Hoxton (**F18**). He was the manager of the Haymarket Theatre 1853–78 (**J14**), and composed numerous pieces for the stage.

BUNN, Alfred (c1796–1860), nicknamed Poet Bunn, was manager of Covent Garden and Drury Lane theatres (**J15**) 1833–48, and author of libretti and verse.

BUNYAN, John (1628–88), preached his last sermon at Whitechapel (**H18**), 1688; died at Snow Hill (**H16**) and is buried in the Bunhill Fields burial ground (**G17**).

BURKE, Edmund (1729–97), statesman and philosopher, lodged at 37 Gerard Street, Soho, 1787–93 (**H14**), and at Duke Street, St James's Street 1793–94 (**J14**).

BURKE, Sir John (1814–92), writer and editor, born in London. He founded *The Peerage and Baronetage of the United Kingdom*, 1826, *The Landed Gentry*, 1846, and *Extinct Peerages*, 1846.

BURKE, Thomas (1886–1945), novelist, born at Kennington (**M15**). Most of his works describe the East End and include *Nights in Town*, 1915, *The Real East End*, 1932, and *The Streets of London*, 1940; he also wrote collections of short stories about China Town, among which is *Limehouse Nights*, 1916.

BURNAND, Sir Francis Cowley (1836–1917), humorist, born in London. Editor of *Punch* 1880–1906; his burlesque *Black-eyed Susan* appeared in 1866.

BURNEY, Fanny (Frances, Madame D'Arblay, 1752–1840), novelist and diarist, moved to London in 1760, lived in Poland Street (**H14**) and attended school in Queen Square, Bloomsbury (**G15**); later lived in a house in the grounds of Chelsea Hospital (**M11**), then in St Martin's Street, Leicester Fields (**J14**). After her marriage in 1793, she lived in Half Moon Street (**J13**) and at 11 Bolton Street (**J14**), off Piccadilly. She died in Grosvenor Street (**J13**).

BUTLER, Samuel (1612–80), author of *Hudibras*, lived for many years at 15 Clifford's Inn (**H16**); died in Rose Street (**J15**) and is buried in the church of St Paul, Covent Garden (**J15**).

BYRON, Lord George Gordon, 6th Baron (1788–1824), poet, born in Holles Street, off Cavendish Square; wrote *Childe Harold*, 1812, while at 8 St James's Street (now Byron House, **J14**).

CAMDEN, William (1551–1623), historian, born in the Old Bailey (**H16**); appointed headmaster of Westminster School, 1593 (**K15**); buried in Westminster Abbey (**K15**). He published his famous *Britannia* in 1586. The Camden Society for historical research, founded in 1838, is named after him.

CAREY, Rosa (1840–1909), novelist, born at Stratford-le-Bow (**F22**), died at Sandilands, Keswick Road, Putney (**P9**). Author of numerous stories for girls.

CARLYLE, Thomas (1795–1881), historian and essayist, first lodged at 33 Ampton Street, off Gray's Inn Road, 1832 (**G15**); resided at 24 Cheyne Row, Chelsea, from 1834 until his death (**M12**).

CARTER, Elizabeth (1717–1806), scholar and poet, died at Clarges Street, Piccadilly, (**J13**), and is buried in Grosvenor Chapel burial ground (**J13**).

CARY, Henry Francis (1772–1844), translator of Dante, was an official of the British Museum Library 1826–37 (**H15**). He is buried in Westminster Abbey (**K15**).

CAUDWELL, Christopher (pseudonym of Christopher St John Sprigg, 1907–37), poet, novelist and critic, born at Putney (**O8**). He wrote detective novels and books on flying, but will be remembered for his studies in Marxist criticism, *Studies in a Dying Culture*, 1938, and *Illusion and Reality: a Study of the Sources of Poetry*, 1939. He was killed in the Spanish civil war.

CAXTON, William (c1422–91), the first English printer, established a press in 1476 at the Sign of the Red Pale in the almonry at Westminster (**K15**); the first known work issued from his press is an Indulgence by Abbot Sant, December 1476.

CHAMIER, Frederick (1796–1870), novelist, born in London. Author of works about the sea and a *Review of the French Revolution of 1848*, 1849.

CHAPMAN, George (c1559–1634), dramatist and translator of Homer, is buried in the church of St Giles-in-the-Fields (**H14**).

CHATTERTON, Thomas (1752–70), poet, came to London in 1770, lived in lodgings first at Shoreditch (**G18**), then Brooke Street, Holborn, (**H16**), where he died; he was buried in the paupers' pit of the Shoe Lane Workhouse (**H16**).

CHAUCER, Geoffrey (c1340–1400), was born on the site of Aldgate Post Office (**H18**); he is buried in Westminster Abbey (**K15**).

CHESTERFIELD, Philip Dormer Stanhope, 4th Earl (1694–1773), statesman and letterwriter, born at London House, St James's Square (**J14**); lived at 18 St James's Square 1727–34 (**J14**). After his marriage in 1734, he moved to 45 Grosvenor Square (**J13**), and in 1749 to Chesterfield House, South Audley Street where he died (**J13**). He also lived at the Ranger's House, Blackheath, periodically from 1748–72 (**N24**).

CHESTERTON, Gilbert Keith (1874–1936), poet and author, born at 14 Sheffield Terrace, Campden Hill (**J10**); moved in 1881 to 11 Warwick Gardens, near Olympia (**L9**), and here published his first book of poems, *The Wild Knight*, 1900; later resided at 60 Overstrand Mansions, Battersea Park (**M12**).

CHEVALIER, Albert (1862–1923), known as the coster laureate, born at Notting Hill (**J9**); lived at 17 St Ann's Villas, Kensington (**J9**). He composed and sang costermonger ballads.

CHEYNEY, Peter (pseudonym of Reginald Southouse-Cheyney, 1896–1951), crime novelist, born in London. He came to fame with *This Man is Dangerous*, 1936.

CHURCH, Richard Thomas (1893–1972), poet, novelist, essayist and autobiographer, born at Battersea (**N12**). A prolific and versatile writer, he received major awards for his 'Porch' trilogy of novels (1937, etc), his three-volume autobiography, *Over the Bridge*, *The Golden Sovereign* and *The Voyage Home* (1955, etc) and a volume of poetry, *The Inheritors*, 1957.

CHURCHILL, Charles (1731–64), satirist, born in Vine Street, Westminster (**K15**). He published satirical pieces among which are *The Apology*, 1761, *The Ghost*, 1762, which attacked Dr Johnson and his circle, and *The Prophecy of Famine*, 1763.

CHURCHILL, Sir Winston Leonard Spencer (1874–1965), statesman and historian, lived at 10 Downing Street (**K15**) when prime minister 1940–45 and 1951–55; he died at 28 Hyde Park Gate (**K11**).

CHURCHYARD, Thomas (c1520–1604), poet and prose writer, is buried in St Margaret's Church, Westminster (**K15**).

CIBBER, Colley (1671–1757), actor and playwright, born in Southampton Street, Bloomsbury (**H15**); died in Berkeley Square (**J13**). He was appointed poet laureate in 1730; the best of his plays was *The Careless Husband*, 1705.

CLARKE, Marcus Andrew Hyslop (1846–81), author, born at 11 Leonard Place, Kensington (**K9**). He went to Australia 1864, where he became the leading author;

his best known work is *For the Term of his Natural Life*, 1874.

CLEVELAND, John (1613–58), the cavalier poet, lived and died at Gray's Inn (**H15**).

CLIVE, Mrs Caroline Archer (1801–1873), author, born at Brompton Grove. She published eight volumes of poems by 'V', and a best-selling novel, *Paul Ferroll*, 1855.

COBBETT, William (1763–1835), writer and politician, was imprisoned in Newgate 1810–12; he started a seed farm at Kensington about 1820 (**K10**).

COCKTON, Henry (1807–53), comic novelist, born in London; lived here until 1841. His books include *Valentine Vox, the Ventriloquist*, 1840.

COKE, Lady Mary (1726–1811), diarist, lived at Aubrey House, Campden Hill, Kensington (**K10**).

COLERIDGE, Samuel Taylor (1772–1834), poet, lived in Buckingham Street (**J15**), Frith Street (**H14**) and Norfolk Street (**J15**), later at 7 Addison Bridge Place, near Olympia (**L9**), and at 71 Berners Street, off Oxford Street (**H14**); retired to 3 The Grove, Highgate, in 1825, where he died (**B13**); his remains now lie in St Michael's church (**B13**).

COLLIER, John Payne (1789–1883), Shakespearian critic, born in Broad Street (**H17**). His *Facts and Particulars concerning Shakespeare* appeared 1835–6 and 1839.

COLLINS, William Wilkie (1824–89), novelist, born at North End, Hampstead (**B11**); entered Lincoln's Inn 1843 (**H15**); lived at 65 Gloucester Place, Portman Square, until 1888 (**H12**), died at 82 Wimpole Street, Cavendish Square (**H13**), and is buried in Kensal Green cemetery (**G7**).

COLMAN, George the Elder (1732–94), playwright, purchased Covent Garden Theatre in 1767 (**J15**), and the Haymarket theatre in 1776 (**J14**). He is buried in Kensington church (**K10**).

COLMAN, George the Younger (1762–1836), dramatist, son of the elder Colman, probably born in London; died in Brompton Square (**K12**) and is buried in Kensington church (**K10**). He wrote or adapted numerous pieces, including *The Heir at Law*, 1797, and *John Bull*, 1803.

COMPTON-BURNETT, Dame Ivy (1884–1969), novelist, lived in Cornwall Gardens, Kensington (**K10**).

CONGREVE, William (1670–1729), dramatist, lived in Howard Street, Southampton Street and Surrey Street (all **J15**); he is buried in Westminster Abbey (**K15**).

COOK, Edward Dutton (1829–83), critic and author, born at 9 Grenville Street, Brunswick Square (**G15**); buried in Highgate cemetery (**B13**). His works include *A Book of the Play*, 1876, *Hours with the Players*, 1881, and *On the Stage*, 1883.

COOK, Eliza (1818–89), poet, born at London Road, Southwark (**K16**); lived at Tavistock House, Tavistock Square (**G14**); died at Thornton Hill, Wimbledon. She issued volumes of poetry in 1838, 1864 and 1865; ran *Eliza Cook's Journal* 1849–54.

CORNWALL, Barry (pseudonym of Bryan Waller Procter, 1787–1874), poet, lived at 38 Harley Street for several years until 1861 (**H12**); lived in Weymouth Street, Cavendish Square, from 1861, and died there (**H13**).

CORY, William Johnson (1823–92), formerly Johnson, poet, lived at Hampstead from 1872 and is buried there (**D11**).

COWLEY, Abraham (1618–67), poet and essayist, born in Fleet Street (**H16**); buried in Westminster Abbey (**K15**). His works include *Poetic Blossoms*, 1633, *The Mistress, or Love Poems*, 1647, and the unfinished epic, *The Davideis*.

COXE, William (1747–1828), historian, born in Dover Street (**J13**), Piccadilly. He published a *History of the House of Austria*, 1807, and histories of the *Spanish Bourbons*, 1813, of *Walpole*, 1798, and of *Marlborough*, 1818–19.

CRAB, Roger (c1621–80), hermit author of *The English Hermite* and *Dagon's Downfall*, died at Bethnal Green (**G19**).

CRAIK, Mrs Dinah Maria (1826–87), novelist, settled at Hampstead after 1853 (**D11**).

CRASHAW, Richard (c1613–49), poet, born in London. His works include a volume of Latin poems, *Epigrammatum Sacrorum Liber*, 1634, and *Steps to the Temple*, 1646.

CRAVEN, Mrs Augustus (1808–91), novelist, born at 36 Manchester Square (**H13**). Her works include *Anne Severin* and *Elaine, Lina and Lucia*.

CREIGHTON, Mandell (1843–1901), historian, became bishop of London 1897; he died at Fulham Palace (**N9**) and is buried in St Paul's cathedral (**H17**).

CRUDEN, Alexander (1701–70), author of the *Concordance of the Holy Scriptures*, died at his lodgings in Camden Passage, Islington (**F16**).

CUNNINGHAM, Allan (1784–1842), Scottish poet and writer, settled in London about 1812.

CUNNINGHAM, Peter (1816–69), writer, born in Pimlico (**L14**). His publications include *A Handbook to London*, *Modern London*, and *The Story of Nell Gwynne*.

DANE, Clemence (pseudonym of Winifred Ashton, 1888–1965), novelist and dramatist, born at Blackheath (**N23**). Her most successful plays were *A Bill of Divorcement*, 1921, based on her novel *Legend*, 1919, and *Will Shakespeare*, 1921. Other well known novels include *Broome Stages*, 1931.

DARLEY, George (1795–1846), poet, lived in London from about 1822.

DARWIN, Charles Robert (1809–82), naturalist, lived at 110 Gower Street 1839–42 (**G14**); he is buried in Westminster Abbey (**K15**).

DAVENANT, Sir William (1606–68), poet, died in Portugal Row (**H15**) and is buried in Westminster Abbey (**K15**).

DAWSON-SCOTT, Catherine Amy (1868–1934), novelist, born in London. Her books, mostly set in Cornwall, include *Wastralls*, 1918, *The Headland*, 1920, and *The Haunting*, 1921.

DAY, Thomas (1748–89), novelist, born in Wellclose Square (**J19**); lived at Lamb House in the Temple 1765–76 (**J16**). He is best known for his *History of Sandford and Merton*, 1783–89.

DAY LEWIS, Cecil (1904–72), poet laureate and novelist, lived at Crooms Hill, Greenwich, from 1954 until his death.

DE BEER, Sir Gavin (1899–1972), scientific writer and biographer, born in London. He produced a series of biographies of famous British scientists, including Charles Darwin, 1963, and wrote many books and articles about Switzerland. He was Director of the Natural History Museum 1950–60.

DEFOE, Daniel (c1660–1731), author, born in the parish of St James's Cripplegate (**H17**); imprisoned in Newgate 1703–4 (**H16**); died in Ropemakers Alley, Moorfields (**G17**); and is buried in Bunhill Fields (**G17**). He also lived in a house on the site of the present 95 Church Street, Stoke Newington (**C17**). *Robinson Crusoe* appeared in 1719, *Moll Flanders* in 1722, and *The Journal of the Plague Year* in 1722.

DEKKER, Thomas (c1570–c1632), dramatist and pamphleteer, was born and spent most of his life in London;

confined to the King's Bench prison for debt 1613–16 (**K17**). His works include *The Shoemaker's Holiday*, 1600, *The Honest Whore*, 1604, and *The Wonderful Year*, describing the plague in London. With Ford and Rowley he collaborated in producing *The Witch of Edmonton*, 1621.

DELL, Ethel Mary (1881–1939), novelist, born at Streatham. Among her books are *The Way of an Eagle*, 1912, *The Keeper of the Door*, 1915, and *Storm Drift*, 1930.

DE MORGAN, William Frend (1839–1917), novelist, born at 69 Gower Street (**G14**), and lived and died at 127 Old Church Street, Chelsea (**M12**). His best known novel is *A Likely Story*, 1911.

DENNIS, John (1657–1734), critic and playwright, born in London. He published *Liberty Asserted*, 1704, *Appius and Virginia*, 1709, and *Reflections, Critical and Satirical* in answer to Pope's *Essay on Criticism*, 1711.

DE QUINCEY, Thomas (1785–1859), essayist, was first in London in 1802, lodging at 61 Greek Street, off Soho Square (**H14**); bought his first dose of opium at 173 Oxford Street (**H14**); returned to London in 1808 and again in 1821, when he lodged in York Street, Covent Garden (**J15**), to begin writing his *Confessions of an English Opium Eater*.

DE VERE, Edward, 17th Earl of Oxford (1550–1604), poet, lived at Oxford Court, Cannon Street 1571–91 (**J17**), and died at Brooke House, Hackney (**D20**).

DICKENS, Charles (1812–70), novelist, lived at a number of London addresses and many parts of the city are associated with him. He was at Bayham Street, Camden Town, 1823 (**F14**); Furnival's Inn, 1834–37 (**H16**); 48 Doughty Street, 1837–39 (**G15**); 1 Devonshire Terrace, Marylebone Road, 1839–51 (**G13**); Tavistock House, Tavistock Square, 1851–60 (**G14**). The Doughty Street house is the headquarters of the Dickens Fellowship and open to the public as museum and study centre. He is buried in Westminster Abbey (**K15**).

DICKINSON, Goldsworthy Lowes (1862–1932), author and humanist, lived at 11 Edwardes Square, Kensington (**K9**).

DISRAELI, Benjamin, 1st Earl of Beaconsfield (1804–81), statesman and novelist, born at 22 Theobalds Road, Holborn (**H15**), moved in 1817 to 6 Bloomsbury Square (**H15**); 1 Grosvenor Gate, Mayfair, 1839–72 (**J13**); and died in his last London house, 19 Curzon Street, Mayfair (**J13**). He continued to write novels until the end of his life, the most successful being *Vivian Gray*, 1826–27, and *Coningsby*, 1844.

DIXON, Richard (1833–1900), poet, born in Islington (**D16**). He also wrote a *History of the Church of England*, 1877–1902.

DOBSON, Henry Austin (1840–1921), poet and essayist, lived at 10 Redcliffe Street, Kensington (**L10**).

DOMETT, Alfred (1811–87), poet, born at Camberwell Grove (**N17**), died at 32 St Charles Square, North Kensington (**H8**). His works include *Ranolf and Amohia*, 1872, and *Flotsam and Jetsam*, 1877.

DONNE, John (1572–1631), poet and churchman, born in the parish of St Nicholas Olave (**J17**); appointed vicar of St Dunstan's-in-the-West, Fleet Street (**H16**); became Dean of St Paul's cathedral in 1621, and is buried there (**H17**). *An Anatomy of the World* was published 1611, *Progress of the Soul*, 1612, and *Divine Poems* (first complete edition), 1899.

DORAN, John (1807–78), miscellaneous writer, born in London and died at 33 Lansdowne Road, Notting Hill (**J9**). He is buried in Kensal Green cemetery (**G7**). His works include *Monarchs Retired from Business*, 1857,

History of Court Fools, 1858, and a melodrama, *Justice, or The Venetian Jew*, 1824.

DOUGLAS, Gavin (1474–1522), Scottish poet, is buried in the Savoy Chapel (**J15**).

DOYLE, Sir Arthur Conan (1859–1930), creator of Sherlock Holmes, practised medicine at 2 Devonshire Place, Wimpole Street (**H13**), in 1891, and lived at 23 Montague Place, Bloomsbury (**H15**). In his last years he maintained a flat at 15 Buckingham Palace Mansions (**K13**).

DRYDEN, John (1631–1700), poet and dramatist, lived at 43 Gerrard Street, Soho, from 1688 until his death (**H14**). He is buried in Westminster Abbey (**K15**).

DU MAURIER, George (1834–96), dramatist, lived at 91 Great Russell Street, Holborn, 1863–68 (**H15**), and at New Grove House, 28 The Grove, Hampstead, 1874–95 (**C11**). He died at 17 Oxford Square (**H12**) and is buried in Hampstead parish churchyard (**D11**).

DUNSANY, Lord (Edward John Moreton Drax Plunkett, 18th Baron Dunsany, 1878–1957), novelist and playwright, born at 15 Park Square, Regent's Park (**G13**). He published nearly fifty books, among them *The Curse of the Wise Woman*, 1933, and *My Talks with Dean Spanley*, 1936, many stories of delicate fantasy and the supernatural, and a dozen plays.

EGAN, Pierce the Elder (1772–1849), sporting journalist and author, probably born in London; died at 9 Regent's Terrace, Thornhill Bridge, Islington (**D15**), and is buried in Highgate cemetery (**B13**). He is best remembered for *Boxiana: or, Sketches of Modern Pugilism*, 1818–24, and *The Lives of Florizel and Perdita*, 1814, in which he satirised the Prince Regent.

ELIOT, George (Mary Ann Evans, 1819–80), novelist, lived with G. H. Lewes at Holly Lodge, 31 Wimbledon Park Road, 1859–60 (**P10**); and at The Priory, 21 North Bank, Regents Park, the house most associated with her and Lewes (**F11**). After her marriage in 1880 she resided at 4 Cheyne Walk, Chelsea, where she died (**M11**). She is buried in Highgate cemetery (**B13**).

ERASMUS, Desiderius (c1466–1536), Dutch humanist and scholar, lived at 15 Cheyne Walk, Chelsea (**M11**).

EVELYN, John (1620–1706), diarist, lived at Sayes Court, Deptford (**L21**); died at his house in Dover Street, Westminster (**J14**).

FARNOL, John Jeffrey (1878–1952), novelist, lived some years in Eltham Road, Lee (**P24**).

FARQUHAR, George (1678–1707), dramatist, is buried in St Martin's-in-the-Fields (**J15**).

FENN, George Manville (1831–1909), boys' story writer, born at Pimlico (**L14**). Editor of *Cassell's Magazine* from 1867; novels include *Hollowdell Grange*, 1867, *In Honour's Cause*, 1896, and *Dick o' the Fens*, 1905.

FIELDING, Henry (1707–54), novelist and playwright, lived for a time at Milbourne House, Barnes Common (**O7**); resided in Bow Street 1748–54 (**H15**), and at Fordhook on the Uxbridge Road (**J4**).

FIRBANK, Ronald (1886–1926), novelist, lived at 40 Clarges Street, Piccadilly (**J13**), and in Curzon Street, Mayfair (**J13**).

FLEMING, Ian Lancaster (1908–65), novelist, born at 27 Green Street, Mayfair (**J13**). He is best known as the creator of James Bond, British Secret Service Agent 007, in a series of twelve enormously successful novels, including *Casino Royale*, 1953, *Diamonds are For Ever*, 1956, *From Russia with Love*, 1957, and *Thunderball*, 1961.

FLETCHER, John (1579–1625), dramatist, shared a house with Francis Beaumont on the Bankside (**J17**); is buried in the church of St Saviour, now Southwark cathedral (**J17**).

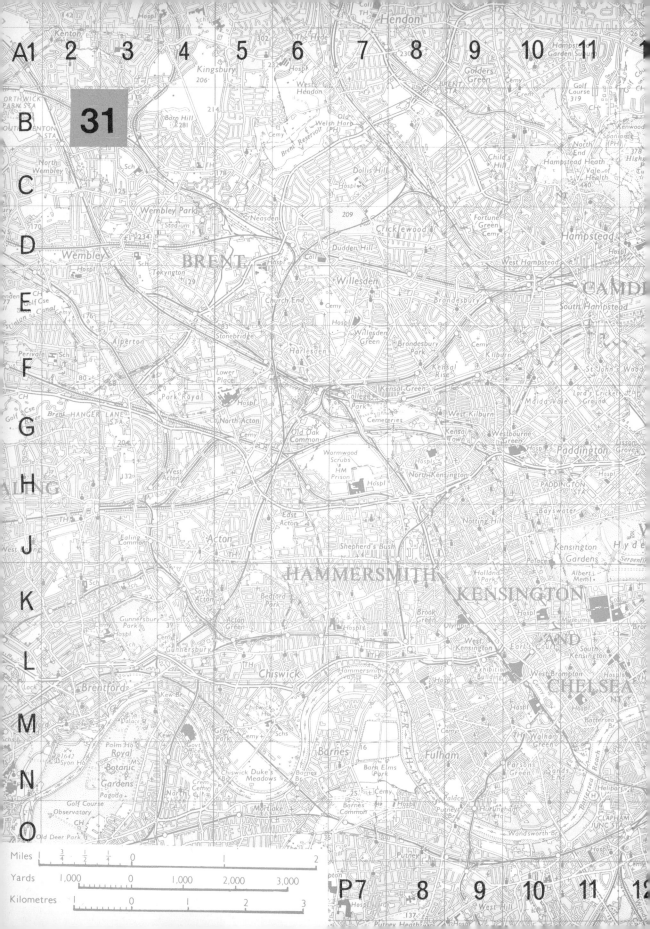

FOLKHARD, Charles James (1878–1963), book illustrator, born at Lewisham (**P20**). His chief success was the creation of 'Teddy Tail', subject of the first British newspaper strip-cartoon (*Daily Mail*, 1915) and of many children's annuals.

FORRESTER, Alfred (1804–72), poet and story-writer who used the pseudonym Alfred Crowquill, born in London; died at 3 Portland Place North, Clapham Road (**N15**); buried in Norwood cemetery. He was the author and illustrator of humorous works.

FORSTER, Edward Morgan (1879–1970), novelist, born in London. His novels, among the most notable of his century, include *The Longest Journey*, 1907, *Howards End*, 1910, *A Passage to India*, 1924.

FORSTER, John (1812–76), biographer of Charles Dickens, lived at 58 Lincoln's Inn Fields, the original of Tulkinghorn's house in *Bleak House* (**H15**).

FOX, George (1624–91), writer and founder of the Society of Friends, buried at Whitecross Street, Bunhill Row (**G17**).

FOX, John (1516–87), author of *The Book of Martyrs*, lived in Milton Street, Cripplegate (**H17**); is buried in St Giles's church, Cripplegate (**H17**).

FRANKLIN, Benjamin (1706–90), statesman and author, worked as a compositor in Bartholomew Close, Little Britain, 1724–26 (**H17**); he was agent for the American colonies here, 1757–62.

FREEMAN, John (1880–1929), poet and critic, born at Dalston (**E18**). He published several volumes of poems, and studies of George Moore, 1922, Herman Melville, 1926, and others.

FREEMAN, Richard Austin (1862–1943), writer of detective stories, born in London: the creator of Dr Thorndyke.

FREUD, Sigmund (1856–1939), founder of psychoanalysis and writer on the subject, lived at 20 Maresfield Gardens, Hampstead, 1938–39 (**D11**).

FROUDE, James Anthony (1818–94), historian, lived at 6 Clifton Place, Sussex Square (**H11**) until 1865, when he moved to 5 Onslow Gardens, Kensington, writing most of his best-known works there (**L11**).

GALSWORTHY, John (1867–1933), novelist and dramatist, lived at Adelphi Terrace until 1918 (**J15**), moving to Grove Lodge, Hampstead, where he died (**D11**). Much of *The Forsyte Saga* series of books were written here.

GARRICK, David (1717–79), actor and dramatist, lived at Garrick's Villa, Hampton, and is buried in Westminster Abbey (**K15**).

GASKELL, Mrs Elizabeth Cleghorn (1810–65), novelist, born at 93 Cheyne Walk, Chelsea (**M12**); lived at 3 Beaufort Street during 1827 (**M11**). Her books include *Cranford*, 1853, *North and South*, 1855, and a life of her close friend Charlotte Brontë, 1857.

GAY, John (1685–1732), author of *The Beggar's Opera*, died at old Queensberry House (**L11**) and is buried in Westminster Abbey (**K15**).

GIBBON, Edward (1737–94), historian, born at Lime Grove, Putney (**O9**), lived at 7 Bentinck Street c1771–83 (**H13**); died at 76 St James's Street (**J14**). His *Decline and Fall of the Roman Empire* appeared 1776–88.

GILBERT, Sir William Schwenck (1836–1911), dramatist, born at 17 Southampton Street, Strand (**J15**); as a child, he lived at 4 Portland Place, Hammersmith (**L9**). He resided at 24 The Boltons, South Kensington, 1876–82 (**L11**), moving to 39 Harrington Gardens where he lived until 1890 (**L11**).

GILCHRIST, ALEXANDER (1828–61), biographer, born at Newington Green (**D17**); died at Chelsea

(**M11**). His wife **Anne** (1828–85), author and journalist, completed his *Life of Blake*, 1863.

GLADSTONE, William Ewart (1809–98), statesman and author, lived in Downing Street (**K15**) during his periods in office as Chancellor of the Exchequer and Prime Minister, and is buried in Westminster Abbey (**K15**).

GLOVER, Richard (1712–85), poet and dramatist, born in St Martin's Lane, Cannon Street (**J15**); died in Albemarle Street (**J13**). His works include *Leonidas*, 1737, an epic, *The Athenaid*, 1787, and his best known ballad 'Admiral Hosier's Ghost'.

GODWIN, George (1813–88), journalist, architect and social reformer, lived at 24 Alexander Square, Kensington (**L11**).

GODWIN, Mary Wollstonecraft (1759–97), miscellaneous writer and mother of Mary Shelley, probably born at Spitalfields (**H18**). She wrote an *Answer to Burke's Reflections on the French Revolution*, 1791, *Vindication of the Rights of Women*, 1792, and *Original Stories for Children*, 1791.

GOLDSMITH, Oliver (1728–74), poet and dramatist, first resided in Fish Lane, near the Monument, in 1756 (**J17**); in 1763 he moved to 6 Wine Office Court off Fleet Street (**H16**), where he wrote *The Vicar of Wakefield*; in the following year he lodged at Canonbury Tower (**E16**); later living at Garden Court in the Temple (**J16**); he resided at 2 Brick Court 1764–74, and died here (**J16**). He is buried in the Temple church (**J16**).

GORDON, Lucie, Lady Duff- (1821–69), translator, born in Queen Square, Westminster (**K14**). She translated from the German Meinhold's *Amber Witch*, 1844, and Feuerbach's *Criminal Trials*, 1846.

GOSSE, Sir Edmund (1849–1928), critic and author, born at Hackney (**D20**); died in London. He was an assistant librarian at the British Museum 1865–75 (**H15**). His critical works include *Seventeenth Century Studies*, 1883, *French Profiles*, 1905, and *Portraits and Sketches*, 1912; he also wrote biographies and histories of literature.

GOSSON, Stephen (1554–1624), dramatist, died at St Botolph's rectory, Bishopsgate (**H18**), and is buried in the church.

GOWER, John (c1330–1408), poet, spent his last years at the priory of St Mary Overies (**J17**) and is buried in Southwark cathedral (**J17**).

GRAHAME, Kenneth (1859–1932), author of *The Wind in the Willows*, lived at 16 Phillimore Place, Kensington, 1901–8 (**K10**).

GRAY, Thomas (1716–71), poet, born on the south side of Cornhill, number 35 (**H17**); lodged in Jermyn Street (**J14**) and Southampton Row, Bloomsbury Square (**H15**).

GREEN, John Richard (1837–83), historian, lived at St Philip's vicarage, Newark Street, Stepney 1865–69 while vicar of St Philip's church (**H19**); lived at 4 Beaumont Street, Marylebone 1869–76 (**H13**), moving later to Connaught Street (**H12**).

GREENAWAY, Kate (1846–1901), book illustrator, born at 1 Cavendish Street, Hoxton (**F17**). She became one of the most influential of all illustrators with the appearance of *Under the Window: Pictures and Rhymes for Children*, 1878, which introduced a style that has become synonymous with her name.

GREENE, Robert (1558–92), dramatist and poet, settled in London about 1589 and died at a house near Dowgate (**J17**).

GROSSMITH, George (1847–1912), actor and author of *Diary of a Nobody*, 1894, born in London.

GROTE, George (1794–1871), historian, lived at 12 Savile Row from 1848 until his death there (**J14**); is buried in Westminster Abbey (**K15**).

HALL, Marguerite Radclyffe (c1886–1943), novelist, is buried in Highgate cemetery (**B13**).

HALLAM, Henry (1777–1859), historian, lived at 67 Wimpole Street 1819–40 (**H13**).

HALLIWELL-PHILLIPS, James Orchard (1820–89), Shakespearean scholar, born in Sloane Street, Chelsea (**K12**). His *Outlines of the Life of Shakespeare*, 1848, was much reissued, and he published a sixteen-volume folio edition of Shakespeare's works.

HARDY, Thomas (1840–1928), poet and novelist, lodged at Westbourne Park Villas 1862–67 (**H11**); lived at 172 Trinity Road, Tooting, 1878–81, and later in The Adelphi, Adelphi Terrace, Westminster (**J15**). His ashes are buried in Westminster Abbey (**K15**).

HARRADEN, Beatrice (1864–1936), novelist, born at Hampstead (**D11**). She is best known for *Ships that Pass in the Night*, 1893.

HAWKINS, Sir John (1719–89), writer and biographer, is buried in Westminster Abbey (**K15**).

HAWTHORNE, Nathaniel (1804–64), American author, stayed at 4 Pond Road, Blackheath, in 1856 (**N24**).

HAYWOOD, Mrs Eliza (1693–1756), novelist, born, lived and died in London. She won much success with *The History of Jemmy and Jenny Jessamy*, 1753.

HAZLITT, William (1778–1830), critic and essayist, lived in Southampton Buildings, Chancery Lane, in 1820 (**H16**), and in Bouverie Street in 1829 (**J16**). He died at 6 Frith Street, Soho (**H14**), and is buried in St Anne's churchyard, Soho (**H14**).

HEINE, Heinrich (1799–1856), German poet and essayist, lived at 32 Craven Street, Westminster, in 1827 (**J15**).

HELPS, Sir Arthur (1817–75), author, born at Streatham; died at 13 Lower Berkeley Street (**H13**), and is buried in Streatham cemetery. His works include *King Henry II: an Historical Drama*, 1843, *A History of the Spanish Conquest of America*, 1855–61, and lives of Pizarro and Cortez.

HENTY, George Alfred (1832–1902), boys' novelist, lived at 33 Lavender Gardens, Battersea (**O13**).

HERBERT, Edward, 1st Baron Herbert of Cherbury (c1583–1648), politician and author, died in London.

HERBERT, Sir Alan Patrick (1890–1971), poet and humorist, born in London; died at 12 Hammersmith Terrace, Hammersmith (**L7**). One of the most prolific contributors to *Punch*, he also wrote operettas, including *Derby Day*, 1932, and *Bless the Bride*, 1947, and his volumes of essays include several collections of *Misleading Cases in the Common Law*. He led the campaign for payment of royalties to authors on library lending as well as on book sales.

HERRICK, Robert (1591–1674), poet, born at Cheapside (**H17**); lived in St Anne's Street, Westminster, 1647–62 (**K14**). One of his best known poems is 'Gather ye rose-buds'.

HILL, Aaron (1685–1750), poet and dramatist, born and died in London. His seventeen dramatic pieces included *Athelwold*, 1731, and adaptations of Voltaire. Pope included him in the *Dunciad*.

HOLCROFT, Thomas (1745–1809), dramatist and novelist, born at Orange Court, Leicester Fields (**J14**); returned to settle in London in 1777; died in Clipstone Street, Marylebone (**H14**), and is buried in Marylebone cemetery (**H13**). *The Road to Ruin*, 1792, and *A Tale of Mystery*, 1802, are among his plays; novels include *Alwyn*, 1780, and *Hugh Trevor*, 1794.

HOOD, Thomas (1799–1845), poet, born at 31 Poultry, City (**H17**); lived at 50 Essex Road 1824–27 (**E17**),

and at Rose Cottage, Winchmore Hill, 1829–31; was at 8 South Place (now 181 Camberwell New Road) in 1840 (**M16**); wrote 'The Song of the Shirt' while residing at 17 Elm Tree Road, St John's Wood, 1841–44 (**G11**). He died at Devonshire Lodge, 28 Finchley Road, Marylebone (**F11**), and is buried in Kensal Green cemetery (**G7**).

HOOK, Theodore Edward (1788–1841), novelist and dramatist, born in Charlotte Street, Bedford Square (**H14**); resided at Egmont Villa, Putney Bridge (**O9**), from 1831 until his death, and is buried in the churchyard of All Saints, Fulham (**N10**).

HOOLE, John (1727–1803), translator and dramatist, born at Moorfields (**H17**); was employed at East India House 1744–83 (**H18**). He published translations of Tasso's *Jerusalem Delivered*, 1763, and *Rinaldo*, 1792, and of Ariosto's *Orlando Furioso*, 1773–83; his dramas include *Cyrus*, 1768, and *Cleonice*, 1775.

HOPE, Anthony (pseudonym of Sir Anthony Hope Hawkins, 1863–1933), novelist, born at Clapton; lived at 41 Russell Square 1903–c1912 (**H15**); is buried in Westminster Abbey (**K15**). He is best remembered for *The Prisoner of Zenda*, 1894, and its sequel, *Rupert of Hentzau*, 1898,

HOPKINS, Gerard Manley (1844–89), priest and poet, born at Stratford (**E24**). His work, much influenced by the early English style of alliterative verse and characterised by its dependence upon stress rather than metre, includes *Windhover*, *The Caged Skylark* and *Pied Beauty*. He died in Dublin. His poetry was published posthumously in 1918 by his friend Robert Bridges, and his *Notebooks* appeared in 1937.

HORNE, Richard Hengist (1803–84), poet and author, born in London. He published *Orion, an Epic Poem*, 1843, and *Ballads and Romances*, 1846, and was a notable correspondent of Elizabeth Barrett Browning, whose letters to him were published in 1877.

HOUGHTON, Richard Monckton Milnes (1809–85), **1st Baron Houghton**, poet, born in Bolton Street, Mayfair (**J13**). His own poetry is insignificant, but he helped greater writers by his early perception of their qualities.

HOUSMAN, Alfred Edward (1859–1936), poet and classical scholar, lived at 17 North Road, Highgate, 1886–1905, and wrote *A Shropshire Lad*, 1896, here (**B13**).

HOWELL, James (c1594–1666), Welsh author and letter writer, was buried in the Temple church (**J16**).

HUDSON, William Henry (1841–1922), writer on nature, lived at Tower House, 40 St Luke's Road, Westbourne Park, from 1890 until his death there (**H9**).

HUGHES, Thomas (1822–96), author, wrote *Tom Brown's Schooldays* in 1856 at The Firs, Ridgeway, Wimbledon.

HUNT, James Henry Leigh (1784–1859), essayist and poet, born in Southgate; lived in many parts of London, including 22 Upper Cheyne Row, Chelsea (**M12**); 32 Edwardes Square (**K10**); the Vale of Health, Hampstead (**C11**); and 7 Cornwall Road, Hammersmith (?**L8**). He died at Chatfield House, Putney High Street (**O9**, but now demolished) and is buried in Kensal Green cemetery (**G7**).

HUTCHINSON, Lucy, writer, born in the Tower of London 1620 (**J18**). Her *Memoirs* of her husband, Colonel John Hutchinson (1615–54), a signatory of Charles I's death sentence, first appeared in 1806.

HUXLEY, Thomas Henry (1825–95), scientist and writer, lived at 38 Marlborough Place, St John's Wood, 1872–90 (**F11**); is buried at St Marylebone cemetery, Finchley.

INCHBALD, Mrs Elizabeth (1753–1821), novelist and dramatist, lived in Frith Street, Soho (**H14**), and in

1812 at 4 Earl's Terrace (**K10**); she died at Kensington House (**K10**) and is buried in Kensington church (**K10**).

INGELOW, Jean (1820–97), poet and novelist, died at 6 Holland Villas Road, Kensington (**K9**); is buried in Brompton cemetery (**M10**).

IRELAND, William Henry (1777–1835), dramatist and forger, born in London. His forgeries included a new version of *King Lear*, and *Vortigern and Rowena*, which he claimed to be the work of Shakespeare; his *Confessions* appeared in 1805.

JACOBS, William Wymark (1863–1943), short-story writer, born at Wapping (**J19**). Publications include *Many Cargoes*, 1896, *Light Freights*, 1901, and *A Master of Craft*, 1900; among his horror stories, *The Monkey's Paw* is best known.

JAMES, George Payne Rainsford (1801–60), novelist and historian, born in George Street, Hanover Square (**J13**). Author of over a hundred popular historical romances.

JAMES, Henry (1843–1916), novelist, settled in London in 1876, living at 34 De Vere Gardens for fifteen years (**K11**); he died at Carlyle Mansions, Chelsea (**M12**).

JERROLD, Douglas William (1803–57), dramatist and humorist, born in Greek Street, Soho (**H14**); died at Kilburn Priory, St John's Wood (**F10**), and is buried in Kensal Green cemetery (**G7**). His most famous work is *Black-eyed Susan*, 1829.

JERROLD, William Blanchard (1826–84), novelist and dramatist, born in London; lived in Thistle Grove, Fulham Road (**M11**); died at 27 Victoria Street, Westminster (**K14**), and is buried in Norwood cemetery. Son of Douglas Jerrold, he succeeded his father as editor of *Lloyd's Weekly Newspaper*, from 1857 until his death; the best known of his dramatic writings is *Cool as a Cucumber*, 1851.

JEWSBURY, Geraldine Endsor (1812–80), novelist, lived in Chelsea from 1854 (**M12**), near her friends Thomas Carlyle and his wife; she died at Burwood Place, Edgware Road (**H12**), and is buried at Brompton cemetery (**M10**).

JOHNSON, Richard (1573–c1659), miscellaneous writer, born in London. His *Famous History of the Seven Champions of Christendom*, 1596, was a favourite work in its day.

JOHNSON, Samuel (1709–84), lexicographer, critic and poet, lived at 17 Gough Square, 1748–59 (**H16**); moved to Staple Inn (**H16**) and elsewhere, and ultimately to Johnson's Court, Fleet Street, 1765–76 (**H16**); he died in Bolt Court (**H16**), now destroyed, and is buried in Westminster Abbey (**K15**). The house in Gough Square is open to the public.

JONES, Ebenezer (1820–60), poet, born in Canonbury Square, Islington (**E16**); became clerk in a City warehouse in 1837. He published his *Studies of Sensation and Event*, 1843, much admired by Browning and Rossetti.

JONES, Harry (1823–1900), novelist, held various incumbencies in London from 1873 and became a prebend of St Paul's cathedral in 1880 (**H17**).

JONSON, Ben (c1573–1637), dramatist and poet, born at Westminster; lived as a child in Northumberland Street (**J15**); lived at Blackfriars in 1607 (**J16**)—the setting of *The Alchemist*, 1610. He is buried in Westminster Abbey (**K15**).

KEATS, John (1795–1821), poet, born at 85 Moorgate (**H17**); became a dresser at Guy's Hospital in 1816 (**J17**); lived at Wentworth Place (Keats House), Hampstead, 1818–20 (**D12**). The house is open to the public.

KEIGHTLEY, Thomas (1789–1872), writer, settled in London in 1824.

KENT, Charles (1823–1902), poet and biographer, born in London; lived at 1 Campden Grove, Kensington (**K10**). His works include *Poets in their Haunts*, 1862, *Charles Dickens as a Reader*, 1872, *Father Prout*, 1881, and *Humour and Pathos of Charles Dickens*, 1884.

KILLIGREW, Thomas the Elder (1612–83), dramatist, died at Whitehall (**K15**) and is buried in Westminster Abbey (**K15**). His best-known comedy is *The Parson's Wedding*.

KINGSLEY, Mary Henrietta (1862–1900), traveller, author and lecturer, born in Islington (**D16**). She lived in Southwood Lane, Highgate, 1863–79 (**B13**); 100 Addison Road, Uxbridge Road, 1893–98 (**K9**); 32 St Mary's Terrace, Kensington, 1898–1900 (**H11**). Her notable books about her travels are *Travels in West Africa*, 1897, and *West African Studies*, 1899.

KINGSTON, William (1814–80), writer of boys' stories, born in Harley Street (**A13**); died at Stormont Lodge, Willesden (**E7**). He published *Peter the Whaler*, 1851, *The Three Midshipmen*, 1862, and *The Three Admirals*, 1877.

KIPLING, Rudyard (1865–1936), author, lived at 43 Villiers Street, Strand, 1889–91 (**J15**), scene of his novel *The Light that Failed*. He died in the Middlesex Hospital, Great Portland Street (**H13**), and is buried in Westminster Abbey (**K15**).

KYD, Thomas (c1557–1595), dramatist, born near Lombard Street (**H17**). He may have been the author of a play, now lost, upon which Shakespeare based *Hamlet*. *The Spanish Tragedy* was produced 1594, *The Rare Triumphs of Love and Fortune*, 1582, and *The Tragedy of Solyman and Perseda*, 1599.

LAMB, Charles (1775–1834), essayist and poet, born in Crown Office Row, Inner Temple (**J16**); lived at Southampton Buildings, Chancery Lane, in 1809 (**H15**); moved to Hare Court, Inner Temple Lane, 1809–17 (**J16**); with his sister **Mary** (1764–1847), he resided at 64 Duncan Terrace, Islington, 1818–27 (**F16**), and at Colebrook Cottage, Islington, 1827–29 (**F16**).

LANDON, Letitia Elizabeth (1802–38), poet and novelist, born at 25 Hans Place, Sloane Street (**K12**). Between 1824 and 1838, she published poems and three novels.

LANG, Andrew (1844–1912), folklorist and poet, lived at 1 Marloes Road, Kensington, from 1876 until his death (**K10**).

LAWRENCE, David Herbert (1885–1930), novelist and poet, lived at 1 Byron Villas, Vale of Health, Hampstead (**C11**) during 1915.

LAWRENCE, Thomas Edward (1888–1935), soldier and author (Lawrence of Arabia), lived at 14 Barton Street, Westminster (**K15**).

LEAR, Edward (1812–88), nonsense writer, born at Bowmans Lodge, Holloway Road (**D15**), and lived at 30 Seymour Street, Marylebone (**H12**). His *Book of Nonsense* appeared 1846, *More Nonsense Rhymes*, 1871, and *Laughable Lyrics*, 1876.

LECKY, William Edward Hartpole (1838–1903), historian and essayist, lived and died at 38 Onslow Gardens, Kensington (**L11**).

LEE, Frederic (1832–1902), poet and writer, was vicar of All Saints church, Lambeth, 1867–99.

LEE, Harriet (1766–1851), novelist and dramatist, born in London. Byron dramatised her story *Kruitzner* in his *Werner*, 1822: other works are a comedy, *The New Peerage*, 1787, and the novels *Clara Lennox*, 1797, and *The Canterbury Tales*, 1797–98 and 1805.

LEE, Nathaniel (c1653–92), dramatist, spent 1682–87 in Bedlam (**H17**); he is buried in the church of St Clement Dane (**H15**).

LEECH, John (1817–64), illustrator, born in Bennett Street, Stamford Street (**J16**); died at Kensington (**K10**) and is buried at Kensal Green (**G8**). He illustrated for *Punch* and the *Christmas Books* of Charles Dickens.

LE GALLIENNE, Richard (1866–1947), poet and essayist, became literary critic of the *Star* newspaper in London, 1891, and remained in London until 1898.

LEIGH, Henry (1837–83), poet, born in London; died at 35 The Strand (**J15**), and is buried in Brompton cemetery (**M10**). He wrote light verse about London and adapted French comic operas for the English stage.

LEMON, Mark (1809–70), editor and humorous writer, born in Oxford Street (**M14**): a founder of *Punch*, of which he was editor from 1843 until his death.

LENIN, Vladimir Ilich Ulyanov (1870–1924), Russian revolutionary leader and writer, lived at 16 Percy Circus, Finsbury (**G15**).

LEVY, Amy (1861–89), poet and novelist, born at Clapham (**O14**). Publications include *A Minor Poet and Other Verse*, 1884, *A London Plane Tree and Other Poems*, and a novel, *Reuben Sachs*, 1889.

LEWES, George Henry (1817–78), miscellaneous writer, born in London; died at the house he shared with George Eliot, The Priory, 21 North Bank, Regent's Park (**G12**); buried in Highgate cemetery (**B13**). Editor of the *Leader*, 1851–54, and of the *Fortnightly*, which he founded, 1865–66. He published a *Biographical History of Philosophy*, 1845, a *Life of Robespierre*, 1848, *On Actors and the Art of Acting*, 1875, and other works including two novels.

LEWIS, Matthew Gregory (1775–1818), novelist, born in London. Known as Monk Lewis: *Ambrioso, or the Monk* appeared 1795, a musical drama, *The Castle Spectre*, 1798.

LILBURNE, John (c1614–57), republican propagandist, born at Greenwich (**M24**). His pamphlets attacked Cromwell's republic as too autocratic; he was repeatedly imprisoned.

LILLO, George (1693–1739), dramatist, born at Moorfields (**H17**); is buried at St Leonard's, Shoreditch (**G18**). Two tragedies are *Fatal Curiosity*, 1736, and *George Barnwell*, 1731; other plays include *Arden of Faversham*, 1759.

LLOYD, Robert (1733–64), poet, born at Westminster (**K14**); died in the Fleet prison (**H16**). *The Actor* appeared in 1760 and a comic opera, *The Capricious Lovers*, in 1764.

LODGE, Thomas (c1558–1625), dramatist and poet, born at West Ham (**F24**); died in London. His *Rosalynde*, 1590, supplied Shakespeare with material for *As You Like It*.

LOGAN, James (c1794–1872), antiquary, lived and died in London.

LOVELACE, Richard (1618–58), poet, born at Woolwich; died in Gunpowder Alley off Shoe Lane (**H16**); buried in old St Bride's church (**H16**). He wrote the poem 'Stone walls do not a prison make' while imprisoned in 1642, and prepared his *Lucasta* while again in prison 1648.

LOWELL, James Russell (1819–91), American poet, was US Ambassador in London 1880–85.

LUCAS, Edward Verrall (1868–1938), essayist and editor, lodged early in his career at Harrington Square, Camden Town (**F14**); his last home was 3 Roberts Mews, Eaton Place (**K13**).

LYTTON, Edward George Earle Lytton Bulwer, 1st Baron (1803–73), novelist and statesman, born at 68 Baker Street (**H13**); buried in St Edmund's chapel, Westminster Abbey (**K15**). He enjoyed immense popularity with such novels as *The Last Days of Pompeii*, 1834, and *Pelham*, 1828.

LYTTON, Edward Robert Bulwer, 1st Earl (1831–91), poet and statesman, son of the 1st Baron Lytton, is buried in St Paul's cathedral (**H17**).

MACAULAY, Thomas Babington, 1st Baron (1800–59), lived at 5 The Pavement, Clapham Common, 1805–36 (**O14**); lived at Holly Lodge, Campden Hill, Kensington, from 1836 until his death there (**K10**); he is buried in Westminster Abbey (**K15**).

MACDONALD, George (1824–1905), poet and novelist, lived at Kelmscott House, Hammersmith (**L7**). William Morris (qv) established a printing press at Kelmscott House in 1890.

MACFARREN, Sir George (1813–87), writer, composer and editor, born at 24 Villiers Street, Strand (**J15**); died at 7 Hamilton Terrace (**G11**) and is buried in Hampstead cemetery (**D9**). His writings include a *Musical History*, 1885; he edited *Old English Ditties*, 1857–80, *Moore's Irish Melodies*, 1859, and *Scottish Ditties*, 1861–80.

MACQUOID, Katherine (1824–1917), novelist, born in Kentish Town (**E14**): the author from 1862 of numerous stories and travel books.

MAHONEY, Francis Sylvester (1804–66), author and journalist, joined the staff of *Fraser's Magazine* in London in 1834, his contributions to which were later re-published as *Reliques of Father Prout*, 1836.

MAIDMENT, James (1794–1879), historian and editor, born at Dowgate Hill (**J17**). His principal work was *The Dramatists of the Restoration* in fourteen volumes, 1872–75.

MALLARMÉ, Stéphane (1842–98), French poet, stayed at 6 Brompton Square, Kensington, 1863 (**L11**).

MALONE, Edmond (1741–1812), Shakespearean scholar, lived at 40 Langham Street, Marylebone (**H13**).

MANLEY, Mrs Mary de la Rivière (1663–1724), dramatist and editor, died at Lambeth (**L15**).

MANNING, Anne (1807–79), novelist, born in London. Her best known works are *Mistress Mary Powell*, 1849, and *The Household of Sir Thomas More*, 1851.

MANSFIELD, Katherine (Katherine Mansfield Beauchamp, 1888–1923), author, lived at 17 East Heath Road, Hampstead (**C11**).

MARRYAT, Frederick (1792–1848), novelist, born at Westminster (**K14**). He wrote *Midshipman Easy*, 1838, while at 8 Duke Street, off Wigmore Street (**H13**), and *Masterman Ready*, 1841, while at 3 Spanish Place, off Manchester Square (**H13**).

MARSTON, John (1576–1634), dramatist, died in Aldermanbury parish (**H17**) and is buried in the Temple Church of St Mary (**H16**).

MARSTON, Philip Bourke (1850–87), poet, born at 123 Camden Road Villas, Camden Town (**E14**); died at 191 Euston Road (**G14**). He published *Song-tide*, 1871, *All in All*, 1875, and *Wind Voices*, 1883.

MARVELL, Andrew (1621–78), poet and satirist, lodged in Maiden Lane, Covent Garden (**J15**); later lived opposite 110 Highgate Hill (**B13**); he is buried in the church of St Giles-in-the-Fields (**H14**).

MARX, Karl (1818–83), Communist philosopher, lived at 28 Dean Street, Soho (**H14**), and died at 41 Maitland Park Road, St Pancras, where he had lived since 1875 (**E12**); he is buried in Highgate cemetery (**B13**).

MASON, Alfred Edward Woodley (1865–1948), novelist, born at Dulwich (**P18**). *The Four Feathers* appeared in 1902, and *At the Villa Rose* in 1910; he created the detective Hanaud of the Sûreté.

MASSINGER, Philip (1583–1640), dramatist, died on the Bankside (**J17**) and is buried in Southwark cathedral (**J17**).

MASSINGHAM, Hugh (1905–71), author and journalist, born in London and died in the Westminster Hospital (**L15**). He wrote several novels and compiled *The London Anthology* with his wife Pauline.

MAUGHAM, William Somerset (1874–1965), novelist, was a medical student at St Thomas's Hospital for six years (**K15**), and a student practitioner in the London slums for a while afterwards. He used this experience for *Liza of Lambeth*, 1897, and *Of Human Bondage*, 1915.

MAYHEW, Augustus (1826–75), novelist, born at 26 Carey Street (**H15**), Lincoln's Inn Fields. He published *Paved with Gold*, 1857, *The Finest Girl in Bloomsbury*, 1861, and *Faces for Fortunes*, 1865.

MAYHEW, Henry (1812–97), journalist and littérateur, born in London; lived at 55 Albany Street, Marylebone (**F13**); died at Charlotte Street, Bloomsbury (**H14**); and is buried in Kensal Green cemetery (**G7**). An originator of *Punch*, 1841. With his brother Augustus, he combined to produce numerous works of fiction, but his most notable work was his own *London Labour and the London Poor*, 1851–62.

MAYHEW, Horace (1816–72), novelist, brother of Augustus and Henry Mayhew (above), born in London; died at 33 Addison Gardens South, Kensington (**K8**), and is buried in Kensal Green cemetery (**G7**). He wrote farces and tales.

MAZZINI, Giuseppe (1805–72), Italian patriot and political writer, lived at 183 Gower Street, St Pancras (**G14**).

MEREDITH, George (1828–1909), novelist and poet, completed *The Ordeal of Richard Feveral*, 1859, while living at 8 Hobury Street, Chelsea (**M11**).

MERRICK, Leonard (1864–1939), novelist, born at Belsize Park (**E11**). Many of his novels have a French background, *The Man who was Good*, 1892, *While Paris Laughed*, 1918, and *The Man who Understood Women*, 1908, a volume of short stories.

MEW, Charlotte (1869–1928), poet, born in Bloomsbury (**G15**). She published *The Farmer's Boy*, 1915, *The Rambling Sailor*, 1929, and was considered by Thomas Hardy the best woman poet of her time.

MEYNELL, Alice (1847–1922), poet and essayist, lived at 47 Palace Court, Kensington, 1890–1905 (**J10**). Her daughter *Viola* (1886–1956), novelist and poet, was born and lived in Kensington (**K10**).

MIDDLETON, Thomas (c1570–1627), dramatist, probably born in London; died at Newington Butts (**L16**).

MILL, John Stuart (1806–73), philosopher, born at 12 Rodney Street, Pentonville (**F15**); lived at 1 Queen Square (now 40 Queen Anne's Gate) 1813–31 (**K14**); lived at 18 Kensington Square 1837–51 (**K10**), where he wrote his *Logis*, 1843, and *Political Economy*, 1848.

MILMAN, Henry Hart (1791–1868), historian and poet, born in Brook Street, St James's (**J13**); became rector of St Margaret's church, Westminster, in 1835 (**K15**); and dean of St Paul's cathedral in 1849, where he is buried (**H17**). His volumes of poetry include *Samor*, 1818, *The Fall of Jerusalem*, 1820, and *Anne Boleyn*, 1822; histories include a *History of the Jews*, 1830, and a *History of Christianity*, 1840.

MILNE, Alan Alexander (1882–1956), novelist and playwright, born at Henley House, Mortimer Road, Kilburn (**F9**). He was assistant editor of *Punch*, 1906–14, before achieving fame with his children's books.

MILTON, John (1608–74), born in Bread Street (**H17**); lived in 1634 at 17 The Barbican (**H17**), and later at 19 York Street, Westminster (**K14**); he wrote the greater part of *Paradise Lost* while living in Jewin Street, Aldersgate (**H17**). He is buried in the church of St Giles, Cripplegate (**H17**).

MOLESWORTH, Mrs Mary Louisa (1839–1921), novelist and children's author, lived her last twenty years in Sloane Street (**K12**).

MONRO, Harold (1879–1932), poet, settled in London in 1911 and founded *Poetry Review* and the Poetry Bookshop, Bloomsbury (**G15**).

MONTAGU, Lady Mary Wortley (1689–1762), letter-writer, born in Arlington Street, Piccadilly (**J14**); lived at 5 Cavendish Square, 1723–30 (**H13**); she died at 44 George Street (**J13**).

MOORE, George (1852–1933), novelist, lived at 121 Ebury Street from 1911 until his death here (**L13**).

MOORE, Thomas (1779–1852), poet, lived at 28 Bury Street, St James's Street, for eleven years (**J14**); lived at Lalla Rookh Cottage, Muswell Hill, in 1817; and at 85 George Street, Marylebone (**H13**).

MORE, Sir Thomas (1478–1535), historian and humanist, born in Milk Street (**H17**); lived at Crosby Place, Bishopsgate (**H18**), and later at Chelsea 1523–34 (**M11**). He was executed in the Tower of London.

MORGAN, Lady Sydney (1783–1859), Irish-born novelist, died in London and is buried in old Brompton cemetery (**M10**).

MORLEY, Henry (1822–94), literary scholar and editor, born at 100 Hatton Gardens (**H16**). He edited Charles Dickens's periodicals 1850–65; produced *English Writers* in eleven volumes, 1887–95, and *First Sketch of English Literature*, 1875.

MORLEY, John (1838–1923), 1st Viscount Morley of Blackburn, statesman and biographer, died at Flowermead, Wimbledon Park.

MORRIS, Richard (1833–94), etymologist, born at Bermondsey (**K18**). He published *The Etymology of Local Names*, 1857, and a *Primer of English Grammar*, 1875, besides editions of old English works, including *Sir Gawayne and the Green Knight*, and the poems of Chaucer and Spenser.

MORRIS, William (1834–96), poet and artist, lived at 17 Red Lion Square, Holborn, 1856–59 (**H15**); after his marriage he went to live at 41 Great Ormond Street, 1858–71 (**G15**).

MOULTRIE, John (1799–1874), poet, born at 31 Great Portland Street (**H13**). His best works are considered to be *My Brother's Grave*, 1820, and *Godiva*, 1820.

MUNDAY, Anthony (1553–1633), playwright, and ballad writer, born in London. He was appointed chief pageant writer for London in 1605. Plays were *The Downfall of Robert, Earl of Huntingdon*, 1601, and its sequel *The Death of Robert, Earl of Huntingdon*, both concerning Robin Hood.

MURRAY, David Leslie (1888–1962), novelist, lived and died at 32 Eton Avenue, Swiss Cottage (**E11**).

MURRY, John Middleton (1889–1957), critic, lived at 17 East Heath Road, Hampstead, with Katherine Mansfield (**C11**).

NEWBERY, John (1713–67), author and bookseller, settled in London about 1744.

NEWMAN, John Henry, Cardinal (1801–90), theologian, poet and author, born in Old Broad Street, City of London (**H17**). His expression of religious thought, of great influence, fills some forty volumes. He also wrote poems, including 'Lead kindly light', the verse text used by Edward Elgar for the 'Dream of Gerontius', 1866, and two novels.

NEWTON, Sir Isaac (1642–1727), mathematician and scientific writer, lived at 35 St Martin's Street, Leicester Square (**J14**), at 87 Jermyn Street (**J14**), and near St Mary Abbot's, Kensington (**K10**).

NEWTON, John (1725–1807), hymn writer, born in London; became rector of St Mary Woolnoth in 1779

(H17). A close friend of Cowper, in conjunction with whom the *Olney Hymns* were produced. He wrote many well-known hymns, including 'Glorious things of Thee are spoken' and 'How sweet the name of Jesus sounds'.

NICHOLS, John (1745–1826), printer and author, born in Islington (D16). His numerous works include *Literary Anecdotes of the Eighteenth Century*, 1812–15, and *The Bibliotheca Topographica Britannica*, 1780–1800.

NORTHCLIFFE, Lord (Alfred Charles William Harmsworth, 1865–1922), founder of the *Daily Mail*, *Daily Mirror*, etc, had his London home at 1 Carlton Gardens, Westminster (J14). He died in a hut sickroom, specially built on the roof of the house next door.

NORTON, Caroline Elizabeth Sarah (1808–77), novelist and poet, and a grand-daughter of Sheridan, born at 11 South Audley Street (J13); died at 10 Upper Grosvenor Street (J13). Her novels were *Stuart of Dunleath*, 1851, *Lost and Saved*, 1863, and *Old Sir Douglas*, 1868.

O'CONNOR, Thomas Power (1848–1929), journalist and parliamentarian, came to London in 1870, died at 5 Morpeth Mansions, Victoria (L14), and is buried in St Mary's cemetery, Kensal Green (G8).

ORTON, Joseph (1933–67), playwright, died at Islington (D16).

OTWAY, Thomas (1652–85), dramatist and poet, died in a tavern on Tower Hill (J18); he is buried in the church of St Clement Dane (H15).

OUIDA, (pseudonym of Louise de la Ramée, 1839–1908), novelist, lived for a time at 11 Ravenscourt Square, Hammersmith (K7).

OVERBURY, Sir Thomas (1581–1613), poet, died in the Tower of London (J18); he is believed to have been poisoned.

PAINE, Thomas (1737–1809), political writer, wrote parts of his *Rights of Man*, 1790–92, while staying at the old Angel Inn, Islington (F16).

PALGRAVE, Sir Francis (1788–1861), historian, born in London; lived at The Green, Hampstead, from 1834 and died there (D11). Appointed Deputy Keeper of Her Majesty's Records, 1838. Among his works are *The English Commonwealth*, 1832, and a *History of Normandy and of England*, 1851–64.

PALGRAVE, Francis Turner (1824–97), poet and critic, son of Sir Francis Palgrave, was brought up at The Green, Hampstead (D11). His best known work remains *The Golden Treasury of Songs and Lyrics*, 1861.

PALMER, John Leslie (1885–1944), novelist and critic, born in London. He wrote thrillers under the names Francis Beeding and David Pilgrim, in collaboration with Hilary St George Saunders.

PALTOCK, Robert (1697–1767), novelist, born in Westminster (K14). His sole major work, *The Life and Adventures of Peter Wilkins, a Cornish Man*, 1751, was praised by Southey and Leigh Hunt.

PARDOE, Julia (1806–62), novelist, historian and travel writer, died at Upper Montagu Street (H12).

PARR, Louisa (c1844–1903), novelist, born in London. Author of numerous stories, including *Dorothy Fox*, 1871, and *Adam and Eve*, 1880.

PATMORE, Coventry Kersey Dighton (1823–96), poet and essayist, lived at 14 Percy Street, St Pancras, 1863–64 (H14).

PEELE, George (c1558–c1597), dramatist, born in London; returned to live here in 1581 and remained until his death. His best work is *The Arraignment of Paris*, 1584; others include *The Old Wives' Tale*, 1595, which probably gave Milton the subject for *Comus*.

PENN, William (1644–1718), Quaker author and founder of Pennsylvania, born on the east side of Great Tower

Hill (J18); he had rooms in Holland House (K9), and lived for a time in Norfolk Street (J15). His best known works include *No Cross, No Crown*, 1669, and *Innocency with her Open Face*, 1668.

PEPYS, Samuel (1633–1703), diarist and administrator, born in Salisbury Court, Fleet Street (H16); 1684–88 lived at 12 Buckingham Street, Strand, and 1688–1701 two doors away (J15); he is buried in the church of St Olave, Hart Street (J18).

PICKEN, Andrew (1788–1833), novelist, settled in London about 1814.

PINERO, Sir Arthur Wing (1855–1934), playwright, born at Islington (D16) and lived at 115a Harley Street, Marylebone (H13). *The Second Mrs Tanqueray*, 1893, is regarded as the beginning of British modern drama.

PINKERTON, John (1758–1826), historian, lived in London 1780–1802.

PLANCHÉ, James Robinson (1796–1880), playwright and herald, born in Old Burlington Street, Piccadilly (J14); died at 10 St Leonard's Terrace, Chelsea (L12). Appointed Somerset Herald in 1866, he wrote the English libretti for Weber's *Der Freischutz*, 1824, and for *Oberon*, 1826.

PLUMPTRE, Edward Hayes (1821–91), poet and translator, born in London. He published verse translations of Sophocles, Aeschylus, and Dante and volumes of his own verse.

POPE, Alexander (1688–1744), poet, born in Plough Street, Lombard Street (J17); lived before 1715 at 9 Berkeley Street (J13). He wrote much of his *Essay on Man*, 1733, at Bolingbroke House, Battersea (N12).

POTTER, Beatrix (1866–1943), author of children's books, born at 2 Bolton Gardens, South Kensington (L11). The first of her famous series of children's books, illustrated by herself, was *Peter Rabbit*, 1900.

PRIOR, Matthew (1664–1721), poet, is buried in Westminster Abbey (K15).

PUTTENHAM, George (c1530–90), poet, died at St Bridget's, Fleet Street (H16).

RACKHAM, Arthur (1867–1939), book illustrator, born in London. Notable works illustrated include *Alice in Wonderland*, *Peter Pan*, *The Ingoldsby Legends* and *Aesop's Fables*.

RADCLIFFE, Mrs Ann (1764–1823), novelist, born in London. She published *The Sicilian Romance*, 1790, *The Mysteries of Udolpho*, 1794, and *The Italian*, 1797. She has been called the Salvator Rosa of British novelists.

RALEIGH, Sir Walter (c1552–1618), explorer, historian and poet, imprisoned in the Tower of London 1603–16 (J18), executed in Old Palace Yard, Westminster (K15), and buried in the church of St Margaret (K15).

RALSTON, William (1828–89); Russian scholar and folklorist, born at York Terrace, Regent's Park (G13); died at 11 North Crescent (H14), and is buried in Brompton cemetery (M10). He published a translation of Turgenieff's *Liza*, 1869, *Songs of the Russian People*, 1872, and *Early Russian History*, 1874.

RANDS, William (1823–82), novelist and 'laureate of the nursery', born in London; died at Luton Villa, Ondine Road, East Dulwich (O18), and is buried in Forest Hill cemetery (P19). Using the pseudonyms Henry Holbeach and Matthew Browne, he wrote poems and fairy tales for children, including *Shoemakers' Village*, 1867, and *Lilliput Lectures*, 1871.

READE, Charles (1814–84), novelist, died at 3 Blomfield Villas, Shepherds Bush (J7), and is buried in St Mary's church, Hammersmith (L9).

RECCORDE or RECORDE, Robert (c1510–58), mathematical writer, died in prison in Southwark (J17).

REED, Talbot Baines (1852–93), boys' novelist, born at Hackney (**O20**); died at Highgate (**B13**). His highly successful *Adventures of a Three Guinea Watch*, serialised in the *Boys' Own Paper* in 1880 and published as a book in 1883, was followed by many popular tales.

REID, Thomas Mayne (1818–83), Irish-born author of adventure stories, is buried in Kensal Green cemetery (**G7**).

RHYS, Ernest (1859–1946), poet and editor, born at Islington (**D16**). He returned to London in 1885 and became editor of *Camelot Classics* and *Everyman's Library*.

RICHARDSON, Henry Handel (pseudonym of Ethel Florence Lindesay Richardson, 1870–1946), Australian novelist, lived at 90 Regent's Park Road, St Pancras (**F13**).

RICHARDSON, Samuel (1689–1761), novelist, lived at 38 and 40 North End Road, Kensington (**L9**), from 1739; he died at Parson's Green (**N10**) is buried in St Bride's church, Fleet Street (**H16**).

RICKMAN, Thomas (1761–1834), bookseller and radical writer known as 'Clio', settled at 39 Leadenhall Street (**H18**) in 1783, then at 7 Upper Marylebone Street where he spent the rest of his life (**H13**).

RITCHIE, Lady Anne Isabella Thackeray (1837–1919), novelist, a daughter of Thackeray, is buried in Hampstead parish churchyard (**D11**).

ROBERTS, Morley (1857–1942), novelist and travel writer, born in London. Books of travel include *Land-travel and Seafaring*, 1891, and *A Tramp's Notebook*, 1904; novels are *A Son of Empire*, 1899, and *The Way of a Man*, 1902.

ROBINSON, Frederick (1830–1901), novelist, born at Spitalfields (**H18**). His works include *Grandmother's Money*, 1860, *Mattie, a Stray*, 1860, and *Woman in the Dark*, 1895.

ROBINSON, William Heath (1872–1944), book illustrator, born at Hornsey (**A15**). His books of weird inventions coined the adjective Heath Robinsonian. His brothers **Thomas** (1869–1950) and **Charles** (1870–1937) were also leading book illustrators.

ROGERS, Samuel (1763–1855), poet, born at Newington Green (**D17**). He was notable for his patronage of other literary men and his famous breakfast talk.

ROLFE, Frederick (1860–1913), novelist, born in Cheapside (**H17**). Calling himself Baron Corvo, he wrote such books as *Hadrian VII*, on which the modern play of that name is based. He died in Venice.

ROSSETTI, Christina Georgina (1830–94), poet, born at 38 Charlotte Street; lived at 30 Torrington Square, Bloomsbury (**G14**), from 1876 until her death, and is buried in Highgate cemetery (**B13**).

ROSSETTI, Dante Gabriel (1828–82), poet and painter, born at 110 Hallam Street, Marylebone (**H13**); lived at 17 Red Lion Square, Holborn, with William Morris (**H15**), and at 16 Cheyne Walk, Chelsea (**M12**). He is buried in Highgate cemetery (**B13**).

ROSSETTI, William Michael (1829–1919), critic and biographer, born at 38 Charlotte Street (**H14**). He edited the works of his brother and sister, Dante Gabriel and Christina Rossetti, and those of other English poets.

RUSKIN, John (1819–1900), writer on art and social issues, born at 54 Hunter Street, King's Cross (**G15**); lived at 163 Denmark Hill, 1842–72 (**O17**).

SALA, George Augustus (1828–95), novelist and journalist, born in New Street, Manchester Square (**H13**); lived in Mecklenburgh Square (**G15**). He wrote articles and stories for Charles Dickens in *Household Words*

and *All the Year Round*. His best known book is *Twice Round the Clock*, 1859.

SCHREINER, Olive Emilie Albertina (1855–1920), author, lived at 16 Portsea Place, Paddington (**II12**).

SCOTT, Clement (1841–1904), critic and novelist, born in London. He was dramatic critic for the *Daily Telegraph*, 1871–98, and edited *The Theatre*, 1880–89. He also adapted many plays from the French.

SCOTT, John (1730–83), poet, born at Bermondsey (**K18**). He is best known for his descriptive poem *Amwell*, 1776.

SCOTT, Sir Walter (1771–1832), spent his last days in London at 75 Jermyn Street, the site of St James's Hotel (**J14**).

SEELEY, Sir John Robert (1834–95), writer and scholar, born in London. His works include *Ecce Homo*, 1865, and *The Expansion of England*, 1883.

SETTLE, Elkanah (1648–1724), poet and dramatist, appointed City Poet in 1691, and died in the Charterhouse (**G16**).

SEYMOUR, Beatrice Kean (d1955), novelist, born in London. Her popular trilogy, *Maids and Mistresses*, appeared in 1932.

SHADWELL, Thomas (c1642–92), poet laureate, died in Church Street, Chelsea (**M12**), and is buried in Westminster Abbey (**K15**).

SHAKESPEARE, William (1564–1616), lodged at the Cripplegate junction of Monkwell Street and Silver Street in 1604 (**H17**); purchased a house in Blackfriars in 1615 (**J16**), and lived in the parish of St Helen's, Bishopsgate, c1596–1600 (**H18**). The Globe theatre, Southwark, in which he had a share, was built in 1599 and destroyed by fire in 1613 (**J17**).

SHANKS, Edward (1892–1953), poet, novelist and critic, born in London. Volumes of verse include *The Island of Youth*, 1921, and *Poems, 1912–32*, 1933; novels are *The People of the Ruins*, 1920, *Queer Street*, 1932, and *Tom Tiddler's Ground*, 1934.

SHAW, George Bernard (1856–1950), dramatist, came to London in 1876; lived at 29 Fitzroy Square (**G14**) before 1898, when he moved to 10 Adelphi Terrace (**J15**).

SHELLEY, Percy Bysshe (1792–1822), poet, lived at 15 Poland Street in his youth (**H14**); was at 23 Aldford Street in 1811 (**J13**), and at 26 Nelson Square, Blackfriars, 1814–15 (**K16**); later in 1815 he was living at 26 Marchmont Street, Bloomsbury (**G15**).

SHERIDAN, Richard Brinsley (1751–1816), playwright, died at 14 Savile Row (**J14**), where he had been living for about a year. A former home had been 10 Hertford Street, Westminster (**J13**).

SHIRLEY, James (1596–1666), dramatist and poet, born in the parish of St Mary Woolnoth, Walbrook (**J17**); he is buried in St Giles-in-the-Fields (**H14**). His best known work is *The Witty Fair One*, 1628.

SIDNEY, Sir Philip (1554–86), poet, was buried in old St Paul's cathedral (**H17**).

SIMS, George (1847–1922), journalist, author and dramatist, born in London. He wrote many books about London, including *Living London*, 1901, *London by Night*, 1906, and *Behind the Veil*, 1913; a series of crime stories was *Dorcas Dene, Detective*, 1897.

SINCLAIR, Catherine (1800–64), children's author, died in Kensington (**K10**).

SKEAT, Walter William (1835–1912), scholar, born in London. His works include editions of *Piers Plowman*, 1866–86, and of Chaucer, 1894–97, besides an *Etymological Dictionary*, 1879–82. In 1873 he founded the English Dialect Society.

184

SKELTON, John (c1460–1529), satirical poet, died in sanctuary in Westminster (**K15**).

SMILES, Samuel (1812–1904), author of *Self-Help*, 1859, lived at 11 Granville Park, Lewisham (**O23**).

SMITH, Charlotte (1749–1806), poet, born in King Street, St James's (**J14**). She also wrote novels, including *Emmeline*, 1788, and *The Old Manor House*, 1793.

SMITH, George (1824–1901), publisher, born in Fenchurch Street (**J18**), moving soon afterwards to 65 Cornhill (**H17**); lived at 112 Gloucester Terrace, 1854–58 (**H11**), at 11 Gloucester Square, 1859–63 (**H11**), at Oak Hill Lodge, Hampstead, 1863–72 (**D11**), and later in Park Lane (**J13**). He established the *Cornhill Magazine* in 1859, and projected and published the *Dictionary of National Biography*, 1885–1900.

SMITH, Horace (1779–1849), and **James** (1775–1839), essayist brothers, born in London; James Smith died here. Their collection of parodies *Rejected Addresses* was written in 1812 for a competition to mark the re-opening of Drury Lane Theatre (**H15**) and became an immediate best-seller. Horace Smith was also the author of historical novels, including *Brambletye House*, 1826, and *The New Forest*, 1829.

SMITH, Stevie (Florence Margaret, 1902–71), poet, and novelist, lived all her life at Palmer's Green.

SMITH, Sydney (1771–1845), clergyman and wit, lived at 14 Doughty Street 1803–6 (**G15**); died at 59 Green Street, near Hyde Park (**K12**), and is buried in Kensal Green cemetery (**G7**).

SMITH, Sir William (1813–93), lexicographer, born in London; died at 94 Westbourne Terrace (**H11**). He produced dictionaries of Greek and Roman antiquities, 1842, Greek and Roman biography and mythology, 1843–49, the Bible, 1860–63, and Christian antiquities, 1875–80.

SMITH, William Henry (1818–72), novelist, born at Hammersmith (**K7**). His philosophical dialogues, *Thorndale* and *Gravenhurst*, appeared in 1857 and 1861.

SMOLLETT, Tobias (1721–71), author, lived in Lawrence Street, Chelsea, 1750–62 (**M12**).

SOMERVILLE, Mrs Mary (1780–1872), scientific writer, lived at 12 Hanover Square, Westminster (**H13**).

SOUTHERN, Thomas (1660–1746), Irish-born dramatist, died in Westminster (**K15**).

SOUTHWELL, Robert (1561–95), recusant poet, died at Tyburn (**J12**).

SPEED, John (1552–1629), historian and cartographer, buried in St Giles, Cripplegate (**H17**).

SPENDER, Lily (1838–95), novelist, born in Portland Place (**H13**). As Mrs John Kent Spender, she produced over twenty novels between 1869 and 1895.

SPENCER, Herbert (1820–1903), sociologist and philosopher, lived at 37 Queen's Gardens, Lancaster Place, 1866–89 (**J15**); he also lived at 2 Leinster Place (**H11**).

SPENSER, Edmund (1552–99), poet, born in East Smithfield (**J18**); died at a tavern in King Street, Westminster (**J14**), and is buried in Westminster Abbey (**K15**). His *Shepheards Calendar* appeared in 1579, and *The Faerie Queen* in 1590 and 1596.

STEELE, Sir Richard (1672–1729), essayist and dramatist, came to London about 1695, lived in Bloomsbury Square (**H15**), on Haverstock Hill (**E12**) and in Villiers Street, Strand (**J15**). He started the *Tatler* in 1709 and the *Spectator* in 1711.

STEPHEN, Sir James (1789–1859), historian and statesman, born at Lambeth (**L15**). His *Essays in Ecclesiastical Biography* appeared in 1849.

STEPHEN, Sir James Fitzjames (1829–94), judge and author, born in Kensington (**K10**). His works include a *General View of the Criminal Law of England*, 1863 and 1890, a *History of the Criminal Law*, 1883, and the *Story of Nuncomar and Sir Elijah Impey*, 1885.

STEPHEN, Sir Leslie (1832–1904), biographer and editor, born in Kensington and lived at 22 Hyde Park Gate (**K11**). He was editor of the *Cornhill*, 1871–82, and of the *Dictionary of National Biography*, 1882–91. He was the father of Virginia Woolf.

STERNE, Laurence (1713–68), novelist, died at 39B Old Bond Street (**J14**) and buried at St George's, Hanover Square (**J13**). His remains were removed to Yorkshire in 1969.

STOW, John (c1525–1605), historian, born in the parish of St Michael, Cornhill (**H17**); buried in the church of St Andrew Undershaft, where his memorial stands (**H18**). His principal work, a *Survey Of London*, appeared in 1598.

STRACHEY, Giles Lytton (1880–1932), critic and biographer, born in London; was living intermittently at 51 Gordon Square, Bloomsbury (**G15**) from 1919. A leading member of the Bloomsbury Group, he pioneered the modern style of writing biography.

STRYPE, John (1643–1737), historian, born at 10 Leyden Street, Middlesex Street (**H18**); died at Hackney (**D20**) and is buried in Leyton parish church (**C22**). His chief preoccupation was ecclesiastical history.

SUCKLING, Sir John (1609–42), poet and dramatist, was living in St Martin's Lane in 1641 (**J15**).

SURREY, Henry Howard, Earl of (1517–47), poet, was executed on Tower Hill (**J18**).

SWIFT, Jonathan (1667–1745), satirist, lodged in Bury Street 1710 (**J14**), and in Church Lane, Chelsea, in 1711 (**M12**).

SWINBURNE, Algernon Charles (1837–1909), poet, born in Chester Street (**L13**); lived with the Rossettis and George Meredith at 16 Cheyne Walk, Chelsea, in 1862 (**M12**); lived with Theodore Watts-Dunton at The Pines, 11 Putney Hill, from 1879 until his death (**P8**): his first series of *Poems and Ballads* appeared in 1866.

TAGORE, Sir Rabindranath (1861–1941), Indian poet, lived at 3, Villas on the Heath, Vale of Health, Hampstead (**C11**).

TAYLOR, Jane (1783–1824), poet, born in Red Lion Street (**H15**); lived in London until 1786. She and her sister Ann were highly popular for their poems for small children, including Jane's 'Twinkle, twinkle, little star'.

TENNIEL, Sir John (1820–1914), caricaturist, born in London. He illustrated such books as *Alice in Wonderland*, *Alice Through the Looking Glass*, Moore's *Lallah Rookh*, and the *Ingoldsby Legends*.

TENNYSON, Alfred, Lord (1809–92), 1st Baron, poet laureate, lodged at several places in London, including Lincoln's Inn Fields (**H15**), and 225 Hampstead Road (**G14**). He is buried in Westminster Abbey (**K15**).

TEY, Josephine (pseudonym of Elizabeth Mackintosh, 1897–1952), novelist and playwright, died in London.

THACKERAY, William Makepeace (1811–63), novelist, lodged as a pupil at Charterhouse at 28 Clerkenwell Road (**G16**); he lived at 16 Young Street, Kensington, 1847–54 (**K10**), and at 36 Onslow Square, Kensington, 1854–62 (**L11**); he died at 2 Palace Green (**K10**) and is buried in Kensal Green cemetery (**G7**).

THIRKELL, Angela (1890–1961), novelist, born in London and lived here until 1917. She wrote her best-selling novels, including *Pomfret Towers*, 1938, *Marling Hall*, 1942, and *Happy Returns*, 1952, after her return to England from Australia in middle age.

THOMAS, Dylan (1914–53), poet, lived at various addresses in Chelsea between 1934 and 1946 (**M11**).

THOMAS, Edward (1878–1917), poet and essayist, born at Lambeth (**L15**); lived at 61 Shelgate Road, Battersea (**P12**). His *Collected Poems* appeared posthumously in 1920.

THOMPSON, Francis (1859–1907), poet, died at the Hospital of St John and St Elizabeth, St John's Wood, and is buried in St Mary's cemetery, Kensal Green (**G7**).

THOMSON, James (1834–82), poet, lived at 7 Huntley Street, Gower Street (**G14**); died in University College Hospital (**G14**), and is buried in Highgate cemetery (**B13**).

THORNBURY, George Walter (1828–76), miscellaneous writer, born in London; died in Camberwell House Asylum, Peckham Road (**N18**). His works include *Shakespeare's England*, 1856, *Songs of the Cavaliers and Roundheads*, 1857, and *Old and New London*, 1872–78.

TOMLINSON, Henry Major (1873–1958), novelist, born at Poplar (**J22**); lived in the East End of London. He wrote popular travel works and some successful novels, including *Gallions Reach*, 1927, and *All Our Yesterdays*, 1930. He was literary editor of the *Nation*, 1917–23.

TOWNLEY, James (1715–78), writer of farces, was headmaster of Merchant Taylors' School from 1759 (**J17**).

TRELAWNEY, Edward John (1792–1881), adventurer and biographer, born in London. He was the close friend of Byron and Shelley, of whom he wrote.

TREE, Sir Herbert Beerbohm (1853–1917), actor-manager and author, lived at 31 Rosary Gardens, Kensington (**L11**).

TREVENA, John (pseudonym of Ernest George Henham, 1870–1946), novelist, born at Lower Norwood. Most of his novels are set on Dartmoor, where he lived from 1903, and include *A Moorland Trilogy* (*Furze the Cruel*, 1907, *Heather*, 1908, and *Granite*, 1909).

TROLLOPE, Anthony (1815–82), novelist, born at 16 Keppel Street (**H14**); lived in Northumberland Avenue (**J15**), and at 39 Montagu Square, Marylebone, 1873–80 (**H12**); died in Welbeck Street (**H13**), and is buried in Kensal Green cemetery (**G7**).

TUPPER, Martin Farquhar (1810–89), poet, born at 20 Devonshire Place, Marylebone (**H13**). *Ballads for the Times, and Other Poems* appeared in 1852, *Three Hundred Sonnets* in 1860, and *Fifty Protestant Ballads* in 1874.

TURNER, Sharon (1768–1847), historian, born at Pentonville (**F16**); died in Red Lion Square, Holborn (**H15**). He published *A History of England from the Norman Conquest to 1509*, 1814–23, *The Sacred History of the World*, 1832, and a poem, *Richard III*, 1845.

TWAIN, Mark (pseudonym of Samuel Langhorne Clemens, 1835–1910), American writer, lived at 23 Tedworth Square, Chelsea, 1896–97 (**L12**).

VANBRUGH, Sir John (1664–1726), architect and dramatist, born in the parish of St Nicholas Acons (**J17**); lived at Vanbrugh Castle, Blackheath, from about 1719 (**M24**); buried in St Stephen's church, Walbrook (**J17**). His plays include *The Relapse*, 1696, and *The Provoked Wife*, 1697.

WALEY, Arthur David (1889–1966), poet and translator, lived at 50 Southwood Lane, Highgate, and died here (**B13**).

WALLACE, Edgar (1875–1932), thriller writer, born at Greenwich (**M24**). A plaque in Ludgate Circus marks the place where he sold papers as a boy (**H16**).

WALLAS, Graham (1858–1932), sociologist and writer, lived at 38 St Leonard's Terrace, Chelsea (**L12**).

WALPOLE, Horace, 4th Earl of Orford (1717–97), writer, born in Arlington Street, Piccadilly (**J13**); lived at 11 Berkeley Square, Mayfair, 1745–79 (**J13**). He published *The Castle of Otranto*, 1765, *The Mysterious Mother*, 1768, and *Memoirs of the Reign of George III*, which first appeared in 1845.

WALPOLE, Sir Hugh Seymour (1884–1941), novelist, lived in Ryde Street, St James's (**J14**), and later in a flat at 90 Piccadilly (**J14**).

WALTON, Izaak (1593–1683), angler and biographer, lived for many years in Fleet Street on the corner of Chancery Lane (**H16**).

WARD, Mrs Humphrey (Mary Augusta Arnold, 1851–1920), novelist, settled in London in 1881.

WARD, Robert Plumer (1765–1846), novelist, born in Mount Street, Mayfair (**J13**). His works include *Tremaine, or the Man of Refinement*, 1825, *De Vere, or the Man of Independence*, 1827, and *De Clifford, or the Constant Man*, 1841.

WARNER, William (1558–1609), poet, born in London. He is chiefly known for his long verse history *Albion's England*, 1586 and 1606.

WATSON, Thomas (c1557–92), poet, born in London. His *Hecatompathia, or the Passionate Centurie of Love*, 1582, comprised 100 poems which he termed sonnets.

WATTS, Alaric (1797–1864), poet, born in London; worked as an usher at a Fulham school, 1812 (**N8**); died at 2 Blenheim Crescent, Notting Hill (**J9**), and is buried in Highgate cemetery (**B13**). His poems were collected as *Lyrics of the Heart*, 1850.

WATTS, Isaac (1674–1748), hymn writer, is buried in Bunhill Fields burial ground (**G17**).

WATTS-DUNTON, Walter Theodore (1832–1914), critic and novelist, lived with Algernon Charles Swinburne at The Pines, 11 Putney Hill, from 1879 and died here (**P8**).

WAUGH, Evelyn (1903–66), novelist, born at Hampstead (**D11**). His gifts for brilliant satire, were first displayed in *Decline and Fall*, 1928, which remains his most widely known work.

WEBB, Maria St John (c1892–1930), children's poet and author, born at West Hampstead (**D10**). Her 'Littlest One' poems, in several collections from 1914, were widely popular.

WEBB, Mary Gladys (1881–1927), novelist, lived at Hampstead from 1921 (**D11**).

WEBSTER, John (c1580–c1625), dramatist, probably born in London; became clerk of the parish of St Andrew's, Holborn (**H16**). His chief work is *The White Devil*, 1612.

WELLS, Charles Jeremiah (c1800–79), poet, born in London. A friend of Hazlitt, Leigh Hunt and Keats, he published *Stories after Nature*, 1822, a drama *Joseph and his Brethren*, 1824, and *Claribel*, 1845.

WELLS, Herbert George (1866–1946), novelist and sociologist, lived at 46 Fitzroy Road, Primrose Hill (**F13**), while a student in South Kensington (**L11**); lived at 28 Haldon Road, Wandsworth, after 1891 (**P10**), and later at 12 Mornington Road (**F13**); was at 17 Church Row, Hampstead, in 1909 (**D11**), then at Chiltern Court Mansions, Upper Baker Street (**G12**); moved in 1937 to 13 Hanover Terrace, Regent's Park, where he died (**G12**).

WESLEY, Charles (1707–88), minister and hymn writer, lived and died in a house on the site of 1 Wheatley Street, Marylebone (**H13**). His sons **Charles** (1757–1834) and **Samuel** (1766–1837) also lived here.

186

WESLEY, John (1703–91), minister and hymn writer, lived and died at 47 City Road, Finsbury (**F16**), and is buried in old St Marylebone churchyard (**H13**).

WHETSTONE, George (c1544–c1587), dramatist, was possibly born in Westcheap (**H17**). His plays include *The English Myrror*, 1586, *The Enemie to Unthriftynesse*, 1586, and *Amelia*, 1593, published posthumously.

WHITEHEAD, Charles (1804–62), poet and novelist, born in London. His recommendation of Charles Dickens to write humorous letterpress for monthly publication resulted in the *Pickwick Papers*. His own writings include *The Solitary*, 1831, *The Autobiography of Jack Ketch*, 1834, and a play in blank verse, *The Cavalier*, 1836.

WHITEHEAD, Paul (1710–74), poet, born at Holborn (**H15**); confined for some years in the Fleet prison (**H16**), from where he issued *State Dunces*, a satire, 1733.

WICKHAM, Anna (1884–1947), poet, lived at Hampstead (**D11**).

WILDE, Oscar Fingal O'Flahertie Wills (1854–1900), poet and playwright, lived at 34 Tite Street, Chelsea, 1884–95 (**M12**).

WILKES, John (1727–97), politician, editor and essayist, is buried in Grosvenor Chapel, Audley Street (**J13**).

WILLIAMS, Charles (1886–1945), critic, novelist, playwright and essayist, born in London. The most successful of his crypto-gothic novels was *Descent into Hell*, 1937.

WILLIAMS, David (1738–1816), writer and pamphleteer, was minister at Southwood Lane, Highgate, 1769–73 (**B13**); set up a school at Chelsea in 1773 (**M11**), and opened a chapel in Margaret Street, Cavendish Square, in 1776, where he lectured until 1780 (**H14**). He founded the Royal Literary Fund in 1788.

WISKEMANN, Elizabeth (1901–71), author and historian, died at Moore Street, Chelsea (**L12**).

WOOD, Mrs Henry (1814–87), novelist, lived from 1866 until her death in St John's Wood Park (**F11**), and is buried in Highgate cemetery (**B13**).

WOOLF, Leonard (1880–1970) and **Virginia** (1882–1941), husband and wife, both leading figures in the Bloomsbury Group, were born in London, Leonard in Lexham Gardens (**L10**), and Virginia at 13 Hyde Park Gate (**K11**). They lived in Brunswick Square, 1912–15 (**G15**), and at 52 Tavistock Square, 1924–39 (**G14**), subsequently destroyed.

WORDSWORTH, Christopher (1807–85), prelate and historian, nephew of William Wordsworth, born at Lambeth (**L15**); created archdeacon of Westminster in 1865. His works include a *Church History* to AD 451, 1881–83, and his great commentary on the Bible.

WRIGHT, Thomas (1810–77), antiquary, died at Chelsea (**M11**).

WYCHERLEY, William (c1640–1716), dramatist, lived at 19–20 Bow Street (**H15**) and is buried in St Paul's cathedral (**H17**).

YEATS, William Butler (1865–1939), Irish poet and dramatist, lived at 23 Fitzroy Road, St Pancras (**F13**).

YOUNG, Arthur (1741–1820), agriculturist and author, born at Whitehall (**K15**); started a monthly magazine, *Universal Museum*, in London in 1762. He published *A Tour Through the Southern Counties*, 1768, and in 1787 began his *Annals of Agriculture*, which appeared in forty-seven volumes.

ZANGWILL, Israel (1864–1926), novelist and playwright, born in London; lived at 288 Old Ford Road, Bethnal Green (**F20**). He published books on Jewish life, including *The Children of the Ghetto*, 1892–93, and *The King of the Schnorrers*, 1894.

Index

1: Of people, in alphabetical order

199

Index

2: Of people, under counties

England

BEDFORDSHIRE

Bloomfield, R. 50
Bunyan, J. 50
Butler, S. (1612–80) 50
Cameron, V.L. 50
Castell, E. 50
Dillingham, F. 50
Dodd, W. 50
Fisher, J. 50
Foster, W. 50
Gascoigne, G. 50
Grey, Z. 50
Henley, W.E. 50
Norton, T. 50
Osborne, D. 50
Pomfret, J. 50
Reynolds, J. 50
Richmond, L. 50
Rowe, N. 50
Rutherford, M. (White, W.H.) 50
Settle, E. 50
Tiptoft, J., Earl of Worcester 50
White, W.H. *see* Rutherford, M.
Wiffen, B.B. 50
Wiffen, J.H. 50

BERKSHIRE

Bacon, P. 28
Baker, W. 29
Blackmore, R.D. 28
Blackstone, Sir W. 29
Blair, E. *see* Orwell, G.
Bridges, R. 28, 29
Butler, J. 29
Carte, T. 28, 29
Collier, J.P. 28
Collins, M. 28
Crowe, W. 28
Day, T. 29
Duck, S. 29
Edgeworth, R.L. 29
Fenton, E. 28
Gibbings, R. 28, 29
Godwin, T. 28
Grahame, K. 28
Hallam, H. 29
Hearne, T. 29
Hughes, J. 28, 29
Hughes, T. 29
Kimber, I. 29
Knight, C. 29
Latter, M. 29
Lawrence, D.H. 28
Lofting, H. 28
Macaulay, C. 28
Mavor, W.F. 28
Merrick, J. 29
Milman, H.H. 29
Mitford, M.R. 29
Montagu, E. 28
Morton, J.M. 28
Morton, T. 28
Newbery, J. 29
Noel, T. 28
Orwell, G. (Blair, E.) 28
Penn, W. 29
Penrose, T. 28
Pocock, E. 28
Pope, A. 28
Pordage, J. 28
Pordage, S. 28
Pusey, E.B. 28
Pye, H.J. 28
Richardson, D.M. 28
Robinson, M. 29
Ruskin, J. 28
Rudyerd, Sir B. 28
St John, H., Lord Bolingbroke 28

Senior, N. 28
Shelley, P.B. 28, 29
Smith, Goldwin 29
Sylvester, J. 28
Talfourd, Sir T.N. 29
Tull, J. 28
Walker, F. 28
Walter, J. (1776–1847) 28
White, W. 29
Whitelocke, B. 28
Wilde, O.F.O'F.W. 29
Willmott, R. 28

BUCKINGHAMSHIRE

Alley, W. 48
Atterbury, F. 48
Aubrey, J. 47
Aubrey-Fletcher, Sir H. *see* Wade, H.
Bentley, R. (fl 1890) 48
Bickersteth, E. (1814–92) 47
Birkett, W.N., Lord 47
Blyton, E. 47
Boyle, Mrs E.V. 47
Brailsford, H.N. 49
Brett, R. 48
Bridges, R. 47
Brooke, R.C. 48
Brooks, C.S. 47
Browning, O. 47
Bunyan, J. 48
Burke, E. 47
Chesterfield, P.D.S., Lord 48
Chesterton, G.K. 47
Churchill, C. 49
Coke, Sir E. 48
Cory, W.J. 47
Cowper, W. 47, 48, 49
Crab, R. 47
Croke, Sir J. 47
Dashwood, Sir F. 49
Davies, R. (d 1581) 47
De la Mare, W.J. 48
Dickens, C.J.H. 48
Digby, Sir K. 47
Disraeli, B., Earl of Beaconsfield 47, 48
D'Israeli, I. 47
Dix, Dom G. 47
Ellwood, T. 47, 48
Fox, G. 48
Fremantle, E. 48
Gibbs, R. 47
Gill, E. 48
Gooch, G.P. 47
Gray, T. 47, 48
Grenville, G.N., Baron Nugent of Carlanstown 48
Greville, C. 47
Grote, G. 47
Hailey, W.M., Baron 48
Hart, Sir B.L. 48, 49
Hayley, W. 47
Herschel, Sir J.F.W. 48
Hession, B. 47
Higgons, T. 47
Hooke, N. 48
Hooker, R. 47
How, R. 49
James, M.R. 47
Jerome, J.K. 48
Jones, H.A. 47
Keach, B. 48, 49
King, H. 49
Lawrence, D.H. 47
Lipscomb, G. 48
Lloyd, R. 47
Machen, A. 47
Martyn, T. 48
Mason, J. 48
Massingham, Harold 48
Milton, J. 47
Newton, J. (1725–1807) 48
Ollyffe, G. 47
Peacock, T.L. 48

Penn, W. 48
Phillips, T. 48
Reynolds, C. 48
Roger of Wendover 49
Rose, W. 48
Scott, T. (1747–1821) 47
Shakespeare, W. 47
Shelley, P.B. 47, 48
Sheridan, R.B. 47
Smedley, F. 48
Spence, Joseph 47
Swinburne, A.C. 47
Ternan, E. 48
Terry, C.S. 48
Todd, H. 47, 48
Toynbee, P. 47
Tyrrell, J. 47
Udall, N. 47
Verney, Lady P. 48
Veryney, M.M. 48
Wade, H. (Aubrey-Fletcher, Sir H.) 47
Wallace, E. 47, 48
Waller, E. 47
Walpole, H., Earl of Orford 47
Whitehead, P. 49
Whitelocke, B. 47
Wiffen, J.H. 48
Wilkes, J. 47, 49
Willis, B. 47, 49
Wilmot, C. 47
Wotton, Sir H. 47
Wotton, W. 48
Wright, T. (1859–1936) 48
Wycliffe, J. 48

CAMBRIDGESHIRE

Anstey, C. 57
Babington, C.C. 57
Blomefield, L. 57
Boyse, J. 57
Brooke, R.C. 57
Byron, G.G., Lord 57
Chambers, J. 57
Cheke, Sir J. 57
Clarkson, T. 58
Cole, W. 57
Collier, J. 57
Cornford, F.C. 57
Cornford, R.J. 57
Crashaw, R. 57
Cumberland, R. 57
Downes, A. 57
Elyot, Sir T. 57
Eversden, J. 57
Fitzball, E. 57
Godwin, W. 58
Gray, T. 57
Henty, G.A. 57
Herbert, A. 57
Hill, O. 58
Housman, A.E. 57
Kingsley, C. 57
Lewis, C.S. 57
Macaulay, R. 57
May, Sir T.E., Baron Farnborough 57
Moore, E. 57
Palmer, E. 57
Paris, M. 57
Pecock, R. 57
Postgate, R.W. 57
Preston, T. 57
Rawley, W. 57
Sayers, D.L. 57
Taylor, Jeremy 57
Tennyson, A., Lord 57
White, H.K. 57
Whitehead, W. 57
Withers, J. 57

CHESHIRE

Abercrombie, L. 95
Ashe, T. 95

Brooke, L.L. 95
Broome, W. 95
Brownswerd, J. 95
Caine, Sir T.H.H. 95
Caldecott, R. 95
Carroll, L. (Dodgson, C.L.) 95
Dod, J. 95
Dodgson, C.L. *see* Carroll, L.
Evans, G.B. 95
Gaskell, Mrs E.C. 95
Heber, R. 95
Henry, M. 95
Higden, R. 95
Holinshed, R. 95
Holme, R. 95
Houghton, W.S. 95
Howson, J.S. 95
Johnson, S. (1691–1773) 95
King, E. 95
Leycester, Sir P. 95
Minshull, E. 95
Owen, W. 95
Parnell, T. 95
Pearson, J. 95
Prince, J.C. 95
Raffald, E. 95
Sinclair, M. 95
Speed, J. 95
Stanley, A.P. 95
Stapledon, W.O. 95
Warburton, R.E.E. 95
Warren, J.B.L., Baron de Tabley 95
Waugh, Edwin 95
Whitehurst, J. 95
Whitney, G. 95

CORNWALL

Attwell, M.L. 12
Beauchamp, K.M. *see* Mansfield, K.
Bond, T. 12
Borlase, W. 12
Buckingham, J.S. 12
Carew, R. 12
Coleridge, D. 12
Crouch, J. 12
Davidson, J. 12
Delany, Mrs M. 12
Ellis, H. 12
Ellis, Mrs H. (Lees, E.M.) 12
Foote, S. 12
Fox, C. 12
Fox, G. 12
Godolphin, S. 12
Grahame, K. 12
Hals, W. 13
Hamley, Gen Sir E. 12
Hardy, T. 12
Harris, John 12, 13
Hawker, R.S. 12
Hocking, J. 12
Hocking, S. 12
Hudson, W.H. 12
Johns, C.A. 12
Kingsley, C. 12
Lawrence, D.H. 13
Lees, E.M. *see* Ellis, Mrs H.
Liddell, H.G. 12
Lowry, H.D. 13
McNeile, H.C. 12
Mansfield, K. (Beauchamp, K.M.) 12, 13
Murry, J.M. 12, 13
Pindar, P. *see* Wolcot, J.
Polwhele, R. 13
Quiller-Couch, Sir A. 12
Redding, C. 12
Scott, R. 12
Spring, H. 12
Temple, W.J. 12
Tregarthen, J.C. 12
Walmsley, L. 12
Walpole, Sir H.S. 13

Evelyn, J. 42
Fawkes, F. 43
Filmer, Sir R. 42
Finch, A., Countess of
　Winchilsea 42
Finlay, G. 42
Firbank, R. 42
Fleming, I.L. 41, 43
Fletcher, P. 42
Foote, S. 42
Ford, F.M. (Hueffer, F.M.) 41
Fowler, H.W. 44
Gethin, Lady G. 43
Gilbert, Sir W.S. 41
Gosson, S. 41
Gower, J. 41
Grossmith, G. 42
Grote, G. 41
Gunning, P. 43
Guthrie, Sir W.T. 44
Hallam, H. 43
Hamilton, C.H.StJ. see
　Richards, F.
Harmsworth, A.C.W. see
　Northcliffe, Lord
Hasted, E. 42, 44
Hazlitt, W. 43
Head, Sir F.B. 43
Herbert, M., Countess of
　Pembroke 43
Hichens, R. 44
Hooker, R. 41
Horne, R.H. 43
Hueffer, F.M. see Ford, F.M.
Jacobs, W. W. 43
James, M.R. 42
Johnson, L.P. 41
Johnson, S. (1709–84) 41
Keats, J. 41
Keyes, S. 42
Lambarde, W. 43
Lamburn, R.C. see
　Crompton, R.
Langdon-Davies, J. 43
Lilburne, J. 42
Linacre, T. 41, 43
Lower, R. 44
Lucas, E.V. 42
Lushington, E.L. 43
Macaulay, C. 44
Marchant, B. 43
Marlowe, C. 41, 42
Mee, A. 42
Mercer, C.W. see Yates, D.
Morris, W.H. 41
Nares, E. 41
Nesbit, E. 42, 43
Nicolson, Sir H. 43, 44
Northcliffe, Lord
　(Harmsworth, A.C.W.) 41
Norton, T. 43
Oldcastle, Sir J. 42
Oxenden, H. 41
Paine, T. 43
Plunkett, E.J.M.D. see
　Dunsany, Lord
Postgate, R.W. 41
Pratt, A. 42
Reynolds, G. 43
Richards, F. (Hamilton,
　C.H.StJ.) 41
Roper, W. 42
Rossetti, D.G. 41
Sacharissa see Sidney, D.
Sackville, C., Earl of Dorset 43
Sackville, T., Earl of Dorset 43
Sackville-West, V. 43, 44
Sandys, G. 41
Sassoon, S. 41, 43
Sedley, Sir C. 41, 44
Shakespeare, W. 42
Sidney, A. 43
Sidney, D. (Sacharissa) 41
Sidney, Sir P. 43
Smart, C. 44
Smith, H. 44
Stevens, W. 43

Tennyson, A., Lord 41, 43, 44
Thackeray, W.M. 44
Theobald, L. 44
Thomas, E. 41, 43
Timbs, J. 42
Twysden, Sir R. 42
Waley, A.D. 44
Waller, E. 41
Welch, D. 42, 43, 44
Wells, H.G. 41, 43
Woodville, A., Earl Rivers 43
Wotton, Sir H. 41
Wyatt, Sir T. 41, 42
Yates, D. (Mercer, C.W.) 44

LANCASHIRE

Agate, J.E. 113
Aikin, J. 114
Aikin, L. 114
Ainsworth, R. 112
Ainsworth, W.H. 113
Arnold, M. 112
Baines, E. 114
Bamford, S. 113
Banks, Mrs L. 113
Barbauld, Mrs A.L. 114
Barrow, Sir J. 112
Beck, T.A. 112
Bellew, J. 112
Billington, W. 113
Binyon, L. 112
Birrell, A. 112
Blundell, Mrs M.F. see
　Francis, M.E.
Bobbin, T. see Collier, J.
Brazil, A. 113
Brierley, B. 113
Brighouse, H. 113
Broster, D.K. 112
Burnett, F.E.H. 113
Byrom, J. 112, 113
Byron, H.J. 113
Chadderton, L. 112
Clarke, C.A. 112
Clough, A.H. 112
Collier, J. (Bobbin, T.) 113
Collingwood, R.G. 112
Crane, W. 112
Crompton, R. (Lamburn,
　R.C.) 112
De Quincey, T. 113
Dixon, W.H. 113
Dunkerley, W. see Oxenham,
　J.
Farington, J. 112
Francis, M.E. (Blundell, Mrs
　M.F.) 112
Gaskell, Mrs E.C. 113
Gladstone, W.E. 112
Golding, L. 113
Gould, N. 113
Gunter, A. 112
Hamerton, P. 113
Hamilton, M.A. 113
Hawthorne, N. 112
Hayman, H. 112
Hemans, Mrs F.D. 112
Hilton, J. 112
Hocking, S. 112
Hodson, J.L. 112
Irving, W. 113
Jackson, H. 112
Jeans, Sir J.H. 114
Lamburn, R.C. see
　Crompton, R.
Lear, E. 113
Le Gallienne, R. 113
Leigh, C. 114
Lempriere, J. 112
Linacre, T. 114
Lingard, J. 112
Linnaeus, C. 113
Lowry, C.M. 113
Monkhouse, A. 113

Morley, J., Viscount
　Blackburn 112
Noonan, R. see Tressell, R.
Oliphant, Mrs M. 113
Oxenham, J. (Dunkerley, W.) 113
Picton, Sir J.A. 113
Potter, B. 113
Richmond, L. 113
Riley, W. 113
Roscoe, W. 113
Ruskin, J. 112
Service, R.W. 113
Smith, E. 112
Spenser, E. 112
Stanley, F., Earl of Derby 113
Swain, C. 113
Tannahill, R. 112
Thompson, Francis 113
Tirebuck, W.E. 113
Tressell, R. (Noonan, R.) 113
Watson, Sir W. 113
Waugh, Edwin 112, 113
Westall, W.B. 112
Whewell, W. 112
Whitaker, T.D. 112
White, J.B. 113
Wilson, Thomas 112
Winstanley, G. 114
Wordsworth, W. 112

LEICESTERSHIRE

Aikin, J. 102
Barbauld, Mrs A.L. 102
Beaumont, F. 102
Beaumont, John 102
Booth, C. 102
Burton, R. 102, 103
Burton, W. 102
Carlyle, T. 102
Cleveland, J. 102
Coleridge, H. 102
Coleridge, S.T. 102
Cooper, T. 102
Crabbe, G. 102
Cradock, J. 102
Dawes, R. 103
Dickinson, W.C. 102
Doddridge, P. 102
Drayton, M. 102
Dyer, J. 102
Fletcher, J. 102
Fox, G. 102
Gardiner, W. (1770–1853) 102
Henley, J. 102
Herrick, R. 103
Herrick, Sir W. 103
Hildersham, A. 102
Jennens, C. 103
Jenner, C. 102
Jewsbury, G.E. 102
Jewsbury, M.J. 102
Johnson, S. (1709–84) 102
Kilbye, R. 103
Lilly, W. 102
Macaulay, T.B., Baron 103
Marriott, J. 102
Marshall, T. 102
Moore, T. 102
Nichols, J. 102
Orton, J. 102
Phillips, Sir R. 102
Porter, E. 102
Potter, T.R. 102
Rogers, S. 102
Rutland, E., Countess of 102
Rutland, R., Earl of 102
Scott, Sir W. 102
Sidney, Sir P. 102
Stone, L. 102
Trevelyan, Sir G.O. 103
Vergil, P. 102
West, Mrs J. 102
Whiston, W. 102
Wordsworth, D. 102

Wordsworth, W. 102
Wycliffe, J. 102

LINCOLNSHIRE

Alington, C.A. 106
Angell, Sir N. (Lane, R.N.A.) 106
Banks, Sir J. 106
Bede, C. (Bradley, E.) 106
Borrow, G. 106
Bradley, E. see Bede, C.
Burton, R. 107
Centlivre, S. 106
Conington, J. 106
de Brunne, R. see Manning,
　or Mannyng, R.
Dyer, J. 106
Eliot, G. (Evans, M.A.) 106
Eusden, L. 106
Evans, M.A. see Eliot, G.
Googe, B. 106
Hadath, G. 106
Hakluyt, R. 106
Horrabin, J.F. 106
Ingelow, J. 106
Kingsley, C. 106
Lane, R.N.A. see Angell, Sir
　N.
Latham, R. 106
Le Neve, J. 107
Manning, or Mannyng, R.
　(de Brunne, R.) 106
Markham, Mrs (Penrose, E.) 106
Marston, J.W. 106
Meres, F. 106
Miller, T. 106
More, Henry 106
Moryson, F. 106
Newton, Sir I. 107
Nicholson, Joseph 107
Palmer, H. 106
Patrick, J. 106
Penrose, E. see Markham,
　Mrs
Pryme, A. de la 106
Scott, Sir W. 106, 107
Scrope, Sir C. 106
Smith, Capt J. 107
Still, J. 106
Stukeley, W. 106
Tennyson, A., Lord 106
Tennyson, C. 106
Tennyson, F. 106
Treece, H. 106
Turner, C.T. 106
Verlaine, P. 107
Wesley, C. 106, 107
Wesley, J. 106, 107
Wesley, S. 106, 107
White, H. K. 107
Winn, H. 106
Wordsworth, C. 106
Wycliffe, J. 106

MIDDLESEX

Andrew, S. (Layton, F.G.) 33
Arnold, M. 32, 33
Ayloffe, J. 33
Banks, Sir J. 33
Baxter, R. 32
Baxter, W. 33
Bedwell, W. 33
Berry, M. 33
Blackmore, R.D. 33
Bowen, E. 32
Byron, G.G., Lord 32
Cambridge, R.O. 33
Cary, H.F. 32
Chace, B. 32
Chapman, G. 32
Churchill, Sir W.L.S. 32
Clarke, C.C. 32
Clarke, M.V.C. 32
Compton-Burnett, Dame I. 33

LONDON

Scotland

Wales